William Lescaze, Architect

THE ART ALLIANCE PRESS AWARD
Community Murals: The People's Art (Alan W. Barnett)
Veiled Images: Titian's Mythological Paintings for Philip II (Jane C. Nash)
William Lescaze, Architect (Lorraine Welling Lanmon)

William Lescaze, Architect

LORRAINE WELLING LANMON

Philadelphia: The Art Alliance Press
London and Toronto: Associated University Presses

Associated University Presses
440 Forsgate Drive
Cranbury, NJ 08512

Associated University Presses
25 Sicilian Avenue
London WC1A 2QH, England

Associated University Presses
2133 Royal Windsor Drive, Unit 1
Mississauga, Ontario
Canada L5J 1K5

The paper used in this publication meets the requirements
of the American National Standard for Permanence of Paper
for Printed Library Materials Z39.48-1984.

Library of Congress Cataloging in Publication Data

Lanmon, Lorraine Welling, 1932–
   William Lescaze, architect.

   Bibliography: p.
   Includes index.
   1. Lescaze, William, 1896–1969.   2. Architecture,
Modern—20th century—United States.   I. Title.
NA737.L45L36   1986   720′.92′4   83-45295
   ISBN 0-87982-506-5 (alk. paper)

Printed in the United States of America

Dedicated to
DPL
EOW and MEW

Contents

Preface

THIS STUDY EXAMINES THE FIFTY-YEAR CAREER OF William Lescaze, architect. It emphasizes his role in the introduction of the European modern style of the 1920s to the East Coast of the United States. It documents his work from the formative period of the International Style in western Europe through its early development in the United States and concludes with his post-war work to his death in 1969.

Prodigious quantities of literature have been written on the International Style. Some have treated its formation, the complexity and individuality of its several expressions within the modern movement, and its dispersion throughout Europe. Others have traced its dissemination to the West Coast of the United States and its thrust through the education programs at Harvard University and the Illinois Institute of Technology. A number of the most recent studies have offered revisionist evaluations of the movement. With the exception of the Philadelphia Saving Fund Society building (PSFS), little consideration has been given, however, to the early development of the International Style on the East Coast of the United States prior to its official sanction by the Museum of Modern Art's International Exhibition of Modern Architecture in 1932.

Five years before that time, Lescaze had made one of the first attempts to introduce the International Style to America in his Capital Bus Terminal built in New York in 1927. Two years later, he succeeded in designing the first International Style school building to be realized in the United States—the Oak Lane Country Day School's nursery school building, built near Philadelphia. His earliest buildings were among the first important

statements of the new architecture in this country. They included: one of the first International Style residences built on the East Coast (the Frederick Vanderbilt Field house at New Hartford, Connecticut, 1930–1931); with George Howe, the first International Style skyscraper built in America (the PSFS building, 1929–1932); the first significant attempt in America to create a large-scale, low-cost urban housing development (the Chrystie-Forsyth project, 1931–1932); with others, the first large-scale, low-cost public housing project built in New York (the Williamsburg Houses, Brooklyn, 1935–1938); the first International Style town house built in New York and one of the earliest uses of glass block and air conditioning in America (his own house at 211 East Forty-eighth Street, New York, 1933–1934); and the first building designed solely for radio programming, performing, and broadcasting (the CBS building in Los Angeles, 1938).

In his own time, Lescaze was widely recognized for his early pioneering of the new architecture. He was selected as the sole American representative to the first meeting of the *Congrès Internationaux d'Architecture Moderne* held in Switzerland in 1928. He was among only nine American architects recognized in 1929 as "New Pioneers" by Henry-Russell Hitchcock in his *Modern Architecture: Romanticism and Reintegration*.[1] In 1931, the firm of Howe and Lescaze was the only American representative in a European traveling exhibition—one that included the work of J. J. P. Oud for Holland; Le Corbusier for France; and Miles van der Rohe for Germany. In 1932, Howe and Lescaze were among only nine "exhibiting architects" in the Museum of Modern

9

Art's International Exhibition of Modern Architecture. In the official publication of that exhibition, Hitchcock wrote that the firm's work "represents an increasingly successful attempt to apply . . . the technical and aesthetic ideas of modern architecture as they have been developed in the last decade in Europe" and considered it to be the "direction in which our better architecture may be expected to advance." He believed the firm's PSFS building to be the one American skyscraper which "is worth discussing in the same terms as the work of the leading architects of Europe."[2] At the same time, Philip Johnson called it "the most interesting piece of architecture in this country, . . . unique in modern architecture of the world."[3]

In 1935 it was reported in *Fortune* magazine that the only architects involved with any frequency in modern architecture in America were Frank Lloyd Wright, Richard Neutra, and Lescaze.[4] The next year *The New Yorker* claimed Lescaze had "taken the lead in Modernist architecture in this country."[5] In 1937 Henry-Russell Hitchcock hailed him as "easily the most prominent architect in the East."[6] In 1940, James M. Richards wrote in his *An Introduction to Modern Architecture*, that the greatest contributions to modern architecture in America in the last twenty years had been made by Lescaze and Neutra.[7] In light of this acclaim, Lescaze's contribution to the modern movement deserves attention.

The primary aim of this study is to document Lescaze's work during the formative period of the International Style in Western Europe through its early development in the United States; to analyze the evolution of his architecture within its historical context; and to establish his role and position in the development of the Style. The development and evolution of the International Style is of particular significance in the history of modern architecture for its traditions have continued to flourish in America, from its inception in the late twenties to the present day. Its early expressions can be seen in the work of George Howe and William Lescaze, Richard Neutra, Rudolph M. Schindler, A. Lawrence Kocher, Albert Frey, and others; next through the work and teaching of Mies van der Rohe at the Illinois Institute of Technology and of Walter Gropius, Marcel Breuer, and José Luis Sert at Harvard; then through the work of the post-war generation under Gropius—Edward Larrabee Barnes, Henry Cobb, Ulrich Franzen, John Johansen, I. M. Pei, Paul Rudolph, Ben Thompson, and The Architects Collaborative group; and most recently through the highly formal and abstract work of Peter Eisenman, Michael Graves, Richard Meier, John Hejduk, and Charles Gwathmey.[8]

Thanks to the many unpublished drawings and documents preserved by Lescaze, the published descriptions, photographs, and criticisms of his work, the preservation of most of his architecture, and the willingness of his contemporaries to recall their association with him, a large amount of documentary evidence is available on which to base an interpretive study of his work. This book is the first full-length study of Lescaze to appear. His major commissions and some of his minor ones are illustrated and discussed in relation to his life and times.

I wish to acknowledge the generous assistance of Ms. Carolyn Davis and her staff at the George Arents Research Library for Special Collections at Syracuse University, Syracuse, New York, who aided my examination of the many documents in the Lescaze archives on deposit there. Also, my thanks to Mr. Robert Johnson, who is in charge of the Records Office, Dartington Hall, Devon, England, where the papers concerning Lescaze's architecture in England are on file.

I am indebted to the architects who shared their recollections of their association with Lescaze with me: Todd C. Bogatay, Mr. and Mrs. Alfred Clauss, Henry Dumper, Albert Frey, R. Buckminster Fuller, Robert Hening, Sidney L. Katz, Norman Rice, and Julian Whittlesey.

The following owners and officers of Lescaze-designed architecture were most gracious in allowing me to visit their buildings: Mr. Jack Badecki, Mr. and Mrs. Cox, Mr. Michael Decent, Mr. John A. Fatula, Mr. Robert Hening, Mr. George Palermo, Mr. Michael Taylor, Mr. Jeff Thornburgh, Mr. and Mrs. Isadore Treatman, Mr. William D. White, and Mrs. William Lescaze. My greatest appreciation goes to the latter, the architect's widow, who not only made quantities of Lescaze's papers and drawings available to me, but whose personal knowledge of her husband's work was invaluable to my research and offered a dimension to the study that it could not otherwise have had.

This volume grew out of a doctoral dissertation presented to the University of Delaware in 1979. I am indebted to Professors George B. Tatum, Damie Stillman, and William I. Homer for their criticisms. My thanks go also to Ronald Cassetti and Edgar Kauffman, Jr. for their suggestions regarding the manuscript.

Finally, I must acknowledge Lescaze's subtle but pointed criticism of those who write about architecture: "I have read several articles, treatises, and books on architecture of late. Oh Gods, help me to remain silent to avoid descriptions with words and let me do drawings only."[9] Certainly the photographs of Lescaze's drawings and completed buildings published herein will speak for themselves and with greater authority than either his or my words.

Unless otherwise noted, all photographs reproduced in this book are courtesy of the William E. Lescaze Archives in the George Arents Research Library of Syracuse University, Syracuse, New York.

NOTES

1. New York: Payson & Clarke, 1929, pp. 201–206.

2. Henry-Russell Hitchcock, "Howe and Lescaze," In Alfred Barr, et al., *Modern Architecture: International Exhibition* (New York: Norton, 1932; reprint ed., New York: published for the Museum of Modern Art by Arno Press, 1969), p. 145.

3. Philip Johnson to Lescaze, 5 August 1932, William E. Lescaze Archives, the George Arents Research Library for Special Collections at Syracuse University, Syracuse, New York; hereafter cited as WELA.

4. "The House That Works: I," *Fortune* 40 (October 1935):59–60.

5. Robert M. Coates, "Profile," *The New Yorker*, December 1936, p. 24.

6. Henry-Russell Hitchcock and Catherine K. Bauer, *Modern Architecture in England*, (New York: The Museum of Modern Art, 1937), p. 39.

7. Harmondsworth, Middlesex, England: Penguin Books Ltd., 1940, p. 90.

8. See Kenneth Frampton, Introduction to *Richard Meier, Architect: Buildings and Projects 1966–1976*, by Richard Meier (New York: Oxford University Press, 1976), pp. 7–8.

9. William Lescaze, Note (handwritten), 2 February 1930, WELA. All drawings and photographs are in the WELA, unless otherwise noted.

William Lescaze, Architect

1

The European Background

WILLIAM LESCAZE'S ARCHITECTURAL CAREER COIN-
cided with the development of modern architecture
in Europe and America. He was born when the
avant-garde experiment of Art Nouveau had
reached maturity; came to manhood at the time
when cubism, futurism, and expressionism were at
their height; studied architecture when the theories
of neo-plasticism and constructivism were being
formulated; entered practice when architectural experiments in expressionism and international functionalism had only just begun; and continued practice for fifty years through the development and
redevelopment of that variable entity called the
modern style.

Born ten years after the leaders of Europe's architectural revolution, the Swiss-born and -trained
Lescaze was one of a few transplanted European
architects who built the new style in America
within ten years of its inception abroad. Experiencing an unusual series of political and economic
events, Lescaze studied architecture during the
time of World War I and entered practice in Europe
at the time of its severe post-war depression. He
began practice in America at the time of its post-
war conservative reaction and established himself in
a partnership at the time of the Great Depression.
In spite of this adversity, Lescaze was instrumental
in introducing the International Style to the East
Coast of America, developed his practice into a
wide sphere of influence before the outbreak of
World War II, and enjoyed a prolific career until his
death in 1969.

Lescaze was born in Onex, near Geneva, Switzerland, on 27 March 1896 (see Chronology, appendix A).[1] His mother's family had emigrated to
Geneva from the south of France; his father's family
had come from Spain. Lescaze was introduced to
the arts as a child. His father was educated at the
University of Heidelberg because of his deep love
and respect for German philosophers, musicians,
writers, and the language—all most unusual for a
French-Swiss. He became a professor of German
language and literature at the Collège de Genève,
the school founded by Calvin in 1559, and was the
author of a number of books on teaching the German language. This background undoubtedly
served William well in his architectural studies in
Zurich, and later in assimilating the German contribution to modern architecture.

The young William had two passionate inter-
ests—playing the violin and painting. With his talented older brother, Adrien, who was an accomplished musician, Lescaze formed part of an
amateur string quartet which met and played regularly. After his brother's untimely death in 1914, at
age twenty-one, Lescaze gave up the violin, playing
only rarely in later years.[2]

The story of Lescaze's painting is happier and
continued to be a satisfying diversion for him
throughout his life. Lescaze's drawings and watercolor paintings, as seen in a sketchbook from his
primary school years, 1904–1910, are not remarkable to be sure, but they are competent first efforts
of a fourteen-year-old. They reflect his interest in

15

Fig. 1. William Lescaze, drawing of a Gothic cathedral, 11 May 1910.

architectural subjects, from Swiss chalets to Gothic cathedrals, and foretell his ability to execute handsome architectural renderings throughout his career (Fig. 1).

Following his primary school education, Lescaze went to the Collège de Genève from 1910 to 1914, where he chose, much to his parents' consternation, the "Section Technique"—the technical rather than the classical course of study.[3] It was there that he studied painting. In 1913 Lescaze painted, in oil, a view of the mountain La Sàleve, as seen from his home. An accomplished work, it not only reveals the influence of Cézanne but also coincidentally compares closely to a 1914 watercolor of *Glärnisch* by Karl Moser, who was to become Lescaze's architectural mentor.[4] Upon his graduation from the Collège de Genève at age eighteen, Lescaze invited his friends to an exhibition of his paintings in his parents' home.[5]

Yet, even with an early interest in painting, Lescaze wrote that he had decided, at the age of six-

teen, without influence of any person, architect, building, or an identifiable cause, to his recollection, to become an architect.[6] He was undecided, however, about where to pursue his architectural studies. At that time he had no desire to attend the conservative Eidgenössische Technische Hochschule (ETH) in Zurich. The École des Beaux-Arts in Paris, where, he later recalled, he thought he would be taught the "art of designing turrets," failed to attract him either. But Paris, the center of his French culture and the international center for avant-garde artists, did.[7]

However, two events of 1914 prevented him from going to Paris. Because of the war and his obligation to military service, he could not leave Switzerland.[8] And, because of the profound grief of the family at the death of his brother, Adrien, Lescaze felt he should remain at home another year. During that time he continued to paint and draw, following the classes at the École des Beaux-Arts in Geneva and taking long painting trips into the Swiss mountains.[9] Characteristic of Lescaze's work in that year is a strong, almost expressionist, charcoal drawing of a nude female figure.[10]

With the appointment of Karl C. Moser to a professorship at Zurich's ETH (or the École Polytechnique Federale, as Lescaze called it), in the second year of World War I, Lescaze immediately decided to begin his study of architecture there.[11] Lescaze later recalled: "I knew and admired his work. I was eager to study with him. I no longer deliberated about my choice of school—only the Poly would do."[12]

This was just the time that the new century's architectural revolution had begun to stir in Central Europe, and Moser, as educator and practitioner, was one of the early advocates of change. Before his arrival at the École Polytechnique, all teaching there was uniformly conservative. In fact, Moser's course in modern architecture was probably one of the first to have been given at any university. Because of his vision of a humanistic architecture, many idealistic students collected at Zurich.[13]

Both Lescaze's early and mature work reveal his exposure to a vitally active period in the evolution of the arts. Non-representational painting was in full bloom; avant-garde architectural treatises and exhibitions of various kinds were being debated. For example, Italy's pre-war contribution to the modern art movement, Futurism, had just begun to influence architectural theories.[14] Thus the ideas of Antonio Sant'Elia, published in *A Manifesto of*

Futurist Architecture in 1914, were to be expressed in Lescaze's stepped-back designs in the late twenties and early thirties.

Knowledge of the native Swiss architect Le Corbusier's experiments in Paris with his Dom-ino house of 1914, his Citrohan houses of 1919–1921, and his theory of Purism published in *Apres le Cubisme* (1918) with Amedee Ozenfant, were undoubtedly brought to Moser's students as well. For Lescaze's mature work of the thirties was clearly dominated by Le Corbusier's influence, as will be noted in a later chapter.[15] Likewise, the ideas of the Dutch expressionists, disseminated through their magazine, *Wendingen*, as well as those of the functionalists disseminated through the magazine *De Stijl* and *Manifesto I*, must have been read by Lescaze.[16] The platform for functionalism was further provided by the controversial journal, *De 8 en Opbouw*, which brought the advanced spirits of both functionalist and expressionist causes to widespread attention. Constructivism, which with neoplasticism was to dominate the arts by the early 1920s, was as well known.[17] To be sure, a combination of expressionist, neo-plastic, and constructivist elements, with varying emphasis, were to characterize Lescaze's work throughout his career.

Knowledge of the dada movement, born in Zurich in 1916, was unavoidable. In addition to its local meetings and activities, its philosophy was widely disseminated after 1917 through its periodical *Dada* and its *Dada Manifesto*. Although Lescaze took no active part in the movement, he discussed the dadaists' plays and paintings with his friends and renewed contact with dadaist Marcel Iancu (Janco), some years later.[18]

The Vienna Secession's Wiener Werkstätte shop in Zurich, designed and operated by Dagobert Peche from 1917–1919, was probably the source of influence on Lescaze's earliest graphic work.

In Germany, the Cologne Deutscher Werkbund Exhibition of 1914 had presented to the public examples of both expressionist and functionalist architecture. In the same year the poet Paul Scheerbart had published his visionary and prophetic *Glasarchitektur* in Berlin.[19] But, probably of foremost influence on the student Lescaze were the utopian and visionary activities of the revolutionary architects and artists, from all over Europe, who gathered together in Berlin at the end of the war to promote architecture as a social art.

Among the more influential publications emanating from the Berlin visionaries during Lescaze's years in Zurich was Bruno Taut's *Architektur-Programm* of 1918, which sought to break down all existing barriers between the arts and to create a new unity wherein each separate discipline would contribute to the art of building. Also calling for a new, utopian architecture, integrated with all the arts, were Walter Gropius, Bruno Taut, and Adolf Behne in their *New Ideas on Architecture*, published in 1919, and Erich Mendelsohn in his *The Problem of the New Architecture* of the same year. Among the more radically inclined theories were those of Paul Scheerbart for a glass architecture, expressed in visual terms by Bruno Taut in his *Alpine Architektur* and *Die Stadtkrone*, also published in 1919.[20] This philosophy was always a part of Lescaze's oeuvre; he became particularly preoccupied with it after World War II.

An architecture of vision rather than reality, most of these projects were executed only on paper. Erich Mendelsohn, having just opened his Berlin office, exhibited his sketches at Cassirer's Gallery in April 1919 under the title "Architecture in Steel and Glass." In the same month the *Arbeitsrät für Kunst* opened its "Exhibition for Unknown Architects" at J. B. Neumann's Berlin gallery. Consisting of sketches by the most advanced architects, artists, and designers in Germany, it was to provide the impetus for one of the most visionary episodes in the history of modern architecture—German expressionism.

A project that became reality was Hans Poelzig's remodeling of a former warehouse and circus into the expressionist Grosses Schauspielhaus, completed in Berlin in 1919. At the same time, in Weimar, the Academy of Fine Art and the Arts and Crafts School were reorganized into *Das Staatliche Bauhaus*, under Gropius's leadership, and its expressionist manifesto was published.[21] Expressionism provided forms that later were to be most influential on much of Lescaze's work.

While only one of these artistic movements, dadaism, originated in Lescaze's Switzerland, most were well known there, for Zurich was a kind of cultural focus for Europe at that time when, culturally and intellectually, a unified Europe no longer existed.[22] The majority of these important new artistic theories were to shape Lescaze's aesthetic sensibility and are reflected in his work throughout his career.

Some of their influence may have come through the teaching of Karl C. Moser, who, Lescaze recalled some years later, was the "teacher who meant the most to me personally."[23] Lescaze believed Moser's lectures to have been "the most inspiring introduction to architecture" he could ever have witnessed.[24] "He challenged you, made things happen in your mind, opened your eyes, helped you to become yourself."[25] In his teaching, Moser adopted an attitude of liberalism which was opposed to that of his colleague at the École Polytechnique, Gustav G. Gull, who more closely adhered to an interpretation of historic tradition. Consequently, the architectural students divided themselves into two groups: the more conservative with Gull, and the more progressive, who were in the majority, with Karl Moser.[26] Lescaze's choice of Moser at the beginning of his architectural education was the first statement of his life-long dedication to the philosophy of a new architecture for a new age.

Moser believed that there were fine old buildings in Switzerland and in all countries of the world, but he encouraged his students only to study, not to copy them, to discover for themselves what made them significant and beautiful in terms of the culture that produced them.[27] Heeding those lessons, Lescaze was later to write:

> My creed in architecture might be said to be: a firm decision to retain only the spiritual value of past cultures and forbid oneself the sterile copy of their forms. A tireless search for the clean and logical expression; the approach to a form which shall belong to the people of this age, their manner of thinking and mode of existence.[28]

Moser advised that "the only lasting quality of good architecture is the change in its appearance which is made necessary through the development of life."[29] These teachings were reflected in Lescaze's lectures and writings throughout his life:

> Good architecture, classic or modern is essentially of its time.[30]

> All good architecture has been living architecture, it has been the modern architecture of its time, growing out of the life of its time, and fully aware of the requirements of that time.[31]

> Modern architecture is architecture designed for modern life.[32]

Further, Moser put particular emphasis on planning—on thinking out the function for which a building was intended and designing it to fulfill that purpose "unhindered by arbitrary notions of orna-

Fig. 2. William Lescaze, diploma project, 1919. Perspective rendering of a large building block in Zurich.

ment or traditional style."[33] These teachings undoubtedly helped to form Lescaze's lifelong belief in a humanistic philosophy of functionalism and to result in the statement that "modern architecture puts MAN first, it exists to serve men."[34] Lescaze frequently expressed the era's notion that "architecture is modern only if it meets in every requirement the needs and purposes of the people living in it."[35] And, in his book, *On Being an Architect*, he wrote: "Living human beings, that's what architecture is made from."[36] Moser also instructed his students not only to solve the problems of a building's function from within, but also to relate them to their environmental context.[37] Likewise, Lescaze was later to write: "The architect's sphere is not a private occupation, . . . it embraces the planning and building of all the community."[38]

In contrast to the hypothetical and formal projects assigned at the École des Beaux-Arts, Moser's assignments stressed the practical. He gave his students problems related to current building needs. They made frequent visits to building sites in Zurich and its surroundings, where managers and laborers on the job offered practical information about particular problems and their possible solutions. Certainly, Moser was the first to provide Lescaze with his rationalist approach to design.

Yet, because new architectural forms rarely kept pace with the evolution of new architectural theories, the waning classicist tradition inherent in Moser's own work was communicated in his teaching.[39] It is reflected in Lescaze's 1919 diploma project—a new theater in a large building block on the site of the old railroad station in Zurich (Fig. 2).[40] The theater portion was to be developed in detail. The remaining space, which was to be used for any other purpose, was to be rendered only by a conceptual sketch.[41] Lescaze's solution prefigured his later modernist stance in that it was a smooth, clear, precise, and rational affair with emphasis on the geometry of its separate functional masses. Yet,

Fig. 3. William Lescaze, Self-Portrait, *6 February 1918.*

evoking German neo-classicism was its monumentality coupled with axial symmetry, a classicist composition including a rusticated ground floor and attic story, and a simplified, original grammar of neo-classical ornamentation. These qualities persisted on the interior as well.[42] This early project was to foretell a long and successful career for Lescaze in theater design: the Trans Lux, CBS, the huge and luxurious Calderone in Hempstead, Long Island, and Cinerama installations throughout the United States.

Although Lescaze was dedicated to the study of architecture while a student at the École Polytechnique, he did not abandon his love for painting and drawing. Several self-portraits in an expressionist vein survive from this period (Fig. 3).[43] Moreover, as president of Zofingue, his university fraternity, he was even called upon to perform as art historian, writing "Réflexions que l'oeuvre, la vie, et la mort de Hodler suggèrent en moi."[44]

Lescaze was graduated from the École Polytechnique when, because of the economic depression following the war, building was at a low ebb

and social reform and the production of low-cost housing were major preoccupations of revolutionary architects. Thus, after the receipt of his Master of Architecture degree on 31 July 1919, Lescaze was attracted by the opportunity to work on the planning and rebuilding of Arras, a town that had been devastated by the war.[45] There he joined the forces of the Committee for the Reconstruction of Devastated France. Lescaze immediately became disillusioned with the Committee, however, because it indulged in the worst kind of "jerry-building" and supported a sentimental effort to build the districts up again much as they had been before the war.[46] The Committee employed few new social concepts, limiting itself to communes based on the theories of Charles Fourier. In Lescaze's opinion, the results were devastating aesthetically, socially, and economically. Enraged by the corrupt administration of the project, and realizing that the latest developments in the industrial production of new standardized housing and in advanced social programs had no hope of being realized, Lescaze soon found himself in open conflict with the Committee.[47]

Consequently, he left Arras after only a few months in order to work for Henri Sauvage, to whom he had been introduced by friends in Paris. A pioneer modernist, Sauvage was at the time noted for his design of the ceramic tile-covered, stepped-back apartment house at 26 rue Vavin (1912), defining in that futurist form a volumetric character which he wanted to extend to the entire neighborhood in order to allow more light and air to penetrate to the streets.[48] Sauvage was dedicated to collective urban housing. He was a specialist in construction methods and a pioneer in prefabrication, advocating factory production of component units to be assembled on the site. Lescaze's experience in Sauvage's office, although brief, reinforced his interest in urban housing and provided an introduction to prefabrication techniques, both of which he was later to help pioneer in the United States.

Lescaze found Paris stimulating, the ideas and theories of Sauvage inspiring, and his draftsman's work in Sauvage's office congenial. But he soon became impatient and discouraged by the slow economic recovery in Europe after the war and the resulting limitation of building opportunities there.[49] The words of his teacher Karl Moser came back to him: "Where are you ever going to find the chance of doing monumental work? Egypt? It's too late—maybe America."[50]

Perhaps Moser did not refer to Lescaze's interest in the "monumental" in the sense of a traditionally monumental style or an inhuman scale but rather to Lescaze's interest in large-scale urban building, housing, and planning projects.[51] Moser noted that preference in a letter of recommendation, stating that Lescaze wished "to utilize his training to solve problems of practical workers' housing."[52]

Lescaze had little knowledge of America; he had not even known any Americans. But he began to think that maybe he could find there what he wanted. Author Paul Wingert reported that

In a general way, . . . he [Lescaze] thought of it as a vast country with a young, uninhibited culture which had produced big business, and new architectural expressions in the skyscraper, grain elevators, and other industrial buildings. He gradually became enthusiastic in his belief that America held at that time a greater future for a young creative architect than Europe could offer. Soon this enthusiasm became a determination.[53]

Lescaze talked about the idea with Sauvage and a young Swiss friend, Gustav Kullmann, who had just returned to Paris from America. Encouraged by Kullmann and Arnold Wolfers, another Swiss friend, Lescaze decided to leave Europe after only a year's professional experience to seek the fulfillment of his dreams in the United States.[54]

It was undoubtedly both the force of the hopelessness of creating architecture in post-war western Europe and a dreamer's and pioneer's spirit that induced Lescaze to go to America. He had no job prospects, very little knowledge of the English language, only a few letters of introduction, and a single letter of recommendation (written in German) from Karl Moser. He had but $500 in his pocket, given him by his father (who opposed his emigration), when he left Switzerland to earn a living building modern architecture in a country which at that time did not know the meaning of the word. Lescaze reasoned that because America was the most progressive country, it must be leading the avant-garde in architectural experimentation and would be the place where his own objectives could be achieved.[55] He was right, but there remained a long struggle to that goal.

NOTES

1. Birth certificate, WELA. Onex no longer exists except for a sectional place-name of a district in Geneva located around St. Pierre, Calvin's church. Lescaze's "Livret de Service" cites Avusy as birthplace, WELA.

2. "William E. Lescaze," Biographical Sketch (typescript for *Architectural Forum*), December 1934, WELA.

3. "William Edmond Lescaze Biographical Sketch" (typescript), July 1931, WELA.

4. See Hermann Kienzle, *Karl Moser* (Zurich: Verlag Der Zurcher Kunstgessellschaft, 1937), Tafel III.

5. Invitation, WELA, announces the "Exposition" from 11 to 23 April 1914.

6. Reply to a questionnaire (typescript), ca. 1950s, WELA.

7. William Lescaze, "On Architecture" (typescript), 3 May 1937, p. 2, WELA; William Lescaze, review of *Switzerland Builds* by G. E. Kidder Smith, in *Saturday Review*, 2 September 1950, p. 39.

8. Lescaze, review of *Switzerland Builds*, p. 39. He rose to the rank of Lieutenant in 1917.

9. See "Biographical Sketch of Lescaze of Howe and Lescaze" (typescript), July 1931, revised 1933, T-Estate-6-C, Records Office, Dartington Hall, Devon, England, hereafter referred to as RODH; "William Edmond Lescaze—Biographical Sketch" (typescript), 1931, WELA; "William Lescaze" (typescript), 1934, WELA. Swiss painters allied to the Parisian avant-garde at that time were Alice Bailly (1872–1938), Gustave Buchet (1899–1963), Jean Crotti (1878–1958), Johannes Itten (1888–1967), Oscar Luthy (1882–1945), and Otto Morach (1887–1973). It is likely that Lescaze knew something of their work through the Falot association, established in Geneva in 1910 to break away from the Geneva and Swiss traditions and to align itself with French schools of Cubism and Futurism. See Will Rotzler, Paul-André Jaccard, and Dominik Keller, "Aufbruch ins Neue 1910–1920: Sechs Schweizer Maler und die Pariser Avant-garde," *Du* 34 (August 1974):10–47.

10. The drawing is in the possession of Charles A. Harris, New York, who was given it by Lescaze when the two men lived in Cleveland from 1920–1923.

11. Moser's own work developed from historicism to modernism by way of *Jugendstil*.

12. William Lescaze, *On Being an Architect* (New York: G. P. Putnam's Sons, 1942), p. 153. Lescaze enrolled in October 1915; Alvin E. Jaeggli to Richard Pommer, 28 July 1973, copy sent to author.

13. Among the students of architecture at the École Polytechnique Federale contemporary with Lescaze were Kamenka, Marcel and Iuliu Iancu, Edouard Calame, Hans Schmidt, H. R. von der Mickel, Werner Moser, and Hans Hofmann. See Gilles Barbey, "William Lescaze (1896–1969)," *Werk*, no. 8 (1971), p. 559.

14. For Futurist theory see Antonio Sant'Elia and Filippo Tommaso Marinetti, "Futurist Architecture," *L'Architettura*, no. 13 (Rome, 1956), p. 516ff, published in Ulrich Conrads, ed., *Programs and manifestoes on 20th-Century Architecture*, trans. Michael Bullock (Cambridge, Mass: MIT Press, 1970), pp. 34–38.

15. Ozenfant had published the principle of Purism from 1915 to 1917 in the review *Elan*. For Le Corbusier's experiments see Le Corbusier, *Towards a New Architecture*, trans. Frederich Etchells (New York: Praeger Pubs., 1970), pp. 209–249; first published as *Vers une architecture* (Paris: Editions Cres, 1923).

16. For De Stijl theory see "De Stijl: Manifesto I," *De Stijl*, No. 1 (November 1918), p. 2, published in Conrads, *Programs and Manifestoes*, pp. 39–40; Theo van Doesburg, "Tot een Beeldende Architectuur," *De Stijl*, 12, no. 6/7 (Rotterdam, 1924), published in Conrads, *Programs and Manifestoes*, pp. 78–80; H. L. C. Jaffe, *De Stijl, 1917–1931* (Amsterdam, 1956); Theodore M. Brown, *The Work of G. Rietveld, Architect* (Ut-

recht: A. W. Bruna & Zoon, 1958).

17. For text of the Realist Manifesto, see Naum Gabo and Antoine Pevsner, *Konstruktive Plastik*, exhibiton catalogue from the Kestner-Gesellschaft (Hanover, 1930), published in Conrads, *Programs and Manifesotes*, p. 56. Also see Stephen Bann, ed., *The Tradition of Constructivism*. Documents of 20th Century Art Series (New York: Viking, 1974).

18. For Dada theory see Hans Richter, *Dada: Art and Anti-Art* (London, 1965); Dawn Ades, "Dada and Surrealism," in *Concepts of Modern Art*, eds. Anthony Richardson and Nikos Stangos (New York: Harper and Row, Pubs., Icon editions, 1974), pp. 109–136. Iancu to Lescaze, 20 January 1935, and Lescaze to Iancu, 28 February 1935, WELA; Mrs. Lescaze, notes to author, June 1977.

19. Paul Scheerbart, *Glass Architecture*, trans. James Palmes (New York: Praeger Pubs., 1972); first published as *Glasarchitektur* (Berlin: Verlag der Sturm, 1914).

20. See Dennis Sharp, *Modern Architecture and Expressionism* (New York: Braziller, 1966), chap. 6 passim; Bruno Taut, *Alpine Architektur* (Hagen, 1919); Bruno Taut, *Die Stadtkrone* (Jena, 1919); Walter Gropius, Bruno Taut, and Adolf Behne, *New Ideas on Architecture* (Berlin, 1919), published in Conrads, *Programs and Manifestoes*, pp. 46–48; Erich Mendelsohn, *The Problem of a New Architecture* (Berlin, 1919), partially published in Conrads, *Programs and Manifestoes*, pp. 54–55.

21. Conrads, *Programs and Manifestoes*, pp. 49–53.

22. Barbey, "William Lescaze," p. 559. Many foreign intellectuals, including Lenin, the German poet-philosopher Hugo Ball, the Rumanian painter and architect Marcel Iancu, the poet Tristan Tzarra, and the Alsatian painter Hans Arp lived in Zurich during Lescaze's university years there. Formulating his revolutionary theory in Zurich, Lenin traveled to St. Petersburg in 1917 to take command of the October Revolution.

23. "William Edmond Lescaze Biographical Sketch" (typescript), July 1931, WELA; "Biographical Sketch of Lescaze of Howe and Lescaze" (typescript), July 1931, revised 1933, T-Estate-6-C, RODH.

24. Lescaze, review of *Switzerland Builds*, p. 39.

25. Lescaze, *On Being an Architect*, p. 154.

26. Barbey, "William Lescaze," p. 559.

27. Lescaze, review of *Switzerland Builds*, p. 39.

28. "Biographical Sketch of Lescaze of Howe and Lescaze," RODH.

29. Kienzle, *Karl Moser*, p. 25.

30. William Lescaze, "The Classic of Tomorrow," *American Architect* 147 (December 1935):11.

31. William Lescaze, "City Home of William Lescaze," *The Technical Engineering News* 16 (June 1935):66.

32. William Lescaze, "Buildings School and Education" (typescript), 3 January 1939, WELA.

33. "William Edmond Lescaze Biographical Sketch" (typescript), WELA.

34. Lescaze, "The Classic of Tomorrow," pp. 11–12.

35. Ibid.

36. Lescaze, *On Being an Architect*, p. 12.

37. Kienzle, *Karl Moser*, pp. 22–27.

38. Lescaze, "The Classic of Tomorrow," p. 13.

39. Kienzle, *Karl Moser*, pp. 22–27. A number of Lescaze's sketches of classical buildings survive which date either from his school years in Zurich or his year in Paris in 1919–1920.

40. Photographs of project drawings were sent to Mrs. Lescaze by Edouard Calame on the request of the author.

41. Edouard Calame to Mrs. William Lescaze, 2 January 1973, WELA.

42. See Barbey, "William Lescaze," p. 559. The existing rendering of the diploma project interior elevation is inscribed on the reverse: "Given to Jean Binet, January 28, 1923, Cleveland."

43. Lescaze considered the German Swiss artist Max Oppenheimer (Mopp), known for his expressionist drawings to be one of the most critical and supportive influences on his artistic development. Mopp was working in Zurich in 1916 and 1917. List of Persons Influential or Supportive to Lescaze's Career (handwritten), July 1966, WELA.

44. *Zofingue Feville Centrale*, 58th Annual (July 1918), pp. 851, 859–865.

45. Dates of enrollment are verified in Alvin E. Jaeggli to Richard Pommer, 28 July 1973; copy sent to the author.

46. For a description of the war devastation in France and the reconstruction proposals, see Shepard B. Clough, Thomas Moodie, Carol Moodie, eds., *Economic History of Europe: Twentieth Century* (New York: Harper & Row, 1968), pp. 58–62, 115–118.

47. Barbey, "William Lescaze," p. 559.

48. Sauvage's stepped tall building was to become a cliché in America, encouraged by New York City's step-back law of 1916. William LeBaron Jenney and William B. Mundie are credited with the initial conception of the set-back as erected in their Manhattan Building, Chicago, 1889–1891. See Donald Hoffmann, "The Setback Skyscraper City of 1891: An Unknown Essay by Louis H. Sullivan," *Journal of the Society of Architectural Historians* 29 (May 1970):181–187.

49. The lack of professional opportunity in Europe was vividly expressed by Richard Neutra in a letter of 20 September 1919 to Rudolph M. Schindler:

> "Now I work in the architect's office shown above [Wernli and Stager, Wadenswil, Lake of Zurich]. But there is little to do. . . . A legion of people in the field of building, literally dead of hunger, forced out of an art which now seems far away as heaven. . . . I have looked zealously for a position for a long time, and in vain. . . . I studied one semester with Professor Moser at the Polytechnic in Zurich."

In another letter to Schindler, Neutra wrote on 17 November 1919:

> "You can hardly imagine how badly timed your idea of returning here seems to me. To say nothing of the material ruin here, the psychological collapse is so total that it affects even the healthiest like a contagious disease. . . . I am not so much broken as deeply uprooted in my whole being. Everything in me cries for impregnation while I am surrounded by the saddest impotence.

See Esther McCoy, ed, "Documentation. Letters between R. M. Schindler and Richard Neutra, 1914–1924," *Journal of the Society of Architectural Historians* 33 (October 1974):221.

50. Reply to a questionnaire, ca. 1950s, WELA. Sheldon and Martha Cheney, *Art and the Machine* (New York: Whittlesey House, McGraw-Hill, 1936), p. 168 quotes Lescaze as having come to America because European architecture was "too damned monumental."

51. During the first months of his residence in America, Lescaze wrote a play for the promotion of sound urban planning. He was among the earliest group of architects to design housing projects in the 1930s, beginning with the Chrystie-Forsyth project of 1932. He continued to build housing projects throughout his career and to serve on numerous State and Federal housing committees.

52. "Recommendation, 3 June 1920: The architect, Willy Lescaze from Geneva, Switzerland intends in America, the land of his very _____[unreadable] wishes, to undertake his work and there to utilize his training to solve problems of practical workers' housing. Lescaze studied four years at the

technical college in Zurich with the undersigned and other professors. His work offers the evidence of his talent and love of the profession. I am asking my honored colleagues to receive with friendship my former student. And I am signing with high respect. Karl C. Moser" (handwritten), WELA; translated from the German by the author.

53. See "William Lescaze: Modern American Architect" (typescript), ca. 1940, p. 12, WELA.

54. Before leaving Paris in 1920, Lescaze completed a competition project for a Maison du Peuple at La Chaux de Fonds, done in collaboration with Eduard Calame. It appears to have been dominated by Calame's more traditional neo-classical vision and/or an effort to please a conservative jury, or an unclear sense of what to propose, or all three.

55. "Biographical Sketch of Lescaze of Howe and Lescaze," RODH.

2
The Formative Years: 1920–1929

LESCAZE ARRIVED IN NEW YORK IN AUGUST OF 1920 eager to build modern architecture, to design workers' housing, and to plan communities.[1] But it was too early for any of these ambitions to be realized in the United States. The "new style" being developed in Europe in the 1910s and 1920s was not built in America until the end of the latter decade.[2] Moreover, the housing and community planning movement, which opened major building opportunities to the planning theorists of the twenties in Europe, did not get underway in the United States until the mid-thirties.

Thus, it is not surprising that in 1920, after making the rounds of architect's offices in New York, Lescaze received no encouragement. He decided to try his luck in Cleveland. He knew nothing about the city, but his friend Gustav Kullmann, who had been to Cleveland as a spokesman for the Swiss student movement, had given him a letter of introduction to the Director of the YMCA there.[3] Further, the much-loved bicycle he had as a boy in Switzerland was a "Cleveland," which he considered a good omen for success in finding employment in a city of the same name.[4] Because of his drawing ability, Lescaze did land a job, on Labor Day weekend, as a draftsman in the architectural offices of Hubbell and Benes, ironically enough one of the more conservative firms in the Midwest.[5] He augmented his $25 a week income by giving French lessons in the evenings at the YMCA where he lived—lessons at which he admitted probably having learned more English than his students did

French.[6] After only a few months, Hubbell and Benes were obliged to cut their staff, and Lescaze, the last hired, was discharged on Thanksgiving weekend. Consequently, in 1921 he went to work for Walter R. MacCornack, Chief of the Bureau of Design for the Cleveland Board of Education, as draftsman for school buildings, planner, and ultimately as designer of a warehouse.[7]

From Lescaze's friendship with MacCornack came much-needed professional encouragement and support. The monthly meeting of the Cosmos Club, held at the YMCA, offered him a touch of European ambience by the opportunity to meet with Russians, British, and Czechs for conversation and dinner. The Cleveland Museum of Art, the Cleveland Playhouse (for which he painted scenery), and the Kokoon Club (a local sketching club established in 1912) also served as social and cultural sustenance to Lescaze in his difficult first years in Cleveland.[8] But most importantly, Cleveland, although a city of modest size, was experiencing exciting new artistic activity in music, theater, painting, and literature.

The celebrated Cleveland Institute of Music, in which the precepts of Emile-Jacques Dalcroze were taught, attracted a colony of musicians. Among those who gathered there were Lescaze's old friend, Jean Binet, who had come from Switzerland to teach eurythmics at the Institute and to study composition with the Cleveland Orchestra's new composer-conductor Ernest Bloch. Lescaze was to establish a close friendship with these men, sharing their interest for music, the theater, and teaching.

He also found fellowship in a circle of readers, writers, and artists who met to talk and browse at Richard Laukhuff's little shop in the Taylor Arcade, which was full of fine books, good prints, and publications unavailable and almost unheard of elsewhere in Cleveland—the "radical stuff."[9] In addition to the musicians Bloch, Binet, Roger Sessions, and Bernard Rogers, the group included the poets Samuel Loveman and Hart Crane and the painters Charles Burchfield and William Sommer.[10]

During his three years in Cleveland, Lescaze painted a great deal to compensate for his lack of opportunity for architectural creativity. His paintings, shown at the Third Annual Exhibition of Cleveland Artists, held at the Cleveland Museum of Art from May third to fifth, 1921, caused much comment.[11] Hart Crane was moved to write to his literary friend Gorham Munson on 16 May 1921:

There is a French-Swiss artist here just eight months from Paris, . . . ; doing very interesting work with a peculiar sharp diabolism in it. Willy E. Lescaze. His work at a local exhibition here recently caused a terrible furor, being in company with Burchfield's the only work worth looking at. . . . I recently sent some of Lescaze's work to The Little Review along with S.'s [Sommer]—but whatever keeps Margaret Anderson so impolitely silent I cannot figure out.[12]

Fig. 4. *William Lescaze*, Richard L., *ca. 1920–1921, oil (Author).*

Seven of the sixteen works submitted by Lescaze were hung—oil paintings entitled *Richard L* (Laukhuff), *The Kingdom of Pan*, and *Love's Fulfillment*; watercolors entitled *Annunciation #1*, *Annunciation #2*, and *Christmas 1920*; and an ink drawing of a chapel (Fig. 4).[13] Lescaze's well-developed personal expression in the expressionist and cubist styles were not at all understood, or at least not accepted, by most Cleveland critics. It was reported that Lescaze had committed six "atrocities . . . three in oil and three in water-colors"; that the portrait of *Richard L* looked as if he had been "buried for months and then dug up, with decomposition far advanced in his head and hands"; that the *Kingdom of Pan* should be retitled "The Kingdom of Pandemonium"; and that *Love's Fulfillment*, a near-geometric arrangement of diamonds and oblongs, was the "most bizarre of all."[14] They were further criticized as "pathological, in need of fumigation, unwholesome, insane, and not suitable for hanging in houses since they were only endurable at a distance of thirty feet or looked at through an opera glass turned wrong end to."[15]

There were favorable opinions as well. *The Cleveland Topics* asserted that Willy Lescaze had excited more comment than anyone else and that for the first time in the exhibition's history, the show leaned toward the "radical." The critic went on to report that "the lifelike portrait of *Richard L* fairly bubbles over with its happy spirit," that "a simple composition entitled *Fulfillment of Love*, which thoroughly explains that age-old perplexing question, [is] the most interesting," and that "*The Kingdom of Pan* leaves little to be asked for in landscape and figure composition."[16] With still more critical insight, L. W. Smith commented that Lescaze "dared to portray his subjects as they appear to him instead of portraying them as they might desire to appear to others."[17] Lescaze's radicalism was not, however, rewarded by the exhibition's judges.[18]

A month after the show closed at the Cleveland Museum of Art, several of Lescaze's paintings were exhibited in Mr. Laukuff's bookstore. A year later, a large exhibition of his work was mounted by Jean Binet and Hubbard Hutchinson on Euclid Avenue.[19] For the Cleveland art world, Lescaze's painting was avant-garde indeed. It was dominated by an expressionist line and cubo-futurist devices of ray-lines and faceting. For Lescaze, as for the majority of Americans, cubism meant little more than sharp lines and acute angles and was seen only in terms of its surface effects. Thus, directional lines and frag-

Fig. 5. William Lescaze, photocopy of Portrait of Hart Crane, *1922 (Author).*

mented shapes were placed upon essentially realistic compositions, resulting in a kind of semiabstract cubo-realism.[20] An allegorical watercolor, painted for Charles Harris, and miscellaneous decorative and advertising materials were still more casually derived from cubist theory. These were not unlike chic Parisian Art Déco's or Vienese Secession's angular, abstract forms spread with a staccato rhythm decoratively over a surface.

Lescaze's drawings continued to be rendered with a sensitive expressionist line. In his portraits, a Kokoschkaesque expressionism can be observed in the rendering of the hands.[21] Under the influence of German-Swiss expressionist Max Oppenheimer (Mopp), Lescaze had perfected his style in a 1918 portrait of his mother. But in contrast to the Impressionist pastel palette used in that painting, the Cleveland palette ranged from analytic cubism's somber play of neutral tones to the fully saturated palette of Italian futurism. His bent toward painterly expressionism was later to become characteristic of both his architectural forms and architectural renderings throughout most of his career.

In 1922 Lescaze sketched a portrait of his friend Hart Crane, which Crane arranged to have published in a 1923 issue of the Paris magazine *Gargoyle*

(Fig. 5). Crane was overjoyed with it. "I have recently had myself futuristically sketched by Lescaze," he wrote Munson. "When I get some money I intend to have a few photographs made of it, and will send you one; I like the thing very much, although most of my friends insist on saying that I never look quite so insane as the picture suggests." Later, he wrote to Munson: "I'm glad you like Lescaze's 'portrait' of me. He *has* an athletic style."[22] Crane was particularly delighted that the right eye was the focus of the composition by reason of the heavy emphasis with which it was drawn. He told his friends that Lescaze had discovered in him Jakob Boehme's visionary man—the right eye focused on the future and eternity, while the left looked backward into time.[23] From this, Crane developed the half-fanciful, half-serious notion that a certain intensity and clarity of expression in the right eye betokened a person of mystic predisposition or power. He alluded to the portrait in the closing lines of the first part of *For the Marriage of Faustus and Helen:*

> Accept a lone eye riveted to your plane, Bent Axle
> of devotion along the companion ways
> That beat, continuous, to hourless days—one
> inconspicuous, glowing orb of praise.[24]

Crane inscribed the drawing: "Willy, thanks for seeing me so nicely, Hart Crane."[25]

Crane not only loved his portrait but he also covered the walls of the tower-room in his parents' Queen Anne-style house with paintings by Lescaze and William Sommer. Crane's and Lescaze's common interest in modern French literature caused the two men to have many good times together driving in the country discussing philosophy and painting. Crane wrote to his friend, Munson: "A friend of mine here, Lescaze the painter, is an excellent literary critic. . . ."[26] A few months later, Crane again remarked:

> My friend, the Swiss-French painter, . . . Willy Lescaze, has proved an inspiration to me. Knowing intimately the work of Marcel Proust, Salmon, Gide, and a host of other French moderns, he is able to see so much better than anyone else around here, the aims I have in my own work. We have had great times discussing the merits of mutual favorites like Joyce, Donne, Eliot, Pound, de Gourmont, Gordon Craig, Nietzsche, etc. After this it goes without saying that I never found a more stimulating individual in New York.[27]

25

It is probably not surprising that Lescaze was called a painter rather than an architect by Crane. For painting was Lescaze's only really creative outlet at the time; he used it as a means of expressing the most personal events of his life. His architectural work as a draftsman for conservatively-styled school buildings depressed him. During this period of eclectic-historicism in American architecture, Gothic or Georgian revival styles were usually considered appropriate for schools. To Lescaze such ideas were an attack on the integrity of his trade. He moped, took long walks, and painted. As an expression of his inner melancholy, he wore a black tie.[28]

Lescaze also instituted a weekly "salon" for his friends to discuss the arts—poetry, painting, architecture, and music. Meeting at various hotels and restaurants for two to three hours on Thursday afternoons, the group consisted of regular members plus the composers and musicians who might be visiting the Institute of Music, the Cleveland Playhouse, or the Opera.[29] The regular members were: Hart Crane (poet), Charles Harris (engineer and poet), Samuel Loveman (poet), Richard Rychtarik (Czechoslovakian artist who designed sets for the Cleveland and the Metropolitan operas), Charlotte Rychtarik (musician), William Sommer (painter), Ernest Nelson (painter and poet), and Gordon Hatfield (composer).[30] "Everybody conversed, and everybody was happy," Sam Loveman recalled; yet Crane complained of the quality of the feminine participation.[31] Of the members, Crane was Lescaze's most constant attendant.[32]

Lescaze's role in fostering appreciation of modern art in Cleveland is best revealed in Crane's letter of 16 May 1922:

Have you seen the amazing satires of Georg Grosz and the beautiful metaphysics of Chirico? My friend Lescaze has put me in touch with a lot of moderns that I fear, off here in Cleveland, I should otherwise never have heard of.[33]

Lescaze kept in touch with the New York art world as well, exhibiting three oil paintings, *Music*, *The King and Dancers*, and *Decision* at the Montross Gallery in New York in April 1922.[34]

Yet, painting and languishing as a draftsman were not Lescaze's dreams for his career in America. This fact was demonstrated by his scenario, "Wealth or The Thrift of the City Plan," written with H. B. Brainerd in December 1920,

soon after his arrival in Cleveland. In keeping with the futurists' call for town planning projects, the authors expressed, in dramatized form their dedication to the need for city planning. Typical of the numerous idealistic city plans of the twenties, their redesign of an industrial city called for harmony between the social order and nature. Illustrating some of their points were examples of the garden city and satellite towns in Germany and England.[35] Because the housing and community planning movement had hardly yet begun in Europe and was not to get underway in America for another decade and a half, the treatise must have been inspired by Lescaze's training under Hans Bernouille at the École Polytechnic Federale and was probably one of the earliest of its kind.

Yet, by 1922 Lescaze's hope of building the monumental, of designing workers' housing, of planning new communities, or of improving human environment in the modern industrial society of America was fading. But in that year, MacCornack made Lescaze responsible for the design of a large warehouse, a greater challenge than his draftsman's job had yet offered. Only an elevation drawing of its principal façade, dated June 1922, is known to survive (Fig. 6). Judging from the rendering, it was a four-story building about 65 feet high and 260 feet long, with raised basement, and of brick construction. Like his earlier Diploma project of 1919, it was a simple, classicist composition. The façade was articulated with light, ground-to-cornice glazed arcading, not unlike that which Moser used in his University of Zurich in 1914. The perimeters of the arcading and the total block were detailed only with gauged brick, and the entrance portal was subordinated almost to disappearance within the central arch. Although a coherent scheme, Lescaze probably found it an unfulfilling challenge within his architectural objectives.

Fig. 6. William Lescaze, warehouse, Cleveland, Ohio, 1922. Elevation rendering of principal façade.

This assumption is corroborated by Hart Crane's statement of June 1922 (the same date as the rendering of the warehouse elevation) that "he [Lescaze] hates Cleveland with all the awareness of the recent description of this place accorded in the last *Masses* or *Liberator*."[36] As Crane's comment might suggest, Lescaze returned to Europe in order to re-evaluate his decision to practice architecture in the United States.

The precise time of Lescaze's visit to Europe is uncertain, but he undoubtedly left sometime in the fall of 1922 (when Crane began to take orders for copies of *Ulysses*, which Lescaze was supposed to smuggle back into the country), and before 7 November, at which time Crane wrote: "I have rather missed Lescaze's stimulation since he left."[37]

Lescaze traveled widely on the Continent, establishing professional contacts and assimilating all the new developments in architecture that he could observe. In Berlin he visited two of his École Polytechnique classmates who were working in the studio of architect and noted furniture designer Bruno Paul.[38] At that time Paul had few architectural commissions, as did most European architects during the long post-war depression. But Paul encouraged Lescaze to stay and head a modern furniture design project that he expected to lead to an architectural studio.[39] Although Lescaze did not stay, his European sojourn was of central importance to his professional education. Berlin was then the center of a turmoil of art movements and architectural activity, with significant ideas, too, developing in Weimar and in Paris, where he also visited. Indeed, between the time Lescaze left Europe in 1920 and his return in 1922–1923, important new projects, treatises, exhibitions, and buildings had been developed all over Europe.

Some of these innovations included the formation of a revolutionary architecture by an active group of visionary and utopian designers in Germany.[40] Their radical expressionist philosophy was promoted from 1920–1922 through Bruno Taut's Berlin and Magdeburg editions of *Das Frühlicht*.[41] In 1923 Mies van der Rohe's visionary second project for a glass curtain wall skyscraper (1922) was published in the Berlin avant-garde art journal *G* (Material Zur Elementaren Gestaltung) and in the *Journal of the American Institute of Architects;* his project for a reinforced concrete office building (1922) had also been drawn.[42] Several expressionist buildings had actually been realized in Germany: in 1921 Erich Mendelsohn's Einstein Tower was completed

in Potsdam, in 1922–1923 Fritz Höger's Chilehaus and Hans and Oskar Gerson's Ballinhaus were built in Hamburg, and between 1920 and 1924 Peter Behrens's I. G. Farben Dyeworks building was executed at Höchst.

By 1923 the radicalism of the early years of expressionism had been tempered by the stabilization of the German economy and the pressing need for housing. Thus, a new rational-expressionism was reflected in Mendelsohn's Berliner Tageblatt building (in collaboration with Richard Neutra and R. P. Henning), his Luckenwalde Factory, and Hugo Häring's Gut Garkau farm buildings at Lübeck, all completed in 1923.

Contradictory philosophies flourished as well. Lescaze had returned to Europe just at the time that the neo-plastic theories of De Stijl were reaching maturity in the Netherlands and being disseminated over the Continent. The periodical, *De Stiji*, launched in 1917, regularly spread the principles of elemental creativity, reaching an ever-widening audience with its publication in German in 1921. Between 1920 and 1923 the painter-writer-polemicist Theo van Doesburg promoted his principles in France, Belgium, and Germany so successfully that neo-plasticism, together with constructivism, succeeded in dominating the whole of modern design by the latter year. Some of its "message" may have come through the Weimar Constructivist-Dada International Conference, led jointly by van Doesburg and the Russian constructivist Eliezar Lissitsky in September 1922. Also convening in Weimar that month was the Berlin *G* group, composed of constructivists, dadaists, and followers of De Stijl, who promoted the essential principles of De Stijl, but with the addition of the constructivist concept of economy of form.[43] These meetings in Weimar and the architectural exhibition held in Berlin in the winter of 1922–1923 signaled the synthesis of neo-plasticism and constructivism, with the critics saying "this is the new architecture."[44] Almost all were to leave an impression on the young Lescaze, as can be seen in his work by 1927.

The focal-point of the avant-garde of Europe in the summer of 1923 was the Bauhaus's exhibition, coupled with an international exhibition of architecture and a show of "free art" at the Landesmuseum.[45] The Bauhaus's only building, "Am Horn," designed by the painter George Muche and constructed under the direction of Adolf Meyer, provided a practical demonstration of the style that had emerged from the functionalist approach.[46] Although Lescaze returned to America a few months prior to the exhibition, its content (shaped by De Stijl and constructivist theory professed by staff members Laszlo Moholy-Nagy, Joseph Albers, Herbert Bayer, and lecturer J. J. P. Oud) must have been well known in Weimar several months prior to its opening. An etching by Lescaze, inscribed "27th March 1923/Geneva Weimar New York/ at Mrs. S. Ford," documents his presence in Weimar at that critical time.[47]

Lescaze had also left Europe prior to the large-scale exhibition of De Stijl work at Leonce Rosenberg's Galerie de l'Effort Moderne in Paris, held late in 1923.[48] A great success, the show was later restaged at the École Speciale d'Architecture in Paris and then traveled to Nancy. Although these exhibitions had not been available to Lescaze first hand, illustrations were published in a 1924 edition of *De Stijl*.[49] At about the same time in Holland, van Doesburg was writing a "rationale of the new architecture, crystallizing in his '16 Points of a Plastic Architecture' some of the architectural ideas that the De Stijl architects had developed since 1917."[50] It was widely disseminated through republications in French and German as well as Dutch.[51] Lescaze's work in the early thirties suggests that he was well acquainted with all the theoretical thrusts of neo-plasticism and constructivism.

Undoubtedly as great an influence at this time as the De Stijl and constructivist activities were the works and writings of Le Corbusier. Working independently, but not uninfluenced by neo-plasticism and constructivism, Le Corbusier was greatly responsible for there being a recognizable International Style, setting out what was to become a large part of its vocabulary. He exhibited his Citrohan house model in 1921; he designed his stylistically fully developed house at Vaucresson and the Ozenfant studio in Paris in 1922; and he completed the La Roche-Jeanneret houses in Paris by 1923. In the same year, he set forth his philosophy of a new architecture in *Vers une architecture*, using much of the content from the essays he had published in *L'Esprit Nouveau* since 1920. Lescaze's oeuvre of the thirties reveals that he was in touch with these developments, too—through his travels, his reading, and his personal and professional associations in Paris and other parts of Europe.[52]

Still, with no large amount of building activity yet underway in Europe, Lescaze decided in March of 1923 to return to America.[53] While enroute, he

Fig. 7. William Lescaze, Simeon Ford house, 2 Sutton Square, New York. Exterior before remodeling of 1923.

received a cablegram from the Simeon Fords inviting him to remodel their soon-to-be-purchased New York town house on the corner of Sutton Place and Sutton Square. Lescaze had met the Fords, as a guest of Jean Binet, at their Christmas party in New York in 1921.[54] Following this offer came a telegram from MacCornack inviting him to return to his Cleveland office.[55] Lescaze was able to accept both proposals. He returned to Cleveland until May when the Fords completed the purchase of the property that was to give him the opportunity he had been waiting for—a chance to establish a private practice.[56]

Lescaze established his own architectural studio on 1 June 1923 at 24 West Eighth Street, New York. His office consisted of only himself and the Simeon Ford commission.[57] Yet, it allowed Lescaze to fulfill the first of two resolutions that he had made to himself during his years in Cleveland: that he would quit whatever salaried job he might have and set out for himself the moment he got his first commission.[58] The Ford job did not allow him much freedom to speculate on new architectural forms, however. Like his Diploma project and the Cleveland warehouse, it continued in the transitional mode of early twentieth-century neoclassicism becoming modern. But it was a substantial commission, one that was to send him on his way toward establishing a successful career in architecture.

The Fords required complete interior renovation of their Sutton Place townhouse and the addition of a fifth floor studio for their daughter, Lauren.[59] Lescaze converted the exterior from its nineteenth century Italianate styling to that of eclectic neo-classicism (Figs. 7 and 8). He changed the heavy, three-dimensional, bracketed roof cornice to a light, thin, cavetto-molding embellished with paterae. In the interest of smooth, planar surfaces, he removed the projecting window pediments, the heavy fielded-panels under the first floor windows, and the high entrance stairs. He changed the sash from bold, single-paned, double-hung windows to small-paned casements with transoms. The original entrance, on the Sutton Place side, was moved to the Sutton Square façade in order to accommodate redesigned interior spaces. In its place Lescaze installed a neo-classical niche. The new entrance was defined with a broken pediment, flanking pilasters, and flat quoin blocks, all composed to give scale and importance to a previously plain wall. These Renaissance Revival details and the figural sculpture rising from the roof on the Sutton Place side served to articulate the two elevations.[60]

The scheme for the fifth-floor studio, like the Sutton Place façade, was affected by the same spirit that inspired Lescaze's neo-classical Diploma project and the Cleveland warehouse. But, compared to those earlier works, the mass was reduced still further and the detailing abstracted to a single unifying fillet, a circle, and a triangle—probably inspired by the new graphic effects being created in

Fig. 8. William Lescaze, Simeon Ford house, 2 Sutton Square, New York. Exterior after remodeling of 1923.

Berlin and Weimar, the centers of De Stijl and constructivist activity, when Lescaze visited them in 1922–1923. Inspiration from the classical past was a school influence that, as an historical image, Lescaze was soon to discard, but as a philosophy of clarity, refinement, and purity of form, he was never to abandon.

For the next six years Lescaze supported himself mainly by jobs that gave little challenge to his talent. For two years his commissions were mostly a series of interiors for Chinese restaurants and night clubs, done in association with other architects. Architect Hugh Tallant asked Lescaze to collaborate with him on the Willow Garden restaurant in Brooklyn because he thought Lescaze might know more about Chinese interiors than he did. Lescaze later wrote: "All I knew of Chinese interiors were those two Chinese screens," which he had admired on the balcony of the Metropolitan Museum of Art.[61]

Expressing the enthusiasm of the twenties for mural paintings, decorative panels, and painted screens—not to mention the Chinese taste—Lescaze, assisted by his friends (including Lauren Ford, Jeanne de Lanux, and Edith Moore), painted the beams of the restaurant with oriental landscape scenes and the window shades with New York elevated railway stations posing as Chinese pagodas. The screens were animated with a melange of Chinese buildings and gardens, the Brooklyn Bridge, Borough Hall, a miscellany of local scenery, stylized natural vignettes, and floral bands.[62] All of the decorations were rendered in an eclectic synthesis of realism and cubo-realism, a style popular in America in the twenties and thirties and one commonly used by Lescaze at that time. The decorative but ill-fated restaurant was closed by Tong warfare the night before it was to be opened, leaving Lescaze with 200 bentwood chairs instead of payment for the job.[63] A similar commission, except that this one opened, was the conversion of the Moulin Rouge restaurant in Brooklyn to the King's Tea Garden. It was done with Herman E. Rufenacht, a Swiss architect who joined Lescaze as draftsman in 1925.[64]

An important association at this period was with William Lawrence Bottomley, who practically supported Lescaze in the lean years from 1923 to 1926 by bringing him jobs for interior designs of restaurants and night clubs. The Lido restaurant, Club Mirador, and Club Montmartre, all in New York, are but a few examples.[65] Robert D. Kohn, who was finishing an addition to the R. H. Macy Company

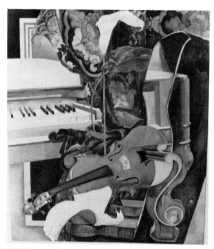

Fig. 9. William Lescaze, Hommage à Consuelo, *1925, oil (Author).*

in 1924, also aided Lescaze by commissioning him to assist with the show rooms, a gallery, and the tea room. Lescaze later wrote: "It was not so much the size or kind of jobs that mattered but the feeling that your elders knew you, had some faith in your ability, did something positive to help you."[66] Lescaze needed this work not only in order to support himself, but because he believed that he had to be active in order to obtain better commissions. He hoped that eventually he would be able to fulfill that second promise to himself—the acceptance only of work in which the client was willing to accept the ideas of the architect.

Unfortunately, his next architectural commission, the addition of a boy's dormitory to the collegiate gothic Edgewood School in Greenwich, Connecticut, gave him little more freedom than did the Ford house.[67] In this dearth of architectural opportunity, painting continued to be the medium in which Lescaze could express himself most freely. Yet, the fact that there are few known paintings from his early years in New York probably reflects his greater satisfaction with life and work there than in Cleveland.[68]

Part of that new quality of life came through the Whitney Studio Club (just a few doors away from his West Eighth Street apartment), where Lescaze met the painter, connoisseur, and modern art collector Albert E. Gallatin, a Genevais, who became a close friend. It may have been Gallatin who introduced Lescaze to Constantin Brancusi during the summer of 1925, a meeting that was to develop into

a lasting friendship with the two men sharing their philosophies of pure form.[69]

Another stimulus came through his visit to the Exposition Internationale des Arts Décoratifs et Industriels Modernes in the summer of 1925.[70] Lescaze's paintings and interiors of 1925–1927 show that he was well acquainted with the eclectic styles exhibited there. His *Hommage à Consuelo,* inscribed "New York 1925 April Lescazes [sic] architect painted this picture for the show at the Whitney Studio Club," reflects the impact of snythetic cubism on his work (Fig. 9).[71] The four tapestries he designed in that year for a theater in New Haven are characteristic of mid-1920s painting in their lyrical expressionism and popularized vocabulary of an exotic Eastern iconography—a subtle melange of primitive, archaic, and classical forms (Fig. 10). A year later, however, Lescaze drew quite a different image, that of a ship's engine housing, in the spirit of the cubist-precisionist painters Charles Demuth and Charles Sheeler (Fig. 11).

Lescaze's interiors of the twenties were also

Fig. 10. William Lescaze, tapestry design for a theater in New Haven, Connecticut, 1925.

characterized by mixed motifs, especially from French sources. In Cleveland, Halle Brothers Department Store, which led the department store promotion of modern design in the Midwest, invited Lescaze to assemble a group of paintings, fabrics, furniture, and accessories, and to design its exhibit for its Art in Industry Exposition, held in August of 1927 in cooperation with the Cleveland Industrial Exposition (Fig. 12).

From Paris and from New York artists and importers Lescaze assembled furniture, sculpture, paintings, mosaics, wood carvings, fabrics, and various objets d'art showing the "modernistic touch."[72] Paintings by Peter Blume, Yasuo Kuniyoshi, Man Ray, Buck Ulreich, and Lescaze hung on the walls of the booth together with murals by Alexandre Tiranoff and mosaics from the Ravenna Studios. Sculptures by Alexandre Archipenko and Warren Wheelock were exhibited as were ceramic figures from the well-known French Lallemant and Primavera studios and from the Viennese Wiener Werkstätte.[73] Fabrics by Bianchini Ferrier, Cheney

Fig. 12. William Lescaze, Halle Brothers exhibit for the "Art in Industry" Exposition, Cleveland, Ohio, 1927.

Brothers, Chambord, and Stehli Silks Corporation, all companies which employed notable artists for designs, were displayed. Furniture from the Paris Studio, the Lescord Shop (which was never a shop but a registered name for Lescaze's interior and furniture design work), and from Paul T. Frankl was displayed in the exhibit.[74] Architectural designs were exhibited by Hugh Ferriss, Frederick Kiesler, Henry Churchill and Herbert Lippmann, Lescaze and Bitterman (a furniture maker who fabricated Lescaze's designs for a short time), Lescaze and Herman Rufenacht (Lescaze's first professionally trained architect-draftsman and a furniture designer), Wilhelm T. Otto, and the firm of Voorhees, Gmelin, and Walker.[75]

The exhibit bore the images of the many sources characteristically utilized in the decorative arts in the late 1920s in America—Egyptian, Mayan, Oriental, and African motifs, the set-back forms from skyscraper design, the Vienna Secession, neo-classicism, constructivism, De Stijl, cubism, Parisian Art Déco, and the dynamism of German expressionism and Italian futurism. The rapid changes of ornamental vocabularies and the ideological complexities of the 1920s, looking both forward to the fourth decade of the twentieth century and backward to the nineteenth century, make it difficult to label the style. But, clearly, it was an expression of a new spirit resulting in free imagery of form, color, and design.

A notable example of this watershed period in design—of looking forward and backward, of tradition becoming modern—was Lescaze's own apartment and studio at 337 East Forty-Second Street, where he had moved in 1925 and probably remod-

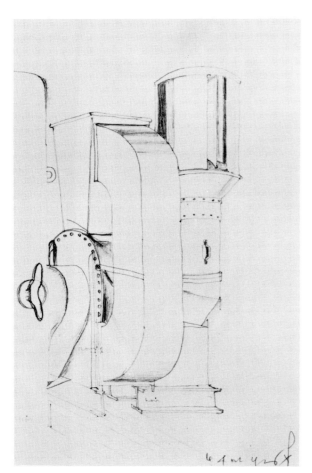

Fig. 11. William Lescaze, ship detail, drawing, October 1926.

Fig. 13. William Lescaze, Lescaze's duplex apartment and architectural office, 337 East Forty-second Street, New York, ca. 1927. Bathroom mural (Arts and Decoration 28 [November 1927]: 50).

eled soon after his return from Spain in 1926. He furnished his bedroom with seventeenth-century Spanish and eighteenth-century French antique furniture and accessories. His expressionist mural paintings, similar to French and German work of the 1920s, decorated the walls. Of particular note was the bathroom, raised three steps from the bedroom so that the tub might be "sunken," decorated with wall paintings composed of a maze of foliage, flowers, and wild animal life, called "modernistic" and "ultra-modern" in the 1927 and 1928 reviews of the apartment (Fig. 13).[76] Like the tapestry designs of 1925, the mural bore allusions to exotic decorative styles that abstracted natural, classical, and primitive prototypes. In a Rousseauesque spirit, the mural recalls that done by Armand-Albert Rateau, in the same year that Lescaze visited Spain, for the bathroom in the Spanish palace of the Duchess of Alba.[77]

On the studio walls, Lescaze painted murals of an entirely different character. He integrated typical Art Déco triangular corner lighting fixtures into one

Fig. 14. William Lescaze, Lescaze's duplex apartment and architectural office, 337 East Forty-second Street, New York, ca. 1927. Office mural.

of the compositions by the application of futurist ray lines appropriate to the light's radiation and symbolic of its energy (Fig. 14).[78] In another, Lescaze celebrated the all-encompassing symbolism of the futurists—speed, mechanization, technical progress, and the metropolis. He utilized some of the most evocative images produced by the modernists—the train, plane, ship, and automobile—not unlike Fritz Lang's "City of the Future" portrayed in the 1926 United Film Artists production, *Metropolis*.[79]

The mixing of modernist and traditional motifs in Lescaze's studio-apartment suggests an exploratory, developmental, experimental period in his career. But, rather than being a symptom of his own indecision, these contrasting spirits probably reflected, in a general way, a confused, divided, and undecided period in the history of painting, architecture, and design. In painting, "the desire to compromise, to strike a balance between the old and the new, led painters to concoct an eclectic synthesis that would combine the best of all possible styles."[80] In architecture, revolutionary modernisms challenged historic traditions with compromising results as well. André Lurçat commented in an article of January 1926 that the new architecture in France was "completely isolated, unknown by the public, and ignored by artists." By the time the article was published in the United States eighteen months later, an amending note explained that "the public seems much more favorable to our movement, apparently recognizing its necessity and truth."[81]

Lescaze was acquainted with the development of the new architecture of which Lurçat spoke, not only by his schooling in Zurich, his work experience in France, and his several months in Germany, but also through his annual visits with friends and professional colleagues on the Continent.[82] In 1926, the year in which Lurçat indicated that the International Style was "unknown by the public, and ignored by artists," Lescaze visited Stuttgart, where the Deutscher Werkbund's Weissenhofsiedlung exhibition was just being completed. The most important housing complex of the decade, it established the dominance of the functionalist philosophy of design for more than another quarter of a century. In the same year, Lescaze again visited Berlin, still the center of the architectural avant-garde.[83] In 1927 he visited Le Corbusier in France and learned of his work in the development of a new architecture.[84] Still, the new style was not yet des-

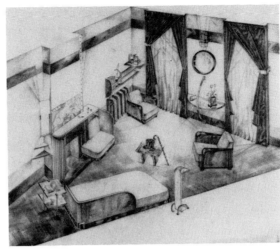

Fig. 15. William Lescaze, R. Colfax Phillips apartment, 19 West Twelfth Street, New York, 1927–1928. Axonometric rendering of living room.

tined to be built on the East Coast of the United States. In fact, Art Déco was not even to reach its height in New York until between 1928 and 1931.[85]

Indeed, neo-classical, cubist, and expressionist Art Déco forms characterized most of Lescaze's work throughout the twenties. In his 1927–1928 scheme for the R. Colfax Phillips apartment at 19 West Twelfth Street, Lescaze painted the entrance wall with geometric forms organized in a cubist-derived composition in an effort to relate a "Chinese" bookcase to the wall and to other architectural elements.[86] In keeping with the new modernism, dark, wide, flat "cornice bands" (to be installed several inches below the ceiling) and wide baseboards were proposed to replace the traditionally-profiled members in order to introduce a bold horizontal direction to the scheme (Fig. 15). French Déco was notable in the geometric, sharply-cut silhouette design of the wall-hung table and in the bulky, curvilinear, upholstered furniture designed by Lescaze and his draftsman, Herman Rufenacht. Triangular lighting fixtures, similar to those in Lescaze's studio, were installed at the juncture of the fireplace and the wall. Their placement, the triangular shelves below, a stepped-leg stool, the drapery treatment and the asymmetrical furniture arrangement all contributed to the "zig-zag" Déco tradition dominant in the twenties.[87] Among the earliest designers of metal furniture in America, Lescaze and Rufenacht specified nickel-plated metal for the framing of a glass table, for a floor lamp, as part of a wall-hung table and wall lamp, as drapery tie-backs at each window, and for the corner of the fireplace.[88] Even drapery material with a metallic look was specified.

In total, the Phillips apartment interior was a bold statement of contrasting values and reflective surfaces—mirrors, chrome, steel, glass, bakelite— all shimmering with light.[89] It represented the angular, cubist decor, a transitional phase between the elegant French Art Déco and the fully realized modern movement. It was perhaps apropos the Phillips apartment that Henry-Russell Hitchcock wrote in his 1929 criticism of Lescaze's interiors:

> But the difficulty of receiving effective cooperation in a city whose "modernism" consists of copying the poorest French models of the New Tradition excuses much, as does also the inherent difficulty of installing completely coherent new Pioneer rooms in old buildings.[90]

It was probably through his "French connections" that a commission of quite a different nature came to Lescaze—a "hunting lodge" in Mt. Kisco, New York, for E. Jean de Sièyes, a French count who was connected with a French bank in New York.[91] De Sièyes required that three separate living areas be incorporated into his small country retreat: a large living room in the center, flanked by a servants' wing and a bedroom-guest wing.

Lescaze's first scheme of October 1927 coupled the simplicity of handcraft precedent with the machine forms of the 1920s (Fig. 16). Its form was dominated by a sheer-walled, stuccoed, central block, penetrated only by a door and a large factory-type window "wrapping" the corner. The principal elevations of the servants' wing and the bedroom-guest wing were also finished with

Fig. 16. William Lescaze, Jean de Sièyes House, Mt. Kisco, New York, 1927–1928. Perspective rendering of first scheme, October 1927.

Fig. 17. William Lescaze, Jean de Sièyes House, Mt. Kisco, New York. 1927–1928, Principal façade.

smooth, white, stucco surfaces, interrupted only by royal-blue-framed horizontal windows. In the purist and constructivist tradition, the massing of the separate parts was conceived with clarity and rendered with crispness and refinement as three carefully proportioned, independent, geometric forms, precisely articulated. The tradition of vernacular architecture was introduced with the texture of shingled gable roofs, a few window shutters (probably used to extend visually the horizontality of the bedroom casement windows), a brick-faced foundation, and a stone wall. All were useful in relating the structure to its picturesque, country, hillside site. This design proved to be, however, both too large and too modern for de Sièyes.

The second scheme modified the first by truncation of the servants' block and the addition of picturesqueness through a wood-railed terrace over the garage, clapboards of irregularly split cypress on the wings, a smaller horizontal window wrapping the living room corner, and more shutters. The result might be compared with the anonymous character of the California Spanish style, the American farmhouse, or the early work of Swiss modernist, Giovanni Panozzo.[92]

As built, the house incorporates the traditionalizing of the second scheme, plus the addition of a Dutch-style gable roof on the center block with a porch overhang supported by thin columns, and awnings at the windows (Fig. 17). Henry-Russell Hitchcock characterized it as "fundamentally traditional even with its large windows and horizontality."[93] A 1929 issue of The Building Developer called it "a combination of old and new" and indicated that "by such transitory stages the public may eventually become accustomed to the new conception of beauty."[94]

The interiors were also a combination of old and new, although here Lescaze was able to exert more effective control over the relationship of furniture to architectural space than in the Phillips apartment (Fig. 18). The de Sièyes house furniture and lighting fixtures reflected the influence of French work, as did the Phillips apartment, but of a quite different type. The new influence came from the 1928 Paris Salon des Artistes-Décorateurs, where the eclectic amalgam of styles exhibited at the 1925 Paris Exposition had largely been abandoned.[95] Lescaze's assimilation of neo-plastic and rationalist forms dominated the de Sièyes interiors, with the French Art Déco aesthetics emerging only incidentally.

The bold, white, asymmetrical fireplace (the first of many of this type Lescaze was to design in his career) and most of the furniture, especially designed for the house, reflected the De Stijl-constructivist philosophies with their emphasis on functional, structural, and spatial concepts rather than the decorative. The neo-plastic design of the lighting fixture over the dining table most surely was derived either from that designed by Walter Gropius in 1923 for his office at the Bauhaus in Weimar or from its prototype designed by Rietveld for Dr. Hartog's study at Maarssen in 1920.[96] Elementarist abstraction characterized the design of the upholstery fabric on the rectilinear couch and the wood-framed chairs, recalling the work of Anni Albers at the Bauhaus in 1927. At the same time, a Rodier patterned fabric covered the French Déco-profiled lounge chairs.

Fig. 19. William Lescaze, Capital Bus Terminal, 230 West Fiftieth Street and 240–242 West Fifty-first Street, New York, 1927. Angle view of exterior (with permission of The Ayer Company, Sag Harbor, New York, successors to Arno Press).

The bedroom wall surfaces, tightly drawn with brass strips and exposed nail heads, expressed the mechanistic, industrial design aesthetic, contemporaneously utilized for railroad cars' and ships' interiors. The bed, storage-headboard, chest, and writing desk, composed of sliding, overlapping and interpenetrating planes, reflected a De Stijl influence. Complex in their composition, they were more typical of French furniture design at that time (that of Rob Mallet-Stevens, for example), than of the simpler and more elemental Dutch or German work. The spirit of Art Déco was interjected via the half-ellipse form of the cabinet, the curvilinear rug, and the richness of the color and grain of quartered gumwood.

Thus, the de Sièyes house was both essentially traditional and modern—certainly traditional in spatial concept, in exterior detailing, and in construction, but modern in its open planning and in some of its interior detailing and furnishings. This "modern" was neither the sophisticated and stylized early Art Déco nor the new functionalism emanating from Germany and Holland. Rather it was a synthesis of both ideas as they were developing just prior to 1930.[97]

Whereas the Phillips apartment posed the problem of an unalterable structure and the de Sièyes house a conservative client, the Capital Bus Terminal commission of the same year presumably allowed Lescaze to express the new European modernism freely. The Terminal, at 239 West Fiftieth Street and 240–242 West Fifty-first Street, repre-

Fig. 18. William Lescaze, Jean de Sièyes House, Mt. Kisco, New York, 1927–1928. Living room.

sented one of the first achievements in interpreting the European International Style on the East Coast of the United States (Fig. 19).

The terminal's flat roof, asymmetrical facade expressing the function of the interior, and unornamented walls bore witness to the new European aesthetic, as did the building's massing, silhouette, rounded corners, overhanging canopy, and window bands at the roof line, all of which reflect an influence from J. J. P. Oud's Kiefhoek housing estate at Rotterdam.[98] Although not a sophisticated statement of the new style, only one vestige of traditional detailing remained in the cornice molding.

Reading the form as symbolic of the machine age, *The New Yorker* magazine reported that the terminal was designed in the shape of a "great bus." Bus transportation was just coming into its own in 1927; not until 1928 did a bus, under one management, make a coast-to-coast trip.[99] A writer for *The New Yorker* found it of interest not only to report that fact but also to comment on two of the seven bus terminals in New York at the time. One of these was Lescaze's Capital Terminal, described as "quite pretentious," having five clerks with offices on the ground floor; bootblack, rest rooms, and Western Union downstairs; and tea at "little tables in the garden."[100]

But it was the competition for a League of Nations building, organized in 1926 and judged in the spring of 1927, that allowed Lescaze his first opportunity to express his youthful dream of designing a monumental building. To Lescaze, not only did this competition represent a part of the burgeoning modern movement in Europe but it was also personally nostalgic in that an internationally important building was proposed for the city of his birth.

The perspective rendering of this project, like his other work of this period, reflects mixed motifs (Fig. 20). Its axial symmetry and its spatial expression of every function reflects Beaux-Arts concepts of planning and composition. The combination of the perpendicular central tower, flanking walls of glass, and the absence of applied decoration emphasized the classicist intent of the design proposal.[101] At the same time, the sculptural, arcaded, stair wing (probably intended to be built of reinforced concrete), the deeply recessed windows, the Corbusian "ship's bridge" atop the central shaft, and the cantilevered corner balconies were visually adventurous.[102] In all, the result was a composite of tentatively modern motifs, characteristic of many of the competition designs. While Lescaze's was not to be numbered among the sea of academically neoclassical projects submitted to the competition, neither was it in a class with the avant-garde, antimonumental concepts of Le Corbusier and Pierre Jeanneret, Hannes Meyer and Hans Wittwer, or Richard Neutra and R. M. Schindler. It is significant that the jury found none of the first-round entries satisfactory for a commission, and they explained the differences in conception by referring to the "evolutionary phase through which contemporary architecture was now passing."[103]

In the same year as the League of Nations project, which had wavered in its commitment to European modernism, Lescaze submitted a far more conservative design to the Soldiers and Sailors Memorial Competition in Providence, Rhode Island. A prismatic shaft of twelve facets, mounted on a granite base, was lighted from within. This scheme was prefigured in German expressionist projects for glass architecture illuminated at night (Fig. 21).[104] It was also related to Hugh Ferriss's

Fig. 20. William Lescaze, League of Nations project, 1927. Perspective rendering of lake façade.

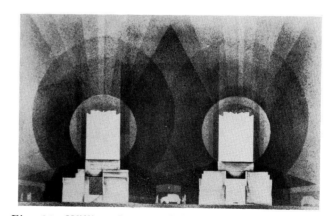

Fig. 21. William Lescaze, Soldiers and Sailors Monument project, 1927. Rendering of two elevations.

Fig. 22. William Lescaze, "Permanent Exhibition," Loeser's Department Store, Brooklyn, 1928. Living room.

project of the same year for a glass skyscraper. Both Ferriss's and Lescaze's projects were exhibited at the Machine Age Exposition held in New York at 119 West Fifty-seventh Street from 16 to 28 May 1927. That exposition was the first major event in the modern movement on the East Coast. It marked the first time that machine parts and products were recognized as significant artistic forms, and the first time that models and photographs of Russian constructivism and the new European architecture were exhibited in America. It gave Lescaze the opportunity to show his projects for a "Modern Living Room Interior" (probably the de Sièyes house), the "Interior of a Modern Apartment" (probably the Phillips apartment), and possibly the model for his League of Nations Project.[105] At the same time, the new architecture in the hands of Richard Neutra and R. M. Schindler had already taken form on the West Coast.

By 1928 Lescaze had executed only two modest architectural commissions, becoming known to the public through his interior design work. Impatient to work with larger problems, Lescaze complained to Le Corbusier that he was commissioned to do nothing but interiors. Le Corbusier replied: "That's the way it always is. I didn't do anything myself for years, besides writing articles and giving lectures. Keep it up."[106] Lescaze did, for throughout 1928 he had no architectural commissions, executing instead a number of exhibition rooms, offices, business showrooms, apartment interiors, and a few architectural projects. His situation was not unique, for throughout the twenties modern design was promoted largely through commercial channels—in department store displays and the redesign of business interiors and façades.

In the spring of 1928, Lescaze designed one of the foremost department store displays of the period for the Frederick Loeser Company in Brooklyn—a living room and a smoking room, which were displayed as a "permanent" exhibition (Fig. 22). Critic Adolph Glassgold reported in *The Arts* that the two rooms were comparable to the finest work seen in New York. Moreover, he considered Lescaze to be a "master of space adjustment" and "completely convinced of the power of simplicity in interior arrangement." He observed that Lescaze's work conveyed a "slight impression of austerity, but so sensitively are the forms disposed and so exhilarating in color that lack of decorative details is insignificant."[107] Probably no critique could have pleased Lescaze more. Glassgold went on to say that Lescaze "turns his attention to the planes of the walls and ceiling which he breaks up into intriguing shapes and transfers this movement of planes to the furniture, etc. and by their placement makes a closely knit unit."[108] Lescaze had apparently succeeded in expressing his dedication to neo-plastic principles of planar unity, in using color to articulate space, and in creating a unity of furniture and architecture where the walls, ceiling, and floor were no longer passive features but active parts of the entire design.

The furniture for the Loeser exhibition was largely borrowed from the designs originally created for the Phillips apartment. In addition, Lescaze introduced three new designs of tubular metal-framed furniture—a table, a stool, and a chair—in the spirit of those shown by Breuer, Stam, Gropius, and Mies in the Weissenhofsiedlung Exposition at Stuttgart in 1927. This metallic modernism, like the Phillips apartment, was rendered in the room's silver-painted wall and metallic-paper-covered folding screen, as well as in silver bowls and various metal sculptures and accessories, all serving as accents to a De Stijl-influenced color scheme of oyster white, gray, and black, with small touches of red and blue.[109]

Less conservative than the Loeser Department Store's exhibition rooms was the controversial penthouse studio-apartment that Lescaze created for Macy's Department Store exhibition in the summer of 1928 (Figs. 23 and 24). Having assumed department store leadership in the promotion of modern decorative art by its 1927 Art in Trade Exposition, Macy's opened in May of 1928 the first

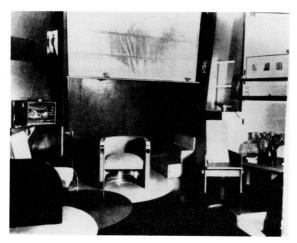

Fig. 23. "Art in Industry", Macy's, New York, 1928. Penthouse studio apartment (Courtesy of Architectural Record, August 1928).

international exhibition of decorative arts shown in the United States—the "International Exhibition of Art in Industry."[110] France, Germany, Sweden, Italy, Austria, and the U.S.A. participated in exhibiting 15 completely furnished rooms, 34 galleries, and more than 5,000 objects. Exhibition rooms were designed by the Austrian Josef Hoffmann; the French Leleu, Maurice Dufrene, Joubert and Petit; the German Bruno Paul; the Italian Gio Ponti; and the Americans Kem Weber, Eugene Schoen, Ralph Walker, and Lescaze.

Lescaze's studio was called the "most unusual," "the most startling in innovation," "the most iconoclastic of any in the exhibition."[111] To be "unusual, startling, and iconoclastic" were undoubtedly purposeful objectives, because publicity was not the least value of these exhibitions. By means of bold color, cubist pattern, and concealed lighting

Fig. 24. "Art in Industry," Macy's, New York, 1928. Penthouse studio apartment (Courtesy of Architectural Record, August 1928).

reflected against metal, Lescaze created a varied and dramatic interior space in which the furniture designed by himself, Ilonka Karasz, and the New Age Studio was displayed.[112] Most of the furniture was of wood with sharply cut profiles, stylistically similar to those being shown at the Paris Salon des Artistes-Décorateurs for 1928. Some were not unlike Alma Buscher's designs done at the Bauhaus in 1924 under Rietveld's De Stijl influence.[113]

In the Macy Exhibition, Lescaze continued to struggle with the problem of indirect, architecturally-concealed lighting. He hoped that lighting fixtures would soon be eliminated entirely and that architecturally-designed lighting systems that would create structural shadows and become an integral part of the whole would prevail. Lighting of this kind, probably originating with German expressionist architects, was to be found in virtually all of Lescaze's interiors after the late twenties.[114] Lescaze and Karasz clearly over-designed their studio in order to show the public as many objects and ideas as reasonably possible within the space available. As Glassgold commented, perhaps they "theorized too much."[115]

The Machine Age Exposition of 1927 and the several department store displays of modernist designs in 1928 soon had their effect on the consuming public. Curtis Patterson reported in the International Studio of September 1929 that in June of 1928 he was able to enumerate exactly twelve consistently modern apartments in New York City; a year later he was able to observe about five times as many.[116] With the advent of new aesthetic criteria, there were a great many problems to be resolved. Lescaze's process of working through some of them can be observed in his commercial and residential interiors and architectural projects of 1928 and 1929.

For Nudelman and Conti, dress manufacturer's showroom, Lescaze designed a customer consultation area and a modeling stage that together expressed a cross between 1925 Art Déco and a later modernist spirit. The same kind of ambivalence is observable in the Amos Parrish and Company's reception room and president's office. In both, only the most essential furnishings (some approximating Paul Frankl's skyscraper-style predilection for verticality) and Rodier fabrics of abstract design were contrasted with contrived manipulations of the interior architecture's interlocking geometric forms.[117]

These modernistic devices almost disappeared in Lescaze's later 1928 commissions: the London shoe

Fig. 25. William Lescaze, Andrew Geller Shoe Factory showroom, Brooklyn, 1928. Corner of showroom.

store, the Andrew Geller shoe stores and factory showroom, and the Leopold Stokowski apartment. The drawing of the London shoe store façade, an understated composition rendered with symmetrically organized vertical and horizontal panels of glass and accented with dark structural bands at the sides and base, only suggests elements derived from the Vienna Secession and the Art Déco styles. In all, the architectural style was simply composed, giving emphasis to plain wall surfaces.

De Stijl aesthetics, now more integrated than in earlier attempts, dominated the design of the Andrew Geller Fifth Avenue shoe stores. They were contemporarily reviewed as being "modern in feeling without a too flagrant display of those ultramodern characteristics that have become a thorn in the public's flesh."[118] Undoubtedly the most sophisticated of Lescaze's commercial interiors at this period was the Geller factory showroom in Brooklyn, which was selected for publication by Albert Morance in the *Encyclopedie des métiers d'art* of 1930 (Fig. 25). It was characterized by an elemental simplicity achieved through the elimination of all but essential display and seating units, the whole designed with cubic severity. All lighting fixtures were omitted in favor of cold white lighting panels installed flush in the soffits. An accented neutral color scheme of grays and blues, diffused lighting, gumwood furniture (similar to that used in the de Sièyes house), and functional display units combined to create an efficient, business-like atmosphere of comfort and dignity.[119]

The De Stijl aesthetic was most successfully achieved in Lescaze's *pied-a-terre* for Philadelphia symphony conductor Leopold Stokowski, on East Seventy-first Street. The *New York World* reported that it was the most "interesting thing in New York City" and the "most perfect small consistently modern apartment in the country." It was undoubtedly Lescaze's most important and successful interior design commission to date (Fig. 26).[120] The apartment consisted of a foyer, a bedroom, and a large studio. The studio served the multiple functions of music room, sitting room, and library. The irregular wall contours became the setting for the built-in look of the studio couch (only just becoming respectable in sophisticated decorative schemes) and its accompanying tables and book shelves. Lescaze's efforts to effect elementarist abstraction are notable in the geometric carpet pattern, furniture design, and arrangement. His practical functionalist philosophy of economically planning for human needs is also clearly expressed. The total effect caused critic Glassgold to call it an "exhilarating" room and a "tribute to beauty and the sanity of modern design."[121] Most importantly, it reflected an enlightened client who demanded something different from the eclectic taste currently prevailing and who provided the means to produce it.

Lescaze soon met other clients who dared to experiment with his functionalist thesis. The Stokowski commission, executed in the early months of 1929, was followed later in that year by

Fig. 26. William Lescaze, Leopold Stokowski apartment, East Seventy-first Street, New York, 1928–1929. Studio.

Fig. 27. Howe and Lescaze (Lescaze, designer), Hattie Carnegie salon, Fifth Avenue at Forty-ninth Street, New York, 1931. Millinery department.

designs of similar style for the Herbert Dreyfus, Ben Herzberg, and Charles Harding apartments. They were notable for their simplicity, unity, comfort, and elegance. They reveal Lescaze's predeliction for architectural lighting, built-in storage and seating furniture, meticulously executed cabinetry, rare and richly grained woods, accented-neutral color schemes, "open planning" with space delineated only by color, light, and screens, roughly textured and abstractly-patterned fabrics, and tubular metal-framed furniture.[122] Lescaze's interest and ability in both furniture and interior design are evident throughout his career. He considered them inseparable from architecture and therefore the architect's responsibility. Particularly notable among his early commissions was the much publicized Hattie Carnegie Salon on Fifth Avenue at Forty-ninth Street (Fig. 27).[123] An architectonic study in chrome and rare woods, it paralleled the interiors of the PSFS (see Chapter 3).

Clearly, Lescaze's early modern style included nearly all the proto-modernisms then current. It changed from that dominated by neo-classicism, to that influenced by the cubist and expressionist sources of Art Déco, to that employing both the sources of Art Déco and some principles of De Stijl, and finally to that dominated by the expressionist and neo-plastic statements of the International Style. This development can be observed most clearly in four projects of 1928, all of which allowed Lescaze an opportunity for experimentation and broadening of his architectural sensibility.

In June of 1928, Lescaze was invited, probably through the influence of his former mentor Karl Moser, to be the sole American representative to the Congrès Internationaux d'Architecture Moderne (CIAM), held at patron Helene de Mandrot's Chateaux in La Sarraz, Canton of Vaud, Switzerland. There, innovative powers in the field of architecture from various national groups met to deal with the problems confronting the progress of the new architecture. Lescaze's attendance at this first meeting of the world's leading modern architects was to have a profound influence on his thinking about the form and structure of buildings. Lescaze's projects moved increasingly toward and finally achieved an integrated modernism, illustrated by his four projects of 1928.

Fig. 28. William Lescaze, apartment house project, Park Avenue at Seventy-second Street, New York, 1928. Perspective rendering of street façade.

Fig. 29. William Lescaze, Christopher Columbus Memorial Lighthouse competition project, 1928–1929. Elevation rendering.

Lescaze designed in the same month as the CIAM meeting an apartment house project to be located on Park Avenue at Seventy-second Street (Fig. 28). Like the League of Nations Project, it was rooted in ambivalent modernist sources. While its bold vertical axis and counterpoint between large and small component parts recalled the Art Déco, its flat roof, cantilevered balconies, slab massing, horizontal window composition, and subtle asymmetry had an affinity with the new International modernism. The result, although a well-integrated design, still stood between one aesthetic philosophy and another.

Fig. 30. William Lescaze, apartment house and garage project, West Fiftieth and Fifty-first Streets, New York, 1928. Perspective rendering of street façade.

Soon after the CIAM meeting, Lescaze entered the Christopher Columbus Memorial Lighthouse competition, opened to the architects of the world on 1 September 1928 and judged in the spring of 1929. His design was a semi-classical structure that expressed the formalist-modernist and the engineer-functionalist in almost equal parts (Fig. 29). While Lescaze's ambivalent solution may have been due to a comparable state of mind or to the prospect of a panel of conservative judges, a contradictory program prescribing grandiose Beaux Arts criteria and at the same time calling for "something fresh and new in spirit and substance as well as form" most probably informed the result.[124]

Exhibiting mixed motifs in a different, and more avant-garde, way was an ambitious November 1928 project for a combined 24-floor apartment house, garage, bus terminal, shops, and restaurant, to be built west of Broadway between Fiftieth and Fifty-first Streets. It appears to be a poorly integrated neo-plasticist building at the base, growing into an expressionist-Déco building at the middle, to a functionalist structure as it approaches the top. (Fig. 30).[125] In sharp contrast to the complexity of forms on the ground floor of the building, the central portion was faced with continuous and uniform rows of balconies cantilevered in a zig-zag pattern, while the façade of the upper portion was penetrated only by doors to railed outdoor corridors (which like Le Corbusier's apartments for a hypothetical city for three million inhabitants of 1922, ran like balconies the length of each stepped-back tier of apartments), and a series of regular, horizontal windows that clearly and simply delineated the separate floors. A stepped-back form, it also reflected both the influence of the earlier work of Sauvage and New York City's zoning laws for skyscraper design.

Finally, in Lescaze's "Future American Country House—An American House in 1938" project, commissioned by the editors of the *Architectural Record*, his evolution from exploration and experimentation with new forms to a synthesis of them was complete (Figs. 31 and 32).[126] Yet, although intended to project the house of 1938, it was not entirely a visionary exercise because, as Lescaze explained, all the mechanical devices, materials, and structural technology incorporated in the house existed in 1928. Some, such as air conditioning, were not in common use, however; nor was its form.

Le Corbusier's call in *Vers une architecture* for one

Fig. 31. William Lescaze, "Future American Country House—An American House in 1938." Project, 1928. Axonometric rendering.

large living room, a large bathroom and dressing room, pleasant servants' quarters, separate garage, built-in storage, ventilating panes to windows in every room, and respect for mechanical conveniences were all incorporated into Lescaze's scheme.[127] Lescaze stated in his introduction to the *Architectural Record*'s publication of the project that the house was practically designed to give man better health, comfort, service, and beauty. For better health, Lescaze, as Le Corbusier had done before him, proposed an unusually large bathroom with southern exposure and adjoining exercise room, glassed porch, ultraviolet-ray lamps, and swimming pool. Vita glass or Quartz Lite were used "to add the special beneficial rays of the sun to customary bathing facilities."[128] Design for the relationship between health and architecture was to some degree typical of all the new architecture—notably in Richard Neutra's Lovell Health House, already under construction at Griffith Park, Los Angeles.

Specifically geared toward comfort in Lescaze's scheme were the generous plan, floors of cork and sponge rubber, soft reflected light, flexible wind screens, and many mechanical services. The latter included air conditioning, electric elevator, and accommodations for meteorlogical instruments. Expressing faith in the futuristic idea of "an airplane in every hangar," that idea, too, was drawn. Lescaze's evocation of a technological and functional idealism, with a formalists's concern for the visual rightness of abstract forms, could hardly have been clearer.[129]

Neither a typical 1928 nor 1938 country house, as it turned out, the project was conceived in what William Jordy has called the "adventurous days of modernism."[130] But Lescaze believed it was concerned with meeting the "actualities of life in the twentieth century" and an "expression in plastic form of a particular mode of living."[131] To be sure, the 1920s were adventurous years in the history of American architecture and design, and complex ones as well. It was a decade in which simplified interpretations of traditional forms and a new vocabulary of stylized decorative detail were introduced, followed by basic new philosophies of structure and form—the Moderne or Art Déco, and the philosophy of International Functionalism or the International Style. It was not an easy evolution, with polarization of positions within the avant-garde and a proliferation of committed groups. Hitchcock wrote in 1929 that there had been "very little conscious adoption of the new manner [International Style] by established architects," but that it was "hardly surprising, considering how slowly America [was] coming generally to accept even the new tradition [Moderne]."[132]

Throughout those difficult years, Lescaze had worked hard to establish his reputation as architect, furniture designer, and interior designer in a society that considered modern to be suspect. Like most

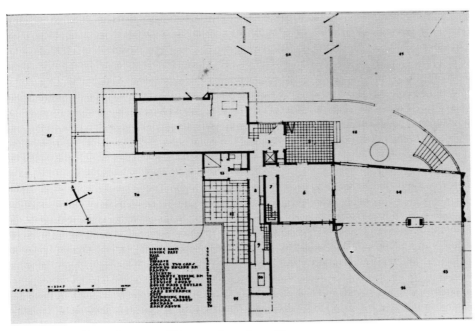

Fig. 32. William Lescaze, "Future American Country House—an American House in 1938." Project, 1928. Floor plan.

modernists in the twenties, Lescaze had few architectural commissions, earning a living from furniture and interior design work. Dedicated to the aesthetic unity of his commissions, Lescaze designed every detail of his interiors including moveable and built-in furniture, lighting fixtures, and carpets.

Further, he displayed his work in most of the significant exhibitions of the twenties and entered national and international architectural competitions. He helped to organize The New School of Architecture and the American Union of Decorative Artists and Craftsmen and was the sole United States delegate to the first international conference on modern architecture.

While the central principles of Lescaze's architecture were rooted in tradition when he entered practice in the United States in 1920, by the end of the decade it had moved from the architectural images of eclecticism to those of modernism, although sometimes remaining ambivalent between the old and new ideologies.

NOTES

1. "Chronology," 1941, WELA. Robert A. M. Stern, in his *George Howe: Toward a Modern American Architecture* (New Haven: Yale University Press, 1975), incorrectly states on p. 91 that Lescaze arrived in America in 1923. He moved to New York from Cleveland in that year.

2. Although Frank Lloyd Wright's work in America during the first two decades of the century was a fundamental influence on the European modern movement as it developed in the 1920s, it was ironically to Europe that America had to look for a continued development of technical, social, and aesthetic architectural expression.

3. Paul S. Wingert, "William Lescaze: Modern American Architect" (typescript), ca. 1940, p. 12, WELA.

4. Ibid., pp. 12–13. The manuscript was read and annotated by Lescaze.

5. William Lescaze, *On Being an Architect* (New York: Putnam's and Sons, 1942), p. 241. According to an interview with Mrs. Lescaze on 6 November 1973, Gilles Barbey was incorrect in stating in his "William Lescaze (1896–1969)" *Werk*, No. 8 (1971), p. 559, that the office of Hubbell and Benes had been recommended to Lescaze before he had left Switzerland.

6. Robert M. Coates, "Profiles," *The New Yorker*, 12 December 1936, p. 45.

7. Lescaze, *On Being an Architect*, p. 241; "Chronology," 7 January 1941, WELA. MacCornack became the Dean of the School of Architecture, Massachusetts Institute of Technology, in charge of the department from 1939 to 1944; William L. Porter to the author, 5 May 1977.

8. Interview with Charles A. Harris, New York City, 14 March 1974. Harris shared a room with Lescaze at the YMCA and later an apartment in Cleveland.

9. Brom Weber, ed., *Letters of Hart Crane* (New York: Hermitage House, 1952), p. 104. Laukhuff was a German organ builder who had come to America some years earlier to practice his craft. When that was not possible, he opened a bookshop. See Wingert, "William Lescaze," p. 13.

10. Wingert, "William Lescaze," p. 13. Charles Coleman and Henry G. Keller were also painting and exhibiting there at this time. See *Third Annual Exhibition of Work by Cleveland Artists and Craftsmen* catalogue in Scrapbook, WELA.

11. The May shows were started in 1919 by William M. Milliken, who was in that year appointed Curator of Decorative Arts at the Cleveland Museum, becoming Director in 1930. The intent was to exhibit local art with an emphasis on an

interpretation of Cleveland and its surrounding country.

12. Weber, *Letters of Hart Crane*, p. 56. Philip Horton, in his *Hart Crane* (New York: Norton, 1937), p. 114, states that Lescaze met Crane in the summer of 1921. It must have been prior to Crane's letter to Munson in which he stated that he recently sent some of Lescaze's work to Margaret Anderson. Lescaze later recalled, in a letter of 22 July 1966 to George Knox, that he probably met Crane at Laukhuff's bookstore, WELA.

13. See Exhibition Catalogue, Scrapbook, WELA. Of these, only the first and the last are known to the author. Only two artists outnumbered him; this record was considered remarkable since Lescaze had been in America for less than a year. See unidentified newsclipping, 21 July 1921, WELA.

14. Criticism of the first two paintings was written by Benjamin Karr in "Work of Cleveland's Artists is Displayed," *Leader News* (Cleveland), 18 May 1921. The criticism of the last appeared in the *Plain Dealer* (Cleveland), n.d., WELA.

15. *Leader News*, 18 May 1921.

16. "Third Annual Exhibit at Museum," *Cleveland Topics*, 1 May 1921, WELA.

17. L. W. Smith, "Art or Insanity—Which" (typescript), 1922, WELA.

18. Judges were: George W. Bellows of New York, Huger Elliott of Philadelphia, and Harold H. Brown of Indianapolis. Exhibition catalogue, p. 2. Scrapbook, WELA.

19. The exhibition was hung for the week of 19 June 1921, unidentified newsclipping, 21 July 1921, WELA. In 1922, a private May Show of Lescaze's paintings was held by Jean Binet and Hubbard Hutchinson at 3738 Euclid Avenue. Shown there on May 18 to 20 were thirteen oil paintings, a charcoal drawing, a pastel, five watercolors, and seven drawings. See typed list and invitation to the exhibition, WELA.

20. Barbara Rose, *American Art Since 1900* New York: Praeger, 1968), p. 85.

21. Kokoschka's work was widely publicized from 1916 to 1918 when Lescaze was in Zurich. Lescaze painted many portraits of his friends, all of which were given to the sitters. Laukhuff returned his to Lescaze because he believed that a creation belonged to the creator. Mrs. Lescaze, notes to the author, June 1977.

22. John Unterecker, *Voyager: A Life of Hart Crane* (New York: Farrar, Straus and Giroux), pp. 210, 243.

23. Horton, *Hart Crane*, pp. 115–116; Unterecker, *Voyager*, p. 260. Also see Bevis Hillier, *Art Deco*, Minneapolis Art Institute Exhibition Catalogue, 8 July—5 September 1971, p. 37, for his interpretation of the symbol of the eye.

24. The lines from "For the Marriage of Faustus and Helen" from *The Complete Poems and Selected Letters and Prose of Hart Crane*, edited by Brom Weber, are reprinted by permission of Liveright Publishing Corporation. Copyright 1933, (c) 1958, 1966 by Liveright Publishing Corporation.

25. A photocopy of the drawing is in the possession of Mrs. Lescaze.

26. Unterecker, *Voyager*, p. 209; Weber, *Letters of Hart Crane*, p. 63, quoting Crane to Gorham Munson, 22 July 1921.

27. Weber, p. 66, quoting Crane to Munson, 6 October 1921.

28. Coates, "Profiles," p. 46, exaggerates both the costume and its symbolism according to Mrs. Lescaze, notes to author, June 1977.

29. Lescaze to Professor George Knox, 22 July 1966, WELA; Horton, *Hart Crane*, pp. 109, 114; Unterecker, *Voyager*, p. 208, quoting a letter from Crane to Munson.

30. Horton, *Hart Crane*, p. 114; Weber, *Letters of Hart Crane*, p. 70; Unterecker, *Voyager*, p. 208.

31. Unterecker, *Voyager*, p. 209.

32. Weber, *Letters of Hart Crane*, p. 70, quoting Crane to Munson, 3 November 1921.

33. Weber, *Letters of Hart Crane*, p. 82, quoting Crane to Munson, 16 May 1922. Lescaze wrote that he had "brought from Europe [to Cleveland] a few folios of reproductions of Braque, Matisse, Cézanne, as well as paintings by others." Lescaze to George Knox, 22 July 1966, WELA.

34. See *Special Exhibition Contemporary Art* Catalogue, Montross Gallery, April 1922, WELA.

35. H. B. Brainerd and W. E. Lescaze, "Wealth or the Thrift of the City Plan, A Photoplay Scenario and Settings," (typescript), 1 December 1920, WELA.

36. Weber, *Letters of Hart Crane*, p. 91, quoting Crane to Munson, ca. 18 June 1922.

37. Unterecker, *Voyager*, p. 262; Weber, *Letters of Hart Crane*, p. 104, quoting Crane to Munson, 7 November 1922.

38. Mrs. Lescaze to author, 23 February 1976. Ellen Kramer in her Landmarks Preservation Commission Designation Report for the Lescaze House, 27 January 1976, states that Lescaze visited Bruno Taut. The author can find no documentation for that occurrence; perhaps the name Bruno Paul was intended.

39. Mrs. Lescaze, interview New York City, 10 October 1974. Paul was one of the earliest designers of low-cost furniture for mass production, commissioned by Karl Schmidt of Dresden in 1907. See Gillian Naylor, *The Bauhaus* (New York: E. P. Dutton Co., 1968), pp. 16, 18.

40. See Dennis Sharp, *Modern Architecture and Expressionism* (New York: Braziller, 1966).

41. In the Magdeburg publications new contributors were: J. J. P. Oud, Mies van der Rohe, Soder, and Martin Machler. See Sharp, *Modern Architecture and Expressionism*, pp. 69, 71; Ulrich Conrads, ed., *Programs and Manifestoes on 20th-Century Architecture*, trans. Michael Bullock (Cambridge, Mass: The MIT Press, 1970), p. 4.

42. Walter Curt Behrendt, "Skyscrapers in Germany," *Journal of the American Institute of Architects*, 11 (September 1923): 365–370.

43. Naylor, *The Bauhaus*, p. 78; Charles Jencks, *Modern Movements in Architecture* (New York: Anchor Press, Doubleday, 1973), p. 117; Banham, *Theory and Design*, p. 187; Conrads, *Programs and Manifestoes*, p. 71.

44. Conrads, *Programs and Manifestoes*, p. 74.

45. Frampton, "De Stijl," p. 148. Dates of the exhibition were 15 August–30 September; see Brown, *Rietveld*, p. 26. Conrads, in *Programs and Manifestoes*, p. 78, states that the exhibition took place in November and December of 1923. See Oskar Schlemmer, "Manifesto for the first Bauhaus Exhibition," published in Conrads, *Programs and Manifestoes*, pp. 69–70; Hans Wingler, *The Bauhaus* (Cambridge and London: The MIT Press, 1969), pp. 67–68.

46. Naylor, *The Bauhaus*, pp. 86–93; Wingler, *The Bauhaus*, p. 385.

47. Wingert, "William Lescaze," p. 15, states that Lescaze returned to New York on 27 March 1923.

48. T. M. Brown, *The Work of G. Rietveld, Architect* (Utrecht: A. W. Bruna & Zoon, 1958), p. 65, states that the Rosenberg exhibition was 15 October–15 November.

49. See *De Stijl* 6, 6/7, 1924.

50. Brown, *Rietveld*, p. 65. See Theo van Doesburg, "Tot een beeldende architectuur," *De Stijl*, 6, 6/7, 1924, pp. 78–83.

51. Brown, *Rietveld*, p. 65.

52. According to Mrs. Lescaze and other documentation, Lescaze visited Paris and other parts of Europe each year after his immigration to the United States. In his book, *On being an Architect*, Lescaze states that one should read as much of Le Corbusier as possible.

53. Nor was there much architectural activity in the new style in America either.

54. Weber, *Letters of Hart Crane*, p. 77, quoting Crane to Sherwood Anderson, 10 January 1922, states that Lescaze was in New York over Christmas. Mrs. Ford's calling card, dated 1921, attached to the planning drama, "Wealth or the Thrift of the City Plan," probably indicates the date Lescaze took it to her. Wingert, "William Lescaze," p. 15, corroborates the meeting date. Lescaze, in *On Being an Architect*, p. 242, states that he received his first New York job two years before setting up his own office, suggesting that the commission had been discussed soon after that first meeting.

55. Wingert, "William Lescaze," p. 15.

56. Ibid.

57. "Notes," 22 April 1938, and the lease for his apartment and studio establish the date, WELA. Wingert, "William Lescaze," p. 15, reports that Lescaze left Cleveland on 1 June 1923.

58. Wingert, "William Lescaze," p. 15.

59. Other Sutton Place houses had been built in 1875 by Effingham Sutton. At that time the area was declining, with coalyards and slaughter-houses moving in and brownstones changing to tenements. In 1921, Mrs. William K. Vanderbilt, who led a movement of socially prominent people to the East Side, rebuilt No. 1 Sutton Place, a few blocks away. The adjoining house was remodeled by J. P. Morgan's sister, Anne Morgan. "A Chapter Ends on Sutton Place," *New York Times*, 7 March 1965, Real Estate pp. 1, 10.

60. See "A Chapter Ends on Sutton Place," p. 1, for photograph that contrasts other Sutton Place houses with their high-rise apartment house neighbors.

61. Lescaze, *On Being an Architect*, p. 242.

62. See Scrapbook, WELA. The screen was signed "Beaute de Moi New York/Quand même 19 XI 1923/De tes Ponts Pleur."

63. Ibid.

64. Rufenacht returned to Switzerland in 1929 and established a private practice there.

65. Bottomley studied with M. Victor Laloux at the École des Beaux-Arts in Paris, and was a prominent architect noted for perfection of proportion.

66. Lescaze, *On Being an Architect*, p. 242.

67. In 1924 Lescaze moved his office to 17 East Forty-ninth Street (as is indicated on the drawings of the Edgewood School Dormitory), retaining the West Eighth Street apartment for his residence. Mrs. Lescaze, "Addresses," WELA.

68. Later, when he got the freedom he wanted in architecture, he painted only occasionally, although his love for painting was apparent in his handsome architectural renderings, some of which were done in his early painting styles.

69. "Chronology," 7 January 1941, WELA, and Notes by Mrs. Lescaze, WELA, state that they met in Paris. Wingert, "William Lescaze," p. 26, states that Lescaze met Brancusi in 1925 at the Wildenstein Gallery in New York: "For some weeks they spent many hours together, riding around the city in Lescaze's old Buick car, top down, discussing American architecture and culture in general; and whenever Lescaze is in Paris these talks are renewed." Mrs. Lescaze, notes to author, June 1977, considers Wingert's statement "completely wrong."

70. "Notes," 22 April 1948, WELA.

71. *Hommage à Consuelo* is in the possession of Mrs. Lescaze.

72. *Halle*, Exhibitors Program, Art in Industry Exposition, 23–28 August 1927, Cleveland, Ohio, Scrapbook, WELA.

73. Ibid. Also see Park, *New Backgrounds*, pp. 52–75.

74. The name was derived from "Lesc" [Lescaze] and "ord" [Ford]. The original idea of the Lescord Shop was that of Lauren Ford. Lescaze was to design furniture; Ford, Mme. Kamenka in Paris, Jean de Lanux, and Consuelo Ford were to buy French fabrics and accessories that could be used for interior design commissions by Lescaze and other designers. This plan never developed commercially. Mrs. Lescaze to author, 16 February 1976; Mrs. Lescaze, notes to author, June 1977.

75. Halle, Exhibitors Program, Scrapbook; "Halle Brothers Exposition Stresses Modernism," *New Review*, 19 August 1927, Scrapbook, WELA.

76. "A Bit of Old Spain in New York," *Arts and Decoration* 28 (November 1927): 50–51; Lillian E. Prussing, *Mid-Week Pictorial*, 12 January 1928.

77. Battersby, *The Decorative Twenties*, p. 47. Lescaze had visited Spain for a month before leaving Europe; Mrs. Lescaze, notes to author, June 1977.

78. Triangular fixtures were prefigured in German Expressionist works such as Walter Gropius's Sommerfeld House at Berlin (1921–1922) and at the night club entrance in the Fritz Lang United Artists film, *Metropolis* (1926).

79. Sets were designed by Otto Hunte, Erich Kettelhut, and Karl Vollbrecht. See Dennis Sharp, ed., *Twentieth-Century Architecture* (Greenwich, Conn.: New York Graphic Society, 1972), p. 59. See Robinson and Bletter, *Skyscraper Style*, pp. 41 5n14, 75n15, for definitions of terminology. In the 1920s in the United States, "modern," "modernist," and "modernistic" generally meant some form of the eclectic style now usually called "Art Déco," with its sources in the Austrian Secession, German Expressionism, Paris Exposition of 1925, Mayan art, etc. After 1928 "modernistic" was the most commonly used term. In 1932, the Museum of Modern Art's catalogue for the International Exhibition of Modern Architecture used the term "modernistic" pejoratively. "Modernist" is now the most used term for the modern architecture movement.

80. Barbara Rose, *American Art Since 1900* (New York: Praeger, 1969), p. 85.

81. Andre Lurçat, "French Architecture," *Machine-Age Exposition Catalogue*, 16–28 May 1927, pp. 22–23.

82. Mrs. Lescaze to author, 23 February 1976. Lescaze's European visits are herein documented in relation to their specific concerns.

83. Annotated train schedules document German visits, WELA.

84. See Robert A. M. Stern, "PSFS: Beaux-Arts Theory and Rational Expressionism," *Journal of the Society of Architectural Historians* 21 (May 1962): 90, 91n35.

85. Robinson and Bletter, *Skyscraper Style*, p. 43.

86. The term "Chinese" is on the drawing by Herman Rufenacht.

87. In common usage during the period, the term "zigzag architecture" was used by Lescaze in his "Modern Architecture for a Modern Nation" (typescript for "The New Deal in Architecture," *New Republic*, 26 July 1933, pp. 278–280), WELA. The term "zigzag moderne" was used by David Gebhard and Harriette van Breton in their *Kem Weber—The Moderne in Southern California, 1920 through 1941* (Santa Barbara: The Art Galleries, University of California, 1969). The triangles and zigzags probably derive from German Expressionism; see Robinson and Bletter, *Skyscraper Style*, p. 53.

88. The glass and chrome table executed for the Phillips apartment was designed by Herman Rufenacht, November 1927. See drawing No. 222, "Phillips apartment."

89. See Kathleen Church Plummer, "The Streamlined Moderne," *Art in America* 62 (January–February 1974): 46–54.

90. Hitchcock, *Modern Architecture*, p. 205.

91. The House was later sold to Samuel Barber and Gian-Carlo Menotti and called "Capricorn."

92. Panozzo's house in Casoro (Tessin) of 1929 is published in Max Bill, *Modern Swiss Architecture 1925–1945* (Bern: Verlag Karl Werner, 1949), p. 111.

93. Alfred Barr, Henry-Russell Hitchcock, Philip Johnson, and Lewis Mumford, *Modern Architecture: International Exhibition* (New York: Norton, 1932); reprint ed., Arno Press for the Museum of Modern Art, 1969), p. 144.

94. Jennie Moore, "Will Modern Change our Houses," *Building Developer*, June 1929, pp. 72–73.

95. Pierre Chareau, Jean Michael Frank, Rene Herbst, Gabriel Guevrekian, Djo-Bourgeois, Robert Mallet-Stevens, J. J. Adnet, René Joubert, Philippe Petit, Eugene Printz, and Francoise Jourdain were among the 1928 exhibitors. Battersby, "The New Modernism," *The Decorative Twenties*, passim.

96. The latter was thicker in section than that designed by Gropius. These were related, as was Rietveld's 1917 red-blue chair, to van der Leck's, van Doesburg's and Mondrian's neoplastic painting experiments of 1914–1917. See Frampton, "De Stijl," pp. 143–147.

97. A few years later the de Sièyes house was restated in the H. F. C. Stikeman house in Sennerville, near Montreal, Quebec. Although formally credited to George Howe, it might be considered a joint work not only for its obvious relationship to the de Sièyes commission, but in a note dated 11 August 1931, Lescaze wrote: "Am going to work tonight on Newark Theatre and GH little house in Canada," "Diary," written on yellow paper, WELA.

98. For a discussion of the phases of the International Style, see William: H. Jordy, *American Buildings and Their Architects: The Impact of European Modernism in the Mid-Twentieth Century* (New York: Doubleday and Co., 1972), pp. 124–129; William H. Jordy, "PSFS: Its Development and Its Significance in Modern Architecture," *Journal of the Society of Architectural Historians* 21 (May 1962):75–78.

99. "The Bus Grows Up," *The New Yorker*, 27 October 1928, pp. 20–21.

100. Ibid.

101. The skyscraper tower had been well established as an appropriate form for important buildings. The composition of central shaft and flanking wings had been utilized by Bertram Goodhue in his Nebraska State Capitol (1919–1924), in several competition drawings for the Chicago Tribune Tower (1922), in Auguste Perret's Notre Dame du Raincy (1922), and in Karl Moser's St. Anthony Church, Basel (1926), to name but a few.

102. The latter two features, expressed here for the first time in Lescaze's work, reappear two years later in the now renowned PSFS building. So, too, do the "different" mid-floors, although undoubtedly for different reasons.

103. Architectural Competition, n. p. The jury, composed of Victor Horta, Karl Moser, A. Muggia, John J. Burnet, Carlos Gato, Ivar Tengbom, H. P. Berlage, Josef Hoffmann, C. Lemaresquier. The commission at a new site, was awarded to Nenot, Flegenheimer, Broggi, Lefevre, and Vago in December 1927. The building was completed in 1936. See Benevolo, pp. 476–477 for further discussion of the competition.

104. Night time illumination of buildings and other structures had become widespread by the time of the 1925 Paris Exposition. There, the Polish Pavilion, by Joseph Czajkowski, had a glass superstructure that was illuminated at night; Lalique exhibited a lighted, faceted fountain. See Robinson and Bletter, *Skyscraper Style*, p. 79n70. The Machine Age Exposition was organized by: *The Little Review*, Jane Heap; Societe des Urbanistes Brussels, Louis van der Swaelmen and M. Gaspard; the U.S.S.R. Society of Cultural Relations with Foreign Countries American Branch; Kunstgewerbeschule, Vienna, Professor Josef Frank; Zclonkowie Group "Praesens" Warsaw, Szymon Syrkus; Architects DRLG Paris, André Lurçat; Advisory American Section, Hugh Ferriss. See *Machine Age Exposition Catalogue*, frontis.

105. Stern, "Relevance of the Decade," pp. 9–10, 9n21. Biographical Data, 18 February 1929, WELA; *Machine Age Exposition Catalogue*, p. 6.

106. Lescaze, *On Being an Architect*, p. 134.

107. C. Adolph Glassgold, "Decorative Art Notes," *The Arts* 13 (May 1928):299.

108. Ibid.

109. Illustration and description in "Modernistic Apartment," *Architecture* 58 (August 1928):89–92. See Battersby, *The Decorative Twenties*, p. 139, regarding silver wallpapers.

110. Both exhibitions were developed with the cooperation of the Metropolitan Museum of Art. See *An International Exposition of Art in Industry, from May 14 to May 26, 1928 at Macy's*, Exhibition Catalogue, WELA.

111. C. Adolph Glassgold, "Art in Industry," *The Arts* 13 (June 1928):379; "The Macy Exposition of Art in Industry," *Architectural Record* 64 (August 1928):137. *Women's Wear Daily*, 26 May 1928; Walter R. Storey, "The Latest Art-in-Industry Exhibit," *New York Times*, 27 May 1928, Magazine Section, p. 19.

112. Believing that the interior architecture of a room should provide most of the decoration, Lescaze incorporated a skylight which leaned inward; one wall covered in blue fabrikoid, one painted yellow, and another white; burnished metal running from floor to ceiling at the corners; and a black floor with blue and vermillion semi-circular inserts.

113. See Brown, *Rietveld*, p. 26; Naylor, *Bauhaus*, p. 97.

114. Indirect lighting with source of light not revealed is, according to Rosemarie Bletter, *Skyscraper Style*, p. 58, a German Expressionist device for creating exaggerated light and shadow and deep spatial effects, and a substitute for light seen through colored glass. Hans Poelzig was among the pioneers in the development of indirect lighting, using it in his Grosses Schauspielhaus of 1919 in Berlin. Reyner Banham has attributed the earliest use of indirect lighting in America to J. R. Davidson of California. In what Banham has called the "Berlin-California" school of lighting, Davidson, in the 1920s, exploited the "left spaces and hollows of normal construction" to provide light without making its sources visible and concealed lighting behind projecting paneling, shining upwards into ceiling coves. See Reyner Banham, *The Well Tempered Environment* (London: The Architectural Press, 1969), p. 201.

115. C. Adolph Glassgold, "Art in Industry," p. 379.

116. Curtis Patterson, review of *The New Interior Decoration* by Dorothy Todd and Raymond Mortimer, in "A Scource Book on Modern Interiors," *International Studio* 94 (September 1929):72–73.

117. Walter R. Storey, "New Art Fashions Office Furniture," *New York Times*, 7 October 1928, Magazine Section, p. 10.

118. "A Modern Shoe Shop," *New York Telegram*, Magazine Section, Scrapbook, WELA.

119. In 1922 Erich Mendelsohn used recessed lighting above glass panels. See Banham, *Well-Tempered Environment*, p. 200; Glassgold, "The Decorative Arts," p. 273.

120. Stokowski had been a client of George Howe in 1926 for an unrealized residential project. Karl K. Kitchen, "Up and Down Broadway," *New York World*, 23 April 1929, Scrapbook, WELA.

121. C. Adolph Glassgold, "The S Apartment," *Architectural Forum* 53 (August 1930):228.

122. The color schemes introduced by Pierre Chareau in the 1919 Salon d'Automne—where he used royal blue, lemon yellow, gray, brown, and beige—were often used in interior commissions of the twenties and early thirties.

123. "New Interiors," *Creative Art* 9 (September 1931); 242–244. It was opened in April 1931, judging from an unidentified

newsclipping hand-dated April 1931, WELA.

124. Albert Kelsey, ed., *Program and Rules of the Competition for the Selection of an Architect for the Monumental Lighthouse* (Pan American Union, 1928), pp. 24, 28; Albert Kelsey, *Program and Rules of the Second Competition for the Selection of an Architect for the Monumental Lighthouse* (Pan American Union, 1930).

125. A November 1928 rendering of the project, which indicates its location, was dedicated to Lawrence Kocher.

126. See William Lescaze, "The Future American Country House," *Architectural Record* 64 (November 1928):417–420.

127. Le Corbusier, "Manual of the Dwelling," *Towards a New Architecture*, trans. Frederick Etchells (New York: Praeger Pub., 1970), pp. 114–119. It was first published as *Vers une architecture* (Paris: Editions Crés, 1923). The first English edition was published in 1927 by the Architectural Press, London.

It was first published in the United States in 1960 by Praeger.

128. Lescaze, "The Future American Country House," p. 417. Also see Le Corbusier, *Towards a New Architecture*, pp. 114–119.

129. A somewhat simplified version of the "Future American Country House"—with gymnasium but without airplane hangar—was designed in the same month and called the "American Home." An undated variation—with airplane hangar but without gymnasium—was captioned "Country House for a Young Couple."

130. Jordy, *The Impact of European Modernism in the Mid-Twentieth Century*, p. 103.

131. Quotations are from Lescaze's Vassar College lecture (typescript), 1934, WELA.

132. Hitchcock, *Modern Architecture*, p. 199.

3

The Partnership of Howe and Lescaze and Their PSFS: 1929–1933

LESCAZE BECAME A NATURALIZED CITIZEN ON 18 March 1929.[1] That year was important not only in this personal respect, but it also marked the turning point in his career. It brought him his first work to be executed in the International Style, the Oak Lane Country Day School's nursery school building; a partnership with George Howe; and the commission that was to establish the international reputation of the firm, the Philadelphia Saving Fund Society Bank and Office building. Unfortunately, these events coincided with a crisis in the economy that caused the natural development of architecture in America to be considerably delayed. Yet, in the years of the Great Depression, Howe and Lescaze managed to evolve a consistent architectural style and to make their most significant contributions to the modern movement in America.

The partnership of George Howe and William Lescaze and their PSFS have been analyzed thoroughly by architectural historians.[2] Still, controversies persist regarding the history of the formation, duration, and dissolution of the partnership and the authorship of its most important building—the PSFS.

According to a note written by Lescaze, probably in 1929, Jeanne de Lanux, a New York interior designer, whose brother and sister Lescaze had known in Paris, was responsible for the introduction of the future partners. De Lanux had met George Howe on 22 June 1928 at the home of a mutual acquaintance, Philadelphia investment broker William Wasserman, whom she had met at a

meeting of the Russian Society on 2 April 1928. De Lanux introduced Lescaze to Mrs. Wasserman on 3 December 1928 and eleven days later she introduced Lescaze to George Howe. On 10 January 1929, Howe, Lescaze, and Mr. Wasserman met in New York for lunch, and about a week later Howe returned to ask Lescaze if he would consider forming a partnership.[3] Lescaze later recalled:

> It was so sudden that I asked him to give me some time to think about it. One thing he had said tempted me very strongly namely, that he had hopes that he might bring to the firm soon a skyscraper project [the PSFS] and since I had come to the U.S. especially because I am attracted to the "monumental," it naturally influenced my decision very much. At the same time a New York architect had asked me to form a partnership but then after a short while, I decided to join forces with George Howe.[4]

A partnership contract between Howe and Lescaze was signed on 10 April 1929; the articles of co-partnership were dated 1 May 1929.[5]

Indeed, Howe did bring the now-renowned PSFS skyscraper commission to the firm soon after its formation. Presumably in anticipation of the commission, Howe sought Lescaze's aid. Although Howe, a Beaux-Arts-trained architect (1908–1913), had been converted intellectually to modernism after leaving the successful Philadelphia firm of Mellor, Meigs, and Howe in 1928, he must have felt not altogether prepared to create the building and, thus, asked Lescaze to join him. Conversely,

48

Lescaze, European-born and -trained at the École Polytechnique in Zurich by the early modernist Karl Moser, had already established a reputation in New York as a modernist designer but had had no opportunity to design a major architectural work.

Lescaze's reputation was undoubtedly known to Howe through the 1928 publications of Lescaze's work in *Architectural Record, The Arts, The New Yorker, The New York Times*, and in a variety of interiors and trade magazines.[6] In that year Howe referred his earlier client, noted conductor Leopold Stokowski, to Lescaze for the commission of a Manhattan *pied-a-terre*. (Fig. 26).[7] Whatever the persuasion, Howe was somehow convinced of Lescaze's ability to help him with the design of PSFS. Not only did he ask Lescaze to join him in partnership, but the articles of co-partnership provided that Lescaze was to assume responsibility for architectural designs while Howe was to be responsible for the conduct of the firm's business.[8] Later, and in another context, Howe underscored the partners' division of responsibilities when he wrote:

> If I felt that this opportunity [PSFS] should be placed at your [Lescaze's] disposal, it was not because I considered you the greatest promoter in the U.S. but because I felt the sincerity of your artistic intentions.[9]

Lescaze's office at 337 East Forty-second Street in New York was the principal location for the practice, even though its foremost commission was in Howe's Philadelphia.

There probably could have been no stronger combination than the pairing of a convert to European modernism with a man trained by an early European modernist and eager to express himself in a monumental work. Both would approach the problem of creating a new architectural form with energy and dedication. Lescaze's ambition is suggested in a note written on 30 December 1929:

> The real fact is that to order a crowd of forms is no longer sufficient. . . . It is giants I want to work with. It is hard to wait with a head and body so impatient.[10]

More importantly, they were to complement each other's strengths and weaknesses productively. Howe offered the convert-modernist's restraint while Lescaze pushed the firm beyond the creative limits of the "old tradition." Together, they contributed significantly to the growth of modern architecture in the United States. The opportunity

Fig. 33. Howe and Lescaze, Philadelphia Saving Fund Society building, Philadelphia, Pennsylvania, 1929–1932. View from Market Street showing north and east elevations.

for this extraordinary partnership to prove itself came with the over $7 million PSFS commission. That bank and office building, completed in 1932, was the most important building of the partnership, if not of both their careers (Figs. 33, 34, 35, 36, 37).

Moreover, as the first International Style skyscraper in the United States, it is a landmark building in the modern movement. In the 1930s, it was heralded as the one American skyscraper which "is

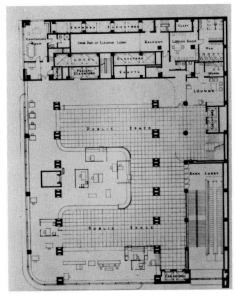

Fig. 34. Howe and Lescaze, Philadelphia Saving Fund Society building, Philadelphia, Pennsylvania, 1929–1932. Second floor plan (banking room).

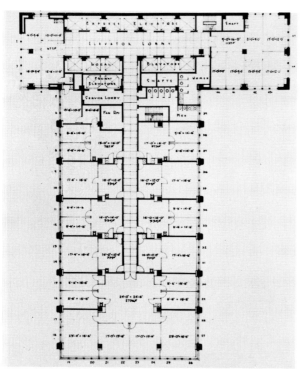

Fig. 35. Howe and Lescaze, Philadelphia Saving Fund Society building, Philadelphia, Pennsylvania, 1929–1932. Typical office floor plan.

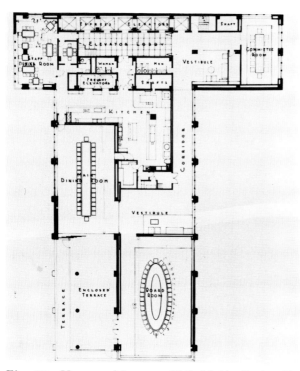

Fig. 36. Howe and Lescaze, Philadelphia Saving Fund Society building, Philadelphia, Pennsylvania, 1929–1932. Thirty-third floor plan (executive board room, dining room, solarium).

Fig. 37. Howe and Lescaze, Philadelphia Saving Fund Society building, Philadelphia, Pennsylvania, 1929–1932. Section. (Reprinted from Architectural Record, *October 1949 © 1949, by McGraw-Hill, Inc. with all rights reserved.)*

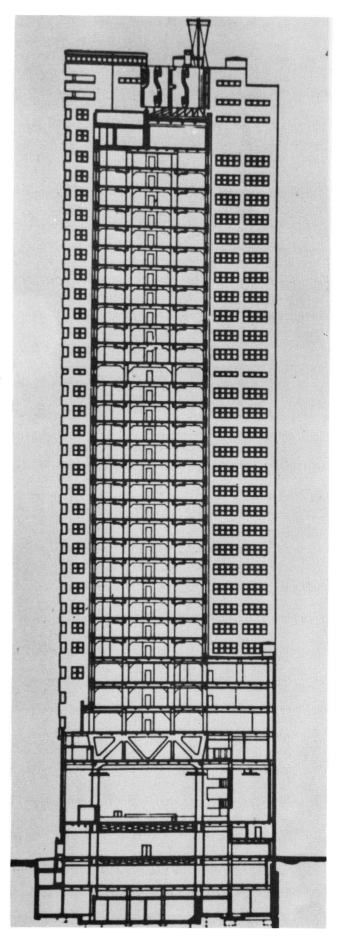

worth discussing in the same terms as the work of the leading architects of Europe," and "the most interesting piece of architecture in this country, . . . unique in modern architecture of the world."[11] The PSFS has more recently been called "the most important tall building erected between the Chicago School of the eighteen eighties and nineties and the metal-and-glass revival beginning around 1950."[12]

As William Jordy has pointed out, PSFS's influence has continued to prevail, prefiguring the design and environmental developments of post World War II skyscrapers. A rectilinear office slab (probably the first), standing on a podium of shops and banking rooms and backed by a subsidiary tower for elevators and services, it anticipated the separation of functions expressed in the 1952 Lever House, New York, and the 1954 Inland Steel building, Chicago, both by Skidmore, Owings and Merrill. It also anticipated the 1957 Harris Trust

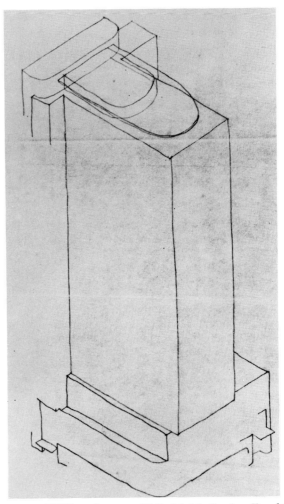

Fig. 39. *William Lescaze, Philadelphia Saving Society building, Philadelphia, Pennsylvania, 1929–1932. Axonometric rendering, 27 October 1929.*

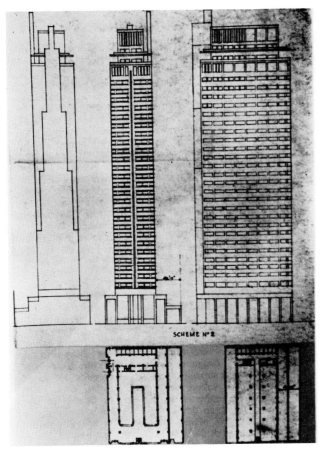

Fig. 38. *George Howe, projected scheme number 2 for the PSFS, Philadelphia, Pennsylvania, 20 March 1929. (Location of the original drawing is unknown to the author. It is reproduced here from William Jordy,* American Buildings and Their Architects, *Vol. 4, New York: Anchor Press/Doubleday, 1976, p. 100, Fig. 40.)*

Block's "different" floor half way up the tower and for the same reason—the economy of installing an air conditioning plant in the center of the slab. The second air-conditioned office building in the United States (the Milam building, San Antonio, 1928, George Willis architect, being the first), its sophisticated Carrier plant was able to adapt to exterior climate changes and compensate for shifting solar heating loads. And, as Reyner Banham has observed, its ceiling, integrating lighting, air conditioning, and acoustical properties, foretold the suspended ceilings of the 1950s.[13]

The discussion of the PSFS is presented here more briefly than its importance justifies because it has been the most thoroughly described, documented, and interpreted building of the partnership; indeed, it may be one of the most frequently published buildings of the early modern movement in America.

To document its design process briefly: Howe's first design for the PSFS was drawn in 1926 and four alternate schemes were dated between the twentieth and twenty-ninth of March, 1929 (Fig. 38). On 27 October 1929, Lescaze's schematic drawing delineated the eventually-realized T-shape, tower, cantilevered offices, banking room, the "notched" area above it, the curved base, and the roof-top pavillions (Fig. 39). On 2 December 1929, Lescaze sketched a rough preliminary design for the base of the building and, on 25 December 1929, he rendered a detailed version of the base. In July 1930, a model of the proposed building, whose façade consisted of alternating horizontal bands of windows and spandrels, was presented to the PSFS's building committee. Between July 1930 and January 1931, the scheme underwent numerous revisions in order to comply with building committee chairman James M. Willcox's wish for it to express structurally its vertical form.[14] In January 1931 ground breaking took place. On 12 August 1931 the building committee authorized air conditioning, which required redesigning the roof pavilions to accommodate cooling towers and designing a PSFS sign to screen them.[15]

It was because of the availability of a highly qualified staff, many of whom were trained in Europe in the tenets of the new modernism, that the design of the PSFS could progress so responsibly and rapidly [Appendix B].[16] Undoubtedly, Alfred Clauss, a disciple of Mies van der Rohe, and Walter Baermann, trained in Munich, were two of the architects in the Howe and Lescaze office who contributed appreciably to the high level of detailing that distinguishes the PSFS. Its distinguished design included not only the architectural spaces but also the furniture and much of the equipment as well. It exhibited a level of comprehensive design equalled in no other contemporary office building.

At once romantic and rational, cubist, constructivist, and expressionist, there was nothing like this slab skyscraper in form, materials, or exquisite finish before this time in the United States. The then recently completed Empire State building was already dated. The most "modern" were the Daily News and McGraw-Hill buildings and the Rockefeller Center buildings, then in process. By 1932, the Bowman brothers had drawn some equally theatrical and technically avant-garde skyscrapers, but they were not destined for realization. The PSFS, a collaborative effort by George Howe and William Lescaze, was a unique work at the time, standing between the European and American phases of the International Style. More than a half-century later, it is still judged a splendid piece of architecture.

Historians William Jordy and Robert A. M. Stern have convincingly argued that the "seed of the eventual design" of PSFS—its structural and functional organization—began with Howe's scheme two of 20 March 1929, which preceeded the partnership's contractual formation by three weeks.[17] Yet, it seems only reasonable to assume that Howe would have sought Lescaze's help in formulating the scheme for the coveted commission that had, after all, presumably caused him to invite Lescaze into partnership. This assumption is particularly compelling in light of the fact that Howe's scheme was drawn more than three months after the meeting of the two men, almost two months after Howe had invited Lescaze to form a partnership, and precisely three weeks before an informal partnership agreement between Howe and Lescaze

Fig. 40. Knud Lönberg-Holm, design for the Chicago Tribune Tower, 1922. Elevation rendering (Walter Gropius, Internationale Architektur, Munich: Albert Langen Press, 1925, pp. 42–43).

composition of base, shaft, and (in lieu of cornice) capping pavillions (Figs. 40 and 41).[20] The side view of Lönberg-Holm's Chicago Tribune entry even provides the prototype for Howe's lower and visually separate volume attached to the front view of his skyscraper composition.

Still more of Lönberg-Holm's ideas for the Tribune building are to be seen in Howe's and Lescaze's 1930 model of the PSFS. The detailing of the windows and juxtaposed balconies at the corner of the spine in the PSFS model recall Lönberg-Holm's Tribune stair shaft fenestration and flanking cantilevered balconies (Figs. 42 and 43). Black and white vertical striping exists in both schemes—in the rear façade of the PSFS model and in the front façade of Lönberg-Holm's rendering. Even the PSFS model's bold value contrasts between dark circulation shaft and light spandrels and the contrasting window patterns relate to Lönberg Holm's scheme (Figs. 40 and 44).

While all of these comparable Lönberg-Holm details were not retained in the final PSFS scheme, other related elements from his drawing are to be noted in the final work. For example, Lönberg-

was signed.[18] One might even wonder if Lescaze's Park Avenue Apartment House project of 1928, (Fig. 28), with its vertical glazing of the circulation core, could have influenced Howe's PSFS scheme of March 1929.

Yet, there remains the distinct possibility that the basis of the design was altogether neither Howe's nor Lescaze's, for stylistic precedents existed for both Howe's structural and functional organization of the building and for Lescaze's scheme for the skin of the building. As Vincent Scully has pointed out, Knud Lönberg-Holm's drawing for the Chicago Tribune competition of 1922 provides a striking parallel for Howe's concept of 20 March 1929.[19] Notable similarities between the two exist in their freestanding towers, nearly symmetrical front elevations and asymmetrical side elevations, central stair shafts, columns rising "four abreast within the slab," horizontal fenestration where the window rhythm alternates "heavy column and light mullion," and a Sullivanesque three-part skyscraper

Fig. 42. Knud Lönberg-Holm, design for the Chicago Tribune Tower, 1922 (J.J.P. Oud, Hollandische Architektur, Munich: Albert Langen Press, 1929, illustration no. 39, p. 61).

Fig. 43. Howe and Lescaze, Philadelphia Saving Fund Society building, Philadelphia, Pennsylvania, 1929–1932. Model, south-east view, 1930.

unnoticed by either Howe or Lescaze. Indeed, it did not, because in June 1929 Lescaze wrote to the Bauhaus requesting personal copies of both Gropius's and Oud's books.[22]

These books, by leaders of the European modern movement, would have been logical sources of architectural inspiration for anyone to turn to when solving the problem of designing America's first modern skyscraper. This is especially true of Lescaze, who had been in close contact with European architectural developments since his student days at Zurich's École Polytechnique and as a young architect working in the atelier of Henri Sauvage in Paris.

Lescaze returned to Europe every year after coming to live in the United States in 1920, and the influences of his European contacts are to be seen in his work prior to PSFS.[23] As discussed in Chapter 2 Lescaze introduced isolated characteristics of the European functionalist style of the twenties in his Jean de Sièyes house drawing of October 1927. His interest in the new European architecture was clearly demonstrated in the Capital Bus Terminal

Holm's debt to De Stijl aesthetics in the typography of his Tribune building's sign and flat wall planes of different colors are reflected in the PSFS sign and planes of black and gray on the south façade (Figs. 41 and 45).

Although Lönberg-Holm's drawings were not officially entered in the 1922 competition, they were available to the architects a few years later through their publication in Gropius's 1925 Bauhaus book, *Internationale Architektur.* They were also published in J. J. P. Oud's 1926 Bauhaus book *Hollandische Architektur* (republished in 1929, the year of Howe's and Lescaze's drawings), where in his essay on the history of modern architecture in Holland he relates his own work to that of a few select buildings abroad, including the Tribune building design of Lönberg-Holm.[21] In the United States, the drawings were published by Henry Russell-Hitchcock in his *Modern Architecture,* also in the crucial year of 1929. This considerable sanction of Lönberg-Holm's work is unlikely to have gone

Fig. 44. Howe and Lescaze, Philadelphia Saving Fund Society building, Philadelphia, Pennsylvania, 1929–1932. Model, north-east view, 1930.

54

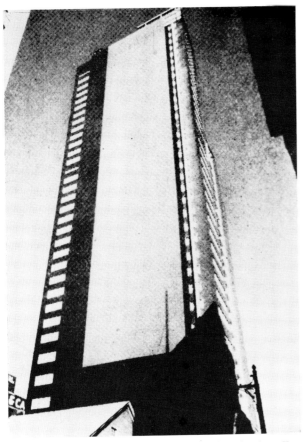

Fig. 45. Howe and Lescaze, Philadelphia Saving Fund Society building, Philadelphia, Pennsylvania, 1929–1932. South view, 1932.

and the League of Nations project of the same year. By 1928 Lescaze's projects, from his Park Avenue Apartment project to his "Future American Country House," moved increasingly toward and finally achieved a modernist functionalism, at least on paper.

Lescaze's contact with European modernism continued after the formation of the partnership even more actively than before. In April 1929, the month in which the partnership agreement with Howe was signed, Lescaze went to Europe to prepare a study on the progress of modern architecture. It might be assumed that his interest was more than that of a general nature; rather it was specifically apropos the PSFS commission. He visited J. J. P. Oud, Johannes Brinkman, Hendrik Berlage, J. W. E. Buys, and A. Boeken in The Netherlands; and Le Corbusier, Auguste Perret, Gabriel Guevrekian, André Lurçat, and Robert Mallet-Stevens in France.[24] Of these contacts, Brinkman appears to have been the greatest influence on PSFS.[25] The tower section of his van Nelle Factory near Rotterdam, which was

nearing completion at the time, is not unlike the July 1930 PSFS scheme (Figs. 46 and 44).[26] Irregular massing, a cantilevered façade, continuous bands of windows, revealed vertical circulation shaft, and low, roof-top pavilions were common to both.[27]

There were other European parallels as well. H. Allen Brooks has noted that Francis Keally's sketch of E. Otto Oswald's design for the Tagblatt-Turm in Stuttgart, published in the February 1929 issue of *Architectural Record*, also prefigures the irregular massing of PSFS, its cantilevered façade, and horizontal window bands.[28] A similar precedent might be seen in Georg Muche's 1924 Bauhaus design for a city apartment building in reinforced concrete.[29]

Jordy has pointed to Max Taut's Chicago Tribune competition entry and Richard Neutra's project of 1926 for a store and office building in his Rush City Reformed as structural precedents which assert projecting columns on the scale and in the manner of the final PSFS solution. Because of the prominence of these projects, Howe and Lescaze were undoubtedly aware of them. The former was readily available in the 1923 publication of the Tribune competition. The latter was published in Neutra's *Wie Baut Amerika?* of 1927 and in Henry-Russell Hitchcock's *Modern Architecture: Romanticism and Reintegration* published in 1929.[30]

Separating the elevator spine from the office tower in Howe's scheme had precedents in Werner Moser's widely published 1924 project for an office building, following Frank Lloyd Wright's project for the National Insurance Company of the same year.[31] Werner Moser was a classmate of Lescaze at Zurich's École Polytechnique and the son of Lescaze's mentor Karl Moser.

A separation of vertical services from cantilevered office slabs was part of still another Chicago Tribune building scheme, by expressionist Hans Scharoun. Moreover, his "overlapping" linkage of spine with base, and an obviously asymmetrical plan, is similar to Lescaze's handling of the same problem in his first drawings of the PSFS base in December 1929 (Figs. 47, 48, and 49). Although Scharoun's Chicago Tribune scheme was not officially entered in the competition, it was published in a 1922 issue of *Das Frühlicht*.[32]

The base of the PSFS can be related to a number of contemporary expressionist works. While Jordy cited Erich Mendelsohn's Shöcken Department Store in Chemnitz, completed a year after Lescaze

Fig. 46. J. A. Brinkman, L. C. van der Vlugt, and Mart Stam, Van Nelle Tobacco Factory, Rotterdam, *1927–1930 (Photograph courtesy of The Museum of Modern Art, New York).*

sketched the initial scheme for the base of PSFS, Mendelsohn's "Universum" Cinema (and the development of which it is a part) in Berlin (1926–1929) is more closely related in form and potentially more influential in terms of its completion date (Fig. 50).[33] Not only does it offer the precedents of curved base, step-backs, and shop windows under a cantilevered masonry band, but it also employs a complex composition of volumes in which a boldly curved base contrasts with a rectilinear vertical slab.

Correspondence between Howe and Lescaze offers new insight into the persisting uncertainties regarding the partners' respective responsibilities for the PSFS design. Excerpts from three letters written by George Howe to Lescaze indicate that Howe considered Lescaze to be in charge of all design decisions for the PSFS. After the PSFS model design had undergone numerous reworkings in compliance with the client's request, Howe wrote to Lescaze:

As you know, I am a pretty fair cooperator and realize

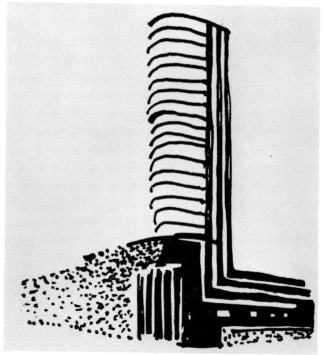

Fig. 47. Hans Scharoun, *study for the Chicago Tribune building, 1922 (Photograph courtesy of the Akademie der Künste, Berlin, Germany).*

Fig. 48. Howe and Lescaze, Philadelphia Saving Fund Society building, Philadelphia, Pennsylvania, 1929–1932. Perspective rendering of first scheme for the base, 2 December 1929.

Fig. 50. Erich Mendelsohn, The "Universum" Cinema, Berlin, 1926–1929. Principal façade (Photograph courtesy of the Akademie der Künste, Berlin, Germany).

that questions of design must be left essentially in the hands of one individual. I do not often interfere even when I am not in agreement.[34]

This was soon followed by Howe's letter stating: "I know how intensely you care about every detail and you no doubt feel inclined to pass on everything yourself."[35] Prompting Howe's comments was the long controversy over the color of the marble to be used in the banking room. Howe preferred a "red" marble called French Gran Antique. Lescaze preferred an ochre color, Jeune Ambre. In the end Lescaze's wishes prevailed.[36]

In a letter of 10 December 1930, Howe declared the PSFS design to be definitely Lescaze's. He wrote:

As we agreed yesterday, it is desirable that I should place my understanding with you on record in case of

my death or disability before the completion of the PSFS building at 12th and Market Streets. In the first place, the design is definitely yours, even more than mine, and as stated in our letter of 9 December 1930 to Mr. Willcox the firm is to receive full credit for the design whatever happens.[37]

The written evidence, most importantly the correspondence between the partners, suggests that Lescaze was the primary creative force behind the PSFS's final design. Although Howe considered Lescaze to be in charge of all design decisions, their correspondence indicates that Howe raised questions, expressed objections, suggested and effected modifications of some of Lescaze's ideas on the basis of personal taste, budgetary restrictions, and harmonious relationships with the Building Committee.[38]

The visual evidence, as documented above, indicates that the PSFS design was a collaborative effort by the two partners. As Howe was later to write to

Fig. 49. Howe and Lescaze, Philadelphia Saving Fund Society building, Philadelphia, Pennsylvania, 1929–1932. Perspective rendering of second scheme for the base, 25 December 1929.

Fig. 51. Howe and Lescaze, Philadelphia Saving Fund Society garage, Twelfth and Filbert Streets, Philadelphia, Pennsylvania, 1929–1933.

Lescaze: "It will be impossible for us to have a succession of jobs like PSFS in which quite effectively and in a very real sense we both participated in the design."[39]

The PSFS bank and office building and the PSFS garage were the only collaborative works of the partnership (Figs. 33 and 51). That fact has been obscured, however, because at the time of the final dissolution of the partnership, some of the Lescaze-designed work was attributed to the firm. The reason for that is explained in a letter of 25 February 1935 from Lescaze to Lawrence Kocher, managing editor of *Architectural Record*. He wrote: "For sentimental reasons, Oak Lane, Field, Hessian Hills School, Curry, and Wilbour Library should continue to be known as joint undertakings."[40] The "sentiment" probably had to do with the fact that those buildings were completed during the partnership years. The attributions to one partner or the other, with a few exceptions, are those jobs commissioned after the first dissolution of the Howe and Lescaze corporation, on 21 July 1933. It is clear, when one analyzes the independent work of Howe and Lescaze, that with the exception of PSFS, Lescaze was the principle author of the work attributed to the firm.

Although professionally and artistically productive, the partnership of Howe and Lescaze had never been one of close personal collaboration. The two men brought contrasting personalities and backgrounds, as well as talents, to the partnership. Howe had a protected childhood, presided over by a "domineering" mother, and enjoyed a life embellished by money, social position, and a classical education at Groton and Harvard with architectural training at the École des Beaux Arts in Paris.[41] Lescaze, the second of three sons, chose a technical education, and at the age of twenty-four (with almost no financial support or benefit of the English language) risked going to a foreign country to pursue his career in architecture. A bold, energetic, and debonair man of action and decision, with a zealous dedication, commitment, and ambition to practice architecture, Lescaze was intensely eager to utilize every bit of his talent in the cause of building. Howe, on the other hand, was, according to his monographer Robert A. M. Stern, "ambivalent, uncertain, indecisive, at times neurotic and plagued by internal conflicts throughout his life."[42] Stern judged him "successful and relaxed," careless with his talents and "content to assume the role of suburban gentleman."[43] Maintaining separate offices—

Howe in Philadelphia and Lescaze in New York—the partners practiced more or less independently of one another with the exception of the PSFS commission. Even then, the partnership began to unravel a year before the PSFS was opened in August 1932.

The first difference between the partners arose over how to conduct further business after the completion of the design of the PSFS. Lescaze preferred to compete in the open market place, employing all the publicity necessary to promote the business of the firm. Howe preferred "an exclusive shop" catering to "fat purses."[44] In regard to that subject, Howe wrote to Lescaze:

The feeling I cannot eradicate from my emotional consciousness is that the whole process of high-power salesmanship, whether of things or ideas, is in fact anti-social and therefore destructive. . . .[45]

He underscored his position with:

As to special activities, social, political, and private, such as mixing with important people or serving on committees, I am sorry to say that I for one, am entirely unfitted for any such work. I went all through it years ago and gave it up as a bad job. It is useless for me to prove to myself once more my unfitness for it.[46]

This is a surprising statement in light of the fact that, according to the terms of the partnership agreement, Howe was to have assumed responsibility for establishing "advantageous business connections, attending meetings, and conferences and conducting negotiations connected with the inception and execution of partnership business."[47] With Howe's share of the partnership responsibility thus abandoned, Lescaze was left to carry out the role himself and to employ the methods he thought to be most productive. Yet Howe did not approve of them.

A difference of opinion soon arose between the partners in regard to the taking on of additional associates or partners. Those that Howe proposed were unacceptable to Lescaze and vice versa.[48] There was yet another problem, probably the most significant one. Howe was suffering a "suppressed nervous condition" that was trying to the partners' personal as well as professional relationships.[49] It seemed to manifest itself first in fatigue. For example, in a letter to Lescaze of 28 August 1931, Howe wrote:

There are a great many questions which can only be settled by one in authority and with the energy to push matters to a conclusion. . . . I am frankly so driven that the very idea turns my stomach. . . .

I haven't got the time or energy to go out to the factories.[50]

A few months later he told Lescaze: "I enjoyed our talk very much the other night and left you, as I always do, feeling a new energy and courage."[51]

But the situation worsened. In a letter of 5 February 1932, Howe wrote to Lescaze:

I wish I didn't get so excited about things when my mind is confused. However, until I have definitely decided on a course of action I do not seem to be able to achieve any peace of mind, and the nervous tension causes me to break out at the most unexpected and seemingly uncalled for moments as yesterday when I get so "het up" about the letter of invitation . . . in the meantime the least incident obviously twangs my nerves drawn taught by the conflict.[52]

On 2 June 1932, Howe told Lescaze of his intent to quit architecture. Lescaze replied:

What's the opposite of a red letter day? Green? Blue. Blue, I guess; blue I call it that June 2nd where you broke the news to me. I had no idea, really. Tell me how long is it that you have arrived at this decision? And is it irrevocable? (I felt it was but I must ask you)

The "inc." suggestion which you made on the following day seems to me better from the angle PSFS and others. Will you wait a little until I have consulted with McCaffrey [Lescaze's attorney] and spoken with you again before saying anything to anyone.

It's always the same thing, hang it all: it's only when about to loose it that one seizes the measure of an affection—of a relationship. Mind you I shall be happy if you do the right thing by you. You understand. But I'll miss you, George, very very much. And I hate to think about that.[53]

As per Howe's suggestion, Howe and Lescaze, Inc. was formed on 28 November 1932; the dissolution of the partnership was made legal by an agreement of 1 December 1932.[54] The corporation was not to last either. Its disintegration began on 19 April 1933 when Howe wrote to Lescaze:

I am afraid I have a bad surprise in store for you. A new circumstance has presented itself. I have just seen my doctor again, who says I must take a six-month vacation. He told me to do so in 1928, but at the time, I could not. I think, therefore, it would be folly not to follow his advice now. He says there is no telling what the cumulative results of a suppressed nervous condition such as mine may be in time, whereas if I take measures now, no ill effects will remain.

Since I had, as you know, intended to retire at the end of the year, it seems best to take the step at the end of the six months' period, on June 1st, as I had originally intended, at which time we had already planned to close the Philadelphia office. Nothing need be said to the world at large about the termination of my architectural activities. I shall simply be taking a rest. You can carry on alone, and at the end of another six months, my official existence will be forgotten, as is the way of the world. There will be no sudden break to the public eye. Also, our joint affairs are now in a most convenient shape to be terminated. All the most current jobs are practically finished and the evaluation of the stock will present no difficulties.

We will talk about it tomorrow. I'm so sorry.[55]

Howe's revelation that he had experienced the same nervous condition in 1928 suggests a relationship between it and the termination of his first partnership with Mellor and Meigs, which took place in that year. Whatever the cause then, it was clear now.[56]

The corporation was subsequently dissolved— for the *first* time—on 21 July 1933.[57] The legal agreement provided that Lescaze would have the "sole and exclusive right to use the name of Howe and Lescaze in and about the carrying on of the profession of architecture," and that Howe would "not undertake any architectural work of any kind . . . without written permission of William Lescaze."[58]

According to the terms of the agreement, Lescaze continued to practice under the name of "Howe and Lescaze." This was a viable arrangement for about fifteen months. Then the question of his practicing under the corporate name arose. Apparently a misunderstanding between the partners occured when discussing the subject. Howe thought Lescaze wanted to give up the name of "Howe and Lescaze," when actually he did not.[59] Howe wrote in reply to Lescaze's surprise at the idea:

The particular question you raised which seemed to me to indicate a desire to abandon the name of Howe and Lescaze was that you said you thought it deplorable that people should say "I was in Philadelphia and I saw the house that you designed and the house that Mr. Howe designed." You stated it was your wish that all work should be said to be designed by Howe and Lescaze. In theory I agree with you, but, as I told

59

you, in practice I have found it impossible to maintain.

Your suggestion in regard to the Welsh House is merely an illustration of what I know will happen. In the case of a house which is avowedly not much to boast of I can assume authorship, in order to relieve the organization of responsibility. In the case of a house designed by you, authorship will automatically be assigned to you as an individual.

That is the way it worked out with Mellor and Meigs.[60]

This confused letter suggests that Howe's nervous condition was upon him again. It was manifested in yet another problem, a misunderstanding regarding what Howe believed to be a $154.97 accounting irregularity in Lescaze's favor. Because of this, Howe informed Lescaze, in a letter of 9 November 1934, that he would prefer to terminate their professional relationship at once.

Out of patience with Howe, Lescaze replied:

You yourself said the other morning that when depressed you wrote letters that you did not mean.

I can only conclude that the enclosed one is another specimen and I am returning it to you so that you yourself can destroy it with your own fingers. This does not come from the George we know and care for. That George would have remembered and taken for granted that his $154.97 will be or has been (I do not tend to those details) automatically credited to him. . . .

I am sorry if you are once more melancholy and upset. But I cannot any longer have you use your letters to me as an outlet for the figments of your irrational depressions. Those letters cause both Mary and myself undeserved and unjustified grief.[61]

Apparently Howe was ready to quit and reaffirmed that he meant what he had said. The final break was cordial, with Lescaze writing a compassionate letter to Howe:

All right George, if you must break completely, good luck be with you always. But that is no reason for us not to behave like well-bred human beings. If you will not be in town to discuss our announcement, make a draft of what you would suggest and send it to me for my opinion.

You really do not know how much I hope you find a way out for you.[62]

Howe responded with: "I wish you and Mary great happiness and yourself every success in your profession."[63]

Subsequent correspondence was cordial, with Lescaze writing such sentiments as: "one of my deep desires is for you to find peace and happiness. The quality of our relationship during five delightful years of working, hoping and planning together is most important to me, and I want to keep it untarnished."[64] Howe responded with: ". . . and like you I want our active and fruitful association to end in a friendly way."[65]

On 1 March 1935 the partners exchanged letters releasing the other from previous agreements, thus protecting each from claims that might arise from their architectural work. The "Certificate of Dissolution of Howe and Lescaze, Inc." was legally effected, for the *second* time, on 20 March 1935.[66]

Clearly the several differences of opinion between the partners on how to carry on the business of the firm ultimately led to the dissolution of the partnership. Yet, presumably, none of these differences, singly or collectively, could have been responsible for the breakdown of such a productive partnership had not Howe's "nervous condition" exaggerated their importance beyond all reasonable proportions. Lescaze was to express a similar opinion when, at the time of Howe's death, he wrote:

George was such a likeable fellow. . . . At the same time, he was as moody as he was likeable. Moodiness makes for many transitory attachments and for unexpected decisions.[67]

Thus, the partnership that produced one of the most important buildings of the twentieth century ended.

Subsequently, the principals in that partnership were never again to equal the achievement of their PSFS building. Perhaps that commission was particularly successful because it was the partners' "moment"—a magical combination of personality, and economic and cultural circumstances. Or the problem may have been uniquely demanding of a great solution. Possibly the enlightened client Mr. Willcox was responsible for causing the architects to produce their best building. Whatever the reason, the work of both men was less accomplished individually.

Howe's short-term partnership with Lescaze was but the first of a series of brief ones to follow: with Norman Bel Geddes, Louis McAllister, Earle W. Bolton, Oscar Stonorov, Louis Kahn, and Robert Montgomery Brown.[68] Lescaze resumed practice alone, establishing a firm under his own name in

1935 which, with associates, continued to flourish until his death in 1969.

NOTES

1. "Certificate of Naturalization," Court of Southern District of New York, Certificate No. 2805320, Petition Vol. 434, No. 13797.

2. See Bibliography, pp. 189–191.

3. The meeting dates and persons involved were recorded by Lescaze on a small piece of blue-bordered paper (hereafter cited as Blue-bordered Note), probably in about 1929, judging from handwriting style and the use of French spellings which he typically used at that time. It reads:

"2 Avril 1928—jl. [Jeanne de Lanux] meet Bill Wasserman (Russian Soc)
22 Juin 1928—jl. meet George Howe (at Wasserman's)
3 Decembre 1928—jl. introduce Marion W. [Wasserman] to Bill Lescaze
14 Decembre 1928—jl. introduce George Howe to Bill Lescaze
10 Janvier 1929—Lunch Howe, Wass., Lescaze
10 Avril 1929—"Signature contract Howe and Lescaze"

According to a letter of 25 January 1962 from Lescaze to William Jordy, William Stix Wasserman, a young Philadelphia stockbroker, was responsible for the introduction. This account is also recorded by Paul S. Wingert, "William Lescaze: Modern American Architect" (typescript), ca. 1940–1941, p. 18. Robert A.M. Stern, in *George Howe: Toward a Modern American Architecture* (New Haven: Yale University Press, 1975), p. 90, claims that Wasserman introduced Howe to Lescaze but also quotes Wasserman's letter of 8 January 1974 stating that Jeanne de Lanux introduced Howe to Lescaze.

4. Lescaze to Jordy, copy of letter, 25 January 1962.

5. The partnership was not formed in 1920 as is stated in R. Pommer, "The Architecture of Urban Housing in the U.S. during the Early 1930s," *JSAH*, XXXVII, 1978, 251. The partnership contract date was recorded on Blue-bordered Note, see footnote 3; "Articles of Co-Partnership between George Howe and William E. Lescaze, 1 May 1929."

6. Selected references include: W. E. Lescaze, "The Future American Country House," *Architectural Records*, LXIV, 1928, 417–420; C. A. Glassgold, "Decorative Art Notes," *The Arts*, XIII, 1928, 296–301; C. A. Glassgold, "The Decorative Arts," *The Arts*, XIV, 1928, 215–217; C. A. Glassgold, "Art in Industry," *The Arts*, XIII, 1928, 375–379; "The Macy Exposition of Art in Industry," *Architectural Record*, LXIV, 1928, 137–143; "Second Macy Art in Industry Exposition Reveals International Progress of Modern Art," *Women's Wear Daily*, 26 May 1928; W. R. Storey, "The Latest Art in Industry Exhibit," *New York Times*, 27 May 1928, Mag. Sect. 18–19; "Nineteen Twenty-Eight Contributes to a Modern American Style," *American Architect*, CXXXV, 1929, 31–48; "Andrew Geller to Move to New Factory," *The Shoe Retailer*, 15 December 1928, 56; "The Bus Grows Up," *The New Yorker*, 27 October 1928, 20–21.

7. K. K. Kitchen, "Up and Down Broadway," *New York World*, 23 April 1929; C. A. Glassgold, "The S. Apartment," *Architectural Forum* 53 (August 1930):228.

8. See "Articles of Co-Partnership."

9. Howe to Lescaze, first letter of two dated 5 August 1931.

10. Translated from the French by Mrs. Lescaze, WELA.

11. Hitchcock, "Howe and Lescaze," p. 145; Philip Johnson to Lescaze, 5 August 1932.

12. William Jordy, *American Buildings and Their Architects: The Impact of European Modernism in the Mid-Twentieth Century*, vol. 4 (New York: Doubleday and Co., 1972), p. 88.

13. Reyner Banham, *The Well-Tempered Environment* (London: The Architectural Press, 1969), pp. 209–212.

14. See Jordy, "PSFS," pp. 67–70, or WELA for photographs of the studies. The last dated study known to the author is 21 January 1931. R. J. Seltzer, real estate consultant, also strongly recommended vertical piers for ease in partitioning the office space. That idea was to prevail in the Rockefeller Center at about the same time.

15. Jordy, *American Buildings and Their Architects*, chapter 2, passim.

16. Some had come from experience with the Chrysler and Empire State buildings, thus little instruction was necessary. Lescaze stated, in response to the "Questionnaire for the Architects' Roster," 16 October 1947, WELA, that the staff of Howe and Lescaze numbered thirty at the time of PSFS. Other sources of Information are: interview with Alfred Clauss and Norman Rice, Philadelphia, 10 April 1974; interview with Julian Whittlesey, Wilton, Connecticut, 20 February 1974; "Summer Schedule for Vacations, Philadelphia and New York offices, 1930," "Bon Voyage Dinner for George J. Peter," 22 July 1931, Lescaze Scrapbook; Lescaze's "284"-PSFS Notes, 24 June 1932; Lescaze to Howe, 16 September 1932; Clauss to author, 10 July 1975.

17. Jordy, "PSFS: Its Development and Significance in Modern Architecture," *Journal of the Society of Architectural Historians* 21 (May 1962):61.

18. Jordy, "PSFS," 61, in stating that the scheme preceded by more than a month the partnership's formation assumes a partnership date of 1 May 1929 instead of the 10 April 1929 documented in footnote 3.

19. *American Art and Urbanism* (New York: Frederick Praeger, Pubs., 1969), 154; and Robert A. M. Stern, *George Howe*, 89.

20. The quoted words are William Jordy's, "PSFS," p. 60.

21. Both Gropius's and Oud's books were published by Albert Langen Press, Munich.

22. Lescaze to the Bauhaus, 18 June 1929. Lescaze also requested furniture and hardware catalogues from the Bauhaus and from Albert Langen Press, 20 June 1929; from S. A. Loevy on 14 June 1930.

23. According to Mrs. Lescaze, Lescaze visited his family in Switzerland and other parts of Europe each year after his immigration to the United States, interviews 1974.

24. Lescaze to Le Corbusier, J. J. P. Oud, André Lurçat, August Perret, Gabriel Guevrekian, Robert Mallet-Stevens, and Christian Zervos, June 1929, all mention Lescaze's having visited in April. Lescaze to A. Sage, 21 June 1929 states that Lescaze interviewed Buys, J. A. Brinkman, Hendrik Berlage, A. Boeken, and J. J. P. Oud. Letters from Lescaze to Mary Hughes and Hughes to Lescaze refer to Lescaze's trip from mid-April to early-June, 1929.

25. In an interview of 9 October 1974, Mrs. Lescaze noted that Lescaze admired Brinkman's work.

26. See Jordy, "PSFS," 76, and Jordy, *American Buildings and Their Architects*, 131–141 for further discussion of the van Nelle factory and PSFS. The van Nelle factory plans were also shown at the Weissenhof exhibition in Stuttgart, where Lescaze had visited shortly before its opening.

27. The certain influence of the van Nelle Factory on Lescaze's work is apparent in the fourth scheme of his Museum of Modern Art project p. 78, commissioned just one month before the model of the PSFS was presented.

28. H. Allen Brooks, "PSFS: A Source for Its Design," *Jour-*

nal of The Society of Architectural Historians (December 1968): 299–302.

29. Hans Wingler, *The Bauhaus* (Cambridge, Mass.: The MIT Press, 1969), p. 389.

30. Neutra (Stuttgart: Hoffman, 1927); Hitchcock (New York, 1929).

31. Henry-Russell Hitchcock compares Wright's project to PSFS in *The Nature of Materials* (New York: Duell, Sloan and Pearce, 1942), p. 81. Moser's project was published in Ludwig Hilberseimer, *Internationale Neue Baukunst* (Stuttgart, 1927), pl. 36; also see Erich Mendelsohn, *Russland, Europa, Amerika* (Berlin, 1929), pl. 142; and "Design for Office Building," *Architectural Record* 68 (December 1930): 489.

32. See Dennis Sharp, *Modern Architecture and Expressionism* (New York: George Braziller, 1966), p. 71.

33. A similar composition was used by Lescaze in his Fox Theater project of 1931. See Jordy, *American Buildings and Their Architects*, 140–145, for discussion of the relationship of the PSFS base to Mendelsohn's Schöcken Department Store, Chemnitz.

34. Howe to Lescaze, 28 August 1931. All Howe and Lescaze correspondence is in the possession of Mrs. Lescaze.

35. Howe to Lescaze, 5 October 1931.

36. See Marble Schedule, PSFS blueprints, PSFS Building, Philadelphia, Pennsylvania.

37. This letter was motivated by Mr. Willcox's position that the employment of Howe and Lescaze as a firm was in form only. Because Willcox's contractual arrangements had been only with Howe (prior to Howe's formation of a partnership with Lescaze), Willcox considered that the agreement existed between PSFS and Howe as an individual as agreed in letters of 9 February 1927 and 10 February 1927. See: Willcox to Howe, 26 November 1930; Lescaze to Howe, 29 November 1930; Howe to Lescaze, 29 November 1930; Howe to Willcox, 29 November 1930; Howe to PSFS, 1 December 1930; Willcox to Howe, 9 December 1930.

38. See Howe and Lescaze correspondence and "284" PSFS Notes in L. W. Lanmon, "The role of William E. Lescaze in the Introduction of the International Style to the United States," (Ph.D. dissertation, University of Delaware, 1979).

39. Howe to Lescaze, 29 October 1934. Spinning off the success of the PSFS was the 1931 project for the Emigrant Industrial Savings Bank, an approximately fifty-five story skyscraper tower planned for New York. Still a viable project as late as 3 February 1933, it remained unrealized. Similar to the July 1930 PSFS scheme, the façades consisted of alternating horizontal bands of windows and spandrels. But this time they were relieved by five setbacks, the uppermost ascending to tower height with a vertical spine at one side. It is tempting to see the composition as a shortened PSFS placed upon four bases.

40. Copy of Lescaze to A. Lawrence Kocher, 12 August 1935, WELA.

41. Stern, *George Howe*, p. 8.

42. Ibid.

43. Ibid., p. 36.

44. The quoted words are in Howe to Lescaze, one of two letters dated 5 August 1931; also see Lescaze to Howe, 10 August 1931; Howe to Lescaze 19 November 1931; and Howe to Lescaze 27 January 1932.

45. Howe to Lescaze, 5 February 1932.

46. Howe to Lescaze, 18 April 1932. The context of this statement was in a letter which again protested the idea of mounting a publicity and promotion campaign for the firm.

47. "Articles of Co-Partnership."

48. See Howe to Lescaze, one of two letters dated 5 August 1931; Howe to Lescaze, 28 August 1931; and interview with Mrs. Lescaze, New York, 17 July 1973.

49. Howe, in a letter to Lescaze, 19 April 1933, mentions that his doctor has recommended a six-month vacation for his "supressed nervous condition." The problem may have manifested itself as early as 1928, according to Howe's letter.

50. Howe to Lescaze, one of two letters dated 8 August 1931. The letter concerned the building and furnishing of the PSFS and the suggestion of taking a junior partner into association.

51. Howe to Lescaze, 5 October 1931.

52. Howe to Lescaze, 5 February 1932.

53. Lescaze to Howe, 5 June 1932.

54. "George Howe with William E. Lescaze, Agreement," 28 November 1932. "George Howe with William E. Lescaze, Agreement," 1 December 1932; Dissolution of Partnership Agreement, 1 December 1932.

55. Lescaze replied to Howe at Jefferson Hospital, Philadelphia, and in care of Dr. Frederick Fraley (a relative of Howe's) at Northeast Harbor, Maine. See letters: Lescaze to Howe, 29 June 1933; 24 August 1933, and 10 September 1933.

56. See Stern, *George Howe*, 79–80, for discussion of Howe's resignation from Mellor, Meigs, and Howe.

57. "George Howe with William Lescaze, Agreement," 21 July 1933. Stern states, ibid, that at the time of the dissolution of the partnership, Lescaze was earning his way as much through the proceeds of the Lescord Shops as through the practice of architecture itself. This is in disagreement with the facts. According to "Howe and Lescaze, Inc. Statement of Assets and Liabilities," 31 May 1933, the worth of the "Lescord shop" was only $2,187.99, as compared with total assets of $22,145.77. Moreover, the considerable PSFS commission was only one year old. Further, Lescase's Job List shows that he received, in 1933, commissions for four buildings that were erected at Dartington Hall, Devon, England; the Roy Spreter Studio and Garage in Lower Merion Township, Pennsylvania; and the Wilbour Library of the Brooklyn Museum.

58. "Howe with Lescaze, Agreement," 21 July 1933. Howe did do architectural work, however, without permission from Lescaze. Howe to Lescaze, 17 November 1933 and Lewis M. Isaacs [Lescaze's lawyer] to Lescaze, 20 November 1934.

59. Howe to Lescaze, 29 October 1934, Lescaze to Howe, 1 November 1934.

60. Howe to Lescaze, one of two letters of 5 November 1934. Howe's reference to theoretically upholding the idea of firm authorship, but believing it wouldn't work in practice, can be attributed to the fact that when Howe's and Meigs' Newbold house was awarded the medal of the New York Architectural League (1925), Meigs claimed full authorship.

61. Lescaze to Howe, 10 November 1934.

62. Lescaze to Howe, 13 November 1934. This does not appear to the author to be the "bitter reply" that Stern, *George Howe*, p. 159, assesses it to be.

63. Howe to Lescaze, 14 November 1934.

64. Lescaze to Howe, 23 November 1934.

65. Howe to Lescaze, 3 December 1934. Compare the tone of these letters with Stern's allusion to an unpleasant separation. Stern, *George Howe*, pp. 158, 159.

66. "Certificate of Dissolution of Howe and Lescaze, Inc.", 20 March 1935. The first dissolution took place on 21 July 1933.

67. W. Lescaze, "Homage to George Howe," (typescript), WELA.

68. Lawrence Wodehouse suggests, in his review of Stern's *George Howe*, that Howe's architectural philandering was possibly a direct result of his unsettled mental state. Lawrence Wodehouse, review of *George Howe: Toward a Modern American Architecture*, by Robert A. M. Stern, in the *Journal of the Society of Architectural Historians* 35 (March 1976): 64.

4

Lescaze's Work during the Partnership: International Modernism, 1929–1933

THE BUILDINGS, WHICH AT THE DISSOLUTION OF THE partnership were attributed to the firm of Howe and Lescaze for "sentimental reasons," yet designed by Lescaze, include some of his most important works. They are primarily characterized by the pure, pristine, volumetric machine forms of the European International Style, developed there almost a decade earlier; an expression of structure, which developed in the Style later in the United States, was tentatively introduced in some.[1]

The principles of De Stijl, the early writings and work of Le Corbusier, rationalist philosophy, and the free plasticity of expressionist architecture were the foremost influences on Lescaze's work during the so called "partnership" years. Lescaze's formal vocabulary at this time reflects his interest in the expressive means of curvilinear forms contrasted with rectilinear forms. That is, he most often organized his buildings in two orthogonally disposed rectangular volumes, joined by a curved volume or plane. Typical of this composition was his nursery school building for the Oak Lane Country Day School near Philadelphia, Pennsylvania. Lescaze had received the commission from Leopold and Evangeline Stokowski, whose New York apartment he had completed shortly before his partnership with Howe was formed.[2] Seeking a European conception of twentieth-century school architecture, Stokowski suggested to the school's headmaster, William Burnlee Curry, that he talk with Lescaze about the project. Although "plans of a more or less conventional building were already well advanced,"

Curry and Lescaze conferred in December 1928.[3] The meeting was not only successful in that early in 1929 Lescaze received the commission for the school, but Lescaze and Curry also became close friends, respecting each other's modernist commitments to educational and architectural experimentation. This was Lescaze's first chance to do what he had "dreamed and longed for—a modern building."[4] Stokowski felt that only a modern building made sense since it was to be for two- and three-year-old children who would find almost everything modern when they grew up.[5]

Oak Lane, like a few schools in Europe, was planned for optimal sun exposure and included

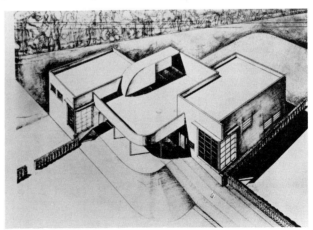

Fig. 52. Howe and Lescaze (Lescaze, designer), nursery school building for the Oak Lane Country Day School, Oak Lane, near Philadelphia, Pennsylvania, 1929. Axonometric rendering of projected scheme, January 1929.

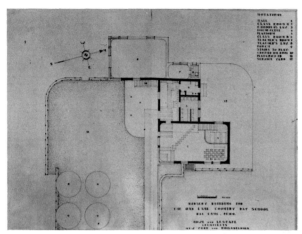

Fig. 53. Howe and Lescaze (Lescaze, designer), nursery school building for the Oak Lane Country Day School, Oak Lane, near Philadelphia, Pennsylvania, 1929. Plan.

both open and covered play areas.[6] As originally conceived, two classrooms, with large south-east corner windows, were to be connected by a hall to give access to a utility core and a teachers' private office (Figs. 52 and 53). The sundeck was fitted neatly into the plan, providing a covered play area that kept light only from the service core, where it was unimportant. Because of budgetary restrictions, only one of the classrooms was built, resulting in more asymmetry than was planned. Budgetary trimming also caused the deletion of the more neo-plastic effects which were to have been provided by flat window hoods and intersecting wall planes at the south-east corners.

In keeping with Maria Montessori's educational philosophy that a human being must be allowed to develop in conformity with his native characteristics rather than with tradition, the building's spaces were planned to encourage initiative, imagination, and individuality and to suggest freedom rather than to imply restrictions. In order that the children might feel an intimacy with their surroundings, the scale was reduced wherever possible to child size. The doors and window-sill heights and the treads and risers of the stairs were scaled to the convenience of two- to four-year olds. The furniture was small and light. To allow better use of the floor for play space, cork tiles were installed for warmth and to reduce injuries. They were laid in geometric patterns to encourage creative and spontaneous use by the children.[7] The architects' dedication to a "functional" flooring material was expressed by Lescaze:

> We wanted it [the nursery school] as nearly perfect as possible. A decision had to be made immediately

about the kind of flooring. We were convinced that the best material was cork, but cork cost five or six hundred dollars in addition to the budget. Frantic telephone calls and wires. All of the trustees were away on vacation. We couldn't let our building, our creation, suffer, so my partner and I decided it would be cork even if we had to pay for it. Which we did.[8]

To Curry, who in previous experience "had always found that the exigencies of the architect's own stylistic prejudices were thought to be more important than the functional needs of the building itself," Lescaze's rational handling of the problem "seemed infinitely more intelligent" than anything he had come across before.[9] To Lescaze, "all the way through, that was a very satisfying job, an enchanting problem plus an extraordinary headmaster, William Curry, and the stimulating interest of Stokowski to work with."[10]

The building revealed a dedication not only to functional planning but to the formal qualities of the new European modern aesthetic as well. In the "ultra-modern" image, as judged by visual standards of the late 1920s, the Oak Lane nursery school articulated most of the fundamental principles of the International Style which were to be defined three years later by Hitchcock and Johnson in their *The International Style:* an architecture of volume rather than of mass, a rhythmic organization of regular units with asymmetrical arrangements predominating, no ornament or texture, and a functionalism that expressed planning for social and economic needs.[11] Moreover, three of Le Corbusier's "Five Points" can be seen in the roof terrace, the window wall, and in the asymmetrical composition of the façade consonant with functional demands of the interior.[12]

Within the spectrum of the International Style's expressive modes, Lescaze's conceptual emphasis for the Oak Lane nursery school centered in the reduction of the building to basic geometric shapes—in "refining, adjusting, simplifying, and perfecting" those shapes and their relationships.[13] It is apparent that he was concerned with the harmonious relationships of the variously shaped doors and windows. He emphasized the building's volume by contrasting colored walls with white ones and by outlining edges with color.[14] The machine precision of smooth, untextured, planar wall surfaces and the drama of contrasting a massive, curvilinear deck parapet against a thin, rectilinear classroom were of utmost importance to him. This emphasis on what Le Corbusier called "contour," "profile," and "primary forms" was to characterize not only the nursery school but also much of Lescaze's work throughout the 1930s.[15]

Although one of the ideological aims of European modernism was to use modern technology as a determinant of form, skeletal framing and mass production were not imperative. Indeed, the structure of the Oak Lane nursery school, like that of Lescaze's Capital Bus Terminal, was not particularly advanced. A concrete block structure covered with stucco, its forms were only symbolic of machine and technological functionalism. Lescaze was not alone in his failure to express structural systems and technological methods in his architecture. Most architects at the time built pseudo-membranous concrete structures for visual effect.[16] Henry-Russell Hitchcock, writing in 1929, observed:

> Engineering may change completely from year to year, but the aesthetic of the New Pioneers has already shown a definite continuity of values separate from, and, even on occasion in opposition to, those derived from the practical and structural.[17]

Yet, Hitchcock considered the Oak Lane nursery school significant in "turning America's attention to new architectural possibilities."[18]

Representing a complete break with American tradition, this first work of the firm of Howe and Lescaze, designed by Lescaze in the spring of 1929 and opened on 23 September 1929, became notable as the first International Style school building in the United States.[19] Moreover, the Oak Lane nursery school was published extensively here and abroad, establishing the firm of Howe and Lescaze as one of the best known of the "New Pioneers" practicing in America. Although the school was a modest statement of the International Style as compared with buildings by the leading Europeans and Richard Neutra working on the West Coast, there were virtually no parallels on the East Coast at the time.

Features of the school's design are to be seen in Lescaze's works that followed in the same year. The bold, sweeping curve of the deck parapet connected to a rectilinear volume, and the window wrapping the corner surmounted by a cantilevered hood, appear similarly but more fully integrated in the base of the PSFS, designed only a few months later (Fig. 48). And the compositions of the large country houses of James M. R. Sinkler and William Stix Wasserman in south-eastern Pennsylvania (designed in the summer that the nursery school was under construction) consisted of Lescaze's ubiqui-

tous, clearly profiled groups of orthogonally-massed, flat-roofed, rectilinear volumes with corner glazing, uncapped walls, roof decks, exposed lally columns, and cantilevered hoods over some of the windows (Fig. 54).[20] Unlike the nursery school, however, they were made picturesque by their relatively rambling compositions and veneers of local stone, brick, and wood siding, which were undoubtedly required by either George Howe, his clients, or both.[21]

Lescaze redrew the Wasserman house a few months later, replacing the traditional facing materials with smooth white stucco that bespoke the new modernism, if only in a superficial way (Fig. 55 and 56). A model of this project was displayed at the New York Architectural League's annual exhibition in February 1930. Most of the critics were united in cautious praise of the scheme. In his review of the exhibition, H. I. Brock dubbed it a "country house in the battleship bridge style."[22] Talbot Hamlin appropriately described the design as "an attempt to give a purely Le Corbusier ab-

Fig. 54. Howe and Lescaze, William Stix Wasserman house project, Whitemarsh, Pennsylvania, 1929–1930. Perspective rendering of entrance façade, scheme two, first version, June 1929.

Fig. 55. Howe and Lescaze, William Stix Wasserman house project, Whitemarsh, Pennsylvania, 1929–1930. Perspective rendering of the garden façade, scheme two, second version, January 1930.

Fig. 56. Howe and Lescaze, William Stix Wasserman house project, Whitemarsh, Pennsylvania, 1929–1930. Perspective rendering of entrance façade, scheme two, second version.

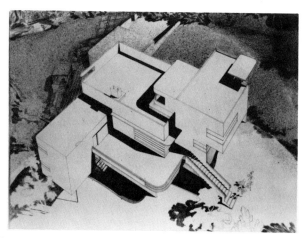

Fig. 57. Howe and Lescaze (Lescaze, designer), Mrs. George French Porter house project, Ojai, California, 1929. Axonometric rendering, October 1929.

stract modern exterior to a conventional plan."[23] Adolph Glassgold saw in it the spirit of Lurçat, Mallet-Stevens, and Le Corbusier but judiciously concluded, in his review of the project, that the International Style had not yet achieved the perfect country residence.[24] Only Henry McBride asserted that Lescaze's Wasserman house model was a forerunner of the coming mode, strictly "in period," and was sure to be much copied.[25]

The project was abandoned as a result of the stock market crash. After the dissolution of the partnership, it was redesigned by Howe and became known as "Square Shadows."[26] This commission might well have been attributed to the partnership; it might even be considered a collaborative effort, for Howe's 1932–1934 version was substantially based on the plan and massing of Lescaze's 1929–1930 scheme.[27]

The house Lescaze designed for Mrs. George French Porter in October 1929 was far more important than either the Sinkler or Wasserman houses in terms of the development of Lescaze's architectural style (Fig. 57). It demonstrates the fact that Lescaze had fully integrated Le Corbusier's formal principles and those of De Stijl's neo-plastic architectonic style, as defined by van Doesburg in his *Tot een beeldende architectuur* ("Towards a Plastic Architecture"), published in 1924.[28]

For the Porter House project (as in his earlier "Future American Country House Project" of 1928), Lescaze specified a steel frame construction that allowed him to compose an asymmetrical complex of interlocking volumes raised on thin columns, to cantilever planes and balconies into space,

and to employ corner and ribbon windows. Thereby he articulated van Doesburg's main point, No. 11, in which he declares:

The new architecture is anti-cubic; that is to say, it does not attempt to fit all the functional space cells together into a closed cube, but projects functional space-cells (as well as overhanging surfaces, balconies, etc.) centrifugally from the centre of the cube outwards. Thus height, breadth, and depth plus time gain an entirely new plastic expression. In this way architecture achieves a more or less floating aspect (in so far as this is possible from the constructional standpoint—this is a problem for the engineer!) which operates, as it were, in opposition to natural gravity.[29]

Lescaze utilized van Doesburg's philosophy of color in architecture by specifying white north and west walls, light blue south and east walls, dark blue sash, and gray roof tiles in order to effect an "organic means of expression."[30] Finally the project was, to use van Doesburg's words, "elemental," "economic," "functional," "plastic," "anti-cubic," and "anti-decorative."[31]

The project's roof terraces, ribbon windows, free plan, free façade, and *pilotis*, also bear witness to Le Corbusier's criteria for a new architecture. Of particular consequence, Lescaze freed the Porter house project from the load-bearing walls that had confined the earlier Oak Lane nursery school to earth-bound volumes and pseudo-corner windows. This project even surpassed his visionary "Future American Country House" project of 1928 in its complexity of spatial composition and freedom of plan.

Yet, there remain compositional and formal similarities among the nursery school and the Porter house project, and the Field and Curry houses to follow. Each was characterized by orthogonally related rectilinear volumes joined by a curvilinear one and the plastic shapes of the expressionists combined with the cubic shapes of the functionalists. Their stylistic syntax included flat roofs, corner and ribbon windows, white and blue stuccoed exterior walls, a lally column at an overhanging open corner, cantilevered hoods and roof terraces.

Although Mrs. Porter's three-level, four-bedroom house remained unbuilt due to the death of her husband, the ideas with which Lescaze experimented in this project were to be realized, on a more modest scale, the next year in one of the first International Style houses to be built on the East Coast of the United States—the Frederick Vanderbilt Field house at New Hartford, Connecticut.

Field, an Asian expert, was engaged in research for the Institute of Pacific Relations. His wife Betty, a recent Bryn Mawr graduate, was a student of anthropology.[32] The house was to be designed as an informal weekend retreat with study and bookcase space (for about 2,000 reference books) for the clients, who were friends of Lescaze.

Fig. 58. *Howe and Lescaze (Lescaze, designer), Frederick Vanderbilt Field house, New Hartford, Connecticut, 1930–1931. Axonometric rendering, September 1930.*

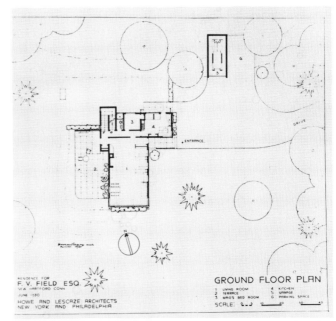

Fig. 59. *Howe and Lescaze (Lescaze, designer), Frederick Vanderbilt Field house, New Hartford, Connecticut, 1930–1931. First floor plan.*

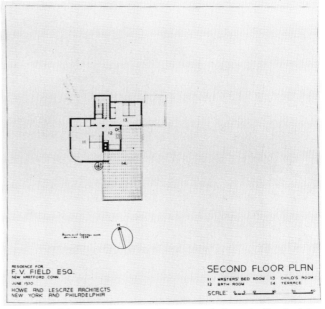

Fig. 60. *Howe and Lescaze (Lescaze, designer), Frederick Vanderbilt Field house, New Hartford, Connecticut, 1930–1931. Second floor plan.*

The first plan, dated June 1930, was only slightly modified for its construction, which took place from September 1930 to December 1931.[33] It was built at a cost of about $35,000 (Figs. 58, 59, and 60). Sited on the highest part of a wooded hilltop property of about thirty-five acres (called Red Hill), the house is dominated by a rectilinear, combination living-dining-library space, banded with windows that

67

frame the view on the south and wrap the corners on the east and west. The service areas adjoin at the north end of the house.[34] Off the living room on the west is a terrace, partly sheltered by the curvilinear, overhanging master bedroom above. A roof terrace, accessible from the master bedroom and child's room on the second floor and reached from the outside by a steel, spiral staircase from the ground terrace, covers the entire living room. Its north end is sheltered by a flat roof cantilevered from the bedroom wall.[35] A detached three-car garage was built to the east of the house.

Lacking the scale of the Porter house project, the curved volume of the Field house, like that of the Oak Lane nursery school, appears overly top-heavy in its first-phase state. Its proportions were visually adjusted in 1936 by the addition of the originally planned west wing (Figs. 61 and 62).[36] Unfortunately, the surfacing shingles of that wing offer a

Fig. 61. Howe and Lescaze (Lescaze, designer), Frederick Vanderbilt Field house, New Hartford, Connecticut, 1930–1931. Exterior view from the south, ca. 1931.

Fig. 62. Howe and Lescaze (Lescaze, designer), Frederick Vanderbilt Field house, New Hartford, Connecticut, 1930–1931. Exterior view from the south after 1936.

texture, visual mass, and picturesqueness that appear unsympathetic with the formal refinement of the earlier stuccoed structure and altogether out of phase with the De Stijl philosophy of smooth, flat, white wall surfaces. Appropriately, they do, however, reflect the later thirties' interest in the "domestication" of the International Style.[37]

Although lacking a completely integrated form and finish, the Field house reflected many features of contemporary European design including all five of Le Corbusier's criteria for a new architecture and much De Stijl theory. Here, for the first time, Lescaze was able to employ a steel frame and concrete slab structure and thereby maintain the structural integrity as well as the visual criteria of the new style.[38] His concern for articulation of the building's frame in cantilevered volumes, proposed in his "Future American Country House" project of 1928 and the Porter house project of 1929, were finally realized, if, however, on a lesser scale.

At the time, few buildings on the East Coast reflected the International Style's technical and aesthetic criteria as well as the Field house.[39] However, on the West Coast the style had already been brilliantly interpreted by Richard Neutra in his constructivist Lovell Health house of 1927–1929 (Fig. 63).

Reviewing the world's architecture in 1932, Talbot Hamlin called the Field house "the most interesting of the purely modernist houses."[40] It was published in the "Master Detail Series" of the *Architectural Forum* and was accompanied by a statement of Lescaze's view that modern architecture "springs from an attitude of mind . . . concerned with human life and human need," and that it should neither be furbished with applied decoration nor pretend to be a part of the landscape. His concluding statement, that modern design was more economical and more easily maintained than traditional design and that the architect should design or specify all the interior furnishings for his buildings wrapped up the period's ideology.[41]

More confidently styled than the Field house was Lescaze's headmaster's house of 1930–1932, built at Dartington Hall in England, where the continental modernist influence had just begun to take form.[42] Located near Totnes, in South Devon, the Dartington Hall estate consisted of 820 acres of land and an abandoned medieval hall when Dorothy and Leonard Elmhirst bought it, in 1925, to begin experiments directed toward bringing economic and social vitality back to the English countryside.[43] As

Fig. 63. Richard Neutra, Lovell "Health" house, Los Angeles, 1927–1929 (Photograph courtesy of The Museum of Modern Art, New York).

a result of their vision and skill, by the 1930s Dartington had gained a position of international importance in the fields of agricultural economics, the arts, and education.[44]

Lescaze's old friend and client William B. Curry, headmaster of the Oak Lane Country Day School and former senior science master at the Bedales School, England, was appointed headmaster of the Dartington School in June 1930. He soon persuaded the Dartington Hall Trustees to allow Lescaze to design the headmaster's residence, to be known as High Cross house (Fig. 64). Lescaze was then unknown in England, but Curry was allowed "to invite him [Lescaze] to stop off in Devon on his next visit to Switzerland."[45]

In order to show Curry that the modern style had even been done in "conservative England," Lescaze sent photographs of a tentatively modernist house at Newbury, Berkshire, by Thomas Tait of Sir John Burnett and partners, London. He sent photo-

Fig. 64. Howe and Lescaze (Lescaze, designer), High Cross house, Dartington Hall Estate, Devon, England, 1930–1932. Exterior view from the east.

graphs, too, of such diverse designs as a house by Albert Chase McArthur for M. D. B. Morgan, completed in 1927 near Phoenix, Arizona, and an illustration of the roof sun terrace of a house at Breslau by Heinrich Lauterback. Lescaze also suggested that Curry look at the German magazine *Die*

Form, the French *Architecture Vivant*, and the American *Architectural Record* in order to familiarize himself with the new architectural style.[46] These measures were seemingly necessary because rigorous modernism had only begun to develop in the work of such English architects as E. Maxwell Fry, Wells Coates, Amyas Connell, Basil Ward, and Colin Lucas. And the European modern style had yet to be imported directly by the European refugees Walter Gropius, Erich Mendelsohn, Marcel Breuer, Berthold Lubetkin, Serge Chermayeff, and others.

In October 1930, Leonard Elmhirst agreed to pay for preliminary drawings for High Cross house, but reserved the right to decide for or against them.[47] The drawings must have been completed in November, for in a letter to Lescaze of 19 December 1930 Curry reported that Elmhirst thought that the preliminary drawings for High Cross house were "ingenious" but that he "missed a sense of balance." Elmhirst had sensed, to his discomfort, one of the basic tenets of the International Style, adopted from De Stijl theory: the abandonment of Beaux-Arts axial symmetry in favor of flexibility of massing and the free façade.[48] Nevertheless, he accepted Lescaze's plans with the result that High Cross house (also called the Curry house) was to become one of Lescaze's most important and successful early commissions. Indeed, Curry thought the house would "rival Dartington's Medieval Hall as a 'showpiece.'"[49]

The house is a bold and uncompromising structure bearing the formal elegance of contemporary European models. The design of its north (roadway) façade, a horizontal block pierced by two ranks of narrow ribbon-windows and two doors, recalls the visual dynamics of Le Corbusier's street façade for the Villa Stein at Garches (Fig. 65).[50] Altogether dissimilar to it, the house's south (garden) façade is not unlike the compositional vocabulary of the Czech architect J. K. Riha's own house of 1930 in Prague (Fig. 66). Whatever the cause for the contrasting elevations, each related well to its own landscape.

Like the Oak Lane nursery school and the Field house, and in keeping with the De Stijl principle that "the new architecture absorbs color organically into itself as a meaningful expressive element of its relationship in time and space," Lescaze specified that the north block be colored and that the color was to be integral with the stucco and not just ap-

Fig. 65. *Howe and Lescaze (Lescaze, designer), High Cross house, Dartington Hall Estate, Devon, England, 1930–1932. Exterior view from the north.*

Fig. 66. *Howe and Lescaze (Lescaze, designer), High Cross house, Dartington Hall Estate, Devon, England, 1930–1932. Exterior view from the south and west.*

plied to the surface.[51] Although the wisdom of using colored stucco was debated for a time, Lescaze was adamant that, if it were not colored, the builder should "make the exterior finish of the walls as smooth and as clean-cut a possible" and "very, very, absolutely white." He underscored the point and his modernist philosophy by asserting: "This is very important to me, I hate rough and uneven surfaces."[52]

Also like the Oak Lane nursery school and the Field house, although more complex, High Cross is massed in two major rectilinear blocks and a curved volume. Spaces push in and out of the garden side of the cubic masses as expressions of function and as parts of an abstract sculpture. The house's gray-blue entrance block contains the reception hall, kitchen, pantry, garage, and lavatory on the first floor and the guest bedrooms, baths, and servants'

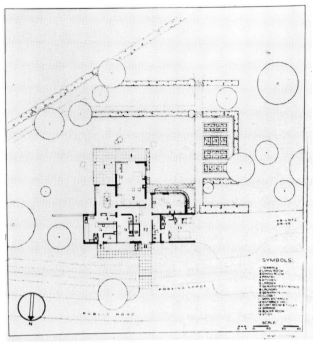

Fig. 67. Howe and Lescaze (Lescaze, designer), High Cross house, Dartington Hall Estate, Devon, England, 1930–1932. First floor plan.

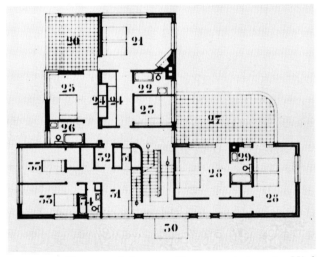

Fig. 68. Howe and Lescaze (Lescaze, designer), High Cross house, Dartington Hall Estate, Devon, England, 1930–1932. Second floor plan.

rooms on the second. The white garden block encloses the living and dining rooms on the first floor and the family's bedrooms and baths on the second floor. The one-story curved volume houses the headmaster's study, which has its own outside entrance for the convenience of school visitors (Figs. 67 and 68).

The house is well sited on sloping ground with all of its main rooms opening to panoramic views over the surrounding fields. An open terrace is accessible

from the living room through glass french doors; a covered terrace is similarly accessible from the dining room. On the second floor, covered terraces serve the master bedroom and child's room; open terraces give off the guest rooms. The roof, partly sheltered and partly open to the sun, is also constructed for terrace use. This De Stijl concept of "opening the walls" and articulating open terrace spaces with closed interior spaces had been applied earlier by Lescaze at the Field house and in the late 1920s residential projects that preceded it.

But here Lescaze employed yet another De Stijl principle of composition—extending the walls beyond the body of the house in every direction so that the "surfaces have a direct connexion to infinite space."[53] To his consternation, the garden wall, which was to extend north from the entrance and terminate in a curve, in sharp contrast to the rectangularity of the north façade, was omitted by the builders for no apparent reason. Lescaze wrote to Curry: "Do you think we just drew this up to make a pretty drawing?" It was subsequently built and was one of Lescaze's favorite features. He later wrote to Curry that he had no objections to landscaping being done at High Cross but added: "As you know I am very fond of the little bit of curved wall and gate at the entrance. Do not touch this."[54]

Typically, Lescaze planned the interior finishes and furnishings with care. The interior color scheme was restricted, according to Lescaze's direction, to the De Stijl color philosophy of neutral black, white, and gray, accented by primary yellow, blue, and red (in this case modified to terra cotta) to form and modulate internal space in an "elementary" and "universal" harmony.[55] In a latent Art Déco luxuriousness, the woodwork throughout the house was handsomely rendered. Lescaze specified American walnut for cabinetry and storage walls in the study, English walnut for the living room, sycamore for the dining room, African walnut for the master bedroom, and pear wood for the child's bedroom. In keeping with the De Stijl principle to emphasize the continuity of the whole wall, Lescaze requested that "when the wood has a decided grain, it should run either vertical or horizontal and in no case should it be bookmatched."[56] Although his specifications for the interiors were carried out, it was not without difficulty. Curry wrote to Lescaze on 9 June 1932:

Unfortunately, now that we have begun to push them, the man in charge of finishing is almost hysterical so that the utmost vigilance is needed to prevent rather foolish things [from] happening. For example, I found one day that he had put deal window sills in the living room and dining room. I at once said they had to come out, and to be replaced by the same wood as the furniture of the rest of the room (is that right?). Then I went down a day or two afterwards and found they had put the steps leading into the dining room in walnut, and was informed that they had done it in order "to be on the safe side." However, the walnut looks very nice.[57]

Elmhirst had wanted the kitchen and laundry to be a model of American planning and equipment. He employed Alice Blinn, an old Cornell University friend of his and Research Editor of *The Delineator* (the publication of the Delineator Home Institute), to consult on the layout and the selection of equipment.[58] After much design, redesign, and correspondence between Miss Blinn, Lescaze, and Curry, Miss Blinn concluded that the resulting kitchen plan was a composite of "American innovations and English arrangements" where the "refrigerator snuggles up against the warming cupboard," where the "sink is in a nice dark corner," where the work table is a considerable distance from the refrigerator, and where the spaces reserved for kitchen and laundry storage would hold enough for a "siege." She deemed the scheme far from acceptable to serve as a demonstration of American planning and asked Lescaze to "make it clear that this kitchen is not 'Delineator' planned."[59]

Because Lescaze believed that "modern architecture . . . insists on architectural furniture" and that "an architect must leave behind him when the building is turned over to the owners a place to live, not a shell that has to be converted into a house," he took great care in the specification of furniture for High Cross house.[60] Furnishings included sofas, cabinets, desks, headboards, tables, storage walls, and lighting designed by Lescaze and chairs by Breuer, Mies, Le Corbusier, PEL, and Curtis Moffat.[61] Unfortunately, the ultimate arrangement of furnishings did not conform to Lescaze's plans.

Also consistent with De Stijl thought, Lescaze managed to convince Curry that picture rails were undesirable. Curry wrote:

I agree about picture rails and we won't have any. If we must have pictures, as you would say, I have no doubt that you would agree that the best way to hang them is by one of those modern inconspicuous hooks behind the picture itself so that neither it or the cord is visible.[62]

Although High Cross house contrived to appear otherwise, it was, for both technical and financial reasons, built as a traditional brick and block structure, with roof terraces of concrete beam-and-slab construction.[63] The "Internationalists" talked about the economy of the style, but it was often expensive and sometimes extravagant in that furniture, hardware, and various detailing materials had to be designed specially because they were not yet in production. Indeed, Curry's house exceeded the contract price of £4,974 by more than £1,000.[64] This was because the style, materials, and some structural details were unfamiliar to the Devon builders. Their slowness was at times exasperating. Curry reported to Lescaze on 9 June 1932: "Building is progressing although we had to get nasty to get Staverton Builders to accelerate. I think the foreman had come to hope that the job would last the remainder of his natural life."[65]

Soon after the completion of the house, in July 1932, Curry wrote to Lescaze:

There are still some who criticize the outside but there is no one who has a word to say against the inside. The living room and study, particularly, are almost perfect and we are delighted with the results of your efforts.[66]

After living in the house for six months, Curry reported to Christopher Hussey:

I find the house's special clarity so particularly restful that I always come back into it with a real sense of relief after having visited a more old fashioned type of house, crowded with furniture and knick-nacs. The large windows make the rooms light even on dull days. And, except for the evenings with the curtains drawn, one never feels so shut off from the outside world as in the ordinary type of room. To me serenity, clarity, and a sense of openness are its distinguishing features. I am disposed to believe that they have important psychological effect on the occupants.[67]

Hussey subsequently observed:

The resulting simplicity [of High Cross house] is decidedly refreshing to minds surfeited with the pseudo and "arty." Indeed, after spending a little time in this house, its effortless common sense tends to make one impatient with much that has been tolerable.[68]

Lescaze's success at High Cross led to later commissions at Dartington—a Junior School project

(Fig. 69), three boarding schools (Fig. 70), a gymnasium (Fig. 71), a central office building (Figs. 72, 73, and 74), seven workers' cottages (Fig. 75), and a house for ballet director and choreographer Kurt Jooss (Fig. 76). The Junior School project and boarding schools contributed to the open-planning concept of school design in England. The first scheme of the central office building, prefigured in Gropius's Bauhaus school at Dessau, was built in a much reduced form, which was necessitated by the Depression. While all of Lescaze's later buildings at Dartington Hall were inferior to High Cross house and add little to the understanding of his architectural development, they consistently reflected his predilection for the planar, geometric, machine forms of the European International Style. The buildings were rendered with flat roofs and pure white stucco surfaces, a material that requires enormous maintenance in a country with heavy rainfall

Fig. 71. William Lescaze with Robert Hening, Foxhole School gymnasium, Dartington Hall Estate, Devon, England, 1933–1934. View from the north.

Fig. 69. Howe and Lescaze (Lescaze, designer), Junior School project, Dartington Hall Estate, Devon, England. Axonometric rendering, April and June 1931.

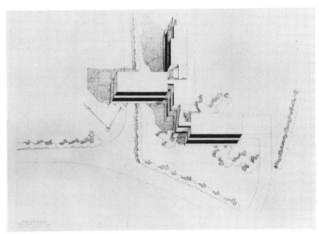

Fig. 72. William Lescaze with Robert Hening, Central Office building, Dartington Hall Estate, Devon, England, 1932–1935. Axonometric rendering of first scheme, 1 March 1932.

Fig. 70. William Lescaze with Robert Hening, Junior School boarding houses and classrooms B and C, Dartington Hall Estate, Devon, England, 1934–1935. Exterior view from the south-west.

Fig. 73. William Lescaze with Robert Hening, Central Office building, Dartington Hall Estate, Devon, England, 1932–1935. Perspective rendering of second scheme, 1 May 1934.

Fig. 74. William Lescaze with Robert Hening, Central Office building, Dartington Hall Estate, Devon, England, 1932–1935. View from the parking entrance.

Fig. 76. William Lescaze with Robert Hening, Warren house (for Kurt Jooss), Dartington Hall Estate, Devon, England, 1934–1935. View from Warren Lane, southwest.

Fig. 75. William Lescaze with Robert Hening, cottages on Warren Lane, Dartington Hall Estate, Devon, England, 1933–1938. Garden side of the three-cottage unit viewed from the two-cottage unit, 1935 and 1933–1934 respectively.

Fig. 77. Howe and Lescaze (Lescaze, designer), Arthur Peck house project, Paoli, Pennsylvania, 1929–1931. Perspective rendering of exterior, August 1931.

and frost; opponents were vocal in their criticism. In order to overcome the technical limitations of the surfacing material, Lescaze's last job at Dartington Hall (in association with Robert Hening), a worker's house, was of conventional brick construction painted white. As with other experiments of this type in England, it was not particularly successful.

Related in compositional method to the foregoing American and English houses, yet changed in fundamental ways, were projects for two large country houses to be built in the United States. The Arthur Peck house project, which came to the firm in 1929, was finally developed in 1931 (Fig. 77). Curvilinear forms emerged from the long, low, horizontal block more boldly than ever before. The typical interplay between voids and solids, heavy volumes raised on thin columns, corner fenestration, roof terraces, and curves contrasted with rectangles, continued to prevail, but now with greater forcefulness of style. Projected as a huge, expensive house to be built in Paoli, Pennsylvania, it was abandoned in 1931 when the clients became "afraid of modern."[69]

A still more expressive development of the Peck house scheme was the residence designed for Mr. and Mrs. Maurice Wertheim. In it, Mendelsohn's philosophy that "real creative power is the result of the interplay of dynamics and function" appears to have affected Lescaze's work.[70] The Wertheim house promised to be a monumental structure sited dramatically on top of a cliff overlooking Quarry Lake near Cos Cob, Connecticut. The first scheme, dated September 1931, was notable for its sweeping horizontality and walls entirely of glass (Figs. 78, 79, and 80). Probably as a concession to greater conservatism, the second scheme renderings, dated October 1931, showed the glazed areas much reduced (Fig. 81). The result, somewhat more static and cubic, is similar to the Peck house project of a few months earlier. As in the case of the Pecks, the Wertheim's fear of the new style prevented either scheme from being built. Although Wertheim was a collector of modern paintings and his wife was interested in modern architecture, they claimed that they did not quite have the courage to go ahead with a modern scheme for their own house. Respecting Lescaze's artistic integrity, they asked him to give up preparing further compromise plans.[71] A comparable scheme and response were to be echoed again in the Wallace house project of 1934.

This new architecture was clearly for the adventurous and progressive, among them the trustees for the Hessian Hills School at Croton-on-Hudson, New York.[72] Schools designed for progressive methods of education were emerging in America in the late twenties (for example, Lescaze's Oak Lane nursery school building), following the revolutionary European examples built earlier in that decade.[73] Although these new schools showed great variety in plan and composition, they had a number of

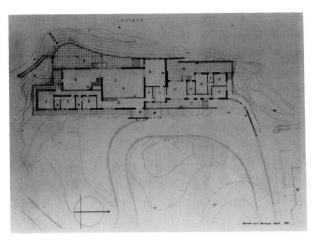

Fig. 79. *Howe and Lescaze (Lescaze, designer), Maurice Wertheim house project, Cos Cob, Connecticut, 1931. First floor plan.*

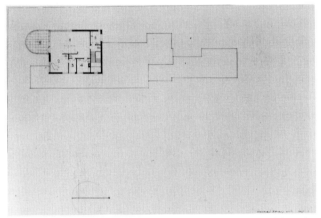

Fig. 80. *Howe and Lescaze (Lescaze, designer), Maurice Wertheim house project, Cos Cob, Connecticut, 1931. Second floor plan.*

Fig. 78. *Howe and Lescaze (Lescaze, designer), Maurice Wertheim house project, Cos Cob, Connecticut, 1931. Perspective rendering of first scheme; view of exterior from the lake side.*

Fig. 81. *Howe and Lescaze (Lescaze, designer), Maurice Wertheim house project, Cos Cob, Connecticut, 1931. Perspective rendering of second scheme; view of exterior from the lake side.*

characteristics in common. All rejected the traditional closed type of structure in favor of a new, open, looser form that would allow more flexible and creative use of space and a closer relationship to nature than the old forms.

Hessian Hills School—housing from 125 to 150 students ranging in age from kindergarten through junior high school—was to include space for nine classrooms, several workshops, a library, an art studio, a music room, teachers' room, and offices.[74] Several schemes were considered for the school, and that which was finally accepted was subsequently altered and ultimately never completed.[75]

The first scheme was a three-story building, its two major blocks joined at an obtuse angle, terraced down the slope of a hillside site, with balconies extending from the upper levels and the lower floor opening onto a covered terrace and a playing field (Fig. 82). To be constructed primarily of steel and concrete, with the entire southern exposure glazed at every level, its unit construction was emphasized by the contrast of black posts, railings, and window framings against white-washed concrete walls. Like Lescaze's other buildings, this one was dominantly horizontal in massing and cubic in form, relieved by a single curved roof at the bend of the angle.[76]

Terraced predecessors, undoubtedly known to Lescaze, were the apartment houses on the rue Vavin and the rue des Amiraux in Paris designed by Henri Sauvage, with whom Lescaze had worked. Lescaze may also have known Sauvage's drawings for an apartment project, a veritable ziggurat, to be built on the banks of the Seine.[77] Other models could have included Richard Döcker's District Hospital at Waiblingen near Stuttgart and Otto Bart-

ning's hospital in Berlin. Yet, the Hessian Hills School bears a closer relationship to Ernst May's Friedrich Ebert School at Frankfurt-am-Main, where the structure, like that of the Hessian Hills scheme, derives its section from the slope of the site.[78] It also parallels Mart Stam and Werner Moser's (with F. Kramer) Budge Home for the Aged, also at Frankfurt-am-Main, where the fenestration design is remarkably similar to that employed by Howe and Lescaze at the Hessian Hills School. Lescaze could have seen the Frankfurt-am-Main buildings on his visit to Europe in April and early May of 1931.[79]

Whatever its source, if any at all, Lescaze's first scheme for the school was abandoned because of the estimated cost of $100,000. A rendering of the second scheme is dated June 1931 (Fig. 83). Handsomely sited on an earth platform held back by a curved concrete retaining wall, it consisted of a two-story classroom wing connected by a large

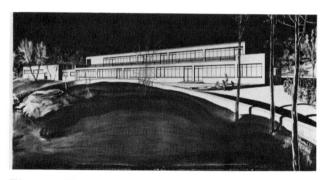

Fig. 83. Howe and Lescaze (Lescaze, designer), Hessian Hills School, Croton-on-Hudson, New York, 1931–1932. Perspective rendering of the second scheme, June 1931.

Fig. 82. Howe and Lescaze (Lescaze, designer), Hessian Hills School, Croton-on-Hudson, New York, 1931–1932. Model of the first scheme, 1931.

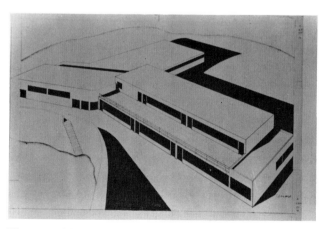

Fig. 84. Howe and Lescaze (Lescaze, designer), Hessian Hills School, Croton-on-Hudson, New York, 1931–1932. Axonometric rendering of the eighth scheme, September 1931.

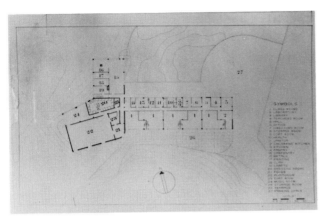

Fig. 85. Howe and Lescaze (Lescaze, designer), Hessian Hills School, Croton-on-Hudson, New York, 1931–1932. Eighth scheme, first floor plan, September 1931.

foyer to a two-story auditorium-music room wing; a smaller one-story shop wing was joined at right angles by connecting hallways. This second scheme was also rejected, probably again because of the estimated cost of $79,000.[80]

The plans were apparently revised several times before scheme eight, of 160,000 cubic feet and at a cost of $60,000, was drawn and ultimately accepted (Figs. 84 and 85).[81] The classrooms and shop wing of scheme eight were identical to those of scheme two, but the foyer was diminished in size and was included in the auditorium-music room block, which was now set at an oblique angle to the other two wings.[82] The ubiquitous curved wall between two rectangular blocks was introduced once again at the south-east "corner" of the auditorium.

The final plans were scheduled to be built in two stages. The first floor of classrooms and the shop wing were built in the late summer of 1931. The second floor of classrooms and the auditorium-music room wing were to be built in 1932. The second floor of classrooms was never built; the auditorium, once more altered in design, was completed in November 1932 (Fig. 86). The construction of the classrooms was reinforced concrete frame, infilled with panels of concrete, and windows and doors of glass framed with blue-painted steel. The auditorium-music room wing was of gray brick, lighted by wide bands of factory sash. The shop wing was built largely of brick with stone facing at the rear of the story-high built-up foundation.

Henry-Russell Hitchcock considered the Hessian Hills School building a marked advance over the earlier Oak Lane nursery school. To him its "frankness of construction" and "simplicity of design" made it comparable to "important European examples" of school design.[83]

Indeed, these qualities were to characterize Lescaze's Trans Lux Theaters, the Wilbour Memorial Library, and his project for a new Museum of Modern Art. For the Trans Lux news-reel theaters, built in New York and Philadelphia in 1931, Lescaze created a plain, controlled, and efficient acoustical box—an interior scheme as new for a theater as their rear projection screens.[84] *The New Yorker* reported at the time of its opening: "This little galvanized-tin thing, like the inside of a submarine, is the most refined—oh, so refined!—little creation the movie world has yet produced."[85] The interior, in contrast to the then current romantic historical themes, was a spartan composition of plain flat walls rendered in different values. The exterior evoked a stylized Déco quality in its extreme value contrasts and typography (Figs. 87 and 88).

Lescaze's belief that every architectural pretense

Fig. 86. Howe and Lescaze (Lescaze, designer), Hessian Hills School, Croton-on-Hudson, New York, 1931–1932. Exterior view from the north.

Fig. 87. Howe and Lescaze (Lescaze, designer), Trans Lux Theater, New York, 1931. Study, interior rendering.

Fig. 88. Howe and Lescaze (Lescaze, designer), Trans Lux Theater, New York, 1931. Study, exterior rendering.

Fig. 89. Howe and Lescaze (Lescaze, designer), Charles Edwin Wilbour Memorial Library, Brooklyn Museum, Brooklyn, New York, 1933–1934. Interior view.

should be avoided in theater design also held true for libraries. The firm's only library commission, the Charles Edwin Wilbour Memorial Library, was devoted to the Egyptological collection of the Brooklyn Museum (Fig. 89). Endowed in 1931 by the collector's son, Victor Wilbour, the room was commissioned in 1933 and opened on 23 November 1934.[86] Located on the third floor, adjacent to the museum gallery devoted to Egyptian objects and directly above the main library (with which it communicates by a self-operating elevator), the library was designed to utilize existing space in an existing building to the greatest possible advantage. The nearly square room was arranged on the alcove system with a balcony on three sides. On the main floor, gray steel stacks especially designed for the space formed the study alcoves, which were furnished with rectangular black-topped metal reading tables and comfortable blue-leather and chrome

arm chairs designed by Lescaze. The balcony, reached by stair and elevator, was screened from the main floor by the backs of the bookcases—sheer, unornamented, lapis-blue enamelled surfaces over seven feet in height.

The visual interweaving of stacks, tables, balcony, and wall planes, in conjunction with the restrained color scheme of white and varying shades of gray with blue and red accents "for the purposes of effecting accentuation, articulation, recession, etc.," was one of Lescaze's most handsome statements of neo-plastic color principles.[87]

While Lescaze's early thirties designs for houses, a skyscraper, a theater, and a library represented new ideas just coming to fruition, his Museum of Modern Art project predicted the development of those yet to come. His 1930 proposals, to build apartments over museum galleries, to light the galleries with natural light, and to paint their walls with dark colors were not to enter museum design with any frequency until almost fifty years later.

In the latter part of 1929, Howe and Lescaze were commissioned by the trustees of the newly organized Museum of Modern Art to make conceptual plans for a new building to house its collections, which were rapidly outgrowing the rented gallery space in the Heckscher Building at 730 Fifth Avenue.[88] Lescaze's earliest known schematic sketch of the museum consists of a tall, narrow circulation spine separated from a shorter, broad gallery slab, and is terminated with a short setback volume surmounted by a penthouse (Fig. 90). Drawn in 1930, it bears an obvious relationship to the massing of the PSFS, which was then in the final planning stages. Further, the cantilevered hoods on the principal façade recall those of the early PSFS sketches of 2 December 1929, 25 December 1929, and the model of July 1930.[89] Of greater significance, the sketch appears to be the prototype for the overall massing of the first concept for the museum and for two of the three commissioned "preliminary schemes."

The earliest plans, dated 1 March 1930, indicate that the first concept (not numbered among the "preliminary schemes"), included a three-story museum combined with two two-story apartments (Fig. 91). The first floor included a reception area, an auditorium, several offices, and service areas. The second floor was devoted to loan exhibition galleries, and the third floor, to permanent exhibition galleries. The living room level of the apart-

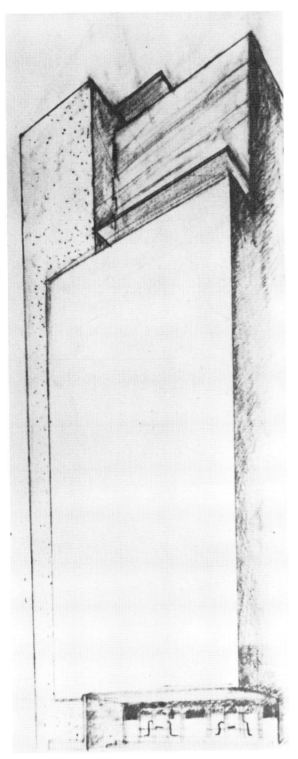

Fig. 90. Howe and Lescaze (Lescaze, designer), Museum of Modern Art project, New York, 1930. Probably schematic sketch for schemes 1 and 2.

Fig. 91. Howe and Lescaze (Lescaze, designer), Museum of Modern Art project, New York, 1930. Perspective rendering of first concept—a three-story museum combined with two two-story apartments, 1 March 1930.

museum galleries in 1983–1984.

Similar in massing, "preliminary schemes" one and two, dated 9 and 10 May 1930, show the circulation spine placed at the side of a six-floor gallery slab, above which rose three more floors and a roof penthouse set back from the main façade (Figs. 92 and 93).[90] A quite different "preliminary" scheme three, dated 11 May 1930, was a single ten-story volume with setbacks at each floor (Fig. 94).

Each of the three schemes offered a different solution to the problem of lighting galleries adequately and effectively. Scheme one provided continuous side lighting through ribbon windows at the top of each floor. Scheme two provided for a reverse ratio of closed and open wall areas, providing lighting through a façade almost entirely of glass. The rendering indicates that glass tubing may have been envisioned. Scheme three admitted light through skylights located at the setbacks of each floor. The façade of scheme three, for which drawings exist in two versions, might well have taken its inspiration from Henri Sauvage's stepback design for the apartment house built in 1912 at 26 rue Vavin in Paris, a building Lescaze probably knew well from his work in Sauvage's atelier.[91]

On 2 June 1930, Howe and Lescaze were com-

ments was on the fourth floor; the bedrooms were designated for the fifth (top) floor—an interesting proposal in light of the Museum of Modern Art's apartment tower, built in the air space over its

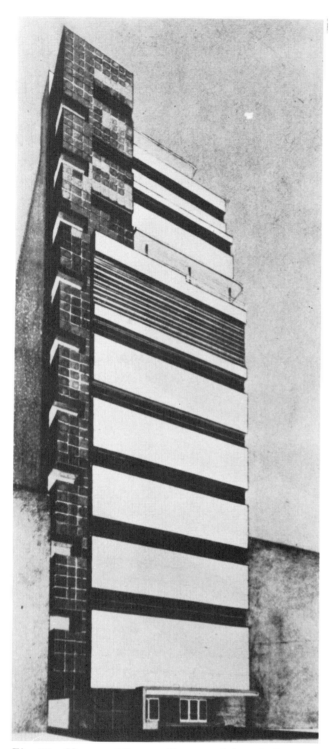

Fig. 93. Howe and Lescaze (Lescaze, designer), Museum of Modern Art project, New York, 1930. Perspective rendering of second scheme, 10 May 1930.

Fig. 92. Howe and Lescaze (Lescaze, designer), Museum of Modern Art project, New York, 1930. Perspective rendering of first scheme, 9 May 1930.

Fig. 94. Howe and Lescaze (Lescaze, designer), Museum of Modern Art project, New York, 1930. Perspective rendering of third scheme, 11 May 1930.

Fig. 95. Howe and Lescaze (Lescaze, designer), Museum of Modern Art project, New York, 1930. Model of fourth scheme.

cross traffic and visual distractions, was organizationally innovative and spatially inventive. The concept was a gravity-defying, technological tour-de-force—Lescaze's most flamboyant experiment in the constructivist idiom. An alternate scheme four included an exterior steel columnar frame (Fig. 96).

Fig. 96. Howe and Lescaze (Lescaze, designer), Museum of Modern Art project, New York, 1930. Model of alternate fourth scheme.

missioned to develop a scheme more completely.[92] Lescaze believed that the correct supply of both natural and artificial lighting and the control of its intensity and direction were of such paramount importance in designing a museum that better and more imaginative lighting solutions had to be explored in scheme four.[93]

Technically adventurous, scheme four was composed of an arrangement of nine horizontal blocks stacked at right angles to each other; five short ones extended east to west and four long ones extended north to south (Fig. 95). The whole was surmounted by a circular penthouse-restaurant.[94] Each block constituted an exhibition gallery. All of them abutted a tall narrow tower which contained elevators, a glass-enclosed main staircase, and fire stairs. The arrangement of the galleries, eliminating

Visionary in their own time, the preformed units set within a grid frame anticipated Moshe Safdie's "Habitat" of 1967.[95]

Scheme four's circular penthouse atop an intersecting stack of rectangular units suggests that Lescaze was well acquainted with Johannes A. Brinkman's, Leendert C. van der Vlugt's and Mart Stam's Van Nelle factory in Rotterdam, The Netherlands, which was nearing completion at the time Lescaze visited Brinkman there in the spring of 1929. Another prototype is T. Warenzow's constructivist housing system for his "city of the future," which was published in El Lissitsky's *Russland: Architektur für eine Weltrevolution* in 1930.[96]

While in schemes one through three the sources of light had been limited to the front walls that faced the street, through the rear walls that faced the court, or through skylights at the ceiling, in scheme four each gallery obtained light from every direction as well as from above. Above each gallery was a light mixing chamber with sides, top, and base of structural glass. The base, acting as a continuous diffusing sash, constituted the ceiling of the gallery. For the regulation of the light, the chamber was equipped with light-controlling blades and reflectors. A photo-electric cell automatically controlled the gradual opening and closing of the blades as daylight fluctuated and finally turned on the electric light in the reflectors as darkness approached.[97]

A year later the firm was asked to prepare two new schemes. These, numbers five and six were further experiments with the problems of light control and traffic circulation.[98] Scheme five, dated August 1931, reverted to the single tower and featured staggered light chambers, giving daylight to the galleries from two directions (Fig. 97). Scheme six, dated September 1931, essentially developed some features of scheme two, incorporating an entire glass front of alternating strips of clear and opaque glass (Fig 98).[99] It offered a novel solution, for that time, to the traffic problem in that visitors were to be taken to the top floor by elevator and were to circulate down through the galleries by means of a quarter-flight of stairs at every exhibition room. This system related to Le Corbusier's "Square-spiral" project of 1930 for The Mundaneum Museum in Geneva, Switzerland, and anticipated by several years the similar circulation systems of Frank Lloyd Wright's Guggenheim Museum (first conceived in 1943) and Edward Stone's Huntington Hartford Gallery of Modern Art of 1964.

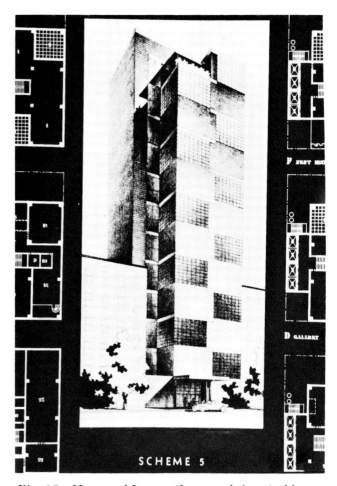

Fig. 97. Howe and Lescaze (Lescaze, designer), Museum of Modern Art project, New York, 1930. Perspective rendering of fifth scheme, August 1931.

Although American museums multiplied as never before in the 1920s and 1930s because of the impetus that European modernism had given to the expansion of the art world, the more than one hundred museums built between 1916 and 1932 were all in the neo-classical eclectic spirit.[100] All of Howe's and Lescaze's Museum of Modern Art project schemes were unprecedented in the history of museum design in both America and Europe. All remained unbuilt. Lescaze was severely disappointed not to have received a commission to construct one of them. A note written by Lescaze in 1930 indicates that Conger Goodyear, then chairman of the Board of Trustees of the Museum of Modern Art, stated that one member of the Board had objected to commissioning Lescaze because he was a foreigner.[101] Whether or not that was the entire reason for the rejection of his scheme, John D. Rockefeller, Jr.'s donation, in 1932, of a house at 11 West Fifty-third Street for museum use put plans

Fig. 98. Howe and Lescaze (Lescaze, designer), Museum of Modern Art project, New York, 1930. Perspective rendering of sixth scheme, September 1931.

for a new museum building in abeyance for three years. At this time, but in another context, Lescaze philosophically wrote:

> The goodness of a thing is not necessarily indicative of its convincing power. However, I must always assume that it is. Otherwise I would never possess a sufficient amount of enthusiasm to be able to create a thing.[102]

Although Lescaze's visionary scheme remained only a project, it tells us a great deal about his architectural conceptions, with a clarity rarely achieved in actual construction.

Philip Goodwin's and Edward Stone's constructed scheme of 1939 was bland by comparison with Lescaze's project.[103] With modest distinction, the former stated the syntax of the International Style as codified by Hitchcock and Johnson including window bands, balconies, port holes, De Stijl graphics, and a cantilevered entrance hood with a diminutive filip of a sign at its end, recalling the type proposed by Lescaze in the earliest schemes of the PSFS.

Probably the greatest architectural challenge of the thirties in the United States was public housing. In 1932 Henry-Russell Hitchcock deemed Lescaze's Chrystie-Forsyth public housing project the earliest significant attempt in America to solve the problem of large-scale, low-cost urban housing in modern social, economic, and aesthetic terms.[104] It was designed for a condemned area of seven blocks between Chrystie and Forsyth Streets on New York's lower east side. The difficult site, a long corridor in a dense slum area, comprised 306,500 square feet of land (Fig. 99).[105] Convenient to City Hall and Wall Street, the area seemed ripe for redevelopment as a white-collar district in the same way that Greenwich Village had been earlier.

Lescaze planned a large scale, low coverage, low density, structural complex sited on a superblock as per the urban housing pattern prescribed by the Housing Division of the Public Works Administration. He proposed twenty-four L-shaped, nine-

Fig. 99. Howe and Lescaze (Lescaze, designer). Housing development project, Chrystie-Forsyth Streets, New York, 1931–1932. Photomontage, aerial view, December 1931.

83

story building units, which would provide three-and four-room apartments for 1,512 families at a rental of $10.95 or less per room per month (Fig. 100). The total cost of constructing the project was estimated at $5,763,000. The construction was to be steel-frame with concrete slab floors exposed on the façade. Where the walls were not of glass, they were of brick, which provided the masonry sheathing the New York Building Code required.[106] The L-shaped residential units, oriented at right angles to one another in alternating directions, were to be arranged on the site in an advancing and receding pattern, creating deep setbacks from the street and forming park-playgrounds spatially related to each unit. For ease of communication from block to block and in order to permit a regular plot plan throughout, some units spanned the east-west streets, increasing the amount of apartment space with east-west exposures and causing little or no detriment to urban traffic flow.

This rationalized layout derived from avant-garde housing forms proposed in England and Europe. The system of the low setback block, which denied the traditional continuity of the street and envisioned the transformation of the city into a continuous park, was first proposed by Ebenezer Howard in 1898. It was developed in Paris by Eugene Henard in his Boulevard à redans of 1903, and in London by Raymond Unwin and Barry Parker in their Hampstead Garden Suburb of 1906. The anti-street models were continued by Le Corbusier in his famous Maison Dom-ino of 1915, in his hypothetical city for three million inhabitants—the "Ville Contemporaine"—of 1922, in his "Plan

Fig. 100. Howe and Lescaze (Lescaze, designer), Housing development project, Chrystie-Forsyth Streets, New York, 1931–1932. Model of two units.

Voisin" for Paris of 1925, and in his "La Ville Radieuse" project of 1929, exhibited at the 1930 CIAM conference in Brussels. Due to the similarity of the Chrystie-Forsyth layout to Le Corbusier's "recessed" apartment buildings in the "Ville Radieuse" project, it was probably from the latter model that Lescaze took his inspiration for the site plan of the Chrystie-Forsyth project.

From Raymond Unwin's *Nothing Gained by Overcrowding* through Le Corbusier's *Vers une architecture* to his *La Ville Radieuse*, it was assumed that an abundance of sun, light, air, and green space was necessary for optimum living conditions, principles that were to remain the stock-in-trade of planners until the 1960s. This philosophy was an important influence on the design of the Chrystie-Forsyth project. The architects proposed that only 13% of the site be built; the remainder was to be retained for open recreation area. For optimum ventilation, the units were designed as free standing slabs, one room deep. In order to capture the greatest amount of sunlight, windows were designed to span continuously the entire width of living rooms and bedrooms, which were to face either east, west, or south.

Many of the project's features, although common in government and industry-supported European housing projects, were innovations in American planning practice and represented a commendable attempt to improve the quality of current housing standards. For example, the separation of street from pedestrian traffic, the opportunity for free circulation over the site at ground level, the garden city emphasis on an intimate scale of the blocks and their corresponding open spaces, the then-considered ease and privacy of circulation on exterior corridors, and the orientation of the units for optimum sunlight and ventilation were outstanding contributions. These ideas, plus the clarity, economy, and unity of the scheme were unknown in American housing design where historicism predominanted.

The architectural means employed in the Chrystie-Forsyth project—*pilotis*, continuous strip fenestration, flat roofs, deck access to apartments, and elevator communication at the corners of the L's—was an attempt to translate Corbusian theory into reality in public authority housing. The units, raised on columns to provide a sheltered playground and uninterrupted circulation at ground level, derive from Corbusian prototypes. The open corridors, which run like balconies the length of each floor of apartments, had their formal source in Le Corbusier's hypothetical city for three million inhabitants—the "Ville Contemporaine" of 1922.[107] The composition of the individual units recalls Marcel Breuer's 1924 model for a small apartment house, published in Gropius's *Internationale Architektur* of 1925, a book Lescaze had ordered from Bauhaus in 1929.[108]

Summarizing the quality of the Chrystie-Forsyth project, Hitchcock wrote:

> The composition as a whole and the handling of the detail indicate an architectural conscientiousness comparable to that of the best European mass housing. . . . The lightness, straightforwardness, and skillful combination of necessarily inexpensive material (for this project) leads to as much architectural distinction as can be hoped for in a building of sociological significance.[109]

And Lewis Mumford found this project "much more convincing as pure architecture" than the PSFS.

Yet, with all of its excellence of design and planning to recommend it, the Chrystie-Forsyth project was not built. On 9 February 1932, the architects presented their plans (dated December 1931) to a gathering of housing experts and builders.[110] On 3 March 1932 the East Side Chamber of Commerce endorsed the project, and the *New York Times* commended it, stating that the proposed plan "seems to meet the social requirements."[111] One week later Lescaze met with city officials in an effort to get their support.[112] On March 25, the *New York Times* reported that the plan, supported by the East Side Chamber of Commerce, sociologists, and architects, was vetoed.[113] In spite of this adversity, in April Lescaze drew four more plans which indicated increased coverage of the site from the original 13% to 47–57%. A scheme of 22 September of the same year shows the corridors enclosed with glass, and plans of 28 September show floor plan revisions to obtain larger rooms. These were again revised in May of 1933. Undaunted, Lescaze developed an entirely new concept in September 1933. In the latter plans, he offered six alternative "recessed patterns," again prefigured by Le Corbusier's plans for his Radiant City.

Still, they were not acceptable because the Chrystie-Forsyth idea was promoted by housing developers without consideration as to why middle class workers would leave their neighborhoods to take up residence in a slum area without benefit of good schools, shops, and neighbors. It proved to be too much of a gamble for entrepreneurs to take. The question of redevelopment of the area, which had begun in 1927, was concluded in 1934 when Mayor La Guardia made it into a park.[114] Although it did not become a reality, Lescaze's Chrystie-Forsyth study was a major contribution to bringing the need for public housing into prominence.

Another design, begun in 1932, was for the vast River Gardens project, a hypothetical study proposed to stimulate planners' minds about lower-middle-class housing needs and solutions.[115] Like the Chrystie-Forsyth project, River Gardens was conceived to replace the slums on the Lower East Side of Manhattan. But in the latter project, it was the high rise residential tower, rather than the low, free standing slab, that was to exert the greatest influence on the scheme's composition. Another anti-street model, its prototypes were Le Corbusier's "A City of Towers," published in his *Vers une architecture* of 1923, his "Plan Voisin" of 1925, and his "La Ville Radieuse" of 1929 (Fig. 101).

The large-scale River Gardens plan consisted of a mix of 103 low, 27 medium, and 20 high cruciform towers, unified with a number of perimeter-defining low garages and stores, and interspersed with recreation and park areas. As in the Chrystie-Forsyth project, some of the units spanned streets, and ribbon windows and flat roofs were basic components of the tower composition. But unlike the Chrystie-Forsyth project, exterior corridors were not utilized at River Gardens, and the towers were raised from the ground on *pilotis* only where they extended into the street to serve as urban *porte cochères*. The residential tower became the accepted housing form of the New York City Housing Authority (of which Lescaze was a member of its architectural board) from the thirties until the sixties.

Fig. 101. Howe and Lescaze (Lescaze, designer). Housing development project, River Gardens, lower east side, New York, 1931–1933. Photomontage, 4 October 1932.

By 1933 housing committees and housing studies began to mushroom. The new interest in housing was expressed in a letter from Mary Hughes Steiner to Leonard Elmhirst, both friends of Lescaze:

The city seethes with luncheons, housing meetings, housing teas, housing committees. Thousands rush in waves from one meeting to another. Thousands who wouldn't have stayed awake three months ago for one sentence about it are now decidedly awake about it and ardently distressed about the need for slum clearance, light and air for the masses. . . . Today the Times says Washington announces that 25 million dollars has been earmarked for New York City Housing.[116]

Lescaze was to participate in this housing "fever," and it was in regard to that twenty-five million federal dollars that the first of New York's truly comprehensive housing studies was to be effected—in the highly publicized Astoria-Queens project. The study of the Astoria district in the Borough of Queens was made early in 1933 to call the authorities' attention to the fact that the money New York was given by the federal government for low-cost housing could be spent much more profitably in that area than in the Lower East Side of Manhattan, where land costs were considerably greater.[117]

Called a "study in realistic city replanning," the project's scope was far broader than previous housing proposals. A major project of the Housing Study Guild, its intent was to show the value of regional studies of housing needs as opposed to the limited model housing approach generally applied to slum clearance at that time. It also argued that comprehensive and integrated housing studies require the collaboration of specialists trained in sociology, economics, city planning, site planning, architecture, and engineering.[118] The associates urged that action to develop Astoria-Queens be taken immediately because the advent of the Triborough Bridge would be accompanied by land speculation which would render prices too high for effective replanning. But, as in the case of the Chrystie-Forsyth project, no immediate action was taken on the proposals.[119] Although Lescaze's early thirties housing projects were not built, they established his reputation in the field which led to later housing commissions in the United States and England.

While Lescaze's schemes for American housing

projects had developed the concept of multiple-family dwellings especially designed for urban settings, the English project at the Churston Estate dealt primarily with a colony of single-family units in a rural setting. Although substantial housing developments had already been built in urban areas of England, they had not been attempted in the countryside until the 1930s. Churston was among the first of these experiments, as well as one of England's earliest housing projects in the International Style. Ambitious and idealistic, its development was to fall before the realism of a conservative English public in a time of economic depression.

The Dartington Hall trustees began planning their experimental housing development in 1932.[120] Located about seven miles from the Hall, on the coast between Paignton and Brixham, the model seaside development was to have been built on the Churston Estate, a 188-acre tract of land at Torbay. The property extended from the sheltered and secluded Broadsands Beach through the smaller and more rugged Elberry Cove. It rose slowly from the Bay to beyond the famous Tor Rocks, which jut out of the high land, up to the main Brixham-Paignton Road, the westerly boundary of the Estate. Spanning the westerly portion of the property is the handsome stone Brunel railway viaduct which carries the Kingswear line of the Great Western Railroad one hundred feet above the ground, with the main road to the beach passing beneath.

No one was then fully aware of the rate at which the natural beauty of the South Coast was being destroyed by speculative building, but there was already some concern. Dartington was sharply criticized for its intention to build on such a beautiful site. It countered that the area would be developed anyway and that it was better to proceed with a carefully planned and well designed scheme than allow it to be littered haphazardly with bungalows of dubious architectural merit.[121]

Several architects were considered by the Dartington trustees to plan the Churston development. Besides Lescaze, they seriously considered Louis de Soissons, who had played an important part in the development of Welwyn, Ebenezer Howard's second garden city. He had designed speculative housing projects for Staverton Builders at Dittesham and Exeter and the Dartington Hall Estate houses at Huxham's Cross and Broom Park in traditional garden suburb style with curving roads and the picturesque charm of pitched roofs, shuttered windows, and textured materials. Oswald P. Milne, architect for several Dartington Hall Estate buildings, was also in the running. Walter Gropius, Werner Moser, Mies van der Rohe, and J. J. P. Oud were considered as possible consultants.[122] After extensive deliberations, the Churston Advisory Committee named Lescaze the official architect for the development early in April 1933.[123]

The notes of the Advisory Committee meeting of 3 May 1933 indicate that the major reason for selecting Lescaze over his major contender, Louis de Soissons, was that Lescaze, "the pioneer of modern architecture in America," had something new to contribute to the house design and the general layout of a rural site. Actually, Lescaze was interested in building flat-roofed houses (as opposed to de Soissons's pitched roofs), which the advisers believed to be the correct type to use at Churston because they would allow the maximum view potential in the smallest amount of space. Probably not unimportant to the Committee was the fact that the flat roof, along with cubic, plain white surfaces had been established as a distinguishing feature of modern European housing at Stuttgart's Weissenhofsiedlung exhibition. The Committee feared, however, that Lescaze would not be able to fulfill its requirements in regard to the economy of planning and building. Since Elmhirst intended that the scheme be a collaborative effort of architect, planner, developer, builder, and buyer, the Committee decided on a collaboration between Lescaze and probably the foremost American planner at the time, Henry Wright. The latter had "studied the work of the leading English town planners and the more recent work carried out in Germany and other places on the continent." Moreover, Wright was considered to be particularly interested in the "human and economic aspects of planning."[124]

Wright's site-plan for Churston, dated 27 July 1933, revised 6 July 1934, was (like his plan of Radburn, New Jersey) a complete, pre-planned community conceived in terms of the English Garden City principles originated by Raymond Unwin and Ebenezer Howard. It included "super-blocks" with houses on traffic-free cul-de-sacs, green spaces crossed by foot paths, pedestrian underpasses and overpasses at the occasional streets, private gardens, landscaped common land, and a community center combining shopping and leisure activities. Also proposed were a hotel, tea house, beach chalets, bathing cubicles, and a car park (Fig. 102).

Fig. 102. Henry Wright, Churston Estate housing development, 1935. Aerial perspective rendering of site plan.

Wright attempted to provide the best orientation, grade, and view of the bay for as many of the houses as possible. Essential in realizing that goal, he argued, was the employment of the flat-roofed house and the location of some of the garages in blocks at some distance from the houses. He also proposed development of the site in five building campaigns so that there would be enough houses built together at one time "to provide the nucleus of an architectural grouping" of houses related to each other and to the landscape rather than a "heterogeneous collection of houses" monotonously sprinkled along a road.[125]

Although Wright's plan may have resulted in a model community of its type, some of its ideals and assumptions were unacceptable to the Churston Development Company. Wright's idea that there should be planning for a communal life was especially odious. F. A. O. Gwatkin, lawyer and friend of the Elmhirsts, one of the first trustees of the Dartington Hall Estate, and an advisor to the Churston Development Company, wrote to Lescaze:

I hope it will never be mentioned to those who may dwell at Churston that they are intended to become a community or that there would be any species of communal life. This would put them off immediately. In this country a person can have a neighbor for the length of his natural life without knowing such next door neighbor.[126]

Executive Director Slater added that no publicity should use the words "community center," for that was one of the problems that stood in the way of the garden city developments in England. He reminded the planners that while the younger and less rigidly minded sector of the population had been attracted to the garden cities, at Churston the residents would be older and more conservative—primarily retired civil servants and military officers (no artists, writers, and university professors)—living on pensions and private incomes. He added that they would not want any American "uplift," "instruction," or "education," but would want to live the way they wished.[127] He also pointed out that "many points that cannot be supported by logic are too deeply rooted in tradition to be influenced by argument." For example, the proposed open landscape plan would not be satisfactory because "an Englishman would not eat or do anything else in his yard if it were not surrounded by a hedge; the fact that it offers but little privacy is of no consequence."[128]

Moreover, the Churston Development Advisors were skeptical of a plan without curbs and sidewalks and believed that so many culs-de-sac were uneconomical in that they were expensive to construct, would adversely affect drainage, and would cause awkwardly-shaped lots that would be difficult to sell.[129]

Walter Gropius, on the other hand, quite approved of the site plan and the layout and design of the first group of houses. However, in order to achieve still greater unity, as in his Dessau Törten district houses, he characteristically favored keeping buildings of the same type together in an unbroken sweep in preference to the uneven grouping proposed by Lescaze at Churston.[130]

Ultimately, the temporary beach facilities were rushed to completion. Although plans for building chalets were abandoned because Wright did not like them, the sea wall, temporary car park, tea house, and bathing cubicles were finished in the summer of 1933.[131] The construction of the proposed Churston houses was delayed for revision and refinement. Their designs were essentially typical of Lescaze's purist, flat-roofed, asymmetrical, cubist compositions that he had done prior to this time. They included roof terraces, penthouses, ribbon windows, iron railings, smooth white wall surfaces, and plain detailing. Of less compositional interest than most of his earlier buildings and projects, these were strictly rectilinear with no curved walls, no

cantilevered volumes, and no open corners supported with lally columns. Lescaze's English collaborator, Robert Hening, called them an example of the "utopian and pristine" International Style.[132]

Public criticism of the development followed immediately. The Torbay Regional Planning Committee reviewed the designs for the first group of houses and reported to the press that the elevations resembled either an "Exeter jail, a sugar box with slits cut in it, or a Lancashire cotton factory."[133] Curry reported to Lescaze that "there are people at Dartington, some of them not devoid of influence," who were upset by the publicity and that they "would be only too happy to see the Churston scheme scrapped and something quite different put in its place."[134]

Although opponents of the International Style were vocal everywhere, and local officials became obstructive in providing necessary permits to build modern buildings, the scheme was not abandoned. The general site plan for the entire Churston development and the plan for siting the houses in the area west of the viaduct (the first section to be developed) were approved by the Regional Planning Committee in January 1934.[135] The initial proposal for the first building campaign called for a mix of villas and terrace houses as at Weissenhof. There was to be a cluster of 20 houses, from eight to ten different types, on a cul-de-sac road on the main Broadsands Road, four terrace houses above Tor Rocks, and an administration building at the main Paignton-Brixham Road. This proposal was repeatedly modified until, finally, the plan called for building only six houses on a cul-de-sac road. By early spring of 1934 the first group of six houses, all of different plans and compromises between the English and American planning traditions, was under construction. They were completed in March 1935 (Fig. 103).[136]

Fig. 103. William Lescaze, Churston Estate housing development, Devon, England, 1932–1936. View of first group of six houses, viewed from the bay side (south-east).

The houses failed to sell for several reasons. The development was generally not favored because the site looked bare and the houses severe and forbidding. One reaction, by a prospective client, was especially revealing:

I was most disappointed on my visit to Churston on the previous day. It was a great shock to see that you proposed to build houses which are more in keeping with the Sahara desert than with a beautiful piece of English scenery. I feel sure that if there is a demand for houses with such exterior design, it is only a passing fancy and that in a few years such houses will be unsalable. This is not only my opinion but that of many who have seen them and consider it a blot on the landscape.[137]

The interiors were praised for their "practical and workmanlike" planning, but criticized for the small size of their kitchens, staircases, storage, and laundry areas. Many did not like the fireplaces, and, while the roof decks were admired, they were generally considered unnecessary.[138]

Although one of the reasons cited for appointing Lescaze the architect of the project had been that he was interested in the new flat-roofed house design, one trustee had cautioned him against introducing new architectural forms to a conservative consuming public:

I want you [Lescaze] to realize that the British public is a very prejudiced one, that it is very insular and that it is very difficult to get it to adopt something new or to get it to live in a house which is different from those that have hitherto been built.[139]

His comments were prophetic. Flat-roofed housing projects in other areas were also selling with difficulty. Not a single house had been sold at the Broadmoor Park development at nearby Torquay, although it had been finished for three years. Similar projects at Dawlish and Teignmouth and the Hay Mills, Harrison Houses, and Elberry, Ltd., in London were having limited success.[140]

The advisors of the Churston Development Company determined that a "softer effect," as at the Frinton Park development, Essex, was needed. They asked Lescaze to add a few curves to the four houses scheduled to be built in the second group in order to give the public what it wants, "without altering the general scheme of architecture."[141] The "curvilinear thirties" had arrived at Churston! In this group the purist idealism and cubic geometry of the twenties' International Style were compromised with softening curves, less clarity in plan and form, and a more picturesque siting than was typical of the earlier group.

The terrace houses, designed in September 1933, were scheduled to be built north of Tor Rocks after the completion of the first group of detached houses (Fig. 104). Probably influenced by Le Corbusier's 1919 Houses of Concrete project, they consisted of a series of small units, unified by bands of windows and garden walls. Because of the slowness of pre-sales, due to a preference for detached houses, their construction was called off in January 1935.[142] In their place, small, detached houses without garages, designed to sell at a lower price than the first six houses, were designed for the lots north of Tor Rocks. Two were started in November 1935 but only one was completed.[143] Thus, only ten of Lescaze's houses were ultimately built at Churston, and four of those were not built as originally conceived.[144]

In a last effort to stimulate sales, a promotional brochure that had been planned since early 1934 was finally published in September 1935. It included a romantic description of the region, maps of the development, elevations and plans explaining the architectural style and structural principles involved, and a long essay justifying why the houses were to be sold on a 999-year lease rather than freehold.[145] Prospective buyers were promised that attractive hotel and country club facilities were planned at the adjoining Elberry Cove.[146]

The club was designed in collaboration with Francis Lorne of the London firm of Sir John Burnet, Tait, and Lorne (Fig. 105). Although not a particularly distinctive design, it typically reflects Lescaze's continued interest in both neo-plastic forms and rectangular forms in opposition to curvilinear. The hotel, a part of the original plan for the development, was one of the most distinguished

Fig. 104. William Lescaze, Churston Estate housing development, Devon, England, 1932–1936. Perspective rendering of proposed terrace houses, September 1933.

Fig. 105. William Lescaze with Francis Lorne. Churston Estate housing development, Devon, England, 1932–1936. Perspective rendering of country club project, November 1935.

Fig. 106. William Lescaze, Churston Estate housing development, Devon, England, 1932–1936. Perspective rendering of Elberry Hotel project, 1935 (Courtesy of the Records Office, Dartington Hall Estate, South Devon, England).

designs of the entire project (Fig. 106). As the first holiday hotel on such a scale to be built in England for many years, this was an adventurous effort for the period. Because there were no guidelines available on the kind or size of hotel which could be run profitably in such a situation, the first schemes were necessarily somewhat "imaginative." One, an undulant form, following the contour of the site, recalls Mendelsohn's expressive use of the International Style vocabulary and Le Corbusier's lineal housing plan for the city of Algiers. The bay façade was articulated by four tiers of cantilevered balconies and bands of windows above a colonnaded ground-floor promenade.

Unfortunately, there were as many factors militating against the consummation of the Elberry Hotel as there had been against the Churston Estate houses, only of a different kind. Most significantly,

the Great Western Railroad Company's Board of Directors, which had been approached to help finance the approximately £197,000 venture, was experiencing dissension between its conservative and progressive elements. It was already developing a hotel in Cornwall; it was being forced to assimilate a great many new expenses imposed by the government; and its restaurant and hotel manager was retiring at the end of 1935.[147] For these reasons the Company felt that it could not make a commitment to the project until after January 1936. But even more importantly, by late 1935 the state of the English economy had worsened to a point where the Railroad became so cautious in its investments that it had to decide against supporting the unsuccessful Churston housing development.[148]

With this disappointment and the continued difficulty of selling the Churston houses, the production schedule of Staverton Builders was slowed nearly to a stop. Builders and salesmen became apathetic toward the project, and management was discouraged. Slater summed up the situation when he wrote:

> There is no doubt that there exists in this area a ring or combine which consists of builders, house agents, builder's merchants, solicitors, architects, landowners, and brickmaking interests. This combine has been dictating the type, method, and development of houses in Paignton, Torquay and along the shores of Torbay for many years.[149]

Numerous additional factors can be identified regarding the failure of the experiment.[150] Those who claimed that the development would spoil the landscape or that the project was an aberration fostered by the progressive educational principles of Dartington Hall undoubtedly biased many against it. Curry later wrote: "We were, I gather, antipatriotic, anti-monarchist, socialist, atheistic, communist, and immoral."[151] The employment of an American architect at a time when Englishmen needed employment was also criticized publicly.[152] Because of the "foreign problem," frustrating delays and expenses in acquiring sources of electrical power and approval to build ensued.

The problem of slow and incomplete communication between the Churston Development Company and the New York-based architect and site planner was aggravated by the hostility of the Staverton Building Company. Its manager had been accustomed to working with de Soisson's traditional plans and did not enjoy dealing with the new style, materials, and construction methods that Lescaze's office specified. The problem was intensified by the fact that the building company was having severe labor problems. The turnover in crew was so great that any experience gained on previous Lescaze buildings, such as High Cross house and the Junior School boarding houses, was lost.

Staverton's salesmen were as negative toward the project as was the building company that employed them. Curry wrote:

What they call selling as applied to Churston is a mere farce. They don't like the houses themselves and cannot understand why anybody should. Their employers betray not the slightest enthusiasm.[153]

The houses were too un-English for the prospective buyers as well. The buying public was of a conservative socio-economic status and in the 1930s had had almost no experience with modern architecture.[154] Thus, the new style alienated the working class that it was meant to attract. The Churston Development Company's director reported that the buyers'

educational level is good but aesthetic development is limited. Most have pronounced views on elevation and planning. . . . Customers are willing to forego interior planning in order to get an exterior with gables, hipped roofs, and features that look expensive. The purchasers from the North and Midlands want to get away from the uniformity to be found in those areas towards something which they describe as old world and rural. It is obvious that anything plain, simple and unostentatious will not attract and merely good internal planning will be completely unsatisfactory as a selling point. On the other hand they are definitely interested in bay windows, balconies, gables, pergolas, and all those other features which tend to make each house appear different from its neighbor although in fact its plan may be identical.[155]

The fact that the houses were being offered with the restriction that no changes be made to the exterior was also incomprehensible to many. Clearly, a housing project financed privately was a struggling enterprise as compared with the government-supported housing projects contemporarily being built in Holland and Germany.

Moreover, the Churston Estate project bore little relationship to Lescaze's earlier housing schemes,

not only in urban versus rural settings but also in quality of design. While there were three rather distinguished villas, proposed terrace houses, and a hotel, the rest were mediocre at best. To be sure, the circumstances for creative building were lacking, and endless compromises seemingly dominated idealistic conceptualizations.

Although Lescaze's work in England—large and expensive houses, school buildings, an office building, low-cost workers' housing, and a housing development—made a significant contribution to the early development of modern architecture in England, there was still an urgent need to have revolutionary architecture and planning projects better understood and accepted, not only in England, but also in America and on the Continent.[156]

To that purpose, Howe and Lescaze displayed their work in numerous exhibitions organized to condition an unsympathetic public to accept the new style. The most important exhibitions in the campaign for a new architecture in America were the Rejected Architects show in April 1931 and the Museum of Modern Art's International Exhibition of Modern Architecture in 1932. The Rejected Architects show, at 903 Seventh Avenue, was a protest on the part of those who supported the International Style against the more traditional "modernistic" architects championed by the New York Architectural League. When men like Oscar Stonorov, Lloyd Morgan, Hazen Sise, William Muschenheim, Walter Baermann, Elroy Webber, and Richard Wood were rejected by the Architectural League's selection committee from their 1931 exhibition, Howe and Lescaze came to their defense by supporting the Rejected Architects' Show.[157]

While Howe's and Lescaze's scheme for the PSFS and first scheme for the Hessian Hills School were shown at the League's 1931 exhibition, their Emigrant Industrial Savings Bank project for New York, the Arthur Peck house project, and High Cross house (then under construction at Dartington Hall) were not accepted by the League for its February 1932 exhibition.[158] Philip Johnson recalled that the League's action was the opportunity Howe and Lescaze had been waiting for, to "strike a blow for progress against reaction."[159]

Howe resigned from the League on 25 February 1932; Lescaze resigned two days later. Their resignations were reported on the front page of the *New York Times* on 28 February 1932 and in newspapers of other cities in America and abroad. Lescaze boldly announced to the press:

> We stand for clarification of architectural principle. We are perfectly willing to fight alone rather than make compromise with the crowd. The issue is too serious to be treated lightly. An architect must be able to practice his profession according to his individual convictions rather than the convictions of the group.[160]

Howe asserted:

> They [the League's jury] are false modernists of the most dangerous kind, mere opportunists and fashion mongers, who have made the modern movement a sort of circus sideshow of their own wares. The League's shows are completely lacking in architectural interest. They are in reality largely trade exhibits and the League takes no attitude at all toward architectural theory.[161]

The League's president, Julian Clarence Levi, replied:

> As I understand it, there are two reasons why Mr. Howe and Mr. Lescaze resigned, the first being that the League was not in sympathy with their artistic principles and, secondly, that if these artistic principles were at variance with the League's principles membership in the League became inadvisable.[162]

Levi continued: "Membership comprises many schools of thought," and does not interfere with the "artistic principles of its members." He noted that Howe's and Lescaze's work was rejected along with about sixty per cent of the material sent in.[163] The result of all this was but little more than a few published comments in support of Howe's and Lescaze's actions.[164]

Nevertheless, Howe and Lescaze received front page attention for the fact that they were receiving much favorable publicity for their work being shown at the Museum of Modern Art's International Exhibition of Modern Architecture, held from 10 February to 23 March 1932. The exhibition was composed of both European and American work. Consisting of ten models and seventy-five photographs of plans collected in 1930, the firm of Howe and Lescaze was but one of only eleven American firms invited to exhibit.[165] In officially recognizing, endorsing, and promoting the International Style, the exhibition probably did for modern architecture in America what the Armory Show did for modern painting almost twenty years earlier.[166]

Illustrations of Howe's and Lescaze's Oak Lane Country Day School's nursery school in Philadelphia, the Hessian Hills School in Croton-on-Hudson, interiors of the Trans Lux Theaters in New York, a model of the Chrystie-Forsyth housing development projected for New York, and the celebrated PSFS (then nearing completion in Philadelphia) were shown. The firm was recognized for its Field House in New Hartford, the High Cross house at Dartington Hall, and the interiors for the Hattie Carnegie salon in New York. Lescaze was personally cited for his project for the League of Nations building, the Capital Bus Terminal, the hunting lodge for the Count de Sièyes, and his "Country House of the Future."[167]

The show was well attended in New York and its influence was extended by a symposium held on 19 February 1932 in connection with the exhibition.[168] An editorial and a report on the proceedings of the symposium were published in April 1932 of *Shelter*.[169] In an effort to disseminate the message of the exhibition still further, the show traveled to twelve other museums and one department store throughout the nation. Howe's and Lescaze's achievements were thus fully recognized.[170]

Henry-Russell Hitchcock commented in the exhibition's official publication: "The work of Howe and Lescaze represents an increasingly successful attempt to apply . . . the technical and aesthetic ideas of modern architecture as they have been developed in the last decade in Europe." He continued:

> They are not nationalists, nor are they importers, they recognize that since the nineteenth century, technics and design have developed differently in America than in Europe. They aim to bring these developments together and to work as a firm of American architects respectful of, but not dominated by, the concepts of the rationalists and the functionalists. Theirs is the direction in which our better architecture may be expected to advance.[171]

Hitchcock nearly proved to be prophetic. Although the partnership did not survive the year, Lescaze's work continued to be dominated by the concepts of rational-functionalism, variously modified by the several aesthetics identified with the International Style—*Le Corbusier's Five Points of a New Architecture*, De Stijl, constructivism, expressionism. In this era of pioneering architectural modernism, no one on the East Coast surpassed his influence; only Neutra, Schindler, and Wright exceeded him in the West. Certainly, the thirties was Lescaze's most productive decade in terms of work in the purist expression of the International Style. Although in relation to the European modern movement his realized work was modest, some of his projects were visionary.

That productive decade was also the time when the partnership of Howe and Lescaze broke up and the decline of the flourishing International Style was signalled by the competition for the Palace of the Soviets, where socialist realism won out over the new modernism.

NOTES

1. Jordy, in *American Buildings and Their Architects* and Robert A. M. Stern, in "PSFS: Beaux-Arts Theory and Rational Expressionism," *Journal of the Society of Architectural Historians* 21 (May 1962) and in *George Howe*, discuss the European and American phases of the International Style.

2. Howe had earlier designed a Stokowski residence project, plans dated 16 May 1926, WELA. Efforts by the Stokowskis to enroll their two-year old daughter, Lyuba, in the day school, which lacked pre-kindergarten facilities, led to an endowment and thus, the commission.

3. William B. Curry, "Modern Buildings for New Schools," *The Graphic Survey*, 1 September 1931, p. 496; William Lescaze, *On Being an Architect* (New York: Putnam and Sons, 1942), p. 243.

4. Lescaze, *On Being an Architect*, p. 243.

5. Ibid.

6. For European school buildings in the new style that preceded the Oak Lane nursery school, see J. G. Wiebenga and L. C. van der Vlugt's Technical School at Gronigen, The Netherlands (1922), Walter Gropius's Bauhaus School at Dessau (1925–1926), and Bruno Taut's Municipal School at Berlin (1927).

7. Curry, "Modern Buildings for New Schools," pp. 496–497.

8. Lescaze, *On Being an Architect*, p. 13.

9. Curry, "Modern Buildings for New Schools," p. 496.

10. Lescaze, *On Being an Architect*, p. 243.

11. Henry-Russell Hitchcock and Philip Johnson, *The International Style: Architecture Since 1922* (New York: W. W. Norton and Co., 1932). The windows of Oak Lane nursery school "wrap" the corner of the building but with the support of a lally column at the corner just inside the windows.

12. The other two were: (1) elevated ground floor on *pilotis* and (2) free design of the ground plan. Le Corbusier and Pierre Jenneret, "Five Points Towards a New Architecture," *Almanach de l'architecture moderne* (Paris, 1926), reprinted in Ulrich Conrads, ed. *Programs and Manifestoes on 20th-Century Architecture* (Cambridge: The MIT Press, 1970), pp. 99–101.

13. Jordy, *The Impact of European Modernism*, p. 128; see pp. 123–245 for a discussion of the modes of the International Style.

14. Exterior polychromy had earlier been used in the European modern movement by Bruno Taut in his housing estates at Magdeburg (1921); by Le Corbusier in his workers' houses at Pessac (1924) and in his exhibition houses at the Weissenhofsiedlung, Stuttgart (1927); by Rietveld in the Schröder house at Utrecht (1924); and by Lurçat at the Casa Guggenbuhl (1926–1927). Cervin Robinson and Rosemarie Bletter, in their *Skyscraper Style* (New York: Oxford University Press, 1975), p. 58, claim that exterior polychromy was a German Expressionist substitute for colored glass.

15. "Contour," "profile," and "primary forms" are part of the language used by Le Corbusier in his *Towards a New Architecture*, trans. Frederick Etchells (New York: Praeger Pubs., 1960). Lescaze was so impressed with Le Corbusier's writings that he later advised students to read "all of Le Corbusier that you can get hold of." *On Being an Architect*, pp. 167–168. At this time Lescaze was even called the "Le Corbusier of America." Curtis Patterson, review of *The New Interior Decoration*, by Dorothy Todd and Raymond Mortimer, in *International Studio* 94 (September 1929):73.

16. Examples of pseudo-membranous concrete structures include Rietveld's Schröder house among many others.

17. Henry-Russell Hitchcock, *Modern Architecture, Romanticism and Reintegration* (New York: Payson & Clarke, 1929), p. 161. Also see William H. Jordy, "Symbolic Essence of Modern European Architecture of the Twenties and its Influence." *Journal of the Society of Architectural Historians* 22 (October 1963):177–187.

18. Henry-Russell Hitchcock, "Howe and Lescaze," in Alfred Barr et al., *Modern Architecture: International Exhibition* (New York: Norton, 1932; reprint ed., New York: published for the Museum of Modern Art by Arno Press, 1969), p. 144.

19. The opening date was announced in the *New York Sun*, the *Philadelphia Inquirer*, and the *Philadelphia Public Ledger* on 22 September 1929.

20. Both were attributed to George Howe by the agreement of February 1935.

21. Stern, *George Howe*, p. 87 states that with the Sinkler house, Howe "hit his stride as a modernist."

22. H. I. Brock, "Modern Architecture in Rural Settings," *New York Times*, 2 February 1930, Special Features, p. 8; a photograph of the model is published there and in Stern, *George Howe*, Fig. 98. Le Corbusier, *Towards a New Architecture*, p. 98.

23. Talbot Hamlin, "Architecture," in *The New International Yearbook*, 1930, ed. Herbert Treadwell Wade (New York: Dodd, Mead, 1931), p. 53.

24. C. Adolph Glassgold, "House of William Stix Wasserman, Esq., Whitemarsh, Pennsylvania," *Architectural Forum* 53 (August 1930):230–232.

25. "Tendencies in City Buildings Illustrated by the Exhibition," *The New York Sun*, 8 February 1930, p. 8.

26. See Stern, *George Howe*, pp. 162–171.

27. See Stern, *George Howe*, Figs. 99–101, for plan and photographs. See Lawrence Wodehouse, review of *George Howe: Towards a Modern American Architecture*, by Robert A. M. Stern, in the *Journal of the Society of Architectural Historians* 35 (March 1976):64, for a discussion of its authorship.

28. Theo van Doesburg, "Towards a Plastic Architecture," reprinted in *Programs and Manifestoes*, ed. Conrads, p. 79, a translation of *De Stijl*, XII, 6/7 (Rotterdam, 1924).

29. Ibid.

30. Ibid., points 14 and 15.

31. All the terms were expressed by van Doesburg in his "Towards a Plastic Architecture."

32. Interview with Mrs. Lescaze, New York, 8 October 1974. Field is a great, great grandson of Commodore Cornelius Vanderbilt, Field to author, 13 June 1977. For the most part it was left to the wealthy, or avant-garde artists and intellectuals, to commission the International Style for private residences in Europe during the twenties and in America during the thirties. Ironically, this was a basic contradiction of CIAM's aims be-

cause the promotion of an architecture of universal validity depended on its acceptance at all social levels.

33. Partial Job List, with dates started and completed, WELA. "Budget for F. V. Field House—Hartford, Conn.," 26 January 1932 (in possession of owner Michael Taylor), indicates the first payments for the "land survey" for the house were made on 12 November 1930 and 14 January 1931. The largest payment for steel frame work was made on 30 August 1931; payment for miscellaneous work was made on 17 December 1931. Charles L. Anderson was the contractor.

34. "Construction Data, F. V. Field House," WELA, "Budget for F. V. Field House," shows a cost of $37,556.25. Stern, *George Howe*, p. 107 states that the cost was $50,000. The name "Red Hill" was told the author by Frederick V. Field in a letter of 13 June 1977. The acreage had been "referred to by that name in an old document or survey." The house was in process of being nominated to the National Register of Historic Places; John W. Shannahan to Michael Taylor, 11 April 1977, copy sent to the author.

35. The *Architectural Record* (November 1931 and November 1932) and the *Architectural Forum* (November 1933) published a 19 September 1930 variation on the original plan. They show a "store room" in place of the "maid's room" and full bath; the child's room is labeled a "guest room." This scheme was not built. F. V. Field to author, 13 June 1977, states that they never had a maid but that the room was useful for children.

36. See "Small House" photograph album, WELA. The wing was nearly completed in August 1936.

37. See Jordy, *The Impact of European Modernism*, chapter 3; William H. Jordy, "The International Style in the 1930's," *Journal of the Society of Architectural Historians* 24 (March 1965): 12, 14.

38. Neutra's Lovell Health house was the first steel-frame domestic building constructed in the United States.

39. Other early works include: Edward Stone's Mandel house, Mt. Kisco, New York, 1933–1934; Paul Wiener's "Contempora House," New City, New York, 1933; and Lawrence Kocher's house for Rex Stout, Conn., designed with Gerhard Ziegler, 1933. See McAndrew, *Guide*, p. 20; *Architectural Record* 73 (April 1933): 288; *Architectural Record* 74 (July 1933): 45–49.

40. Talbot Hamlin, "Architecture," in *The New International Yearbook 1932*, ed. Frank Vizetelly (New York: Dodd, Mead & Co., 1933), p. 52.

41. "Modern House," Master Detail Series, *Architectural Forum* 59 (November 1933): 393–394. This practice was, of course, not new, having been done brilliantly by many for centuries before him.

42. See Henry-Russell Hitchcock, *Modern Architecture in England*, New York: The Museum of Modern Art, reprint edition by the Arno Press, 1969, pp. 26–41, for a complete discussion of early modern architecture in England.

43. Dorothy Whitney Straight Elmhirst was the daughter of William C. Whitney, the well-known American financier and statesman. He died in 1904 leaving Dorothy, at age 17, with an independent fortune. Dorothy married Willard Dickerman Straight on 11 September 1911. Straight died on 28 November 1918. Leonard K. Elmhirst, the son of a Yorkshire parson, was a graduate in history and theology of Trinity College, Cambridge. After the first World War he studied agriculture at Cornell University (class of 1921) and from 1921 to 1924 worked with Rabindranath Tagore in India, establishing a department of Rural Reconstruction to train students and carry out research. It was at Cornell, where Dorothy W. Straight was arranging to have a Student Union built as a memorial to Willard Straight (a Cornell graduate), that she met Leonard Elmhirst. He helped her work out the plan for what is now

known as Willard Straight Hall, designed by the New York firm of Delano and Aldrich. The Elmhirsts married in 1925. See Victor Bonham-Carter, *Dartington Hall* (London: Phoenix House, 1958), pp. 19–22.

44. Those contributing to the very vital and active years of expansion were A. E. Malbon, who developed Staverton Builders, at first a subsidiary of Dartington Hall Ltd.; C. F. Nielsen, a Dane who introduced new methods of intensive dairy production at Dartington's Old Parsonage Farm; Jack Currie, who made Dartington the cornerstone of what today is known as the International Association of Agricultural Economists; and Wilfred Hiley, who developed the many acres of woodlands on the Estate and scattered around Dartmoor as pioneer experiments in progressive and economic forestry management. Among the artists in residence were Kurt Jooss and his ballet company; the dancers Margaret Barr, Louise Sollber, and Rudolph Laban; dramatists Ellen van Volkenburg and Michael Checkov; sculptor Willi Soukop; musicians Hans Oppenheim and Fritz Cohen; potter Bernard Leach; composer Alan Rawsthorne; puppeteer Richard Odlin; painters Hein Heckroth and Mark Tobey; and film maker William Hunter. See Bonham-Carter, *Dartington Hall*, chapter 4, passim.

45. Curry (1900–1962) was educated at Alnwick Grammar School and received his Bachelor of Science and Master of Arts degrees from Trinity College, Cambridge. William B. Curry, "The School," in Bonham-Carter, *Dartington Hall*, p. 162; Curry to Jerome J. Rothchild, 16 October 1930, T-School-1A, Records Office, Dartington Hall (hereafter cited as RODH).

46. Lescaze to Curry, 17 June 1930, T-13-Folder A, RODH. The Tait house was published in "An Essay in the Architecture of Protest," *Architect and Building News* 121 (September 1929): 311–315. The roof terrace of Lauterbach's house was illustrated in Howard T. Fisher, "New Elements in House Design," *Architectural Record* 66 (November 1929): 401. According to the Architectural Association's *Guide to Modern Architecture in London* (1957), the first example of Continental modernism in England was Easton's and Robertson's Royal Horticultural Hall, completed in 1927. A conservative version of the Continental modernism had been imported in 1926 with Peter Behrens's Northampton house, New Ways, built for the inventor Basset-Lowke; also in Thomas Tait's Crittall Housing Estate, Silver End, near Chelmsford, Essex, England (1927–1928). The first major house in England to reflect the fully developed style was Amyas Connell and Basil Ward's High and Over, Amersham, Bucks (1929–1930) for Bernard Ashmole. It and the Royal Corinthian Yacht Club at Burnham-on-Crouch, built by Joseph Emberton in 1930–1931, represented England in the Museum of Modern Art's 1932 International Exhibition of Modern Architecture. Contemporary with Curry's High Cross house was Connell's and Ward's New Farm near Haslemere, Surrey, England (1932). See Anthony Jackson, "The Politics of Architecture: English Architecture (1929–1951)," *Journal of the Society of Architectural Historians* 24 (March 1965): 97–99, for a discussion of the earliest publications in England on modern architecture.

47. Curry to Lescaze, 22 October 1930 (quoting a cable from Leonard Elmhirst), T-13-Folder A, RODH.

48. Curry to Lescaze, 19 December 1930, T-13-Folder A, RODH. See Theo van Doesburg, "Towards a Plastic Architecture," *De Stijl* XII, 6/7, (Rotterdam, 1924), points 12 and 13, in *Programs and Manifestoes*, ed. Conrads, pp. 79–80.

49. Curry to Lescaze, 1 September 1931, T-1-A, RODH.

50. Alfred Clauss, project director for this job, stated in an interview in Philadelphia, 10 April 1974, that he was primarily responsible for the design of the north façade.

51. Van Doesburg, "Towards a Plastic Architecture," point 14, quoted in Theodore M. Brown, *The Work of G. Riet-*

veld Architect (Utrecht: A. W. Bruna & Zoon, 1958), p. 69.

52. Lescaze to Curry, 16 September 1931; Lescaze to Curry, 22 October 1931, T-13-A, RODH.

53. See van Doesburg, "Towards a Plastic Architecture," points 5, 8, and 11, in *Programs and Manifestoes*, ed. Conrads, pp. 78–79.

54. Lescaze to Curry, 5 October 1932, T-13-B, RODH; Lescaze to Curry, 29 January 1934, T-14-B, RODH. Curved walls extending beyond the structure were planned for Oak Lane nursery school before this.

55. See Dr. Schoenmaekers' philosophy set forth in *The New Image of the World*, cited in Frampton, "De Stijl," p. 141.

56. Lescaze to Curry, 26 February 1932, T-13-B, RODH. See Schoenmaekers, *The New Image of the World*, cited in Kenneth Frampton, "De Stijl," in *Concepts of Modern Art*, ed. Anthony Richardson and Nikos Stangos (New York: Harper & Row, 1974), p. 141.

57. Curry to Lescaze, 9 June 1932, T-13-B, RODH.

58. Alice Mary Blinn graduated with a B. S. degree from the College of Home Economics at Cornell in 1917 and was an extension instructor in charge of home economics publications there until 1926. She began writing for *The Delineator* in 1924 and became research editor in 1926. She was appointed assistant editor of the *Ladies Home Journal* in 1934.

59. Alice Mary Blinn to Lescaze, 15 October 1931, T-13-A, RODH. Other correspondence regarding the kitchen plan is: Lescaze to Blinn, 18 August 1931, T-13-A; Curry to Lescaze, 1 September 1931, T-13-A; Curry to Lescaze, 24 September 1931, T-13-A, all RODH.

60. William Lescaze, "The Modern House," *Architectural Forum* 59 (November 1933): 393–394. See F. L. Wright's introduction to the first Wasmuth volume where he wrote: ". . . it is quite impossible to consider the building one thing and its furnishings another. . . . Heating apparatus, lighting fixtures, the very chairs and tables, cabinets and musical instruments, where practical are of the building itself." Quoted here from Kenneth Frampton, "De Stijl," p. 141.

61. Curtis Moffat, an American photographer who had lived for some time in Paris and had opened a gallery in 1929 at 4 Fitzroy Square, London, was one of the few active disciples of modernism in England. In the early thirities, he was in charge of the English agency of the French Décoration Intérieure Moderne (DIM). Martin Battersby, *The Decorative Twenties* (New York: Walker & Co., 1969), p. 166; Battersby, *The Decorative Thirties* (New York: Walker & Co., 1971), pp. 85–87.

62. Curry to Lescaze, 6 November 1931, T-13-A, RODH. The seventh point of van Doesburg's and van Eesteren's Manifesto, "Towards a Collective Construction," *De Stijl* VI, 6 (July 1924), pp. 89–91, stated: ". . . we assert that painting separated from the architectonic construction (i.e. the picture) has no right to exist." Quoted here from *Programs and Manifestoes*, ed. Conrads, p. 66.

63. Construction data is from "Description of Residence for Mr. William B. Curry, Headmaster, Dartington Hall, Devon, England" (typescript), WELA.

64. G. F. Ventriss to Dr. W. K. Slater, 19 October 1932, T-13-B, RODH.

65. Curry to Lescaze, 9 June 1932, T-13-B, RODH.

66. Curry to Lescaze, 26 August 1932, T-13-B, RODH.

67. Curry to Christopher Hussey, 30 January 1933, T-13-C, RODH.

68. Christopher Hussey, "High Cross Hill, Dartington, Devon, The Residence of Mr. W. B. Curry," *Country Life*, 11 February 1933, p. 147.

69. Interview with Mrs. Lescaze, New York, 8 October 1974. Lescaze's rendering of the house in an early stage of development is dated 21 June 1931. The plan is published in *Architectural Record* 70 (November 1931): 369. Stern, in *George Howe* p. 107, states that the cost was estimated to be $147,000.

70. Erich Mendelsohn, "Architecture of our Own Times," lecture delivered to Architectural Association in London, May 1931, published in Dennis Sharp, *Modern Architecture and Expressionism* (New York: Braziller, 1966), pp. 126, 129. Mendelsohn had previously expressed the same idea in a letter to his wife in ca. 1920, Ibid., chap. 9, No. 6, citing *Briefe eines Architekten*, Munich, 1921, p. 57.

71. Lescaze, Note (handwritten), 2 October 1931, WELA. In 1934 the job went to Ralph Pomerance (a relative), of Pomerance and Breines, New York; McAndrew, *Guide*, p. 19.

72. The local architect Harvey Stevenson was first considered but deemed too conservative. See Stern, *George Howe*, p. 99, and George Howe, "Will Erect Functionalist Building," *Art Digest* 5 (1 June 1931): 10.

73. For outstanding examples among them see Chap. 4, footnote 6 and Johannes Duiker's Open Air School in Amsterdam (1928–1930); Ernst May's Friedrich Ebert School in Frankfurt-am-Main (1931); Irving Gill's Kindergarten in Oceanside, California (1931); and André Lurçat's school in Villejuif, Seine, near Paris (1931–1933).

74. "Notes on the Hessian Hills School" (typescript), May 1931, WELA; Curry, "Modern Buildings for New Schools," p. 498; Howe, "Will Erect Functionalist Building," p. 10.

75. Stern, in *George Howe*, discusses only two schemes and refers to scheme eight as scheme two. See Stern, *George Howe*, p. 99, figs. 67, 68.

76. The use of a curved roof canopy at the angle related to that used by Oud at Kiefhook.

77. See Dennis Sharp, *A Visual History of Twentieth Century Architecture* (New York: New York Graphic Society, 1972), p. 62.

78. Stern in *George Howe*, p. 100, states that there were no precedents for a building deriving its section from the slope of the site.

79. His visit to Europe at that time is documented by a letter from Howe to Lescaze, dated 1 April 1931, stating "you must be nearly arriving on the other side." Receipt of the letter was indicated in pencil as "Geneva, April 17." Lescaze's "282"-PSFS Notes indicated that he sailed from New York on 27 March 1931 and returned to New York on 10 May 1931, WELA.

80. Stern, in *George Howe*, p. 100n35, quotes Elizabeth Moos: "the financial limit was $65,000." Elizabeth Moos, unpublished "Statement," 14 November 1931. Howe archives, Columbia University.

81. Stern, *George Howe*, p. 100n35 quotes Elizabeth Moos: "The amount of building we now have [the first stage] cost us $40,000." Stern states, p. 100, that the cost as built [presumably after the second stage] was $47,000.

82. In both schemes two and eight the plans specify an "auditorium" and "music room" and not a combination auditorium-gymnasium. However, the large dressing room space adjacent to the auditorium suggests a gymnasium use as well.

83. Hitchcock, "Howe and Lescaze," p. 144.

84. In New York the theaters were located at Fifty-eighth Street at Madison Avenue and Forth-eighth Street at Broadway; in Philadelphia there was one at Eighteenth Street and Market. See "Trans-Lux Theater an Innovation in Film Projection," *Architectural Record* 70 (August 1931): 118–120.

85. "The Current Cinema," *The New Yorker*, 28 March 1931, pp. 75–76.

86. Charles Edwin Wilbour (1833–1896) was an observer, recorder, and collector of Egyptology. Susan A. Hutchinson, "The Wilbour Library Room," *The Brooklyn Museum Quarterly*

22 (January 1935):23.

87. See Hutchinson, "The Wilbour Library Room," pp. 24–25, for details on the original color scheme. Kenneth Frampton, "De Stijl," p. 149; van Doesburg, "Towards a Plastic Architecture," point 15, in *Programs and Manifestoes*, ed. Conrads, p. 80.

88. Howe was chairman of the Junior Advisory Committee of the Museum of Modern Art in 1930. The time is determined by drawings dated early in 1930 and a letter from Mary Hughes to Lescaze, 22 October 1929, which mentioned the Museum of Modern Art job, WELA. Because the trustees had no specific site yet in mind, the architects prepared preliminary schemes for an unspecified site. The architects assumed a typical city plot 100 feet deep, approximately 60 feet wide, on the north side of a street 60 feet wide. See George Howe and William Lescaze, *A Modern Museum* (Springdale, Conn., 1930), WELA. Howe and Lescaze were commissioned to draw plans only; a building commission was not to be assumed. Interview, Mrs. Lescaze, New York, 29 June 1977.

89. See Jordy, "PSFS," pp. 63–64.

90. There were undoubtedly other drawings bearing different dates; Stern, *George Howe*, Fig. 72, cites scheme one as being dated 14 May 1930.

91. See pp. 13, 14 above. Sauvage's apartment house was published in Platz, *Die Baukunst der neuesten Zeit*, p. 471.

92. Howe and Lescaze, *A Modern Museum*, p. 5, WELA. "A Proposed Museum of Contemporary Art for New York City by Howe and Lescaze, Architects," *Architectural Record* 80 (July 1936):44, states only that on 2 June 1930 the architects prepared drawings for a Museum of Contemporary Art; no mention of a trustees' commission was made.

93. A preliminary sketch is dated 3 August 1930, WELA; drawings of a model are dated 18, 19, 20 September 1930; window revisions are dated 2 October 1930.

94. The plans were published in Howe and Lescaze, *A Modern Museum*, p. 15; "A Proposed Museum of Contemporary Art for New York City by Howe and Lescaze, Architects," p. 47.

95. See Moshe Safdie, *Beyond Habitat* (Cambridge, Mass.: MIT Press, 1971).

96. Wien: Verlag Anton Schroll & Co., p. 43.

97. "A Proposed Museum of Contemporary Art," pp. 44, 46.

98. Albert Frey to author, 24 April 1974, states that he developed plans, elevations and renderings for variations five and six of a multi-story art museum. Frey, a 1924 graduate of the Institute of Technology at Winterthur (near Zurich), Switzerland, subsequently worked in Zurich, Brussels, and in 1928–1929 in Paris with Le Corbusier. He states that from August 1931 to July 1932, he worked half days for Howe and Lescaze. Alfred Clauss to author, 9 August 1977, corroborates Frey's role and states that he (Clauss) also worked on both MoMA schemes.

99. An annotation on the reverse of schemes five and six (numbered one and two) states that five studies were prepared and that the fifth was accepted by the Museum of Modern Art. This probably can be interpreted to mean the last scheme or number six. Lescaze probably counted schemes one and two as one concept, WELA.

100. See Laurence Vail Coleman, *Museum Buildings* (Washington, D.C.: The American Association of Museums, 1950), p. 36.

101. Lescaze, "Things which have hurt, should be filed away and forgotten," 31 October 1930 (typescript), WELA.

102. Lescaze to Curry, 4 December 1931, T-13-A, RODH.

103. Albert Frey to author, 24 April 1974, states that he was "designer with Philip Goodwin who in a joint venture with Edward Stone was doing the Museum of Modern Art."

104. Hitchcock, "Howe and Lescaze." According to Stern, *George Howe*, p. 103n39, the Carl Mackley Housing project, built in Philadelphia in 1934 by Oscar Stonorov, Alfred Kastner in association with W. Pope Barney, was, in terms of style, the first modern public housing project built in America. See Richard Pommer, "The Architecture of Urban Housing in the United States during the Early 1930s," *Journal of the Society of Architectural Historians* XXXVII (December 1978):235–264, for a comprehensive discussion of urban housing in the thirties.

105. The City of New York acquired title to the area on 27 August 1929. It was to have been ceded at a low cost. *East Side Chamber News* 5 (February 1932), pp. 7–9.

106. Ibid.

107. Le Corbusier, *Towards a New Architecture*, trans. Etchells, p. 57, shows an illustration of a "Town Built on Piles, 1915." Michael Brinkman's Spangen housing and J. J. P. Oud's "Tussendijken" block, built in Rotterdam in 1920, were the first to utilize an elevated deck to provide access to mass housing. Unlike the Corbusian and Chrystie-Forsyth projects, the Spangen blocks utilized only one deck at the third floor level.

108. See p. 54 above.

109. Hitchcock, "Howe and Lescaze," p. 146.

110. See "Explain Houses on Stilts," *New York Times*, 10 February 1932, p. 43.

111. "Model Housing," Editorial, *New York Times*, 4 March 1932, p. 18.

112. Stern, *George Howe*, p. 103.

113. Franklin D. Roosevelt vetoed the "Dunnigan Bill," sponsored by New York City Administration, which would have given city authorities the right to mortgage the fee of excess lands obtained through condemnation and lease them to private corporations for housing purposes. "Governor to Veto City Bill to Lease Land for Housing," *New York Times*, 25 March 1932, p. 1.

114. Anthony Jackson, *A Place Called Home* (Cambridge, Mass: The MIT Press, 1976), p. 194.

115. It was planned in cooperation with Carol Aronovici, city planner; George E. Strehan, structural engineer; and E. I. Daugherty and Company, mechanical engineers. Exterior and interior renderings are dated 4 October 1932, 21 October 1932, and February 1933.

116. Mary Hughes Steiner to Leonard Elmhirst, 5 January 1933. Mary Connick Hughes married photographer and film maker Ralph Steiner in 1927; she married Lescaze in September 1933.

117. "Realistic Planning," *Architectural Forum* 61 (July 1934):49–55.

118. Queensbridge Dwellings Reports, WELA.

119. The Astoria-Queens project was revitalized as "Queensbridge" in 1937, and four blocks of six-story, Y-shaped, apartment units were built in 1939 from the plans of Frederick G. Frost, William F. Ballard, Henry Churchill, and Burnett C. Turner. See "Queens Project Urged to House East Side Poor," *New York Herald Tribune*, 25 July 1937, p. 4; "New Colony Urged as Slum Solution," *New York Times*, 25 July 1937, general news, p. 5. McAndrew, *Guide*, p. 65; Talbot Hamlin, "Architecture," in *The New International Yearbook 1938*, ed., Frank Vizetelly (New York: Dodd, Mead, 1939), p. 38.

120. The date is established by Elmhirst's letter to O. P. Milne, 1 July 1932, C-Churston-8-G, RODH.

121. Nicolas Cottis, "Time to Preserve This for the Future?," *Dartington Hall News*, 28 March 1969, p. 6.

122. Correspondence concerning possible architects in-

cludes: Elmhirst to Milne, 1 July 1932, C-Churston-8-G; Slater to Gwatkin, 28 December 1932, C-Churston-8-G; Gwatkin to Elmhirst, 6 January 1933, C-Churston-8-G; Mary Steiner to Leonard K. Elmhirst, 5 January 1933, T-Estate-6-C; Gwatkin to Elmhirst, 6 January 1933, C-Churston-8-G; Gwatkin to Elmhirst, 17 January 1933, C-Churston-8-G; Charles Ross Jr. to Elmhirst, 25 January 1933, T-Estate-5-C; Henry Wright to Elmhirst, 9 November 1933, T-Estate-5-E, all RODH.

123. Documents regarding early plans for Churston are Lescaze's personal notes of 20 December 1932, 10 January 1933, 12 January 1933, 13 January 1933, 17 January 1933, WELA. The date of Lescaze's appointment is documented by: Lescaze to Slater, 24 March 1933, Slater to Lescaze, 6 April 1933, and Lescaze to Slater 21 April 1933, C-Churston-8-G. In the latter Lescaze mentions having received the appointment by cable in "the meantime" (since Slater's letter of April 6.) Judging from letters of Lescaze to Howe, 25 March 1933, and Howe to Lescaze, 27 March 1933, Lescaze had apparently hoped to elicit Howe's assistance in securing the commission. But Howe indicated in his letter of 19 April 1933 that he would take a six months rest and then retire, WELA.

124. Also appointed at that meeting of the Churston Advisory Committee were Mrs. Beatrice Farrand, American landscape architect and consultant at the Dartington Estate, named consulting landscape architect; and the young English architect Colin Penn, of the Howe and Lescaze office in New York, who was designated resident architect for the Churston development. After a year, Robert Hening, who had been supervising Lescaze's work at Dartington, took over the resident architect's duties at Churston as well. In order to administer the planning and construction of the project, the Churston Development Company was formed with Dr. W. K. Slater as Executive Director. "Report of the Churston Advisory Committee," 3 May 1933, C-Churston-8-A. Organizational Chart, C-Churston-8-G, RODH.

125. General Property layout Subdivided in Sections," June 1934, revised 6 July 1934, drawing no. 346-32. Wright to Slater 11 October 1933, T-Estate-5-E, RODH.

126. F. A. O. Gwatkin to Lescaze, 30 August 1933, C-Churston-8-B, RODH.

127. "Memo on the Churston Development" (Probably written by Slater), September 1933, C-Churston-8-C, RODH.

128. Ibid.

129. "Report on the Churston Development" (Probably written by Slater), 27 September 1933, C-Churston-8-B; Wright to Slater, 9 November 1933, C-Churston-8-B, RODH.

130. Penn to Lescaze, 19 July 1933, C-Churston-9-J, RODH.

131. Drawings for the teahouse were filed 24 May 1933, for the bathing cubicles 6 June 1933. See Churston Development Co., Ltd., "Index of Drawings," Section 5, WELA. Slater to Lescaze 9 June 1933, C-Churston-8-A; "Notes for Elmhirst" by Slater, 3 May 1933, C-Churston-8-A, all RODH.

132. Interview with Robert Hening, Dartington Hall, 16 June 1973.

133. Slater to Lescaze, 11 July 1933, C-Churston-8-B, RODH.

134. Curry to Lescaze, 5 September 1933, T-14-A, RODH.

135. Slater to Lescaze, 6 January 1934, C-Churston-9-A, RODH.

136. These were plan types C, L, M, K, J, and H on lots 64, 63, 62, 61, 55, and 54 respectively. Lescaze to Slater, 11 October 1933, C-Churston-9-A RODH; "Houses in Group #1 at Churston" (typescript chart), WELA; site plan, drawing no. 346, SPI, 3 October 1933, revised 23 February 1934, 21 June 1934, and 9 July 1935; WELA; Slater to Lescaze, 31 March

1935, C-Churston-9-A, RODH.

137. J. G. Brodie to Staverton Builders, 9 August 1935, C-Churston-7-G, RODH.

138. Memo, Helen Elmhirst (Mrs. J. V.) and Miss McGregor, C-Churston-7-G; Salesmanager to Slater, 31 October 1935, C-Churston-2-C; Slater to Lescaze, 8 March 1935, C-Churston-8-E, all RODH.

139. Gwatkin to Lescaze, 30 August 1933, C-Churston-8-B, RODH.

140. Salesmanager to Slater, 31 October 1935, C-Churston-2-C. RODH.

141. "Managing Director's Report," 15 May 1935, C-Churston-2-C, RODH.

142. Slater to Lescaze, 22 January 1935, C-Churston-9-C; Director's Report, 6 February 1935, C-Churston-2-C, all RODH.

143. It was completed in February 1936. Hening to Slater, "Building Report for February," 9 March 1936, C-Churston-7-B reads: "Type 1, lot 70 is started but as per your instructions, work on this house has been stopped. Type 1, lot 74 is complete." Inspection of the sites showed that a Type 1 house was indeed built on lot 74 but that no Lescaze house was built on lot 70. The owner of the house built north of Tor Rocks was in the process of constructing a garage when the author visited in the summer of 1973.

144. Site plan, drawing no. 346, SPI, 3 October 1933, revised 23 February 1934, 21 June 1934, and 9 July 1935, indicates that a Type R house was built on lot 6 and a Type 1 on lot 70. Inspection of the sites indicates that these were not built. Also, see: Slater to Lescaze, 19 October 1935, C-Churston-7-B; Hening to Slater, 7 November 1935, C-Churston-7-B; and Hening to Slater, 9 March 1936, C-Churston-7-B, all RODH.

145. Slater to Lescaze, 13 February 1935, C-Churston-9-A; Slater to Lescaze, 19 September 1935, C-Churston-9-A, RODH. Lescaze provided the essay for the rationale of modern design in: "Why We Have Adopted Modern Architecture" (typescript), 23 November 1934, WELA.

146. Perspective renderings of the exterior of the hotel are in the RODH in an album marked "Miscellaneous." Renderings of the ground floor plan, main entrance, and lounge interior were published in the *Architectural Record* 81 (May 1937): BT 32.

147. Slater to Lescaze, 3 October 1935, C-Churston-9-E; Slater to Lescaze, 29 November 1935, C-Churston-8-E, all RODH.

148. "Director's Report," 17 October 1935, C-Churston-2-C, RODH.

149. "Director's Report," Churston Development Company, 6 February 1935, C-Churston-2-C, RODH.

150. Sources for the factors accounting for the failure of the project were compiled from the author's sense of the correspondence written throughout its planning and development. Some specific references are: Hening, "Memo on Building Organization," 27 March 1935, T-Estate-3-A; "Notes," C-Churston-10-A; "Managing Director's Report," 7 May 1935, C-Churston-2-C; "Memo on architectural services for Churston Estate," 3 March 1936, C-Churston-2-D; Malbon to Slater, 5 March 1937, C-Churston-7-A, all RODH.

151. Curry to Lescaze, 14 March 1936, T-Estate-13-C, RODH.

152. *Torbay Herald Express*, 3 July 1933, WELA.

153. Curry to Lescaze, 14 March 1936, T-Estate-13-C, RODH.

154. See Anthony Jackson, "The Politics of Architecture: English Architecture, 1929–1951," *Journal of the Society of Architectural Historians* 24 (March 1965): 97–99.

155. "Director's Report," February 1937, C-Churston-2-D, RODH.

156. Nikolaus Pevsner, *Buildings of England, South Devon* (Harmondsworth, Middlesex: Penguin Books, 1952), p. 101.

157. Philip Johnson, "Rejected Architects," *Creative Art* 8 (June 1931):433–435; Stern, *George Howe*, pp. 151–153.

158. A penthouse apartment, its rooms to be designed by Ely Jacques Kahn (man's room), Eugene Schoen (dining room), Henry F. Bultetude (bedroom), Otto Teegan (boudoir), Norman T. Newton (garden), Bill Lam (living room), Lescaze (solarium), Joseph Urban (backdrop), and Ralph Walker (chairman) was to have been exhibited in the Vanderbilt Gallery as a part of the League's February 1932 exhibition. It was called off because of the depressed economy at that time.

159. Philip Johnson, speech to the Architectural League, 26 May 1965, printed in the League's *News Bulletin* (ca. September 1956), p. 104, cited here from Stern, *George Howe*, p. 151.

160. "Howe and Lescaze Quit League to 'Fight Alone' Rather than 'Compromise with Crowd,'" *New York Times*, 28 February 1932, pp. 1, 22. Howe had expressed similar feelings in Howe to Lescaze, 5 February 1932.

161. *Philadelphia Public Ledger*, 30 March 1932, cited in Stern, *George Howe*, p. 157.

162. "Denies League Curbed Architects Who Quit," *New York Times*, 1 March 1932, p. 43, quoted in Stern, *George Howe*, p. 156; see Stern, *George Howe*, pp. 155–157, for further details of the event.

163. "Denies League Curbed Architects Who Quit," p. 43.

164. See Henry-Russell Hitchcock, "Architecture," *Arts Weekly*, 11 March 1932, pp. 12–13; Harold Steiner, "The Architectural League," *Arts Weekly*, 18 March 1932, p. 13; Lewis Mumford, "The Skyline: Organic Architecture," *The New Yorker*, 27 February 1932, pp. 45–46.

165. Clauss and Daub, R. G. and William Cory, Frederick Kiesler, Kocher and Frey, Thompson and Churchill, and Oscar Stonorov (with Tucker and Howell) were represented in the quantitaive "extent of modern architecture" part of the exhibit. The work of Frank Lloyd Wright, Raymond Hood, Howe and Lescaze, Richard Neutra, and the Bowman Brothers was shown in the qualitative, "exhibiting architects," part of the exhibition. See Barr, et al., *Modern Architecture*, pp. 129–177; A. Conger Goodyear, *The Museum of Modern Art: The First Ten Years* (New York: The Museum of Modern Art, 1943); Lewis Mumford, "The Sky Line: Organic Architecture," *The New Yorker*, 27 February 1932, pp. 49–50; Stern, *George Howe*, p. 154n37.

166. Lynes, *Good Old Modern* (New York: Atheneum, 1973), p. 189.

167. Hitchcock, "Howe and Lescaze," pp. 147–148.

168. Lynes, *Good Old Modern*, p. 87, states that 33,000 people saw the show, but that as attendance went for other shows held that season, it was not a large number.

169. "Symposium: The International Architecture Exhibition," *Shelter* 2 (April 1932):3–9.

170. The exhibition was shown at the Pennsylvania Art Museum, Wadsworth Atheneaum (Hartford, Conn.), Buffalo Fine Arts Academy, Cleveland Museum of Art, Milwaukee Art Institute, Cincinnati Art Museum, Rochester (New York) Memorial Art Gallery, Carnegie Institute (Pittsburgh), Toledo Museum of Art, Fogg Art Museum, Worcester Art Museum, Art Institute of Omaha, and the Gallery of Bullocks Wilshire (Los Angeles). See Lynes, *Good Old Modern*, pp. 86–87.

171. Hitchcock, "Howe and Lescaze," p. 145.

5

Post-Partnership Years: International Modernism, 1933–1940

AFTER BREAKING OFF WITH HOWE, LESCAZE'S PRAC-
tice grew in both number and variety of commissions as the nation recovered from its severe
financial depression and the new architecture
gained acceptance throughout the world. His work
developed to encompass new architectural forms,
experimental structures, and a new architectural
type. Although some of it changed stylistically as
the International Style was modified to include a
variety of materials, textures, and a complexity of
form, much of this work remained consistent with
his earlier expressions of rationalism and the
volumetric nature of skeletal construction. While
residential work continued to be an important part
of his practice, public and commercial buildings
and large-scale housing projects were realized in increasing numbers. Several major commissions and
projects of the thirties, designed for diverse loca-
tions, illustrate the on-going early International
Style in Lescaze's oeuvre.

Lescaze's first new job in private practice was his
own house, at 211 East Forty-eighth street. Completed in June 1934, the combined residence and
architectural office is an extraordinary reinterpreta-
tion of the nineteenth century New York town-
house. Moreover, it is distinguished as one of the
"first modern city houses in the United States," the
first International Style residence in New York,
and probably the first residence in New York in
which structural glass-block and central air conditioning were employed (Figs. 107, 108, and 109). It
was designated an historic landmark in 1976 by the

Fig. 107. William Lescaze, William Lescaze house, 211
East Forty-eighth Street, New York, 1933–1934. Street
façade.

Fig. 108. William Lescaze, William Lescaze house, 211 East Forty-eighth Street, New York, 1933–1934. Garden façade.

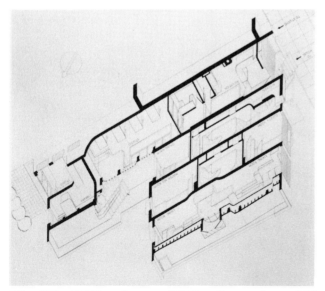

Fig. 109. William Lescaze, William Lescaze house, 211 East Forty-eighth Street, New York, 1933–1934. Plan.

Landmarks Preservation Commission.[1]

By highly imaginative planning, Lescaze was able to claim from a lot only a little over 16 feet wide by 100 feet deep a maximum amount of well lighted, conveniently organized, and aesthetically satisfying spaces for both residence and business, with private outdoor living spaces provided as well. The four-story, flat-roofed, smooth, white-stuccoed street façade was articulated by a blue lally column, blue enamel doors to the residence and office, carefully proportioned panels of glass-brick and -blocks at the first, third, and fourth floors, and a single, continuous strip of casement windows at the second floor.[2]

Various types of structural glass were specified according to their specific properties in relation to the function of the interior plan. Just below street level, and recessed to the plane of the façade of the original 1865 brownstone that the house replaced, is the entrance to Lescaze's office-reception room with drafting rooms extending beneath the residence and terraces almost to the rear of the lot. A solid glass-brick wall, specified for security and privacy, shields the office from the sights and sounds of the street yet allows natural light to penetrate.

As in its brownstone predecessor, a high stoop at the left side of the building, sheltered by a flat canti-levered hood, leads to the residence entrance. At this second-floor level, the kitchen and servants quarters are lighted by a band of clear glass in steel-framed casement and fixed sash which wrap around the curved corner of the stairwell wall. The dining room, on the private garden façade of this level, has access to the two-level walled-terraces through two wide glass doors in a wall of clear plate glass. The lower terrace provides a visual extension of the dining room to include a planting of flowers, a tree, and a pool. The upper terrace, which extends almost to the property line, provides a sunny outdoor living area. The garden wall is faced with a matt-glazed, light-gray brick like that of the garden façade of the house. Areas of vault-lights, later changed to tiles, were installed in the pavement of the terraces to bring light into the office and the drafting studios below.[3]

The guest room, on the third floor street façade, is shielded from the noise and view of the street by a vacuum glass-block wall and ventilated by two casement window openings set into it. The master bedroom on the garden facade of this level is distinguished by a curved wall that projects from the face of the building and admits the morning sun through a band of casement windows that provide a view of the Turtle Bay gardens to the east.

The living room, on the top floor, where it is the most isolated, extends the full depth and width of the house. The street end is opened to light but closed to sound, dirt, and the view of a nine-story apartment house across the street. It is also insulated against heat and cold by a wall of vacuum glass-block that is interrupted only by steel strips, which serve to strengthen the panel (Fig. 110). The garden end is open to the view through a wide band of fixed-sash and casement windows which allow ventilation when air conditioning is not necessary or desired.[4]

The house was significant for its introduction to New York, if not the United States, of a high-style architecture utilizing large areas of so-called "glass bricks," which Paul Scheerbart had prophesied in 1914 "make a wall material which may well become an interesting speciality of glass architecture."[5] Lescaze later explained:

> When we built our house in 1934, glass bricks had not yet been used in this country. Unbelievable but true. I had seen a few of them in Europe, and they seemed to me an excellent new material to do a job I was anxious to have done. They added to the amount of daylight without adding to the fuel bill, they let daylight through yet obscured the uninteresting view of the nine-story apartment house across the street, and they deadened street noises. An enterprising manufacturer agreed to make the first American glass blocks for us in his plant in Illinois. But what an epic battle we had with the Code: it lasted at least three months, back and forth. Three months of agony.[6]

Although the use of glass blocks was uncommon, yet not unknown in this country, there were many examples to be seen in Europe.[7] The foremost prototypes were Le Corbusier's apartment house at Boulogne sur Seine, built in 1932, and the remarkable Dalsace house, "Maison de Verre" of 1927–1932, by Pierre Chareau and Bernard Bijvoet, which had casement sash incorporated in its glass block façade, as does the Lescaze house. An event in its own time, the "Maison de Verre" was treated as a trend-setting structure in professional publications of the 1930s. In addition to these sources, by 1929 at least two publications featured the advantages to be gained by designing in glass. Konrad Werner Schulze's *Glas in der Architektur der Gegenwart* outlined glass brick building techniques, and Arthur Korn's *Glas im Bau und als Gebrauchsgegenstand* provided a catalogue of examples of glass architecture.[8]

The design of the Lescaze house was shaped by a second technical innovation, the installation of a central air conditioning system.[9] In the 1930s central air conditioning for commercial buildings was still in its infancy and was almost unheard of for private residences, finding its way into general use in the American home only in the 1950s.[10] The four major rooms of the Lescaze house—living room, dining room, master bedroom, and studio-office—were air-conditioned by Carrier's Nesbett System, one which cools and dehumidifies in the summer and warms and humidifies in the winter.[11]

As in his earlier interiors, Lescaze's house was elegantly finished with an accented neutral color scheme. All the furniture, with the exception of the piano and two Alvar Aalto bentwood chairs in the living room, was designed by Lescaze. It was typically characterized by the use of chrome, leather, mohair, and fine woods.[12] Unlike the bare-bulb and globe lighting tradition favored by the Bauhaus and Le Corbusier, indirect lighting, designed as an integral part of the building, was incorporated throughout the house. In the living room, a large, round, centrally located skylight glows with natural light in the daytime and artificial light at night. At the couch and at both ends of the fireplace, lighting is concealed in alcoves. At the desk and bookcase, incandescent bulbs are concealed behind narrow baffles. Direct lighting fixtures, designed by Lescaze, are located at the sofa and the reading chair. Over the dining table, Lescaze installed a suspended lighting trough of steel, which indirectly lighted the table by reflection from the ceiling. Lescaze concealed the guest-bedroom lighting in the headboard, and the master bedroom lighting behind a baffle over the headboard. The office reception room employs the Pass and Seymour lighting fixtures that Lescaze had designed for the PSFS.

Designed for simplicity in housekeeping, the house incorporates a dumb-waiter and an inter-room telephone system. In addition, the air conditioning reduces dust to a minimum, the metal furniture and finishes are nontarnishable, and the wood furniture is treated with an alcohol-proof finish. As George Daub, Lescaze's chief construction supervisor, wrote to Lescaze on 14 November 1933:

> There was not much point in building a building unless it was thoroughly modern from the point of view of equipment and living qualities, because we want to

Fig. 110. William Lescaze, William Lescaze house, 211 East Forty-eighth Street, New York, 1933–1934. Lescaze and glass-block wall of living room.

show our clients what we believe in, what we advocate, how the materials will wear, and to show them the job that this particular equipment accomplishes.[13]

Arts and Decoration magazine reported that "almost no one who has had the opportunity to inspect the Lescaze house from top to bottom goes away with his faith in the Traditional approach unshaken."[14] *Architectural Forum* speculated on the Lescaze house's economic and social implications to the city, noting that "it requires no prophet to see the great possibilities for the reclamation of much deteriorated housing if the slogan about walking to work can be amended to read, 'walk downstairs to work.'" For the ambitious Lescaze, this was a particularly satisfactory arrangement, for, as he wrote in a note to himself: "day on routine things, late PM, evenings and weekends for design."[15]

Lescaze's model was immediately convincing. Critic Lewis Mumford wrote in *The New Yorker:* "All in all, Mr. Lescaze has done a very useful piece of individual pioneering. I should not be surprised if his ingenious treatment of plot and site started a wave of renovation in old brownstones."[16] The use of glass block was quickly adopted by architect Morris B. Sanders, Jr., in his own house of 1934–1935 at 219 East Forty-ninth Street.[17]

Mumford's prophecy was to be realized in a series of distinguished New York town-houses that Lescaze designed in the thirties. Soon after the completion of his own house in 1934, Lescaze prepared plans for Mr. and Mrs. Raymond C. Kramer at 32 East Seventy-fourth Street (Fig. 111). Mrs. Kramer, a personal friend of the Lescazes, wanted her house to be as much like theirs as possible. Although numerous internal changes were made for the living requirements of the Kramer family, the façade, furniture, and interior finishes were similar to the Lescaze house.

Also for friends, Lescaze remodeled the interiors and designed the furniture for the Benjamin J. Buttenwieser town-house at 17 East Seventy-third Street. Completed in 1935, it was designed in the spirit of its predecessors, the Lescaze and Kramer houses. In it, as in the other houses, the interior was characterized by an understated elegance, neutral color scheme, rich woods, custom designed cabinetry, the division of space by furniture arrangement, and architectural lighting.

Although there was an unrealized town-house project of 1935 for Howard Froelich, the fourth and

Fig. 111. William Lescaze, Raymond C. Kramer house, 32 East Seventy-fourth Street, New York, 1934–1935. Street façade.

last of Lescaze's rebuilt New York town-houses was that designed in 1940 for Mr. and Mrs. Edward A. Norman at 124 East Seventieth Street (Fig. 112).[18] They, like the Kramers, admired Lescaze's house and wanted one of similar character.

After working through several preliminary schemes, Lescaze finally faced this four-story house with a grime-resistant surface—dark gray glazed brick, white marble, and white glazed brick. The change from a white stucco street façade, used at the Lescaze and Kramer houses, to glazed brick was probably inspired by the difficulty in maintaining the former in the city. This assumption is supported by the fact that by 1940 Lescaze had painted his own house dark gray with a white entrance reveal.[19] By the time of the Norman house, the glass block was handled more decoratively than functionally. Instead of being the wall, large glass block panels only surround areas of clear, movable and fixed sash at each level. Designed for the special needs of a professional writer, the plan is also very different from those of the Lescaze and Kramer

Fig. 112. William Lescaze, Edward A. Norman house, 124 East Seventieth Street, New York, 1940–1941. Street façade.

houses. Completed in November 1941, the Norman house was included in the 1944 Museum of Modern Art exhibition of outstanding architecture and awarded the New York State Association of Architects Certificate of Merit Award for 1947.[20]

The most challenging commission that Lescaze received in the thirties was for a very special building type—a radio studio for the Columbia Broadcasting System. While most industries were foundering during the depression, the radio broadcasting industry, which started operation in 1921, was beginning to boom.[21] Although the growth of radio broadcasting was one of the most rapid in the history of American industry, no one knew in the beginning whether the future of radio would be "the novelty of a rapid and rather mysterious form of communication, or as it has turned out to be—an educational and entertainment institution, developed on highly commercial lines."[22] For this reason and because of the financial depression, the industry adapted itself to growth and change in

the most economical fashion possible. First came the inevitable makeshifts—legitimate theaters, garages, and other existing buildings converted to broadcasting studios.

In 1934 the Columbia Broadcasting System, embarking upon a period of unprecedented expansion, leased the empty Avon Theater at 251 West Forty-fifth Street, rechristened it the CBS Radio Playhouse, and commissioned Lescaze to effect, with a minimum of expense, the necessary remodeling to provide seating for large studio-audiences. In these first reconstructions a number of highly ingenious solutions to the numerous mechanical and acoustical problems of radio broadcasting were worked out. In this one, two units—one for controls, the other for participants—were erected on opposite sides of the proscenium arch. They were built of plywood and composition board, with double windows set in metal frames, slanted to prevent reflections and glare. Extensions of the units covered the lower part of the proscenium arch and connected them with the front of the balcony, giving the effect that considerably more remodeling had been done than was actually the case. Curved screens, designed to correct acoustical defects, were set at the edge of the stage. Two clocks, Stand-by and On-The-Air signs, and the CBS logo, all designed by Lescaze, punctuated the smooth, white wall treatment.[23]

In a similar manner, Lescaze remodeled New York's Hammerstein Manhattan Opera House for CBS's use as a radio theater. In it, however, with Dr. E. E. Free as consultant acoustical engineer, Lescaze replaced the screens of the type used at the Avon with an acoustically regulating three-part canopy projecting from the proscenium arch toward the audience. He also improved the earlier design of the clocks and Stand-By and On-The-Air signs. The editors of *Architectural Forum*, obviously impressed, published in their October 1936 issue that "the somber and dramatic shell, historically memorable in the annals of New York, contrasted with the dynamic expressions of new forms and clean colors, invites the attention of the artist and the philosopher alike."[24]

Lescaze next redesigned the main CBS studios and offices at 485 Madison Avenue in New York.[25] These were followed a few months later by plans for an entirely new CBS building to be built in New York and to be designed specifically for the purpose of radio broadcasting activities. Never realized, the project was dated December 1935 (Fig.

Fig. 113. William Lescaze, CBS office building project, New York, 1935. Perspective rendering.

113). A bold departure from any of Lescaze's earlier work, this building was composed of two large, plain, rectangular blocks, one raised on piers above and at right angles to the other. The elevated five-story block was sheathed with curtain walls of glass on all four sides; the lower four-story block was predominately opaque with two bands of glass on the entrance façade. The sheer planes of the volumes were relieved only by a cantilevered hood at the entrance and the joints of the sheathing material.

In the 1936 Chicago and the 1937 San Francisco studios of CBS, Lescaze continued the development of standard forms, repeating many of the designs and treatments used in the New York studios—an example of the importance of design in establishing corporate identity. Remodeling and reorganization of existing structures did not, however, remain a satisfactory solution to the industry's ever-increasing technological and spatial requirements.

In early 1936, shortly after CBS had acquired the facilities of station KNX in Hollywood with a view to expanding it into a key station for the origination of a chain of programs on the West Coast, Lescaze was called in to discuss the possibilities of adapting the existing facilities to achieve the ideal conditions desired. A few months of study revealed that instead of remodeling the old premises, a new CBS Pacific Coast center should be built in order to accommodate properly the specific problems of radio broadcasting by creating architecture and equipment as acoustically perfect as was technically possible at the time. Thus, within fifteen years from the inception of commercial broadcasting in America, Lescaze was instrumental in evolving a new building type designed for a very specific and

technologically demanding function.[26] His CBS buildings for station KNX in the Hollywood district of Los Angeles, designed in 1936–1937 and completed in 1938, were the first buildings in the United States to be designed solely for radio programming, performing, and broadcasting (Fig. 114 and 115).

Fig. 114. William Lescaze with Earl T. Heitschmidt, Columbia Broadcasting System, Station KNX, Hollywood District, Los Angeles, California, 1936–1938. View of four-building complex from Sunset Boulevard.

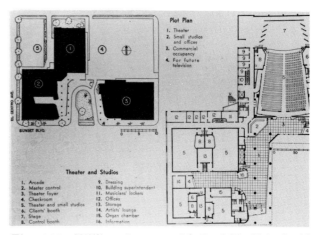

Fig. 115. William Lescaze with Earl T. Heitschmidt, Columbia Broadcasting System, Station KNX, Hollywood District, Los Angeles, California, 1936–1938. Plot plan and first floor plan of studio-office-theater group.

The Hollywood buildings were located on the site of the old Christie Comedy studios on Sunset Boulevard between Gower and El Centro Streets, where the first film studios sprang up. Six preliminary sketches indicate some of the solutions proposed by Lescaze and Earl T. Heitschmidt (associate architect) for the various requirements that were set up and subsequently changed.[27] All were plain white geometric masses relieved only by sharply incised fenestration and a sans serif CBS logo. Scheme six, the penultimate design, with drawings dated August and September 1936, was modified in the final plans of May 1937 by incorporating *pilotis* and by replacing a glass curtain wall on the office building with ribbon windows.[28]

Occupying most of an entire block, the reinforced concrete buildings enclosed three sides of a landscaped patio facing Sunset Boulevard. Retaining the separate elements which characterized the earliest schemes, the main building complex was divided into three structural masses: a rectangular five-story office building, a low, partly one- and partly two-story studio building, and a theater building, devoted to seating over 1,000 public theater-goers. After plans had been under way for six months, CBS decided to develop the rest of the property. A two-story business building was erected which made possible the courtyard between it and the main building complex and provided space for CBS management, a talent agency, a restaurant, a bank, shops, and a possible future expansion of the CBS facilities. A complex building program was, thus, compartmentalized into just four large autonomous but related volumes.

The office-studio-theater group is particularly interesting. A plan to provide for complex circulation requirements, an earthquake-resistant structural design, and acoustical control were the noteworthy features of the structures. The fundamental problem in plan was to provide for efficient circulation of traffic within the buildings, particularly on the first floor where large numbers of visitors, actors, guest stars, musicians, song pluggers, salesmen, advertising agency people, technicians, and movers of heavy equipment had to be accommodated. The studio unit was provided with a staff corridor, completely encircling the building, which did not cross the circulation of the public or office traffic at any point. For visitors there was a large entrance lobby featuring a glass-enclosed master control room and an uninterrupted view through a glass wall into the courtyard.

Lescaze's scheme to resist earthquake forces included the combination of a tier-type office structure with the exceptional rigidity of a bearing-wall structure of the windowless concrete box that formed the adjacent studio building. The slender columns of the office building became structurally

advantageous, for they could act as a "hinge" to throw seismic forces into the rigid walls and roof of the studio block. The theater portion remained a separate unit, having an eight-inch wide separation joint which completely detached it from the other structures. At the exterior walls, this joint was closed by a stainless steel plate.[29]

The acoustical design was based on several objectives—the reduction of noise levels in the studios, the elimination of multiple echoes between parallel walls, and the control of reverberation and room resonance.[30] Sound insulation and isolation were attained by several means: separating the floors, walls, and ceilings of each studio from the main structure of the building by means of flexible supports, clips, and hangers, resulting in a "room-within-a-room" structure; double-door entrances to the studios; isolating rotating or vibrating machinery by means of flexible supports; a honeycomb structure of absorptive cells in the ventilating ducts; acoustical plaster in all corridors, lobbies, and public spaces in the vicinity of studios and in the theater; walls of ten percent slope and sound absorptive materials in a particular ratio to reflective materials in the studios.[31] The three-unit studio complex (excluding the business building) was built at a cost of about $1,500,000.[32]

Like the PSFS building, Lescaze designed much of the furniture and equipment for the CBS building and left his mark with both the machine imagery of stainless steel and the Déco elegance of handsome wood surfaces on the interiors. On its completion in April 1938, the complex was described by CBS Vice-President Thornburgh as an "ideal radio workshop."[33] Lescaze was satisfied with it, too. Writing to Mrs. Mabel Dodge Luhan, at the time of the building's opening, he commented: "By the way, I hope you'll have a chance to see that building sometime. I am very pleased with the way it has turned out."[34] In 1939 Lescaze received an honor award from the southern California chapter of the American Institute of Architects for its design. Lescaze's association with the CBS lasted until 1949. With only minor changes, the complex is still in use, housing KNX News Radio, KNX/FM Radio, KNXT Television, and Columbia Records.[35]

In 1939, Lescaze returned to the PSFS *parti* for the design of Washington, D.C.'s first modern building of any importance—the two million dollar, reinforced concrete Longfellow office building at

Fig. 116. William Lescaze, Longfellow Building, Connecticut Avenue at Rhode Island Avenue, Washington, D.C., 1939–1941. Axonometric sketch, 13 August 1939.

Fig. 117. William Lescaze, Longfellow Building, Connecticut Avenue at Rhode Island Avenue, Washington, D.C., 1939–1941. View showing west and south elevations.

Rhode Island and Connecticut Avenues.[36] Like the PSFS, designed ten years earlier, its first scheme consisted of a large office block interlocked with a separately articulated service spine (Fig. 116). As completed, the spine is invisible on the exterior, yet, recalling the 1930 model for PSFS is the exploitation of the cantilever and unrelieved piles of window bands. Balconies on the west side were designed to serve as sun screens (Fig. 117).[37] In composition, finish, and detail it did not begin to equal its prototype. Yet, its contemporary critics, on its completion in 1941, asserted that "Lescaze's Longfellow Building would stand out in any city as a first-rate piece of work; against the Washington background its effect is explosive."[38] Offering the supreme compliment, Joseph Hudnut, former Dean of the Harvard Graduate School of Design, called it "quite the best building in town." He hoped that when it was finished it would be taken over for the sessions of the Supreme Court because "it would help to restore the somewhat faded dignity of that harassed body."[39]

Although Lescaze had important commissions throughout the thirties, modernism was generally making little progress in the United States. *Fortune* magazine reported in October 1935 that there were no more than fifty residences, two large office buildings, a dozen theaters, three schools, four small clubs, and two airports in the country that could be equated with European modernism and that the only architects involved with the new style in any frequency were Frank Lloyd Wright, Richard J. Neutra, and Lescaze.[40] Demonstrating the struggle that architects had in developing the International Style in America, even in the late thirties, are the evolution of Lescaze's Brooklyn Children's Museum project and the justifications given for the winning entries of three important architectural competitions.

Because of his success with the Brooklyn Museum's Wilbour Memorial Library of 1933, the next year Lescaze remodeled the Brooklyn Museum's ground floor and was commissioned to design a new children's museum. The projected one-million-dollar museum was to have been built on Brooklyn Avenue between Prospect Place and St. Marks Avenue to replace the 1867 Italianate mansion then housing the museum in Brower Park. Lescaze's first known scheme, dated 6 February 1935, contrasted an asymmetrical composition of large one- and two-story window-banded rectilinear blocks raised on columns with a low, more child-scaled curved entrance pavilion (Fig. 118).[41] The second scheme, dated 1 August 1935 and September 1935, shows a ground-born plan unified on the cross axis to create a nearly symmetrical organi-

Fig. 118. William Lescaze, Children's Museum project, Brooklyn, New York, 1934–1937. Perspective rendering of first scheme, 6 February 1935.

Fig. 119. William Lescaze, Children's Museum project, Brooklyn, New York, 1934–1937. Perspective rendering of second scheme, September 1935 (American Architect 147 [December 1935]: 17).

Fig. 120. William Lescaze, Children's Museum project, Brooklyn, New York, 1934–1937. Perspective rendering of third scheme, 13 October 1936.

zation of six wings. The asymmetrical entrance façade was delineated with window bands, smooth limestone facing, and an entrance portal supported on thin columns and announced by a large mural. The scheme was approved on 13 August 1935 by the Municipal Art Commission of the City of New York, the Brooklyn Institute of Arts and Sciences, the Department of Parks of the City of New York, and the Department of Buildings of the Borough of Brooklyn.[42] Seeking $532,400 from the City of New

Fig. 121. William Lescaze, Children's Museum project, Brooklyn, New York, 1934–1937. Perspective rendering of fourth scheme.

York and $436,600 from WPA funds for the museum's structure, the trustees of the Brooklyn Museum submitted the plans to the Allotment Board in Washington for approval. They were not endorsed (Fig. 119).[43]

The plans were revised still further under the direction of Park Commissioner Robert Moses.[44] The third scheme, drawings dated 16 September 1936 and 13 October 1936, show a similar composition but with emphasis on the heightened central entrance block, approaching an almost symmetrical arrangement (Fig. 120).[45] Probably in a last effort to get Washington's approval, these plans were again reworked to render them closer to the tradition of the thirties' "stripped" classicism with latent Déco decoration. The fourth scheme shows the central entrance block with a vertically disposed zig-zag surface, a weighty hood protecting the entrance, and sculpture panels surmounting the doors and decorating the window bands. This design was approved by the Municipal Art Commission by 16 September 1937 (Fig. 121).[46] In two years, Lescaze's proposals had moved from an asymmetrical, horizontal, volumetric scheme raised on *pilotis* to a nearly symmetrical, decorated, massive structure— a compromise lying between the modern and traditional ideals of that time.

Although Edward C. Blum, president of the museum, predicted that "we shall be able to secure appropriations to erect the new building promptly," the funds were not forthcoming.[47] Perhaps it was just as well that the last scheme was not built, for it would have been entirely different from Lescaze's architectural intent and an undistinguished compromise.[48]

The architectural competitions of the late thirties might have been particularly propitious occasions in which to promote modern solutions to architectural problems. But such solutions were seldom selected as the winners even at the end of the decade; witness three competitions of the period—the Oregon State Capitol Building of 1936, the Wheaton College Art Center of 1938, and the Goucher College Campus Plan of the same year. Lescaze entered all three and placed in none.

His entry for the $2½ million Oregon State Capitol Building competition offered an intelligent and handsome solution to a complex problem. The two main areas of governmental activity were expressed in different and separate forms—a tall, seven-story office block for the business of the executive branch of the state department, and a low, partly two- and partly three-story building for the business of the legislature.[49] The two units were connected by a glass corridor (Fig. 122). The legislative unit was composed of three major volumes expressing the functions of housing the legislative assembly chambers, the committee offices, and the legislative offices. The plan separated daily from intermittent activities and public from private activity by a composition of spaced pavilions, which provided ease of circulation, economy of maintenance, and provision for expansion.

The exteriors of the two units were typically expressive of Lescaze's International Style vocabulary. Both were finished with smooth white wall surfaces and large areas of glass. The tall executive block was banded with windows wrapping one corner, recalling the treatment of his Hollywood CBS office building, which was designed in the same year. The long, low legislative unit was dominated by a central glass-walled volume projecting over the entrance, with bands of windows extending across

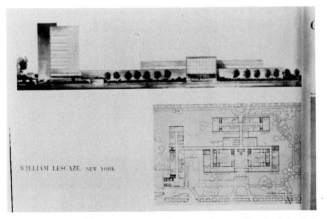

*Fig. 122. William Lescaze, Oregon State Capital building competition, 1936. Elevation rendering of principal façade (*Architectural Forum *65 [*July 1936*]:n.p.).*

the wings. This was not unlike the third scheme for the Brooklyn Children's Museum, also designed in the same year. Flat roofs, an over-all asymmetrical composition, and no applied ornamentation of any kind rendered the idiom complete.

The Oregon jury announced the winner of the competition—Trowbridge, Livingston, and Francis Keally Associates of New York—and five award-winning "mention" entries, out of a field of 123, after only two days of deliberation.[50] In reporting on the jury's choice, Walter Thompson of Philadelphia, one of the two architect members of the jury, stated only that Oregon had made a most "fortunate choice." David Allison of Los Angeles, the other architect member of the jury, cited the winning entry as "the outstanding one presented." Supreme Court Justice John L. Rand called the scheme "beautiful and artistic without gaudiness," while Justice Henry Beam said only "grand." The *Oregon Journal* reported that the winning design was "beautiful without being ornate; useful without being extravagant."[51] The jury chairman defended the winning entry with: "It looks like a capitol . . . and we like a lobby."[52] The minutes of the jury stated that one of the architect-members of the jury justified the selection with:

> Always there is a great deal of modernistic tendency. You know we have had a World's Fair in Chicago that was very modern, and that was echoed in a number of drawings here. We have kept some of the modern thought subjects on the back wall. . . . In the winner we feel you have something that has a modern flavor, based upon good, sound traditional Greek thought. . . .[53]

Thus, with little apparent enlightened critical judgment, jury, justices, and newspapermen alike sanctioned an aesthetic stance somewhere between modernism and traditionalism which was to replace an old neo-classical building with a new neo-classical building, and to continue the tradition set by the nation's capital.

Although Lescaze did not place among the award-winning entries, all of which were either in the 1930s' neo-classical modern style or in a colonial idiom, his scheme was recognized by its publication in *Architectural Record* and *Architectural Forum*.[54]

The 1938 Wheaton College Art Center competition, sponsored by the Museum of Modern Art and *Architectural Forum*, was organized to "present architecturally as well as educationally the most forward looking ideas of today."[55] Even with that specific objective and an illustrious group of specially invited participants—Walter Gropius and Marcel Breuer, Richard Neutra, Maynard Lyndon and Eberle Smith, and William Lescaze—the jury awarded first place to Richard Bennett and Caleb Hornbostel, whose entry leaned strongly toward the thirties' neo-classically flavored modernism. Gropius and Breuer's more elegant, not to mention Internationalist, design placed second. Lescaze's entry is unknown.

A few months after the Wheaton College competition was announced, Goucher College organized a competition to select an architect to prepare a general development plan for its Towson, Maryland, campus and to design and supervise the construction of one principal building. Again, Lescaze was invited to participate. In the manner of his late thirties' houses and small public buildings, Lescaze's was a modernist design enriched by a partial stone facing (Fig. 123). The jury awarded the first prize to John C. B. Moore and Robert S. Hutchins of New York for a design that might best be characterized as creatively eclectic. As in the Wheaton College Competition entry, the more modernist scheme (by Eliel and Eero Saarinen) was awarded second place.[56] Apparently the judges of the Wheaton and Goucher competitions wished to recognize the newest ideas but were not brave enough, or for some other reason, unable to build them. Nor were the critics ready to accept them. A reviewer of the Museum of Modern Art's important 1938 Bauhaus exhibition wrote that the furniture shown was "stark and uninteresting," the pottery and textiles made only the "mildest appeal," the paintings were "dull abstractions," and the architecture was "most disappointing of all."[57]

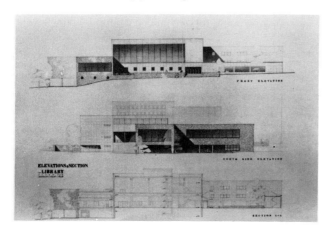

Fig. 123. William Lescaze, Goucher College Campus competition, 1938. Elevation and section rendering of library.

At the turn of the decade the European modern movement was more readily acceptable, but not without change. Some of its early expressions were transformed into a new image, tempered and transformed by regional traditions—the wood-frame vernacular of New England domestic building, the West Coast redwood variation of the International Style, and Frank Lloyd Wright's "Usonian" houses. Lescaze's work changed as well.

NOTES

1. Ellen Kramer, "Designation Report," Landmarks Preservation Commission, 27 January 1976, No. 1 LP-0898, WELA.

2. The rendering of the Lescaze house, dated August 1933 (probably the first scheme), shows no glass brick fenestration and a wall facing of either scored stucco or some other material laid up in large blocks.

3. See undated, untitled press release (typescript), WELA.

4. In 1941 Lescaze bought the neighboring town house, No. 209, and remodeled its top floor as a bedroom and playroom for the Lescazes' son, Lee Adrien, born 8 December 1938. Its access is from the stair at the fourth floor living room level.

5. Paul Scheerbart, *Glasarchitektur* (Berlin, 1914), quoted in Dennis Sharp, trans., *Glass Architecture* (New York: Praeger Pubs., 1972), p. 50.

6. William Lescaze, *On Being an Architect* (New York: G. P. Putnam's Sons, 1942), pp. 205–206. Lescaze was mistaken about glass bricks not having been used before in America. Reyner Banham, in his *Well-Tempered Environment* (London: The Architectural Press, 1969, p. 201), reports that J. R. Davidson was one of the first to use regular commercial glass bricks, back-lighted, as part of the exterior scheme of his own Los Angeles office, built in 1925. Although Lescaze states that a firm in Illinois manufactured these glass "bricks," the Macbeth-Evans Company, founded in 1899 in Pittsburgh, is credited (in a two-page advertisement featuring the Lescaze house in the December 1934 issue of *Architectural Forum*) with their manufacture for the Structural Glass Corporation. An undated, untitled typescript, written for a publicity release on the Lescaze house, ca. 1934 or 1935, WELA, reports that the glass bricks were provided by the Structural Glass Brick Company.

7. See Banham, *The Well-Tempered Environment*, p. 164; Dennis Sharp, *A Visual History of Twentieth-Century Architecture* (New York: New York Graphic Society Ltd., 1972), p. 124. Some European structures utilizing glass block, built prior to this time, were: the orthopedic clinic of Dr. Van Neck, 53 rue Waffelaerts, St. Gilles, Brussels, Belgium, designed by Antoine Pompe in 1910; Bruno Taut's Glass House (utilizing Luxfer prisms) for the 1914 Werkbund Exhibition in Cologne; Mohr's City Hospital, Potsdam; Max Taut's Publishing House, Berlin; Otto Haesler's School in Celle; the Paris Werkbund Exhibition of 1930 by Gropius, Breuer, Bayer, and Moholy-Nagy; and Le Corbusier and Jeanneret's House at Geneva, Switzerland of 1932.

8. Konrad Werner Schulze, *Glas in der Architektur der Gegenwart* (Stuttgart: Wissenschaftlicher Verlag Dr. Zaugg and Co., 1929), particularly pp. 47–66 which outline the Luxfer, Solfac, and Keppler glass brick designs; Arthur Korn, *Glass in Modern Architecture* (London, 1969), originally published as *Glas im Bau und als Gebrauchsgegenstand* (Berlin: Pollak, 1929). Neither of these publications illustrate plain, unprismed or unpatterned glass blocks, however.

9. Carrier had installed one in his own house in 1929; see Banham, *The Well-Tempered Environment*, p. 164.

10. See Banham, *The Well-Tempered Environment*, p. 183; M. Ingles, *Willis Carrier, Father of Air Conditioning* (Garden City, New York, 1952); Realto Cherne and Chester Nelson, "Preliminary Planning for Air Conditioning in the Design of Modern Buildings," *Architectural Record* 75 (June 1934): 536–548.

11. William E. Lescaze House Description (typescript), WELA; Daub to Lescaze, 14 November 1933, WELA.

12. William E. Lescaze House Description (typescript), WELA.

13. Daub to Lescaze, 14 November 1933, WELA.

14. Herbert Williams, "The Home of an Uncompromising Modernist," *Arts and Decoration* 51 (April 1940): 41.

15. "City House of William Lescaze, New York," *Architectural Forum* 61 (December 1934): 388; Lescaze, note to himself (handwritten), WELA.

16. Lewis Mumford, "The Sky Line," *The New Yorker*, 15 September 1934, p. 101.

17. See "House for Morris B. Sanders," *Architectural Forum* 64 (March 1936): 157–166. Also note 212 East 49th Street.

18. A photograph of the Froelich rendering is in "Photographs of Renderings" (Scrapbook), Package 2, WELA. Dorothy Norman is author of several books on Alfred Stieglitz and on symbolic art and Jawaharlal Nehru.

19. Williams, "Uncompromising Modernist," p. 6.

20. Certificate of Merit, WELA.

21. Bureau of the Census, *Historical Statistics of the United States Colonial Times to 1970*, Part II (Washington, D.C.: U.S. Government Printing Office, 1975), p. 792.

22. William Lescaze, "Plant for CBS—Hollywood," *Architectural Concrete*, 4, no. 3, n.d. (ca. 1938), p. 3.

23. Illustrations were published in *Architectural Forum* 63 (August 1935): 721–722.

24. See "Columbia Broadcasting Studio." *Architectural Forum* 65 (October 1936): 372–373, for complete details.

25. Illustrations were published in *Architectural Forum* 64 (June 1936): 479–483.

26. See William Lescaze, "Radio Stations," *Forms and Functions of Twentieth Century Architecture*, ed. Talbot Hamlin (New York: Columbia University Press, 1952), 4: 169–189.

27. Sketches of schemes 1, 4, 6, and the final design were published in *Architectural Forum* 68 (June 1938): 454.

28. Two drawings of scheme 6, dated 16 and 18 August 1936, and the final elevation drawing are in the Royal Institute of British Architects Drawings Collection, London, nos. 8/j/25, 1-5 and 125. A photograph of the 14 September 1936 preliminary rendering is in "Photographs of Renderings" (Scrapbook), Package 2, WELA.

29. Fred N. Severud of New York was the structural engineer; S. B. Barnes of Los Angeles was the associate structural engineer.

30. Acoustical consultant was Dr. Vern O. Knudsen of the University of California, Los Angeles.

31. Structural information is from "Design for Broadcasting," *Engineering News-Record* 122 (5 January 1939): 12–15; Lescaze, "Plant for CBS—Hollywood," pp. 4–7.

32. Commission CBS, Station KNX (typescript), 13 April 1937, WELA. Another typescript, KNX-515, lists the cost exclusive of the business building as $400,000. *The Southwest Builder and Contractor* 91 (27 May 1938): 14 reported that the cost was about $700,000 excluding equipment. "The New Home of the Columbia Broadcasting System," *California Arts and Architecture* 54 (July 1938): 28, published the cost at $1,750,000. A typescript of 14 March 1942, WELA, lists the cost at $1,250,000.

33. "The New Home of the Columbia Broadcasting System," p. 29.

34. Lescaze to Mable Dodge Luhan, 17 May 1938, WELA.

35. William D. White to the author, 3 September 1976.

36. "Regarding Longfellow Building, Washington, D.C., #617," (typescript), 24 March 1942, WELA. Drawings dated 13 August 1939 and September 1939 are in Box 2, Folder 6, WELA. Drawings dated 14 August 1939 are no. 8/j/23, RIBA Drawings Collection, London.

37. In the design stage, the building was tested on the Loomis "sun machine" to check the effect of the sun on the air conditioning system. Lescaze to Mrs. George Baltus, 3 November 1966, WELA.

38. "Longfellow Building, Washington, D.C.," *Architectural Forum* 74 (June 1941): 396.

39. Joseph Hudnut to Lescaze, 29 January 1941, WELA.

40. "The House That Works" I, *Fortune* 40 (October 1935): 59–60.

41. Photographs of elevations and perspective renderings are in "Photographs of Renderings" (scrapbook), Package 2, WELA.

42. The approval is noted on the first floor plan, Avery Library, Columbia University; *Report for the Year 1935, Museums of the Brooklyn Institute of Arts and Sciences* (Brooklyn, New York, 1936), p. 108.

43. *Report for the Year 1935, Museums of the Brooklyn Institute of Arts and Sciences*, p. 108.

44. "Children's Museum, Brooklyn," *New York Herald Tribune*, 16 September 1937, WELA.

45. WELA, The Avery Library card catalogue, Columbia University, lists a revised plan of 16 September 1936 as "missing."

46. "Design Approved for New Museum," *New York Times*, 6 November 1937; *New York Herald Tribune*, 16 September 1937, clippings (scrapbook) hand-dated and unverifiable, WELA.

47. *New York Herald Tribune*, 16 September 1937, WELA. The new Children's Museum, by Hardy, Holtzman, and Pfeiffer opened in 1977.

48. See Ada Louise Huxtable, "Architectural Drawings as Art," *New York Times*, 12 June 1977, "Arts and Leisure," p. 25.

49. The heights of these buildings, judged from unscaled elevation drawings, may not be accurate.

50. The jury consisted of Carl Gould, technical advisor; Walter Thompson, Philadelphia architect; David Allison, Los Angeles architect; T. H. Banfield and Mrs. Gordon Vorhees, members of the Capitol Commission; E. B. MacNaughton, banker and chairman of the jury. "Oregon State Capitol Competition; Winning Design by Trowbridge and Livingston and Francis Keally, with five of the runner-up designs," *American Architect* 149 (July 1936): 27–34.

51. All quotations above are cited in "All Not Quiet on the Western Front," *Architectural Record* 8 (August 1936): 76.

52. Ibid., p. 13.

53. Ibid., p. 15.

54. See "Oregon State Capitol Competition," *Architectural Forum* 65 (July 1936): 10; "All Not Quiet on the Western Front," p. 76.

55. *The Bulletin of the Museum of Modern Art*, No. 2 5 (February 1938): 2–3; "Competition to Select an Architect for Proposed Art Center for Wheaton College," *Architectural Forum* 68 (February 1938): 6a–6d.

56. Photographs of Lescaze's plans are in Picture Box No. 3, WELA. Third place went to Fred G. Frost, Sr. and Jr., New York, and fourth to John A. Thompson and Gerald Holmes of Thompson, Homes and Converse, Inc., New York.

57. A. Conger Goodyear, *The Museum of Modern Art: The First Ten Years* (New York: Museum of Modern Art, 1943), p. 70, quoting "R. C.," *Herald Tribune*, 11 December 1938.

6

Post-Partnership Years: International Modernism in Transition, 1934–1940

IN CONTRAST TO THE RATIONALISM OF LESCAZE'S early thirties work, by mid-decade some of it was transformed by a variety of building materials, textured surfaces, color, and complexity of form, "extending and loosening the sanctions" of the International Style to become more "domesticated, vernacularized, diversified, and adapted to popular taste."[1]

Actually, Lescaze had experimented with this aesthetic as early as 1931 when he employed textured siding and a picturesque composition for the Psi Upsilon Fraternity house project at Dartmouth College (Fig. 124). Breaking with the cubic, pure white volumes of the International Style was Lescaze's Spreter studio and garage of 1934, built in

Fig. 125. *William Lescaze, Roy F. Spreter studio and garage, Conshohocken State Road at Mill Creek Road, Lower Merion Township, Pennsylvania, 1934. View in landscape.*

Lower Merion Township, Pennsylvania, for the illustrator Roy F. Spreter, notable for his Camel cigarette advertisements and later as a portraitist (Figs. 125 and 126). The plain geometry, subtle curves, and clear expression of functions that typified Lescaze's earlier work were retained in the Spreter studio, only now the form was made more complex. The typically planar, white, stucco walls were juxtaposed with contrasting texture, color, and mass of native stone—yet clearly and separately delineated as stone garage and stucco studio. Lescaze's specification of stone in combination with stucco and greater complexity of form in the Spreter studio was probably not solely due to an avant-garde aesthetic sensibility but to a combination of idealism and practicality. The first rendering of the

Fig. 124. *William Lescaze, Psi Upsilon Fraternity House project, Dartmouth College, Hanover, New Hampshire, 1931. Perspective rendering.*

Fig. 126. William Lescaze, Roy F. Spreter studio and garage, Conshohocken State Road at Mill Creek Road, Lower Merion Township, Pennsylvania, 1934. View from garage side.

Fig. 127. William Lescaze, Roy F. Spreter studio and garage, Conshohocken State Road at Mill Creek Road, Lower Merion Township, Pennsylvania, 1934. View of studio corner.

Fig. 128. William Lescaze, Roy F. Spreter studio and garage, Conshohocken State Road at Mill Creek Road, Lower Merion Township, Pennsylvania, 1934. View at stair corner and end of garage and studio.

studio, dated 8 July 1933, indicated an all stucco-surfaced building.[2] Lescaze later reported that the stone taken from the excavation was used for economy and that the form resulted from the practical considerations of utilizing the old barn road for easy access to the garages and, at the same time, providing a northern exposure for the studio above.[3] Nevertheless, Lescaze capitalized on the situation. Probably his most Corbusian work, the Spreter studio stone work recalls Le Corbusier's at the Madame de Mandrot house at Le Pradet (1930–1931), and the Swiss Students' hostel in Paris (1930–1932); the corner-window evokes Le Corbusier's skylight in the Ozenfant studio of 1922 (Figs. 127 and 128).

Similar to the Spreter studio and garage was the larger Garret A. Hobart III house and studio built at Tuxedo Park, New York, in 1938. The massing of the Hobart studio was oriented at a slight angle to the main block of the house in almost the same way that the Spreter garage was oriented to its studio, but this time for no apparent pragmatic reason (Fig. 129). Again, stone from the site was used for the first floor of the house and the entire two-story sculpture studio. The second floor of the house was finished with white stucco. A brick terrace laid in a herring-bone pattern, a Renaissance Revival balustrade at the edge of the promontory overlooking the lake, and elaborate stairs descending to the formal gardens below—all retained from the earlier building on the site—were further evidence of the acceptability of the enrichment of the International Style by color, pattern, form, and texture.[4]

The demand for large country houses was, however, something of an exception to the widespread need in the mid-thirties for low-cost commercial manufacture of prefabricated housing. In 1935, *Architectural Forum* noted 33 available prefabrication systems.[5] The depression caused the greatest effort in American housing to be directed toward the design of the less-than-$5,000 house. The August 1935 and February 1936 issues of the *Architectural Record* were entirely devoted to the subject of low- and moderate-cost housing. These were not the multiple-unit projects like the Europeans were building, but small, single-family detached houses. By the end of 1936, it was reported in the *Architectural Forum* that "not only was it [low-cost housing]

Fig. 129. William Lescaze, Garret A. Hobart III house and studio, Tuxedo Park, New York, 1938. Entrance view.

the largest building boom; it was pretty nearly the whole boom all by itself."[6]

Purdue University's housing research project, organized in 1935, contributed to the design and construction of the needed small houses. Nine houses costing less than $5,000 were to be built and studied to determine how costs could be reduced and how low-cost houses could be improved in plan, construction, and equipment. Each of the houses was to be designed with a different basic construction representing materials and methods then available. The stucco surface was all but abandoned. In 1937, it was reported in the *Architectural Record* that the first five houses—those built of wood, of steel-frame and prefabricated panels, of steel, of reinforced concrete, and of wood-frame and stucco—had been completed.[7] Lescaze's scheme for Rostone panels (a man-made stone composed chiefly of shale, alkaline earths, and a high percentage of stone chips) bolted

Fig. 130. William Lescaze, Vincent K. Cates house, Melrose, Massachusetts, 1935. Angle view showing street façades.

to a steel frame was among those that remained untried.[8]

In the same year Lescaze designed a "small house" for Vincent K. Cates of Melrose, Massachusetts (Fig. 130). Cates, an engineer from the West Coast, was familiar with modern design there, and had seen Lescaze's work in a magazine. He asked Lescaze if he could design an inexpensive house.[9] At a cost of $7,200, Lescaze's solution was a modestly scaled, compact, three-bedroom, wood-framed house complete with built-in bookcases and storage cabinets. Because the house was to be sited on a small suburban lot, Lescaze organized the plan for privacy for both indoor and outdoor living areas. The service spaces were located on the street side, and the living room and bedroom decks were placed on the garden side. Only one window opened to the entrance (street) façade. High, long fences provided privacy for the garden and the service yard. They also offered a bold horizontal line to the simple, rectilinear composition of the house, which relied on its proportioning in relation to the fences and the window openings for its compositional success. Its crisp, cubic forms, strip windows, blue lally column, and free plan marked the house as Internationalist. Yet, its painted white clapboards and board fence acknowledged the regionalism of New England. While the "austere lines" of this modern house were softened by the texture and shadow of clapboards, it retained the graphic tautness of the purist mode of the International Style.

The media offered mixed reactions. The *Boston Evening Transcript* reported that the Cates house was shocking to a Boston suburb accustomed to traditional architecture.[10] Yet, only a month later, the *Melrose* (Mass.) *Leader* claimed that although the house had caused "no end of comment . . . new visitors have come to appreciate the simplicity and practicality of the structure."[11] *House Beautiful* magazine supported the project by stating that "modern design need not be limited to city skyscrapers nor enormous mansions."[12]

The Cates house was but the first of a series of minor works in wood, brick, and stone designed by Lescaze. A similar, but slightly freer composition was built in Rochester, New York, for his old Cleveland composer-friend Bernard Rogers (Fig. 131). As the decade wore on and the economy improved, these "small" houses grew larger and more varied in composition.

Fig. 131. William Lescaze, Bernard Rogers house, Rochester, New York, 1937. View from street.

Of a similar type, but exhibiting still greater compositional freedom, were Lescaze's Lloyd Good and William Butler houses, designed in 1936 in collaboration with George Daub and built between the Atlantic Ocean and Barnegat Bay at Harvey Cedars, New Jersey.[13] The widespread interest in the "domesticated" modern was reflected the next year in Lescaze's Howard Markel house at Redding, Connecticut, and in the house designed for Minneapolis book and art dealer Frederick V. Nash (Fig. 132).

Lescaze was not to cease his design of large houses employing plain stuccoed surfaces, however. The unbuilt G. W. Hartmann and W. K. Wallace projects were just such schemes. So was the Fred S. Dunn house, built in 1936–1937 at Woodbridge, Connecticut. Similar to most of the schemes of Lescaze's houses of this period, the Dunn house is distinguished by its orientation to its

Fig. 132. William Lescaze, Frederick Nash house, Wayzata, Minnesota, 1937. Perspective rendering of entrance façade, 18 June 1937.

wooded suburban setting, long continuous banks of casement windows, terraces, and a second-floor deck. Unlike the others, the plan was most generous, including four spacious family bedrooms, a maid's and a governess's quarters, a guest suite, four bathrooms, laundry, living room, dining room, and large entrance hall. It was particularly well laid out for ease of circulation and personal privacy. The house was built at a cost of $13,859 (Fig. 133).[14]

In his 1938 Dunn guest cottage and Stacey May project, Lescaze introduced the mono-pitched roof to his vocabulary of cubic forms (Fig. 134).[15] Also, for the house of Harold Spivacke, Director of the Music Department at the Library of Congress, Lescaze abandoned cubic forms to design a building of

Fig. 133. William Lescaze, Frederick S. Dunn house, Woodbridge, Connecticut, 1936–1937. Garden façade.

trapezoidal shape. The plan, too, was notably "different," including a greenhouse and a living room of a size to accommodate piano concerts. Begun in 1939, the house, built at Rowland and Quebec Places, N. W., Washington, D.C., was completed in 1940.

Undoubtedly the most technically inventive of Lescaze's buildings in the 1930s was the Alfred Loomis house, designed and built at Tuxedo Park, New York, in 1936–37 (Fig. 135).[16] Loomis, although a trained lawyer, loved science (especially physics), and built a laboratory in conjunction with his house, where he invited scientists to work. He wanted to build a house to verify certain theories of air conditioning, humidity control, and sound control.[17] After erecting posts on the four corners of where he thought the house should be sited, Loomis did not know what to do next. So, he asked

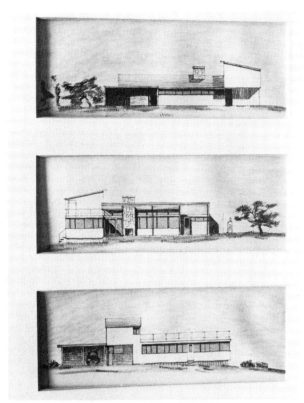

Fig. 134. William Lescaze, Stacy May project, Martha's Vineyard, Massachusetts, 1938. Elevation renderings, December 1938.

Fig. 135. William Lescaze, Alfred Loomis house, Tuxedo Park, New York, 1936–1937. Garden façade.

the editors of *Architectural Forum* to recommend an architect. He was invited to look at pictures of current architects' work to see what he liked. He saw Lescaze's work, reacted favorably, and asked him to collaborate on the project. Lescaze was intrigued. He expressed his delight in a letter to Leonard Elmhirst:

Alfred Loomis has recently asked me to help him with

an experimental house in which he will test some of his ideas on air pressure and air conditioning. By the way, this is turning out to be one of the most exciting little things I have done.[18]

Probably a unique design, the building has double exterior walls, constructed about two feet apart, with a similar space between the ceiling and roof (Fig. 136). Because of this house-within-a-house construction, it was possible to control the temperature and humidity within the inner house both accurately and economically and without moisture and condensation on its glass walls. The inner house is equipped with both heating and air conditioning systems; the shell-space has a separate heating system only. The exterior walls are of brick with light-section metal frames supporting large areas of glass; the interior walls are wood-framed and plastered, where there are not large areas of glass.

The double construction also insulates against outdoor noises. Noise control within the house was further facilitated by mineral wool insulation, vibration dampers on mechanical equipment, a cork-insulated air conditioning room, insulated air ducts, and acoustical materials throughout the house. An awning (which extends the full length of the house), the doors, and the screens all operate electrically. A V-form supports a terrace hood, recalling that used by Le Corbusier at the 1931 Salvation Army hostel in Paris.

On the interior, a neutral color scheme, polished fine woods, skylights, indirect lighting, built-in furniture, a bold fireplace design, and spatial divisions by furniture arrangement reflect the hallmarks of Lescaze's 1930s interior schemes. Unlike previous works, a large hall, which acts as a small conserva-

Fig. 136. William Lescaze, Alfred Loomis house, Tuxedo Park, New York, 1936–1937. Wall section.

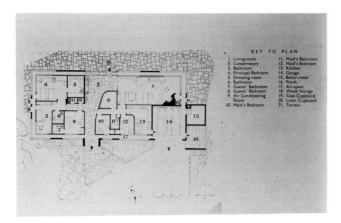

Fig. 137. William Lescaze, Alfred Loomis house, Tuxedo Park, New York, 1936–1937. Plan.

tory, bisects the plan and divides the private rooms from the public areas (Fig. 137).

In a general way, the house expresses the prevailing ideology of the thirties—the scientific attitude as a way of life and the belief in technology for a better society. In this regard Loomis invented a "sun machine" to record the angle of the sun's rays at different times of the year in relation to the topography (Fig. 138).[19] In order to site his house most favorably in relation to the sun, models of the house were placed on the machine and the amount of sun that came through the windows at any time of the day during the entire year was recorded. Loomis's "scientific" attitude was further manifested in his effort to create a highly controlled, artificial environment. Numerous experiments to that end were also forwarded in the thirties by the projects of R. Buckminster Fuller, Frank Paul, Norman Bel Geddes, George Fred Keck, the Luckhardt brothers, and others.

Probably coincidentally, the Loomis house partially realized the research and writings of the German visionary Paul Scheerbart. In his *Glasarchitektur*, published in 1914, Scheerbart wrote: "As air is one of the worst conductors of heat, the double glass wall is an essential condition for all glass architecture. The walls can be a metre apart—or have an even greater space between."[20] However, Scheerbart was concerned neither with air conditioning systems nor humidity control, as was Loomis. And, contrary to Loomis's solution, Scheerbart advised against heating the space between the walls.

In the same year that Lescaze was commissioned to collaborate on the experimental Loomis house, he received perhaps an even more "challenging"

Fig. 138. Alfred Loomis, sun machine, ca. 1936 (Mrs. Lescaze, New York).

proposal from Frank Walton of Chicago, one that Lescaze found to make "even a bad Monday worth while." Walton wrote to Lescaze on 15 December 1936:

I wish to commission you to draw up plans for a residence to be built just out of Live Oak, Florida. This land is sand and subject to "lime-sinks" or cave-ins and I should like to have this possible hazard negated. Here is a list of hazards I should like you to keep in mind in drawing up plans:
1. Fire
2. Tornado
3. Earthquakes
4. Flood
5. Lime-sinks
6. Insects
7. Armed-invaders
8. Bombs and shells
9. Meteors (small)
10. 300° heat
11. -200° cold

Such a house would of course have to be built somewhat under the ground. I shall have a flower garden and lounging patio over it, surrounded by a heavy wall, of course. It is in this garden that I would do my living and entertaining in fair weather, below in foul. House to be large enough to cache food supplies for 10 years. I have an oil well on this property running pure crude, and I wish to use this to create electric power for cooling, heating, lighting, etc., when needed, to supplement wind power. I want every moving part in this house-machine to be manufactured to last for 100 years, everything as completely automatic as possible. Spare no expense.

If you are interested, let me know. I read about you in *The New Yorker.*

Frank Walton

This is the ultimate house, I think. I see no other way out.

F. W.[21]

Unfortunately, Lescaze's reply of 17 December 1936 to Walton's parody is unknown to the author, but no commission ensued!

While Walton was an unusual prospective client, indeed, most of Lescaze's early clients were somewhat atypical. They all valued the freedom of individual expression and were willing to experiment with new artistic ideas. As per CIAM's aims, the clients were not limited to any social class or profession. Yet, they were reasonably well-established, enlightened clients, as was the case throughout Europe and the United States. They included musicians Stokowski, Spivacke, and Rogers; artists Spreter and Hobart; writers Field and Dorothy Norman; educators Curry, Elmhirst, and Dunn; scientific patron Loomis; collectors Wertheim, Wilbour, and Nash; and business persons Jean de Sièyes, Hattie Carnegie, the directors of the PSFS, CBS, and others.

By the mid-thirties Lescaze's reputation was well established as a leader in modern architecture in the United States. *The Architect and Building News* stated that for some years Lescaze had "been among the leaders of the modern movement in America." *The New York World-Telegram* reported that he had "stepped out ahead of the front ranks."[22] He was characterized as "one of the foremost contemporary American architects," a "well known exponent of modern design," a "brilliant architect," and was acclaimed as the architect that

we modernists look to as a sign and portent of a better day in American architecture. . . . An architecture . . . of design based on use not on fantasy—an architecture which is more sound science and less art. . . .[23]

Noting Lescaze's reputation both as "avant-garde architect and campaigner," Robert Coates claimed in *The New Yorker* that he had "taken the lead in Modernist architecture in this country."[24] Henry-

Russell Hitchcock hailed him as "easily the most prominent architect in the East."[25]

Because of his growing reputation and the increasing acceptance of the International Style in America by mid-decade, Lescaze received large commissions from business, industry, education, and government throughout the late thirties. Although not ranking among the period's outstanding architectural achievements, they do have merits worth mentioning.

One was the Ansonia High School in Connecticut. Already known for the design of the Oak Lane Country Day School's nursery school building near Philadelphia, the Hessian Hills School at Croton-on-Hudson, New York, and the Dartington School boarding houses, Lescaze (in association with Vernon Sears) won the commission to design the Ansonia High School. Evolving through several preliminary schemes for three different sites, the final plan was drawn in November 1935. With construction begun in August 1936 and completed in March 1937, it was probably the first large school in the International Style built on the East Coast (Figs. 139 and 140).[26]

Unlike Lescaze's earlier white buildings, this steel-framed structure was sheathed with limestone and red brick, banded with large areas of glass, and accented with gray lally columns and glass block. It was planned to accommodate 750 students at a cost of $410,334.[27] The building was distinguished for its clear articulation of three principal units—auditorium, classrooms, and gymnasium—and its intelligent site plan which maximized the use of a corner site. The J-shaped plan consisted of a gymnasium at one end and an auditorium at the other,

Fig. 139. William Lescaze with Vernon Sears, High School, Ansonia, Connecticut, 1935–1937. Perspective rendering.

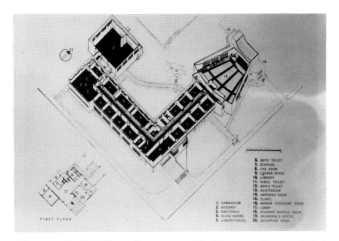

Fig. 140. William Lescaze with Vernon Sears, High School, Ansonia, Connecticut, 1935–1937. Plan.

Fig. 141. William Lescaze, Kimble Glass Company administration building, Vineland, New Jersey, 1936–1937. Rendering of angle view showing entrance façades.

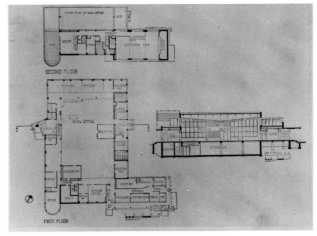

Fig. 142. William Lescaze, Kimble Glass Company administration building, Vineland, New Jersey, 1936–1937. Plan and section.

connected by two two-story classroom blocks, turning the corner at right angles.[28] The classroom block on the entrance side was raised on columns, forming a passage, so that the auditorium, gymnasium, and athletic field could be easily accessible from the street for student and public use in the evenings or other times that classes were not in session.[29] For further flexibility of use by both students and the public, each unit of the building had its own entrance so that it could be used independently of the others.

For months after the school's completion, the town was split between those who liked it and those who did not.[30] *The Bridgeport Post* reported that "the architect's drawings of the new school disclose a structure looking something like a cross between a factory, a garage, a jail, and a sewage disposal plant."[31] At the same time the *Architectural Forum* printed: "If this [Ansonia] is modern architecture, U.S. school children, their teachers and the whole community have everything to gain by its general adoption."[32] In 1940, it was judged a "thoroughly modern large school building, comfortable, convenient, well lighted, superior in nearly every way to what most school boards are still building."[33] Although additions and alterations have obscured its former spatial qualities, it continues to function well for many more students than were originally planned for.

In 1936 Lescaze had the opportunity to design the plant administration building for the Kimble Glass Company of Vineland, New Jersey (Figs. 141 and 142). The problem was to provide space for a clerical staff, offices for executives, and rooms for various employee services. Developing features of

one of the Ansonia High School's preliminary schemes, its complex massing of one- and two-story, curved and rectangular volumes expressed a well-organized plan. An entrance lobby opened onto a central general office which was lighted through an inverted trussed roof and clerestory; at the periphery were private offices, conference rooms, drafting room and lounges. A projecting wing was devoted to employee services with conference rooms and auditorium above.[34] Like Ansonia High School, the concrete and steel-framed structure was faced with brick and limestone slabs. Broad bands of glass block emphasized the sweeping horizontality of the façades, recalling that feature of the Peck and Wertheim projects of 1931.

The building was completed in February 1937 at a cost of $250,000. Herman K. Kimble, president of the company, praised the structure as being "modern without being modernistic," and called its "functional operation . . . as perfect as the building is beautiful."[35] A satisfied client, indeed!

Experimenting still further with a variety of architectural forms and structures was Lescaze's scheme for Unity House, summer camp of the New York branch of the International Ladies' Garment Workers Union, near Bushkill, Pennsylvania. The camp's site dates back to 1919 when 750 acres of wooded land, together with a two-mile lake, were acquired. The following year an existing resort hotel on the site was remodeled and the grounds converted to their new purpose. The increasing popularity of the camp as a vacation center brought the need for increased facilities. In August 1934 Lescaze was engaged to work out plans for a $280,000 expansion of the camp to accommodate 1,000 persons.[36] He proposed an "unassuming, comfortable, and attractive" scheme which included plans for road layouts, a main social hall, dormitories, a bowling alley, tennis courts, cottages, service buildings, and landscaping (Fig. 143).[37] Eight of the twelve buildings that Lescaze proposed in his master plan were completed in 1936—the main social hall, a dormitory for single persons, and six cottages for families.

The most interesting unit of the complex was the social hall (destroyed by fire in 1967). Designed to serve as the focus of all social activities, it included a

Fig. 144. William Lescaze, Unity House camp, near Bushkill, Pennsylvania, 1934–1936. View of main building.

dining room, terrace pavilion, tea room, lounge, children's dining room, kitchen, and lobby, all spaciously designed to accommodate the large crowds that would gather there. Its wood-trussed, vaulted roof and native stone foundation once again expressed Lescaze's late modernist style (Fig. 144).

Also in the mid-thirties, Lescaze's early interest in building large-scale public housing finally came to fruition. He was one of five senior architects who participated in the design of Brooklyn's Ten Eyck Houses (later called the Williamsburg Houses).[38] It was the country's first federally-financed (PWA), low-rent, public housing development in New York and the largest and best effort to rebuild slum areas neighborhood-by-neighborhood, based on concepts similar to those of the National Resources Planning Board's plan for better cities. Commissioned in 1935, its construction was begun 3 January 1936 and completed in 1938. The $12,783,000 housing development occupied a twelve-block, twenty-five-acre site bounded by Maujer Street, Leonard Street, Scholes Street, and Bushwick Avenues in the Williamsburg area of Brooklyn.[39]

Chief architect Richmond Shreve asked Lescaze to be in charge of planning the site and designing the exteriors of 1,622 living units (floor plans had been prescribed by the Federal government), plus community meeting rooms, play rooms for pre-school children, and shops. The scheme consisted of four-story buidings of concrete construction exposed at the floor levels, brick-faced walls, and corner windows (Fig. 145).

As in the site plans of his earlier housing projects, and following the English and German planning

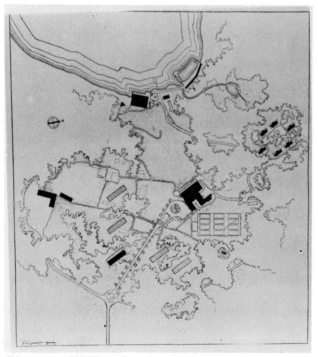

Fig. 143. William Lescaze, Unity House camp, near Bushkill, Pennsylvania, 1934–1936. Plot plan.

Fig. 145. William Lescaze and others, Ten Eyck Houses (Williamsburg Housing development), Brooklyn, New York, 1935–1938.

Fig. 146. William Lescaze and others, Ten Eyck Houses (Williamsburg Housing development), Brooklyn, New York, 1935–1938. Aerial view.

principles developed in the 1920s and 1930s, Lescaze separated foot from vehicular traffic and provided large open green spaces by closing two east-west streets to regroup the twelve-block area into four "super-blocks." His first scheme, in keeping with the earlier designs prepared by architects for PWA projects, consisted of U-shaped, four-story housing units grouped around the perimeters of the block. His second scheme employed connecting H-shaped housing units placed on an angle to the street. The third and final plan, developed from scheme two, was composed of H-shaped and T-shaped housing units laid out at angles to the street (Fig. 146). The angled plan, a variation on the German *Zeilenbau*, was proposed in order to keep living spaces as far from traffic as possible and to provide an orientation to maximum winter sunlight and pre-

vailing south-west summer breezes. The plan also avoided distinction between fronts and backs of the buildings and afforded maximum privacy.

Discussing the scheme in 1937, Talbot Hamlin commented that "the design was economical and clever . . . and certainly there was a sense of size and space in passage from court to court, and a variety in the actual views obtained, which was a real virtue."[40] A year later, however, he claimed that following the street pattern would have given as much actual sun in the rooms and avoided the "jagged rhythm," "restlessness," lack of "continuity," "the formlessness" and "disintegration" that resulted from the angled plan. Although Hamlin believed the system in the plan was observable to the trained and sophisticated eye, he thought it would bring pleasure to "only the esoteric few and not the people."[41] A champion of the plan, Walter Gropius commented that the Williamsburg Housing "seems to have solved the problem of space and light very economically, and it has the great advantage of being spread over enough land to make it worthwhile as a sample of a planned development."[42]

At the close of the decade, Lescaze participated in two world's fairs. For the monumental and modernistic 1936 Texas Centennial Exhibition in Dallas, Lescaze designed the Magnolia Petroleum Company pavilion. His initial scheme was a single geometric block raised on *pilotis* with a sweeping entrance ramp rising from a formal courtyard, which contained standards bearing the flags of Texas.[43] The final scheme was more a conservative but no less formal statement in which the familiar glass brick, portholes, cantilevered stairs, lally columns, and tubular railings characterized the geometric composition.

Lescaze was the only architect to design two buildings for the 1939 New York World's Fair—the Swiss Pavilion and the Aviation Building. Designed in association with John R. Weber of Switzerland, the Swiss Pavilion was composed of two pavilions. The exhibition space in the Court of Peace was linked to the main building by a flower-bordered footbridge which spanned the avenue between the two units. The main pavilion contained some exhibits but was primarily devoted to recreation and dining—an auditorium for Swiss music, a theater, a bar, a restaurant, and a very popular beer-garden and cheese cellar. The concrete structure bore an irregular silhouette, varying roof and floor levels, and a variety of open and closed spatial relationships. It was enlivened by the use of contrasting materials—stucco, vertical wood siding, stone, gravel, tiles, colored glass—and made festive with flags of the cantons, checkered table cloths, umbrellas, and murals. The skillful job of landscaping, the use of a variety of textures, and the variation in scale of the separate volumes precluded the effect of an "enlarged architectural model," characteristic of most of the fair buildings.[44] The architects were awarded a silver medal for their efforts.

For the Aviation Building, Lescaze proposed an ingenious scheme of refined form and structural sophistication. The three-part plan, consisting of entrance lobby and restaurant, exhibition area, and cyclorama, was particularly interesting for the relatively new type of imbrication of volumes which Lescaze proposed. Here, the cubic composition of the Swiss pavilion was replaced by a formal vocabulary appropriate to the necessity of providing vast interior spaces. In designing three separate volumes, self-supported from sweeping curves which interlocked with each other, Lescaze and J. Gordon Carr, his associate, stated that the building was conceived "in terms of forms which carry forward the illusion of space and embodies the idea of presenting flight in space" (Figs. 147 and 148). It was likened by others to a "blimp nosing into a band concert shell."[45]

The problem of providing a low-cost, rigid shell was solved by the use of two structural systems—shop-fabricated, solid-section hinged arches for the exhibition space, and open-web arches of more usual design in the half dome. The former was

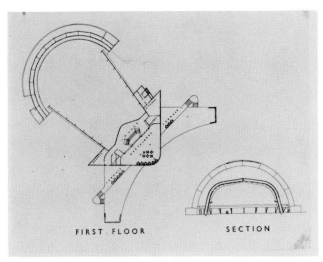

FIRST FLOOR   SECTION

Fig. 148. William Lescaze with J. Gordon Carr, Aviation Building, New York World's Fair, 1937–1938. Plan.

sheathed on the exterior with aluminum-covered corrugated asbestos. The latter, covered with canvas, was painted on the exterior and stuccoed on the interior. A huge stressed-canvas canopy arched across the entire front, laced to a system of braced tubular steel columns and anchored with tie-rods to concrete blocks at each end.

The 8 February 1938 New York Herald Tribune reported that inside the half dome of the $250,000 building a large transport plane was suspended by invisible means, propellers turning, lights flashing, and ailerons moving, with cloud forms, sunset, moonlight, and stars projected behind it. Special effect lighting created further illusions of space. An airport control tower and a chamber equipped with an instrument panel offered visitors an opportunity to play "pilot." Models of wind tunnels, famous airplanes, relics of historic flights, and full-scale models of planes of the future (which could be entered by the visitor) filled the exhibition hall. A clipper ship was displayed outside. Demonstrating his interest in the synthesis of the arts, Lescaze commissioned Arshile Gorky to paint a mural in the building.

Cited as "probably the best fair-built building" (which excludes the Finnish-financed Alvar Aalto building), and "as successful as any at the fair," the Aviation Building symbolized the "World of Tomorrow" in American architecture.[46] In a similar spirit was Lescaze's project for a "House for the Year 2039," drawn in the same year as the Aviation building (Fig. 149).[47] Like his "Future American Country House" project of ten years earlier, the

Fig. 147. William Lescaze with J. Gordon Carr, Aviation Building, New York World's Fair, 1937–1938. View from north-west.

Fig. 149. William Lescaze, House for the Year 2039 project, November 1938. Perspective rendering.

most futuristic aspect of it was the provision for air transportation—this time a helicopter pad on the roof. But tomorrow's world was to be interrupted by World War II. Thus, the most productive decade for the new architecture in America, and Lescaze's most important work aesthetically, came to an abrupt and unfulfilled end.

NOTES

1. Henry-Russell Hitchcock, "The International Style Twenty Years After," *Architectural Record* 110 (August 1951): 89–97; William Jordy, *American Buildings and Their Architects: The Impact of European Modernism in the Mid-Twentieth Century,* vol. 4 (New York: Doubleday and Co., Inc., 1972), p. 167.

2. See plans dated 8 July 1933, 19 July 1933, September 1933, 9 March 1934 in WELA. An addition was made by George Daub in 1951. Further changes were made by the owners in 1971.

3. See "Spreter Studio Construction Data," (typescript), WELA; "Lighthouse for a Painter," *Arts and Decoration* 42 (January 1935): 49.

4. "Spreter Studio Construction Data," WELA. Supergraphics were painted by William Tapley in 1971 on the ceiling and one wall of the living room; see *Progressive Architecture,* 53 (May 1972): 123.

5. "Prefabrication," *Architectural Forum* 63 (December 1935): 544–576.

6. "Men and Deeds," *Architectural Forum* 65 (October 1936): 74, 82.

7. Benjamin F. Betts, "Purdue Completes Year of Structural Research," *Architectural Record* 81 (March 1937): BT34–35. *The Architectural Record* 79 (February 1936) was entirely devoted to low-cost small housing.

8. Photograph, WELA. One was exhibited at the Chicago Fair in 1933–1934.

9. Interview with Mrs. Lescaze, New York, 10 October 1974.

10. *The Boston Evening Transcript,* 25 June 1935.

11. *Melrose* (Massachusetts) *Leader,* 5 July 1935.

12. "New . . . in New England," *House Beautiful* 78 (December 1936): 64–65.

13. Prior to 1940, eight more houses were added to this group by George Daub and three by J. Joshua Fish. See John McAndrew, ed., *Guide to Modern Architecture: Northeast States* (New York: Museum of Modern Art, 1940), p. 45.

14. Plans and documentary data are in WELA.

15. The Cates, Good, Butler, Dunn, Nash, Markel, and Rogers houses are illustrated in a photograph album, "Small Houses," WELA.

16. Blueprints are dated 19 February 1937, Box 2, Folder 111, WELA.

17. Interview with Mrs. Lescaze, New York, 9 October 1974.

18. Lescaze to Elmhirst, 15 June 1936, T-13-C, RODH.

19. Interview with Mrs. Lescaze, New York, 9 October 1974.

20. See Sharp, *Glass Architecture,* p. 42.

21. Lescaze published Walton's letter in his *On Being an Architect,* pp. 146–147.

22. "A House in New York City," *Architect and Building News* 143 (5 July 1935): 19; Allan Keller, "They Build New York," *New York World-Telegram,* 19 February 1938, p. 1.

23. *House and Garden* 69 (January 1936): 54; *House Beautiful* 78 (December 1936): 65; *Arts and Decoration* 46 (October 1937): 9; *Trend* 3 (March–April 1935): 28.

24. Robert M. Coates, "Profile," *The New Yorker,* 12 December 1936, p. 44.

25. Henry-Russell Hitchcock, "Modern Architecture in England," in *Modern Architecture in England* (New York: The Museum of Modern Art, 1937), p. 37.

26. The rendering, dated 14 November 1935, was only slightly modified in the final scheme; laying of the cornerstone was announced in "Ansonia Goes Modernistic," *Bridgeport* (Conn.) *Post,* 6 August 1936. Construction began in December 1935; its progress was photographically recorded, WELA.

27. "Commission 419," WELA; the school was built with the aid of a PWA grant of $190,632. See Harry L. Liftig, "Ansonia Builds a Modern High School," Dedication Program, 1936, p. 15. W. J. Farley, "The Ansonia High School—a P. W. A. Project," Dedication Program, 1936, p. 17 records the cost at $461,000.

28. Undated photographs of a preliminary scheme show a similar articulation of the parts but with the entrance oriented to the adjacent street. The penultimate scheme, dated 14 November 1935, proposed a three-story building of almost identical plan and elevation as the final scheme. A symmetrical alternative plan was drawn in March 1936. See "Photographs of Renderings" (scrapbook), Package 2, WELA.

29. The open passage was filled in for additional classroom space in 1961. A new wing, now occupying the playground space, was built at the same time.

30. Keller, "They Build New York," p. 19.

31. *Bridgeport* (Conn.) *Post,* 6 August 1936.

32. "Ansonia High School, Ansonia, Connecticut," *Architectural Forum* 67 (December 1937): 489.

33. McAndrew, *Guide,* p. 19.

34. Renderings of preliminary schemes, dated 21 September 1936 and 20 October 1936, show the auditorium and employee services block to be on opposite axis from the final scheme and, thus, projecting from the façade at the second floor to form a covered porch entrance. Photographs of renderings are in "Photographs of Renderings" (scrapbook), Package 2, WELA. The perspective rendering published in *Architectural Record* 82 (August 1937): 124, is of the preliminary scheme. The plan published there is the revised version, which was built.

35. Herman K. Kimble to Lescaze, 22 April 1938, WELA.

36. McAndrew, *Guide,* p. 91; List of Works—Date Started and Completed (typescript), WELA. The camp opened on 22 June 1935.

37. McAndrew, *Guide,* p. 91.

38. Chief architect was Richmond H. Shreve. Associates

were James F. Bly, Matthew W. Del Gaudio, Arthur C. Holden, William Lescaze, Samuel Gardstein, Paul Trapani, G. Harmon Gurney, Harry Leslie Walker, and John W. Ingle, Jr..

39. "Housing Project Shown in a Model," *New York Times*, 19 December 1935, p. 9; "New York Williamsburg Houses, Brooklyn," *Architectural Forum* 68 (May 1938):356.

40. Talbot Hamlin, "Architecture," in *International Yearbook 1937*, ed. Frank H. Vizetelly (New York: Funk and Wagnalls, 1938), p. 40.

41. Talbot Hamlin, "New York Housing: Harlem River Homes and Williamsburg Houses," *Pencil Points* 19 (May 1938):286–287.

42. H. I. Brock, "A Modernist Scans our Skyline," *New York Times*, 11 April 1937, Magazine Section, pp. 12, 24.

43. Photographs of the perspective rendering are in "Photographs of Renderings" (scrapbook), Package 2, WELA.

44. F. A. Gutheim, "Buildings at the Fair," *Magazine of Art* 32 (May 1939):287.

45. *New York Herald Tribune*, 8 February 1938, WELA. Richard Wurts and others, *The New York World's Fair 1939–1940 in 155 Photographs* (New York: Dover Publications, 1977), p. 35.

46. Gutheim, "Buildings at the Fair," p. 288; Paul F. Norton, "World's Fairs in the 1930s," *Journal of the Society of Architectural Historians* 24 (March 1965):30. Lescaze was also commissioned to design a world's fair pavilion for the Libbey-Owens-Ford Glass Company. Potentially an opportunity to realize Scheerbart's and Bruno Taut's dreams of expressing the fragility, lightness, and transparency of glass, Lescaze's solution was a disappointingly conventional scheme of glass curtain walls and wide strip windows. The project remained unrealized.

47. Original drawings for the "House of 2039" are in the Avery Library, Columbia University. One is published in David Gebhard and Deborah Nevins, *200 Years of American Architectural Drawing* (New York: Whitney Library of Design, 1977), p. 211. It is misidentified there as the "House of 2089."

7

The Late Years: 1941–1969

WHILE THERE WERE FEW ARCHITECTURAL COMMISsions to be had during World War II, it was not an idle period for Lescaze. He seized the opportunity to write, lecture, and teach; to plan visionary projects; to experiment still further with new forms, materials, structural systems, low-cost housing projects, regional planning studies, and new building types—all in readiness for post-war building and still another phase of the International Style.

The first new forms evolved from his small houses of the late thirties and were developed throughout the forties in his F. V. Field caretaker's cottage, and the Clarence Levey, Jerome Crowley, Sidney Kaye, and Henry Englander houses.[1] In these, Lescaze abandoned the flat-roofed cube and seamless surfaces in favor of the mono-pitched and butterfly roofs, combinations of wood siding (popularly redwood after the California vernacular), and large areas of glass interspersed with those of stone. Missing were the machine aesthetic of industrial production and the free use of curvilinear forms. These houses were tougher, more rugged and varied than their tautly drawn, thin-walled, stuccoed predecessors of the thirties. Lescaze, like Le Corbusier, Breuer, and others had abandoned the delicate, light, flat, flowing continuity of the early International Style in favor of texture, mass, and weight contrasted with transparency. The idealism of the twenties and thirties International Style aesthetic was now mostly dead, giving way to a new eclecticism. The dogma of the International Style had been broken to utilize once again the organic

principles of Sullivan and Wright—principles that had never quite been lost.

In the Levey house, Lescaze incorporated a mono-pitched roof with stone and redwood walls, interspersed with large areas of glass (Fig. 150). The Crowley house bore the current butterfly roof, redwood siding, and the still popular wide window bands (Fig. 151). And the Kaye house, although a direct descendant of the European modern style of the twenties, might almost be considered a "ranch house" of the Bay Area's persuasion with its natural grained wood exterior and horizontality stretched onto a broad stone foundation. Lescaze's associate Henry Dumper was primarily responsible for the

Fig. 150. William Lescaze, Clarence Levey house, Candlewood Lake, Connecticut, 1946–1947. View from lakeside.

125

Fig. 151. William Lescaze, Jerome Crowley house, South Bend, Indiana, 1948–1949.

design of these domestically scaled wooden structures of the forties. They reflect his ease with the American "humanistic" modification of the European "functionalist" modern. A larger version of the idiom was realized in the sprawling, one-story, wooden, butterfly-roofed Crossett, Arkansas Health Center.[2] The old spirit was not completely dead, however. At about the same time, Lescaze's remodeling of the picturesque and shingled Dune Deck Hotel at Westhampton, Long Island, to include a sleek, flat-roofed, regular cubic form complete with smooth, vertical white siding and horizontal window bands, reflected the earlier version of the Style.

Because of the few building opportunities available during the war, much of Lescaze's work consisted, as it had twenty years earlier, of interiors, alterations, furniture and industrial design, and planning projects. He was particularly frustrated by not being able to participate directly in the war. His articles, "How Can I Be Useful?" and "Building for Defense," expressed his feeling of being wasted; he pleaded to be allowed to help the war effort.[3] A few months before Pearl Harbor, he wrote in his "Journal:" "My God, what I wouldn't give for having some other ability besides architecture. If I had a tool factory, if I could be doing something which would be useful now, in the times we live in, for my adopted country."[4] A few weeks later he reflected ". . . I am haunted by the desire to do something positive, something tangible for the defense of our country, even though it may be modest, say like small parts of a shell or ammunition."[5]

Although his energy could not be used directly in the war effort, Lescaze was gratified to have his

120-unit, 2-story brick, "Woods End" apartments built for war workers in Roselle, New Jersey and his 215-unit "Chestnut Gardens" apartments constructed in Bridgeport, Connecticut in the early forties. He also contributed to architecture by exhibiting, writing, and lecturing on the importance of planning for post-war building, and by teaching at Harvard University, Columbia University, Pratt Institute, and The New School. In a report issued in 1940 by Columbia University, Lescaze urged fellow architects, engineers, and builders to organize themselves and prepare for the modern and rational building that would be demanded for housing, schools, and plants after the war was over.[6]

At this time, too, Lescaze published a book on his philosophy of architecture, *On Being An Architect*, employing anecdotes from his architectural experience.[7] Albeit a prolific writer and lecturer for the cause of modern architecture, Lescaze's most overriding passion was for building. "I love to draw, I love to plan and build buildings," he wrote. "It's not the articles you write or the articles which are written about you which count, its the buildings you build."[8]

Although he protested his "inglorious role of [a] helpless and incongruous civilian . . . left behind, idle and useless in the loneliness of empty drafting rooms," Lescaze kept occupied with urban planning studies for Schenectady, Scarsdale, and Manhattan.[9] A plan for East Harlem, the James Weldon Johnson houses, focused on the well-being of children—a community where health care, education, and recreation would be provided.[10] His proposal for West Harlem's urban rehabilitation was based on the theories of his earlier Williamsburg site plan, consisting of "super blocks" and "super building" units, diagonally plotted on the site.[11]

Support for these plans was not forthcoming. Lescaze expressed his discouragement in a letter of 1943 to his former partner George Howe, then involved with Federal housing: "I have been trying to do some kind of planning for a small part of Manhattan and it's been hellish to make progress without any financial help. . . . Shall we of the building industry be altogether unprepared when peace comes?"[12] With little preparation, federal- and state-aided public housing burst upon the landscape in the post-war era. Lescaze's plans for the Chelsea Housing development (later called the Elliott Houses), designed in 1941 for the Chelsea area of Manhattan and halted by the war, were im-

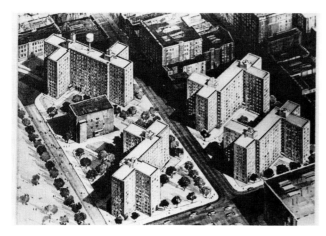

Fig. 152. William Lescaze with Archibald M. Brown, Chelsea Housing development, for New York Housing Authority (Elliott Houses), New York, 1941–1946. Aerial view rendering.

Fig. 153. William Lescaze, "Spinney Hill Homes," Manhasset, Long Island, New York, 1950–1952.

mediately revived (Fig. 152).[13] Like the earlier Williamsburg Houses, the brick-clad towers were sited at an angle to the block.

By the fifties, Lescaze finally had the opportunity to build the workers' housing projects he had envisioned as a student at the Polytechnique in Zurich. For Long Island's north shore, he designed the 66-unit "Harbor Homes" at Port Washington and the 102-unit "Spinney Hill Homes" at Manhasset (Fig. 153). Of residential scale, the two-story, flat-roofed, row houses reflected the popularization of "natural" materials (redwood and brick) and were planned for a suburban garden-apartment site. In the same spirit, Lescaze designed the gabled, brick and wood "Hillview Homes" in Salamanca, New York; "Pond View" in Manhasset and "Laurel Homes" in Roslyn, Long Island. In 1960, his large

1,273-unit "Manhattanville Houses" were built between 129th and 133rd Streets, Broadway to Amsterdam Avenue. Like the early post-war Chelsea Houses, they were brick-clad towers prepared for a cleared site.

In the post-war years there were practical breakthroughs in building technology which heretofore had existed only in the minds of architects and designers before the war. The idea that a new architecture would result from a mechanized industry of materials and processes—architecture as an industrial product—was undoubtedly consequential to Lescaze's war time research on prefabricated window components, walls, and houses.

Ever since steel and concrete frames reduced the wall's function to a "skin," the concept of a "curtain-wall" has intrigued designers and was to dominate constructional style by the 1950s. Lescaze's "metal-clad insulating wall" system, developed with Bob Davidson for the non-profit New York Housing Trust, was a theoretical study, made in 1946 before an industry existed. Five years later, Lescaze was retained by the Curtain Wall Committee of the Porcelain Enamel Institute to study criteria for metal curtain-walls and to develop a porcelain-enamel wall system.[14]

Prefabricated housing experiments, intended to help solve the nation's post-war housing shortage, were inevitable. Lescaze designed a model house for Finestra Steel as early as 1942. A few years later, Lescaze designed for the Reliance Steel Products Company a five-room, aluminum-sheathed steel-framed house in only seven factory-fabricated sections (Fig. 154). They could be bolted together by a five-man crew in under two hours, for each section

Fig. 154. William Lescaze, Reliance Homes, 1946. Model.

was structurally complete with all heating, wiring, plumbing, and wall finishes factory-installed. Site operation was limited to preparing a slab foundation and hooking up the utilities. Projected designs ranged from a studio model to a three-bedroom house and garage. Flat or gable roof was optional. The first model was built in 1946; production began in 1948. By the next year, the houses were being produced at the rate of six per day, at a retail price of about $5,500.[15] In spite of its promise, this scheme, like others, failed because of its unpopular design and the building union's opposition.

The Durisol Corporaton retained Lescaze in still another effort to produce an economical house by industrial means. He and two other architects designed experimental housing models (built near Garrison, New York), constructed of cement and chemically mineralized wood-shavings precast in blocks and panels of various sizes and shapes. Developed in Europe in the early thirties, the product was promoted as being insulating, fire-resistant, sound-absorbing, lightweight, and termite and moisture proof. It could be nailed, screwed, clipped, or mortared into place and could be sawed and molded into most building forms. With all this to recommend it, plus labor saving construction, it was not successful because of production problems, a module that did not correspond with standard window sizes and common sill heights, and an industrial look that consumers found unacceptable for small houses.[16]

Lescaze's post-war planning also included a scheme for regulating building along highways. Writing in his *On Being an Architect* that "some form of control might conceivably regulate at least 500 feet on each side of highways," Lescaze prophetically called for service plazas that would provide snack bars, restaurants, space for recreation and dancing, lawns, restrooms, sales areas, and auto servicing.[17] His proposal for such a unit, published in *Architectural Forum*, argued for such highway regulation in the interest of improved aesthetics, safety, and economic vitality.[18]

Lescaze's twenties' and thirties' visionary drawings of residences with airplanes on every roof did not materialize. However, the rapid rise of car-ownership, the proliferation of expressways after the war, the need for large commercial buildings that could not be built during the war, and the expansion of the economy brought a significant change in urban life at the end of the forties. Soon

after the War, in the era often called the "third skyscraper age," the construction of huge apartment and office blocks with curtain walls of glass, regular shapes, and repetitive units proliferated. Large commissions from business, institutions, and government ultimately resulted in a corporate building type, representative of the requirements of anonymous clients for flexible building spaces. Not since the late 1920s had modern commercial buildings been built on such a grand scale. Lescaze's youthful desire to build "monumental" architecture was now to be realized in the large office, apartment, and public buildings that dominated his work from the war to his death.

Lescaze's earliest post-war public buildings were essentially newer versions of earlier schemes. The Sydenham Hospital project of 1947 related directly to his Los Angeles CBS building of ten years before. His 1950s office buildings at 711 Third Avenue and 30 West Broadway, plus several projects of this time, recall the horizontal layering of floors in the 1930 model for the PSFS building in Philadelphia (Fig. 155). Some of these projects were also predicated upon the PSFS's vertically projecting

Fig. 155. William Lescaze, office building, 711 Third Avenue, New York, 1952–1956. Photomontage.

mullions and a composition of slab raised cross axis upon a podium base. Others were simply towers set upon low bases. One scheme, a project for 2 Broadway, was a single layered slab with a "different" floor part way up, as in the tower section of PSFS. As James Marston Fitch observed, it must have been for Lescaze a "source of great satisfaction to have evolved so early an idiom of expression as satisfactory now as it was then."[19]

Lescaze's early interior design work continued after the war in large commercial contracts and in the ongoing J. Walter Thompson commission in the Graybar building.

Although Lescaze vigorously disagreed with the concept of designing architecture as sculpture, his Sutton House apartment project, the apartment building for 200 East 58th Street, and the Churchill apartment house in Los Angeles all reflect the sculptural fifties, albeit conservatively (Fig. 156).[20]

At the end of the fifties, Lescaze's style moved toward Miesian symmetry, skeletal expression of structure, and rectilinear patterns emphasized by strong value contrasts. This classicistic regularity was first expressed in his Embassy of Switzerland

Fig. 157. William Lescaze with Kahn and Jacobs, High School of Art and Design, New York, 1953–1960.

Fig. 158. William Lescaze with Matthew W. del Gaudio, the Civil Courthouse and Municipal Courts Building, New York, 1945, 1953–1960.

building in Washington, D.C., his High School of Art and Design (with Kahn and Jacobs) in New York, and the Civil Courthouse and Municipal Courts Building (with Matthew del Gaudio), New York (Figs. 157 and 158). Each was characterized by cubic forms and symmetrical division of at least one façade in open and closed planes. An increasing emphasis on the skeletal structure is evident in his Brotherhood House on Seventh Avenue and

Fig. 156. William Lescaze, Sutton House project, New York, 1951. Perspective rendering.

Fig. 159. William Lescaze, Brotherhood House, Seventh Avenue at Fortieth Street, New York, 1959–1960.

Fig. 160. William Lescaze and Associates, First National City Bank, New York World's Fair, 1964. Perspective rendering.

Fig. 161. William Lescaze, office building, 777 Third Avenue, New York, 1961–1965.

Fig. 162. William Lescaze and Associates, Chatham Center, Pittsburgh, Pennsylvania, 1964–1965.

climaxed in the axial and formal First National City Bank built for the 1964 World's Fair (Figs. 159 and 160). The architect's rendering of the latter even illustrates Mies's Barcelona chairs in the banking room. Thus, from the Corbusian cast of his early work, Lescaze entered the sixties with a Miesian stance.

By the last decade of his practice, Lescaze had become a very successful commercial architect, building large office towers, apartment houses, public housing, and government and institutional buildings. In 1964 Lescaze was ranked in the first 25% of *Architectural Forum's* list of the 100 top-volume architectural firms in America with from $60,000,000 to $75,000,000 worth of buildings put in place in 1963.[21] In 1964, the firm name was changed from William Lescaze to William Lescaze and Associates. Associates were to include Henry A. Dumper, Apollinare Osadca, George Daub, Alvin Hausman, Nevio Maggiora, Frank Preston, and Sidney Rappaport.[22]

This was Lescaze's most successful period financially, if not aesthetically. Typical of the work at this time is the 38-story office building at 777 Third Avenue (Fig. 161). In it any reference to

rage for 2,200 cars, and a 600-seat cinema (Fig. 162).

Lescaze's last major commission was the 50-story office building at 1 New York Plaza (Fig. 163). In it, the tower's curtain walls were articulated in an essentially square grid with rather prosaic results.

Fig. 163. William Lescaze and Associates, office building 1 New York Plaza, New York, 1965–1969. Model and Mr. Lescaze.

horizontality gave way to vertical packaging with emphasis on the mullions of the curtain walls. Having wide application, variations on the theme can be seen in his office building at 300 East 42nd Street, New York; the Church Center for the United Nations, New York; and 1 Oliver Plaza in Pittsburgh, Pennsylvania, among others.

Still, Lescaze did not altogether abandon the PSFS's directional contrasts nor its cubist interlocking forms. The Chatham Center in Pittsburgh recapitulates his earlier architectural vocabularies, useful because of the complexity of its program which consisted of a 19-story apartment house, 9-story office with a surmounting 11-story hotel, ga-

NOTES

1. Client Jerome Crowley, president of a paint company in South Bend, Indiana, commissioned Lescaze on the basis of his published work in magazines, Crowley to author, 29 July 1980. Sidney Kaye, lawyer for CBS, Los Angeles, knew Lescaze's work from that commission.

2. Henry A. Dumper, associate, was primarily responsible for the design of the Kaye, Crowley, and Englander houses, and the Crossett Health Center; Henry A. Dumper to author, 8 October 1980.

3. *Pencil Points*, 21 (September 1940), n. p. and *Architectural Forum* 74 (June 1941): 127–128.

4. "Journal" (typescript), September 1, 1941, WELA.

5. "Journal" (typescript), September 28, 1941, WELA.

6. Typescript, 1940, WELA.

7. New York: G. P. Putnam's Sons, 1942.

8. Notes to self (handwritten), 25 February 1940 and 22 March 1956, WELA.

9. Lecture, Worcester Art Museum (typescript), 16 February 1943, WELA.

10. "We're Planning a City for Children" (typescript), WELA.

11. See "A Plan for Harlem's Redevelopment," *Architectural Forum* 80 (April 1944): 145–152; "Uplifting the Downtrodden," New York: Revere Copper and Brass Inc.; drawings and photographs in WELA.

12. Lescaze to Howe, 8 October 1943, WELA.

13. Photographs of perspective renderings are in "Photographs of Renderings" (scrapbook), Package 2, WELA. Also see "Worth Fighting For: Decent Housing for All," *PM's Daily Picture Magazine*, 13 April 1943, p. 1.

14. "Porcelain Enameled Curtain Wall Design Recommendations," *Architect and Engineer* 198 (July 1954): 10–11.

15. See Bibliography.

16. "Four Experimental Houses," *Architectural Forum* 91 (November 1949): 86–89. The other two architects were Edward Stone and Armand Bartos.

17. New York: G. P. Putnam's Sons, 1942, pp. 208–209.

18. "Service Station," *Architectural Forum* 78 (May 1943): 132–133.

19. James Marston Fitch, "William Lescaze," *Architecture Formes et Fonctions*, 6 (1959): 86–103.

20. See "What is Architecture?" (typescript), 31 January 1962, WELA.

21. "100 Largest Architectural Firms in the U.S.," *Architectural Forum* 120 (April 1964): 13–15.

22. Names of these associates were provided by Lescaze's accountant, Samuel Roth. Roth to author, 15 December 1980.

8

A Summation

ALTHOUGH NOT WITHOUT VARIETY, LESCAZE'S WORK bears a continuity and identifiable quality throughout his career. There is a continuity of style from the PSFS to the New York office buildings of twenty years later. There is a sustained interest in designing with structural glass from the time of his own house in 1933–1934 to his latest work in the 1960s. A coherent design relationship among architecture, interiors, furniture, and accessories was maintained from the 1923 Ford house to the postwar speculative office towers (Appendix E). Lescaze believed that an architect was not a "store window dresser, forced to design a new change every week."[1]

From his diploma project of 1919 to the Long Island Calderone Theater of thirty years later, Lescaze designed all sizes and manner of theaters and pioneered new schemes in the thirties for radio broadcasting and film projection. In the fifties, he designed cinerama theaters across the nation from New York to California.

His constant interest in large public housing projects persisted from his college years with Hans Bernouille in the second decade of the century to the New York City Housing Authority's projects of the sixties.

Finally, Lescaze's avocation of painting and his promotion of the integration of the arts (like that of De Stijl theory and the twenties' visionaries in Berlin and at the Bauhaus), were maintained throughout his life. He argued that the collaboration of artists in the creation of buildings should begin early in the course of the commission. He wrote in 1938: "As you probably know, mural paintings and sculpture are unfortunately too often an afterthought. They come after everything else is settled. . . . That situation must change."[2] Almost a quarter of a century later, he publicly decried the fact that the muralist and two sculptors for the New York Civil Courthouse and Municipal Courts building had been retained outside his control.[3] He urged early collaboration of artist and architect in the same way that structural and mechanical engineers were retained.[4]

Lescaze's belief in the importance of integrating the arts ultimately led to his commissioning a mural by Arshile Gorky for the 1939 World's Fair Aviation Building, a mosaic mural by Max Spivak for the Calderone Theater of 1949, a José de Rivera sculpture and Hans Hofmann mosaic mural for the 711 Third Avenue office building in 1956, a Beverly Pepper sculpture for the entrance of the office building at 777 Third Avenue in 1964, and a large ceramic tile mural by Pierre Soulage for the lobby of 1 Oliver Plaza office building in Pittsburgh of 1968. Only in the last commission, however, was the artist retained right from the start.[5]

Lescaze's work covered the widest possible range of architectural problems; his solutions were rarely without a touch of distinction. He believed that "to be an architect was something beautiful, frightfully important. One had to burn with the fire of conviction."[6] That conviction led him to become one of the century's leading architects; also a successful

132

furniture and interior designer, painter, musician, writer, lecturer, and educator.

In spite of the adversity of his early career—a world war, conservative post-war reaction, economic depression, and another world war—Lescaze reminisced that "all in all practicing architecture has been a wonderful thing for me."[7] He remarked:

> We have to work out our own destiny and we have to work it out in our own way. There are a lot of things that have to be done and we have to do them. We can't look to Europe for any solution. It is simply up to us.[8]

Indeed, he worked it out in his own way, but not without looking to Europe. Lescaze's early style developed from that dominated by neo-classicism and the eclectic sources of Art Déco, through that influenced by some of the principles of the International Style, to that dominated by the International Style alone. A number of labels, such as rationalist, expressionist, functionalist, romanticist, and French formalist have been used to characterize Lescaze's architecture. Indeed, his exact style is difficult to define because it synthesized all of these. It reflects both a technological and functional idealism along with the formalist's concern for abstract forms—indeed, the International Style as premiered by Le Corbusier, Gropius, Mendelsohn, and Mies is evident.

Lescaze participated in both the pre-war and post-war phases of the International Style in the United States; in the former he made his finest contribution. Lescaze's work falls into four periods. The first, from 1920–1929, was concerned with exploration, discovery, and finding himself in the new style. Although his efforts were sincere, results were minimal. The second, from 1929–1940, was his most contributory and influential period as a leader in introducing European modernism to the United States. The third, the war years of 1941–1945, consisted of writing, teaching, designing war housing, and proselytizing for the future of architectural design and planning. The fourth, from 1946–1969, never had the vitality of the pre-war work, probably reflecting the deterioration of the modern style in general. While successful in terms of big business, the work of these last years was no longer especially innovative.

Although Lescaze's work fell in the shadows of the foremost leaders of the modern architectural movement in the sense of creating its new theories or structural systems, Lescaze was among the best of the supporting cast. Dedicated to the idealism of the International Style, he was one of the most influential and articulate exponents of the early modern movement in America, introducing the newest design ideas from the Continent to an American clientele. He was considered the leading modern architect in the eastern United States in the thirties.

His earliest buildings were among the first important statements of the new architecture in this country. They include: the first International Style school building in the United States (the Oak Lane Country Day School's nursery school near Philadelphia, 1929); one of the first International Style residences built on the East Coast (the Frederick Vanderbilt Field house at New Hartford, Connecticut, 1930–1931); with George Howe, the first International Style skyscraper built in America (the Philadelphia Saving Fund Society building, 1929–1932); the first significant attempt in America to create a large-scale, low-cost urban housing development (the Chrystie-Forsyth project, 1931–1932); with others, the first large-scale, low-cost public housing project built in New York (the Williamsburg Houses, Brooklyn, 1935–1938); the first International Style town house built in New York and one of the earliest uses of glass block and air conditioning in America (his own house at 211 East Forty-eighth Street, New York, 1933–1934); and one of the earliest modern residences, schools, and housing developments in England (the headmaster's house at Dartington Hall, 1930–1932; the boarding schools at Dartington Hall, 1932–1934; and the Churston Housing Development near Paignton, 1932–1936). All are important landmarks in the history of modern architecture.

A talented and skilled architect, Lescaze is historically important because he worked to bridge the ideologies between turn-of-the-century design ideals and those of later modernism, producing a long list of innovative "firsts" in the twenties and thirties. They represent his promotion of the modernist ideology with a missionary zeal, an acute business sense, and a facility to utilize new developments in building technology. He is still remembered as a pioneering modernist. He will probably be best remembered for his most famous work, with George Howe, the PSFS.

For Lescaze, like the Europeans, architecture was both a social and artistic pursuit. He believed that the form and symbol of the International Style was dedicated to the idea of a new architecture resulting in a better society. The Ruskinian view that building should be the record of a community's life; van Doesburg's "moralist's view" that "visual order . . . will ultimately lead to personal and social good"; and the artistic view that "beautiful spaces and forms are ends in themselves" shaped his work.[9]

Lescaze's commitment to a modern architecture of strong simple forms can be traced from his first to his last project. He summarized his life's philosophy of design in his last public interview:

> Mais d'après moi, on ne doit pas s'amuser avec l'architecture, et construire pour étonner et susciter des bravos.
>
> Avant tout, on doit bâtir des immeubles fonctionels et disciplinés.
>
> La logique engendre automatiquement la beauté, une beauté durable que traverse les modes et les époques.
>
> C'est ma conviction profonde après un demisiècle d'architecture.[10]

To the very end, Lescaze was eager to work. Less than a month before his death, on 9 February 1969, he wrote: ". . . how I wish I knew when I am scheduled to be removed from this earth. How much can I finish before. How much should I dare to start before. . . ."[11]

That Lescaze made a significant and lasting contribution to the modern architecture movement in America, there is no doubt. He was an architect who worked in a great tradition and added something of importance to it. Yet, Lescaze noted at the end of his career:

It is strange when you look back and you see how much you have been ignored, how much silence has been built around you, . . . One wonders? When did it begin? I can't really say. It is difficult to put a finger on it and say: this is it—it's so silent, like fog. And it's been going now for years and years—yet I still hope that sweet history will show that I created more than they acknowledge and that I did influence the current of modern architecture more than they are admitting today.[12]

NOTES

1. Note to self (typescript), 21 August 1963, Sharon, Connecticut, WELA.

2. Lescaze to Mabel Dodge Luhan, 7 June 1938, WELA.

3. "Art and Politics Skirmish in City," *New York Times*, 30 April 1961, p. 82.

4. William Lescaze, "Thoughts on Art and Architecture," *Art International*, XII/2 (February 1968): 50.

5. William Lescaze, "Apropos Soulages Mural No. 1 Oliver Plaza" (typescript), 23 August 1967, WELA.

6. William Lescaze, "On Architecture" (typescript), 3 May 1937, p. 2, WELA.

7. William Lescaze, "Notes" (typescript), 26 January 1965, WELA.

8. Maury Maverick, quoted in Lescaze, "On Architecture," p. 4, WELA.

9. The quoted words are Theodore M. Brown's in his review of *Schindler*, by David Gebhard, in the *Art Bulletin 55* (June 1973): 310.

10. From an interview with Christian Vellas, 14 February 1969, published in the *Tribune de Genève;* quoted here from Agnoldomenico Pica, "Lescaze," *Domus* no. 476 (July 1969), p. 1.

11. Note to self (handwritten), 16 January 1969), WELA.

12. William Lescaze, Note to self (handwritten), early morning 30 November 1960, WELA.

Appendix A
Chronology

1896	27 March, born at Onex, Switzerland.
1910–1914	Collège de Genève.
1914–1915	Student of drawing and painting at Beaux-Arts de Genève.
1915–1919	Eidgenössische Technische Hochschule (École Polytechnique Federale), Zurich. Graduated as Master of Architecture in July 1919.
1919	About September–November, worked for the Committee for the Reconstruction of Devastated Areas of France, Arras.
1920	About January–August, worked in the office of Henri Sauvage, Paris. Immigrated to the United States in August.
	September–November, draftsman in the office of Hubbell and Benes, Cleveland.
1921–1922	Draftsman in the office of Walter R. MacCornack, Chief of the Bureau of Design for the Cleveland Board of Education.
	Exhibited paintings in the Cleveland Museum of Art's shows for Cleveland artists.
	Exhibited paintings at the Montross Gallery, New York.
1922–1923	Summer 1922–March 1923, traveled in Europe.
1923	April–May, returned to Cleveland, office of MacCornack.
	June, established independent architectural practice in New York City, firm of William Lescaze.
1923–1926	Period of remodeling and interior design commissions.
	Exhibited paintings at Whitney Studio Galleries and Montross Gallery, New York.
1927	Capital Bus Terminal, New York, first building executed in private practice.
1928	14 December, met George Howe.
1929	18 March, became a naturalized citizen of the United States.
	10 April, partnership contract with George Howe signed.
	1 May, partnership legally formed; firm of Howe and Lescaze established.
	September, opening of Oak Lane Country Day School's nursery school, Lescaze's first building in the International Style and the first school in the Style in the United States.
1929–1932	Philadelphia Saving Fund Society Office Building, first International Style skyscraper built in the United States, opened in August 1932.
1930–1931	Frederick Vanderbilt Field house, New Hartford, Connecticut, one of the first International Style houses built on the East Coast of the United States.

1930–1932	Headmaster's house (High Cross house), Dartington Hall, Devon, England, one of the earliest houses in the International Style built in England.
1932–1936	Churston Estate Housing Development, Devon, England, one of earliest International Style housing developments built in England.
1932	27 February, resigned from New York Architectural League.
	2 June, Howe told Lescaze of his intent to give up architectural practice.
	28 November, legal agreement to form Howe and Lescaze, Incorporated.
	1 December, legal agreement to dissolve partnership of Howe and Lescaze.
1933	21 July, legal agreement to dissolve corporation of Howe and Lescaze; Lescaze retained corporate name.
	29 September, marriage to Mary Connick Hughes of New York.
1933–1934	Lescaze house, 211 East Forty-eighth Street, New York, first International Style town house in New York; one of earliest uses of glass brick and air conditioning in the United States.
1935	20 March, second legal agreement to dissolve corporation. Lescaze discontinued use of corporate name. Firm of William Lescaze established.
1936–1942	Visiting Critic, Columbia University.
1937	Awarded silver medal by the International Jury at the Paris Exposition for the PSFS.
1938	8 December, son Lee Adrien born.
1939	Honor award by Southern California Chapter of the American Institute of Architects for the Columbia Broadcasting System building in Los Angeles, California.
	Awarded Gold Medal by the Philadelphia Chapter of the American Institute of Architects for the PSFS.
	Awarded silver medal for the Pavilion of Switzerland at the New York World's Fair.
1940	Awarded silver medal by the Pan American Congress of Architects, Montevideo, Uruguay, for the PSFS.
1943–1945	Taught industrial design at Pratt Institute.
1947	Certificate of Merit Award, New York State Association of Architects, for the Norman house.
1948	Fellow, Royal Society of Arts, England.
1949–1959	Member of the State Building Code Commission.
1951	Fellow, American Institute of Architects for achievement in design, education, and public service.
1955	Citation of Honor and Merit, Temple University, Philadelphia, Pennsylvania.
	Citation Award, *Progressive Architecture*.
1964	Citation, Church Center for the United Nations.
	Firm of William Lescaze and Associates formed with Henry Dumper, associate.
1966	Apollinare Osadca joined the firm as an associate. Other associates included Nevio Maggiore, Frank Preston, George Daub, Alvin Hausman, and Sidney Rappaport.
1969	Philadelphia Chapter, A.I.A. Building of Century Award for PSFS.
	9 February, died, New York.

Appendix B
Howe and Lescaze Staff for PSFS

Name	Responsibility	Dates of employment	Name	Responsibility	Dates of employment
Afazada, Girard	Draftsman		Heebner, Ronald M.	Chief Draftsman	Throughout
Baermann, Walter (trained in Munich)	Interiors	ca. Feb. 1931–Sept. 1932	Maas, Henrick Pieter	Draftsman and engineer	?–1934
Ball, Richard G.	Draftsman		McAllister, Louis	Assistant to Howe, Philadelphia	Throughout
Bolton, Earle W., Jr.	Drafting room mgr. in charge of dwgs. and specifications	Fall 1930 to end of project	Peter, George J.	Manager and engineer	1930–30 July 1931
Brach, Walter J.	Draftsman	"	Pollack, Ralph	Draftsman	
Brown, Morrison J.	Draftsman	"	Rice, J.	"Contact" man	
Colby, Charles	Draftsman	"	Rice, Norman (worked in Le Corbusier's office in Paris)	Coordinator of design details	Late spring 1931–1932
Clauss, Alfred (trained under Bonatz at Stuttgart Technical college)	Design, building schemes in 1930; furniture in 1931–32	Feb. 1930–Late 1932	Shapiro	Draftsman, Phila.	?–Sept. 1932
Daley, Robert House	Draftsman	"	Sinn, Gus	Draftsman	"
Daub, George	Chief, construction contracts and supervision, N.Y.	Throughout	Sturges, Walter Knight	Draftsman	"
			Sun	Draftsman	"
Dobson	Secretary, Philadelphia	Throughout	Whittlesey, Julian	Apprentice, draftsman	1931–16 Sept. 1932
Ehrlich	Design draftsman, Philadelphia	"	Zimmerly, Dick,	Draftsman	"
Fantl, Ernestine	Secretary, N.Y. (later a Curator, MoMA)	"			
Frey, Albert (trained in Winterthur, Switzerland; worked with Le Corbusier in Paris)	No work on PSFS	Aug. 1931–July 1932, half days.			

Appendix C
Allocation of Buildings Commissioned during the Years of the Howe and Lescaze Partnership and the Corporation

Howe and Lescaze	George Howe	William Lescaze	Howe and Lescaze	George Howe	William Lescaze
Oak Lane Country Day School	J. M. R. Sinkler House	Roy F. Spreter House	PSFS Garage	William Wasserman House	All new English work
Frederick V. Field House	American Battle Monuments	Lescaze house	Wilbour Library, Brooklyn Museum		Editorial Publications
Hessian Hills School	H. R. S. Stikeman House	Columbia Broadcasting System Studios	Chrystie-Forsyth Housing Development		South Philadelphia Housing
William B. Curry House	Welsh House	R. C. Kramer House			Boston Small House
PSFS Bank and Office Building	M. J. Speiser House	B. J. Buttenwieser House			Unity House

Appendix D*
Job List

Job No.	Date	Client	Description	Location
	1923			
131		Sutton Place [Sutton Square, No. 2]		
132 a, b, c, d		Mrs. C. Berens		
133		Willow Garden Restaurant		
134		Lalo		
135		La Bouterie		
136		van Biene		
137		Gidding		
138		Mrs. William R. Shephard		
139		Lido Restaurant		
140	1924	Club de Montmartre		
141		Hall at New Smyrna		
142		Garden Misses Hatwany and Miracle		
143		Exhibition rooms) R.D. Kohn		
144		Macy Gallery)		
145		Alteration to 3 University Place		
146		House near Geneva, Switzerland		
147		le Paradis, Washington		
148		O'Rourke, Astoria, L.I.		
149		Philadelphia, Ch. Chambers		
150		Garden at Sutton Place		
151		Burns Bros. Coal		
152		Miss M. Dreir, Silverlake, White Plains		
153		Dr. F.L. Stanton		
154		Macy Tea Room, R.D. Kohn		
155		J. Fraser-Apartment and studios		
156		A. Constantin		
157		Thorley Flowers		
158		Mrs. Tripp, Rye, N.Y.		
159		Karha Farm		
160		Andre, New York		
161		Mrs. D. Bulkley		
162				
163				

*Job numbers 107B (the first recorded) through 130 have been omitted because they were George Howe's commissions. The dates indicated before job number 510 are the author's judgment; after that they were written in the job list. Minor variations exist among the various copies of the job list. Editorial changes have been made for stylistic consistency in dates, place names, abbreviations, and capitalization. States were not always indicated. When only a street address is recorded, it may be assumed to be in New York. Bracketed entries are unrecorded but otherwise documented by the author. Numerical gaps and chronological inconsistencies exist in the job list. They have not been altered by the author.

Job No.	Date	Client	Description	Location
164				
165				
166				
167				
168				
169				
170				
171				
172				
173				
174				
175				
176				
177				
178				
179				
180				
181				
182				
183				
184				
185	1925	[Moulin Rouge, King's Tea Garden, Fulton Street, Brooklyn]		
186				
187				
188				
189				
190				
191				
192				
193				
194				
195				
196				
197				
198				
199				
200	1926	[Lauren J. Ford, Alteration to cottage, Rye, N.Y.]		
201				
202				
203				
204				
205				
206				
207				
208				
209	1927	[Capital Bus Terminal, 239 W. 50th St. and 240-242 W. 51st St., New York]		
210				
211				
212				
213				
214		Alice Ferguson Apartment House, New York [Faro de Colon]		
215		Miss N. Mclaren	Bathroom	New York
216		Madame Rubenstein	Shop	New York
217		R. B. Rathbone	Residence	White Plains, N.Y.
218		Dr. Campbell	Alteration	Dobbs Ferry, N.Y.
219		Saks and Company	Window	New York, N.Y.
220		Jean de Sièyes	Residence	Mt. Kisco, N.Y.
221		Alice de LaMar	Fireplace & kitchen	New York
222		R. Colfax Phillips	Apartment	New York
223		Marc Peter, Jr.	Drawings	
224		Best and Company	Window	New York
225		University Film	Building	Cambridge, Mass.
226	1928	Fred Loeser	Exhibition rooms	Brooklyn, N.Y.
227		Darcy Tea Set	Park Ave. galleries	New York
228		Amos Parrish & Co.	Offices	New York
229		James Converse	Alterations, residence	New York
230		Juan Kunzler	Bathroom	Douglaston
231		James Breese	Modern garden	Southampton, L.I.
232		Macy Exhibition	Penthouse	New York
233		Harper's Bazaar	Offices	New York
234		Best and Company	3rd floor annex	New York

Job No.	Date	Client	Description	Location
235		Miss Wiborg	Apartment	New York
236		Nudelman & Conti	Showroom	New York
237		Namm	Windows	Brooklyn, N.Y.
238		Best and Company	Article	
239		S.T. Meyers	Foyer	New York
240		L. Franke	Dining room	New York
241		L. Stokowski	Apartment	New York
242		A. Boni	Library	New York
243		Channel Bookshop	Interior	New York
244		R. Steiner [Boni Library]	Furniture	New York
245		Landay and Steinberg	Store	New York
246		Grauer	Store	New York
247		London Shoe	Store	New York
248		de Zemler	Showroom	New York
249		Welte Mignon		
250		Hugh Ferris		
251		Geller	Showroom	New York
252		Garage and apartment	Building	
253		Ravenna Mosaics	Booth	New York
254		Andrew Geller	Factory	Brooklyn, N.Y.
255		Maison Bertie	Beauty parlor	New York
256		Arden Gallery	Background	New York
257		Home Making Center	Floor	Grand Central, Pa.
258	1929	Oak Lane School	School	Philadelphia, Pa.
259		Unity Lap Robe Co.	Showroom	New York
260		H.E. Peter	Cabinet	Washington, D.C.
261		Judson Campbell	Building	New York
262		Wm. Stix Wasserman	Room	Philadelphia, Pa.
263				
264		Rayon Institute	Furniture	New York
265		Herbert Dreyfus	Room	New York
266		Orville Bullit	Dining room	Whitemarsh, Pa.
267		Samuel A. Crozer	Morning room	Chestnut Hill
268		J.L. Handy	Office	New York
269		Miss Montgomery	Studio	New York
270		Mrs. Chas. Harding	Salon	New York
271		Saks-34th Street	Store	New York
272		Briggs Haberdashery	Store	New York
273		Mr. Alex Chatin	Apartment	New York
274		Mr. Charles Denby	Offices	Philadelphia, Pa.
275		H.M. Dreyfus	Bedroom suite	New York
276		Ben Herzberg	Apartment	New York
277		Mrs. Porter	Residence	Ojai, California
278		H.M. Dreyfus	Bedroom and bath	New York
279				
T-280		Marc Peter	Legation, residence	
281		[Brill]	[Apartment]	Philadelphia, Pa.
282		Yarnell	Alterations	
283				
284		PSFS	Bank & office	Philadelphia, Pa.
285				
286		Peck	Residence	[Paoli, Pa.]
287		Peck	Chapel	
288				
289		Howe and Lescaze	Office	Philadelphia, Pa.
T-290		AP	Fashion building	
291		Hunt	Room	
292		Mrs. Charles Russell	Residence	
293		Mrs. L. Isaacs	Theatre	
294				
295		Museum of Modern Art	Museum	
296		Sturgis Ingersoll	Picture gallery	
297		PSFS	Garage	
298		PSFS	South Branch	
299			Philadelphia park development	
T-300		Mr. Howe	Studio	
301	1930	Frederick V. Field	Residence	New Hartford, Conn.
C-302			Theatre	
303		PSFS	Temporary branch	
304		Dartington Hall	Headmaster's house	England
304-B		Dartington Hall	Junior school	

Job No.	Date	Client	Description	Location
305	1931	Hattie Carnegie, Inc.	Store	
306		Mr. Lescaze	Apartment	
307		Trans Lux Movies, Inc.	Theatres	
308		PSFS	Temporary office	
T-309)1			Warehouse, Worcester	
)2A.B.				
T-310			Emigrant Savings Bank	
T-311			Apartment house	
312		Hessian Hills School	School building	Croton, N.Y.
313		Frank Vance Storrs	Offices	
314		Wm. Stix Wasserman	Office	
T-315		Major John Zanft	Conservatory	
T-316		Hattie Carnegie, Inc.	Front shop	
T-317		Trans Lux Movie, Inc.	Theatre-PSFS	
318		Fox	Theatre	
319		Harry F.S. Stikeman	Residence	Canada
320		Pennsylvania Museum	Furniture	Philadelphia, Pa.
321		M. Wertheim	Residence	Connecticut
322		Project-Chrystie-Forsythe Streets hsg. development	Housing development	
T-323		Leonard K. Elmhirst	Various offices	Dartington Hall, England
E-324		Architectural League exhibition	Solarium	New York
E-325		Pennsylvania Museum exhibition		Philadelphia, Pa.
T-326		Lincoln Hotel		New York
T-327		Gotham Hotel		New York
T-328		Trans Lux Corp.	Theatre	Philadelphia, Pa.
T-329		Museum of Natural Science		Philadelphia, Pa.
T-330		Trans Lux Corp.	Theatre	Grand Central, N.Y.
T-331		Fifty small houses		
T-332		Fleetwood system	Small store front	New York
T-333		Trans Lux Corp.	Theatre	18th & Market, Pa.
T-334		Project	Housing development	Danbury, Pa.
T-335		Psi Upsilon fraternity	Club house	Dartmouth, Hanover, N.H.
T-336		Project-L (River Gardens)	Large scale housing	
T-337		Vassar College	Gymnasium	Poughkeepsie, N.Y.
T-338			Gas station	New York
339		Dorothy Gray	Store front	New York
T-340	1932	Astoria	Development	New York
341		59th St. & Park Ave.		New York
342		Mr. William Lescaze	Shanty	Bridgewater, Conn.
343		Stonebridge Bldg.	New York	New York
344		405 E. 57th St. Bldg.		New York
345		Project-Laurel Hill	Housing Dev.	New York
346		Churston Estate Co.	Housing Dev.	Devon, England
347		Leonard K. Elmhirst	Boarding House #1	Dartington Hall, England
348		Queen's Blvd.	Competition	New York
349		Springfield Museum	Directors Room	Springfield, Mass.
350		Buckingham Hotel	Alterations	New York
351		180 Madison Ave.		New York
352		Bensonhurst	Housing Dev.	Brooklyn, N.Y.
353		Phelps Stokes	Competitive hsg.	New York
354	1933	Mr. William Lescaze	Alteration to house	211 E. 48th St.
355		Dartington Hall	Nursery school	England
356		Dartington Hall	Gymnasium	England
357		Dartington Hall	Offices & laboratory	England
358		Dartington Hall	Piggery	England
359		Dartington Hall	Yarner housing	England
360		Roy Spreter	Studio & garage	Ardmore, Pa.
361		Dr. G.W. Hartman	Small house	State College, Pa.
362		Connecticut College	General layout & auditorium	New London, Conn.
363		Robert McLean	Electric sign	Evening Bulletin
364		Dr. J. Campbell White	Children's Haven	New York
365		Frank Darling	Radio City	New York
366		Philip Youtz	Wilbour library	Brooklyn, N.Y.
367		Housing Research	Data	
368		Waldo Adler	Low cost housing	Philadelphia, Pa.

Job No.	Date	Client	Description	Location
369		L.K. Elmhirst	4 cottages	Dartington Hall, England
370		C. Bauer	Low cost housing	Philadelphia, Pa.
371		L.K. Elmhirst	Boarding houses 4 & 5	Dartington Hall, England
372		Gimbel's	Consultation	New York
373		U.S. Government	Housing	
374		Villa	Alterations	Geneva, Switzerland
375	1934	Dartington Hall	Old building	Devon, England
375-B		Dartington Hall	Theatre	Devon, England
376		B. Altman	Apartment	New York
377		Queensbridge	Housing	New York
378		Public Library	New building	New York
379		R.C. Kramer	Town house	New York
380		Wm. Kay Wallace	Country house	Bedford Village
381		Elmhirst (Offices)	Alterations (Ed. Publications)	New York
382			Housing	Philadelphia, Pa.
383		Boarding Houses B & C		Dartington Hall, England
384		R. Ullman	Alterations	New York
385		Whitney Estate	Camp Togus	Adirondacks
386		Brooklyn Museum	Children's Museum	Brooklyn, N.Y.
387		Metropolitan Museum	Exhibition room 1934	New York
388		N.Y.C. Housing	Williamsburg	New York
389		Theatre Arts Monthly	Project theatre	
390		Mrs. Rossin	Apartment	New York
391		Auditorium	Brooklyn Museum	Brooklyn, N.Y.
392		Robert McLean	Wine cellar alt.	Brooklyn, N.Y.
393		Dartington Hall	Jooss house	Dartington Hall, England
394		Arthur Levy	Small house	Providence, R.I.
395		Mrs. A.J. Connick	Air conditioning	New York
396		Mrs. B.J. Buttenwieser	Town house	New York
397		Unity House	Camp A-Bldg. A, Main Dining hall B-Dormitory C-Bowling alley D-Survey & Road layout E-Tennis courts F-Cottages G-Canopies H-Interiors I-Color scheme J-Social hall K-Landscaping L-Toilets M-Pump house	Bushkill, Pa.
398		CBS	Theatre	45th St., N.Y.
399		L.K. Elmhirst	Alteration to 1125 Fifth Ave.	New York
400		L.K. Elmhirst	Rock Creek housing	Washington, D.C.
401		E.C. Blum	Bedroom	Brooklyn, N.Y.
402		Design	Cocktail shaker	New York
403		H.M. Dreyfus	Interior of apartment	New York
404	1935	CBS	Radio studio	New York
405		CBS	Studio 485	New York
406		Brunswick-Balke-Collender	Billiard tables	Chicago, Ill.
407		Vincent Cates	Boston small house	Boston, Mass.
408		J. Walter Thompson	Office for Miss Ruth Waldo	New York
409		Howard Froelick	Town house	New York
410		CBS	Little theatre	New York
411		Silvray, Inc.	Lighting signs	New York
412		CBS	Studio #5	New York
413		CBS	Misc. reception rooms	New York
414		CBS	Studio #4	New York
415		CBS	Chairs & music stands	New York
416		John Hammond	Gas station	New York
417		CBS	Display room	New York

Job No.	Date	Client	Description	Location
418		CBS	Misc. accessories	New York
419		City of Ansonia	High school	Ansonia, Conn.
420		Mrs. Mittleman	Alteration to apt.	New York
421		S.T. Kootz	Alteration to office and living room	New York
422		Property Management	Theatre and store	Boston, Mass.
423		Mr. Schwefel	Bar, George Washington Hotel	New York
424		John Hammond	Residence	Bryn Mawr, Pa.
425		WEL	Consultant housing	New York
426		CBS	CBS	New York
427		Mrs. Field	Bleecker St.	New York
428		CBS	Soundlocks	New York
429		CBS	Colors	New York
430		CBS	Floor patterns	New York
431		CBS	Microphone	New York
432		Mr. Good	Weekend house	Harvey Cedars, N.J.
433		CBS	Alterations	New York
434		Purdue University	Small House	Purdue, Ind.
435		Herzberg	Apartment	New York
436			Ransom project	New York
437		Mrs. Williams	Residence	Norfolk, Conn.
438		Alan Wolfe		New York
439		Greenwich House Guild		Greenwich, Conn.
440		Magnolia Petroleum	Exposition bldg.	Dallas, Tex.
441		EL	Consultant	New York
442		Mr. Hiter King	Movie Center	Greenwich, Conn.
443		CBS	Studio #7	New York
444		CBS	Elevator study	New York
445		CBS	Materials research	New York
446		Nassau College, N.Y.U.	Study	Hempstead, L.I.
447		British Broadcasting Co.	Offices	New York
448		Mr. Roth	Leather	New York
449		Mrs. De Kay	Couch	New York
450		Churston Dev. Co.	Hotel	Devon, England
451		Churston Dev. Co.	Second batch houses	Devon, England
452		Churston Dev. Co.	Shops and bank	Devon, England
453		Churston Dev. Co.	Administrative bldg.	Devon, England
454		Churston Dev. Co.	Third batch houses	Devon, England
455		Churston Dev. Co.	Fourth batch houses	Devon, England
500	1936	Rex Allen	Consultation	New York
501		CBS	WBBM-Chicago	Chicago, Ill.
502		Samuel Kootz	Cigarette lighter	New York
503		Ralph Steiner	Fan	New York
504			Restaurant	New York
505			Glass house	Newark, N.J.
506		Competition	Oregon State Capitol	
507		F.V. Field	Apartment	New York
508		CBS	Majestic Theatre	New York
509		Prof. F.S. Dunn	House	Woodbridge, Conn.
510	Apr.	CBS	Maintenance	New York
511		CBS	Scheme 34	New York
512		John Gustavson	House	Harvey Cedars, N.J.
513		Church		Ansonia, Conn.
514		F.V. Field	Addition to house	New Hartford, Conn.
515	May	CBS	New studios	Hollywood, Calif.
516		J. Walter Thompson	Offices	New York
516 A		General consultation		
B		Radio Reception room		
C		Radio department		
D		Miss Taylor's office		
E		Miscellaneous		
F		Elevator lobby		
G		Old reception room		
517		Alfred Loomis	Experimental house	Tuxedo Park, N.Y.
518	June	Time, Inc.	Offices	New York
519		Bernard Rogers	House	Rochester, N.Y.
520	July	W.H. Fain [Williams]	House	Greenwich, Conn.
521		CBS	Manhattan Theatre	New York
522		Louis Seidman	Development	New York
523		Kimble Glass Co.	Office bldg.	Vineland, N.J.

Job No.	Date	Client	Description	Location
523 A		Arch.		
B		Structural		
C		Mechanical		
		1. Heat & air conditioning		
		2. Plumbing		
D		Electrical		
E		Air conditioning in other bldgs.		
524		Owens Illinois	Recreation room	Bridgeton, N.J.
525		John J. Nesbitt	Unit	Philadelphia, Pa.
526	Aug.	Samuel Kootz	Penthouse	New York
527		Good Housekeeping	Model apartment	New York
528		CBS	Studios	Cincinnati, Ohio
529		Paul Keston	Apartment	New York
530		CBS	Music Box Theatre	Hollywood, Calif.
531		CBS	Studios	San Francisco, Calif.
532		Fred Nash	Country house	Minneapolis, Minn.
533	Sept.		Apartment house	New York
534	Oct.	CBS	Consultation	New York
535	Nov.	CBS	Alteration, 12th floor	New York
536		Frank Zermann	Proposed house	Long Island City, N.Y.
537		Nathan Straus	Offices	New York
538	Dec.	CBS	Office building	Hollywood, Calif.
539		Mr. Buttzman	Industrial design	New York
540		Herman Kimble	Apartment	Ventnor, N.J.
541		Major Bayette	House	Florida
542		CBS	Park Ave.	New York
543	1937	Howard Markel	Country house	Redding, Conn.
544		CBS	Golden Theatre	New York
545	Feb.	Mrs. Mali	Bedroom	New York
546		Time, Inc.	Offices	New York
547	Mar.	J. Walter Thompson	Layout	New York
548		Kimble Glass Co.	Supt. office	Vineland, N.J.
549		CBS	Studios	San Francisco, Calif.
550				
551				
552				
553				
554				
555				
556				
557				
558				
559				
560				
561				
562				
563				
564				
565				
566				
567				
568				
569				
570	Mar.	CBS	Lobby, 799 Seventh Ave.	New York
571	Apr.	Mrs. Mali	Alteration to house	New York
572	May	Mrs. Boorum	House	Auburn, N.Y.
573	June	CBS	World's Fair	New York
574		Osgood Field	Alt. to house	New York
575		Kimble Glass Co.	Furniture, Kimco Club	Vineland, N.J.
576	July	Mr. Bentayou	Design perfume bottle	New York
577	Sept.	Mrs. Katz	Music school	New York
578		Felix Green	Apartment	New York
579	Oct.	CBS	Alt. 485 Madison Ave.	New York
580	Nov.	McCall's magazine	Layout of model house	New York
581	Nov.	Mrs. Gellhorn	Apartment	New York
582	Nov.	World's Fair	Aviation building	New York
583	Nov.	Pass and Seymour	Fixtures	New York
584	Dec.	LOF World's Fair	Building	New York
585	1938	W.B. Osgood Field	House	Putnam Valley, N.Y.

Job No.	Date	Client	Description	Location
585 a				
b				
c				
d				
e				
586	Jan.	Mr. Weinberg	Bridge approach	New York
587	Jan.	Alfred Stern	Penthouse	New York
588		Garrett A. Hobart, III	House	Tuxedo Park, N.Y.
589	Mar.	B.J. Buttenwieser	Room for son	New York
590		Macey-Fowler	Furniture design	New York
591		Miss Rosenblatt	House	Yonkers, N.Y.
592		Wheaton College	Competition	Norton, Mass.
593		F.V. Field	Alteration 16 W. 12th St.	New York
594		Switzer-Sonnenberg	World's Fair gadgets	New York
595	Apr.	Knowles	Queens hsg. project	New York
596	May	AGA	Competition	Baltimore, Md.
597	June	Switzerland	World's Fair pavilion	New York
598	June	Goucher College	Competition	Baltimore, Md.
599		Treasury department	Competition	Washington, D.C.
600	June	WCAU - CBS	Alt. to auditorium	Philadelphia, Pa.
601	July	World's Fair	Glass house	New York
602	Aug.	W. Lescaze	Guest room furniture	New York
603	Aug.	W. Lescaze	Additional floors	New York
604	Nov.	F.V. Dunn	Cottage	Woodbridge, Conn.
605	Nov.	Yonkers Project		Yonkers, N.Y.
606	Dec.	Stacy May	Cottage	Martha's Vineyard, Mass.
607		WCAU	Facade	Philadelphia, Pa.
608	1939	Switzerland	Office of consul	New York
609	Jan.	Margaret Lamont	Utopia Children's House	New York
610	Feb.	John Stuart, Inc.	Display floor	New York
611	Feb.	Osgood Field	Kitchen, 18 W. 12th St.	New York
612	Feb.	Competition	[Smithsonian]	Washington, D.C.
613	Apr.	Aviation building	Restaurant	New York World's Fair
614	June	B.J. Buttenwieser	Alteration	Bedford, N.Y.
615	June	Betty Barclay	Restaurant	New York
616	June	Thonet Brothers	Furniture design	New York
617A	July	Cherry Lawn School	Alteration to old building	Darien, Conn.
617B	July	Cherry Lawn School	New boys' dorm	Darien, Conn.
618	July	George Marshall	House	New York
619	July	Project	Office building [Longfellow]	Washington, D.C.
620	July	G. Mittelman	Alteration	New York
621	Sept.	Newspaper Guild	Alteration	New York
622	Sept.	Harold Spivacke	House	Washington, D.C.
623	Nov.	Metropolitan Museum	Exhibition	New York
624		Dr. Bernard Bernard	Room	New York
625		Switzerland	Pavilion	New York World's Fair
625 a		Parade ground pavilion		
b		Restaurant and cheese cellar, interior		
c		Locker and storage bldg.		
d		Dolder cheese cellar, interiors		
e		Oelikens		
626	Dec.	Republic Aviation	Factory	Farmingdale, L.I.
627		Johnson & Johnson	Plant	New Brunswick, N.J.
628	1940	Edward A. Norman	Residence	New York
629	Mar.		Apartment house study	New York
630		Mrs. George Crawford	Guest house	Greenwich, Conn.
631	Apr.	Unity House	Alteration to bldg. A	Bushkill, Pa.
632	Apr.	Osgood Field, Jr.	Alteration, 3rd floor 18 W. 12th St.	New York
633	Apr.		Industrial design	New York
634	May	Garrett A. Hobart, III	Alteration, bath & dressing room	Patterson, N.J.
635	May	Frederick V. Field	Alteration, 4th floor 16 W. 12th St.	New York
636	May		New city buildings	Troy, N.Y.
637	May	Frederick V. Field	Apartment house study 63 E. 79th St.	New York
638	May	Mr. Joseph Barnes	Sketches, alteration apt. house lobby	Washington, D.C.

Job No.	Date	Client	Description	Location
639	June		Alteration, apt. house	Washington, D.C.
640	June	Kellogg Mann	Gas Station	Buffalo, N.Y.
641	June		Project "F" St.	Washington, D.C.
642	July	N.Y.C.H.A.	Chelsea houses	New York
643	July	Mrs. Joseph Barnes	Alteration, W. 22nd St.	New York
645	July	Field	645 Fifth Ave.	New York
646	July	Dr. White	Apartment house project	New York
647	Sept.	Swiss Legation	Project	Washington, D.C.
648	Oct.	Maurice Stone	Bedroom	New York
649A	Oct.	Ferdinand Sonneborn	Residence	Greenburgh, N.Y.
649B		Ferdinand Sonneborn	Garage building	Greenburgh, N.Y.
649C		Ferdinand Sonneborn	All other buildings	Greenburgh, N.Y.
650	Oct.	Wickett	House	Greenborough, N.Y.
651	Dec.		Proposed apartment house, Fifth Ave.	New York
652	Nov.		Alteration, Westchester Van & Storage Co. bldg.	Mt. Vernon, N.Y.
653	Jan. 1941	Mary Morris Steiner	Industrial design	New York
654	Feb.	University Settlement	Alt. gymnasium	New York
655	Mar.	John C. Drake	Office bldg. Conn. & N.	Washington, D.C.
656	Mar.	Vincent Gallagher	Taxpayer	Albany, N.Y.
657	Apr.	George L. Michel	Taxpayer	Forest Hills, N.Y.
658	Apr.	Fred V. Field	Guest house	New Hartford, Conn.
659	Apr.	Fred V. Nash	New addition	Minneapolis, Minn.
660	May	Johnson & Johnson	Signs	New Brunswick, N.J.
661	May	Fred Field	Caretaker's cottage	New Hartford, Conn.
662	May	Ralph Steiner	Cottage	Warren, Conn.
663	May	John C. Drake	Metropolitan project	Washington, D.C.
664	May	Harold Sothoron	Oak Gardens	Washington, D.C.
665	July		Defense house	
666	July		Defense housing, plot plan and typical house	Hartford, Conn.
667	July		Defense housing, plot plan and typical house	Hartford, Conn.
668	Aug.	Paul Herzog	Alteration	Hartsdale, N.Y.
669	Aug.	Maurice Stone	Consulting services	New York
670	Aug.	Competition	Mid-River vent. bldg.	New York
671	Sept.	William Lescaze	Alteration, 209 E. 48th St.	New York
672	Aug.		Defense housing, plot plan and typical house	West Springfield, Mass.
673	Oct.	Benjamin Buttenwieser	Daughter's bedroom	New York
674	Oct.	University Settlement	Alterations	New York
675	Oct.	Mrs. Mittleman	Room	New York
676	Nov.	J.B. Williams Co.	Alt. to offices	Graybar Bldg., N.Y.
677	Nov.	Messers. Flory and Grant	Office	New York
678	Dec.		Defense housing, plot plan and typical house	Massena, N.Y.
679	Jan. 1942		Dormitory project	Washington, D.C.
680	Mar.		Defense houses	Roselle, N.J.
681	Apr.	Maurice Stone	Consulting services	44 W. 12th St., N.Y.
682	May	Mr. Throgmorton	Dormitory project	Arlington, Va.
683	July	Museum	Brooklyn Children's Museum	Brooklyn, N.Y.
684-P	July	Station WLW	Broadcasting studios	Cincinnati, Ohio
685-P	July		Studies	Schenectady, N.Y.
686-P	July		Studies	New York
687	Aug.	Helena Rubinstein	Apartment	New York
688	Sept.	Pass & Seymour	Lighting fixtures	Syracuse, N.Y.
689	Sept.	Dr. B. Bernard	Apartment	New York
690	Oct.	Stanley McAllister	Honor Roll	Scarsdale, N.Y.
691	Dec.		War housing project	Montgomery City, Md.
692	Jan. 1943	Monsanto	Designs in plastic	New York
693	Jan.	Mrs. R.C. Kramer	Repairs to house	New York
694	Feb.	Kawneer Company	Consulting services	Niles, Mich.
695	Mar.	Architectural Forum	Design for filling station	New York
696	Mar.	American Aircraft	Plant	Secaucus, N.J.
697	Mar.	Mrs. John Jessup	House	
698	Mar.		Manhattan planning study	New York
699	Mar.	Chestnut Gardens, Inc.	War housing project	Bridgeport, Conn.
700	Apr.	Spelman Prentice	Alt. to farmhouse	St. Johnsbury, Vt.
701	May	M.L. Goldman	Apartment interiors	New York
702	May	Maurice Stone	Removal of violation	W. 46th St. Theatre

Job No.	Date	Client	Description	Location
703	May	Revere	Design for ad (Leisure Center)	
704	May	J. Walter Thompson	Layout of offices	New York
705	June	Edward Zimmer	War housing	New Jersey
706	Aug.	CBS	Theater	W. 53rd St.
707	Aug.	Mrs. Maurice Stone	Apartment 930 Fifth Ave.	New York
708	Aug.	Paul Herzog	784 Park Ave., 18th Floor	New York
709	Sept.	L. Seidman	Small housing	Bridgeport, Conn.
710	Sept.	C.E. Halback	Warehouse	Brooklyn, N.Y.
711	Sept.	Robert W. Dowling	Amusement center	New York
712	Oct.	Industrial design	Lighting fixtures	New York
713	Oct.	Emerson	Radio cabinet	New York
714	Oct.	City Athletic Club	Local law 29	New York
715	Oct.	CBS	Executive office	New York
716	Nov.	Hamilton school	Private school, 15 E. 81st St.	New York
717	Dec.	Hope's Windows	Research	Jamestown, N.Y.
718	Jan. 1944	Bob Highfield	Small housing	Silver Spring, Md.
719	Jan.	Pittsburgh Plate Glass	Commercial	Pittsburgh, Pa.
720	Feb.	Johnson & Johnson	Personnel dept.	New Brunswick, N.J.
721	Feb.	Vincent Gallagher	Housing development	Albany, N.Y.
722	Mar.	CBS	Theatre #2	New York
723	Mar.	Cherry Lawn School A. Manor House B. Boys' Dormitory C. Steinhall D. Lab Building E. Swedish Cottage F. Boys' Cottage	Additions	Darien, Conn.
724	Apr.	Mrs. Prashker	Alteration to residence	Palisades, N.J.
725	Apr.	Filene	Parking terminal	Boston, Mass.
726	Apr.	Mrs. Samuel Duryee	Apartment	New York
727	May	CBS	Office (Dr. Stanton)	New York
728	May	Spelman Prentice	Addition to residence	Lyndonville, Vt.
729	May	Universal Housing & Development Corp.	Linwood Heights	Washington, D.C.
730	May	Universal Housing & Development Corp.	Landover	Maryland
731	June	WOR	Building sign	New York
732	June	Bloomingdale's	Green room	New York
733	June	Hamilton School	Addition in rear	New York
734	June	J. Walter Thompson	Layout of art & traffic depts.	New York
735	June	Pioneer Williams Co.	Elm Terrace Gardens	West Haven, Conn.
736	June	Pioneer Williams Co.	Lawnside	New Jersey
737	June	J. Walter Thompson	North "L", 11th floor	New York
738	July	Johnson & Johnson Co.	Research; Ind. bldg.	New Brunswick, N.J.
739	Aug.	Maurice Stone	Dining room	New York
P-740	Aug.	Planning Study	City for Children	East Harlem, N.Y.
741	Sept.	J. Walter Thompson	Research; furniture standards	New York
742	Sept.	Mrs. Wm. McCleery	Interiors	New York
743	Sept.	Dr. Bernard	Consulting	New York
744	Sept.	City Athletic Club	Alterations	New York
745	Sept.	Mrs. William Paley	Alterations	New York
746	Sept.	Project	Recuperative hospital	Washington, D.C.
747	Oct.	J. Walter Thompson	Key floor plans	New York
748	Oct.	Mr. Jos. McCaffery	Alt., Films for Ind.	135 W. 52nd St.
749	Oct.	NYCHA	Changes to Elliott houses	New York
750	Oct.	George G. Woodman	Residence	Chappaqua, N.Y.
751	Oct.	CBS	Microphone	New York
752	Oct.	Univ. Housing & Dev. Corp.	North Kenilworth	Maryland
753	Nov.	City Athletic Club	Alteration, washrooms	New York
754	Nov.	Federal Mfg. & Eng. Corp.	Industrial design	Brooklyn, N.Y.
755	Dec.	Rockland Realtors Corp.	Office	Fort Lee, N.J.
756	Dec.	Universal Housing & Development Corp.	Chestnut Heights, Garden, apt.	Washington, D.C.
757	Dec.	Bausch & Lomb	Optician's office (adv)	Rochester, N.Y.
758	Jan.	Dr. Eugene Lowenberg	Doctor's bldg.	Norfolk, Va.
759	Jan.	Scarsdale	Planning study-recreation	Scarsdale, N.Y.
760	Jan.	Crossett	Health Facility Center	Crosset, Ark.
761	Mar.	Chicopee Sales Corp.	Offices	New York
762	Mar.	Consumers Cooperative	Restaurant	New York
763	Mar.	City Athletic Club	Addition	52 W. 54th St.

Job No.	Date	Client	Description	Location
764	Mar.	Mr. Hardwick Moseley	Apartment	New York
765	Mar.	Mr. Joseph Barnes		New York
766	Mar.	Godmothers League	Babies' Shelter	West 71st St.
767	Apr.	Dr. Calderone Theatre	Theatre	Hempstead, L.I.
768	May	White House	Radio room	Washington, D.C.
769	May	White House	Radio cabinets	Washington, D.C.
770	May	Samuel Kootz	Art gallery	New York
771	May	Mrs. Meloney	Alteration	New York
772	May	Johnson & Johnson	Recreation & First aid room	New Brunswick, N.J.
773	June	Hudson Guild	Alteration	New York
774	June	Maurice Stone	Bookshelves, apt.	New York
775	June	Mrs. Kazan	Alteration	167 E. 74th St.
776	June	David Heyman	Living room alt.	Armonk, N.Y.
777	July	Iceland State Broadcast Service	Broadcasting station	Reykjavik, Iceland
778	July	Vanadium Corporation	Alteration offices	New York
779	July	Columbia Broadcasting System	Mobile unit	New York
780	July	Alfred Loomis	Residence	Easthampton, N.Y.
781	July	Photographic Trade News	Camera store (Adv.)	New York
782	July		Housing	Buffalo, N.Y.
783	July	Teck Construction Co.	Department store	Silver Springs, Md.
784	Aug.	Herzog	Alteration-residence	Washington, D.C.
785	Aug.	Board of Education	Elementary school	Norwood, N.J.
786	Aug.	City of New York	City & Municipal Courts Bldg.	New York
787	Sept.	Board of Education	P.S. 14	Richmond, N.Y.
788	Sept.		Alteration, Mineola Theatre	Mineola, L.I.
789	Sept.	Crown Central Petroleum Corporation	Filling station	Baltimore, Md.
790	Sept.	Mr. & Mrs. D. Greenberg	Residence	Hopewell Junction, N.Y.
791	Sept.	Jerome Crowley	Residence	South Bend, Ind.
792	Sept.	Walter Erb	Small house design	Madison, Wis.
793	Nov.	Dr. Kingsley Roberts	Bedroom furniture	New York
794	Nov.	Westchester Conservatory of Music	Preliminary sketches	White Plains, N.Y.
795	Nov.	Henry Englander	Residence	Jamaica, N.Y.
796	Nov.	Morris Schoenfeld	Laun-Dry-Ette	New York
797	Nov.	Werner Gubelin	Jewelry Store	New York
798	Nov.	Borgenicht	Showroom & offices	New York
799	Dec.	William Walton	Apartment-Gramercy Park	New York
800	Mar. 1946	N.Y. Housing Trust	Research prefab	New York
801	Dec.	Reliance Steel Corp.	Design for prefabricated houses	Pittsburgh, Pa.
802	Dec.	C.D. Williams	Addition to house	Norfolk, Conn.
803	Dec.		Frozen foods	
804	Dec.	KLM Royal Dutch Airlines	Survey and recommendations	New York
805	Dec.	Mr. & Mrs. Thos. Clyde	Residence	Southhampton, L.I.
806	Jan. 1946	J. Walter Thompson	Alt. to Wall St. office	New York
807	Jan.	City Athletic Club	Alteration	New York
808	Jan.	Mr. Buttenwieser	Alteration to town house	New York
809	Jan.	Mr. Vincent Gallagher	Residence	Delray Beach, Fl.
810	Jan.	Mrs. Levey	Residence	Candlewood Lake, Conn.
811	Jan.	CBS	Maxine Elliott Theatre alt.	New York
812	Mar.	Vincent Gallagher	County club & dept. store	Albany, N.Y.
813	Apr.	Belmont Hill School	Proposed additions	Belmont, Mass.
814	Apr.	Schwarz Laboratory	Site plan	New Rochelle, N.Y.
815	Apr.	CBS	Alvin Theatre	New York
816	May	Hugh Bennett	Residence	Huntington, L.I.
817	May	Longfellow Bldg.	Alternations for store rental	Washington, D.C
818	May	Fred Nash	Addition to residence	Minneapolis, Minn.
319	May	Congress Theatre	Inspection, recommendations	Saratoga, N.Y.
820	May	Mr. Harney	Liquor store	New York
821	May	Mr. Stavros Niarchos	Alteration, 441 E. 57th St.	New York
822		Paul Kern	Alteration, residence	New York
823		Fred Field	Residence	Putnam County, N.Y.
824	June	J.W. Thompson	New kitchen, new coatroom	New York
825	July	Clarence Hornung	Alteration	New York
P-826	Aug.	Harry Nagin	Hotel	Atlantic City, N.J.
827	Aug.	Community Center	Alteration	New York
828	Aug.	J. Walter Thompson	Office panelling	New York
829	Sept.	WINS	Alteration	New York
830	Sept.	KNX	Traffic study	Hollywood, Calif.

Job No.	Date	Client	Description	Location
831	Oct.		Second stage, wall research	
832		Fred V. Field	Lila's room	16 W. 12th St.
833	Jan. 1947	John C. Drake	Conn. Ave. and N Project	Washington, D.C.
834	Jan.		Project	New York
835	Jan.	Richard Wright	Alteration	13 Charles St.
836	Jan.	20th Century Garage	Alteration	48th St.
837	Feb.	Mesker Windows	Advertisement	St. Louis, Mo.
838	Feb.		Professional building	Hempstead, L.I.
839	Feb.	Harmony Hotel	Fire Dept. compliance	New York
840	Feb.	Editorial Publications (New Republic)	Reception room counter	New York
841	Apr.	J. Walter Thompson	Soundproof room	New York
842	Feb.	Frank Calderone	Alteration to residence	Kings Point, L.I.
843	Apr.	N.Y. State Division of Housing	Consultant	Astoria, L.I.
844	May	Hospital S	Addition	New York
845	May	Hudson Guild	Elevator	New York
846	June	J. Walter Thompson	Miscellaneous furniture	New York
847	June	Bernice Jay	Store and apartments	Washington, D.C.
848	July	Webb & Knapp	Offices - 383 Madison Ave.	New York
849	July	North Hempstead	Housing project	**Manhasset, Port Washington, L.I.**
850	July	CBS	Color consultation	New York
851	Aug.	Maytag Atlantic	Building alteration	Long Island, N.Y.
852	Sept.	Mr. Spelman Prentice	Alteration	1 E. 94th St.
853	Sept.	Mr. A.F. Cook	Alteration	Seaford, L.I.
854	Sept.	CBS - KNX	Additions	Hollywood, Calif.
855	Oct.	Somerton [Reliance]	Site planning	Philadelphia, Pa.
856	Oct.	Philmont [Reliance]	Site planning	Philadelphia, Pa.
857	Nov.	[Reliance]	Demonstration house	Pittsburgh, Pa.
858	Mar. 1948	J. Walter Thompson	Mail room	New York
859	Mar.	Dalton School	Alteration	New York
860	Mar.	Ruskin Apartments	Apartment house	Pittsburgh, Pa.
861	Mar.	12 E. 65th St., Child Study Assoc.	Alteration	New York
862	May	Durisol, Inc.	House	Aberdeen, Md.
863	June	Falklands	Alterations	Pennsylvania
864	June	E.A. Jacobs - Jay Realty	Apartment house	Montgomery, Md.
865	June	E.A. Jacobs - Jay Realty	Veterans housing	Prince Georges Cty., Md.
866	June	John Stuart, Inc.	Store alteration	478 Fourth Ave.
867	June	Mrs. Dorothy Paley	Alteration	36 E. 74th St.
868	July	Ralph Steiner	Alteration	174 E. 72nd St.
869	Aug.	Saul Nesbitt	Alteration	508 E. 87th St.
870	Aug.	Chalmers Dale	Residence	Cold Springs, N.Y.
871	Oct.	J. Walter Thompson	South L 1008	New York
872	Oct.	Mrs. W. Lescaze	Alteration	Sharon, Conn.
873	Oct.	Hy Chessler	Dune Deck Hotel	Westhampton, L.I.
874	Oct.	Sydney Kaye	House	Cornwall Bridge, Conn.
875	Oct.	Fred Field	Office	23 W. 26th St.
876	Dec.	CBS	Color television	New York
877	Jan. 1949	J.W. Thompson	Overall plan	New York
878		Mr. Ferry	Residence	Bronxville, N.Y.
879		J.W. Thompson	Art dept.	New York
880		Ralph Schoolman	Residence	Cold Spring, N.Y.
881		J.W. Thompson	Color layout room 1025	New York
882		Aug. Austin	Houses	Yonkers, N.Y.
883	June	J. Walter Thompson	Dining room	New York
884	June	G. Piccione	Residence	Rockville Centre, N.Y.
885	June	J. Walter Thompson	Rec. room 10th floor	New York
886	June	Mr. & Mrs. Chas. Grimes	Residence	3 E. 92nd St.
887	July	Henry C. Flower	Living room	25 East End Ave.
888	June	Dr. Frank Calderone	Boathouse	Kings Point, L.I.
889	Sept.	Condoulin Corp.	Prefab	Albany, N.Y.
890	Sept.	John Flory	Residence	Pondridge, Conn.
891	Sept.	Richard Scheuer	Residence	Mamaroneck, N.Y.
892	Sept.	Atlantic - Reliance Homes, Inc.	Prefab	Margate City, N.J.
893	Oct.	Fred V. Field	Alterations	New Hartford, Conn.
894	Oct.	N. Tulchin	Alt., theatre	8th Ave. & 51st St.
895	Dec.	J. Walter Thompson	Alt., 10th floor, North L	New York
896	Dec.	J. Walter Thompson	Miss Waldo's office	New York
897	Dec.	Frank Stanton	60 E. 79th St.	New York
898	Jan. 1950	Wm. S. Paley	Alterations	North Hills, L.I.

Job No.	Date	Client	Description	Location
899	Jan.	Webb & Knapp	Alterations	New York
900	Oct. 1949	SBCC	Building code	New York State
901	Mar. 1950	Richard Nesbitt	Whse. & Display Rm.	New Hyde Park, L.I.
902	Mar.	Mr. Kalmanoff	Residence	Harrison, N.Y.
903	Apr.	J. Walter Thompson	12th fl., North L, accounting	New York
904	Apr.	Mrs. J. Borgenicht	1 E. 93rd St., alterations	New York
905	May	Skouras Theatres Corp.	Valentine Theatre Lobby alterations	Fordham Road Bronx, N.Y.
906	May	Skouras Theatres Corp.	David Marcus Theatre Lobby alterations	3464 Jerome Ave. Bronx, N.Y.
907	May	Maurice Stone	Front alterations	18 E. 49th St.
908	May	Maurice Stone	Front alterations	14 E. 44th St.
909	May	J. Walter Thompson Co.	South & North T Tubl. Rel. & Repr., 12th fl.	New York
910	May	J. Walter Thompson Co.	Traffic South L, 10th fl.	New York
911	May	J. Walter Thompson Co.	North L art dept., 10th fl.	New York
912	May	J. Walter Thompson Co.	South L library, cafet., etc. 12th fl.	New York
913	May	J. Walter Thompson Co.	Copy dept., 10th fl. South & North T	New York
914	May	Project	Hotel	Washington, D.C.
915	July	J. Walter Thompson Co.	Radio dept., 11th fl., North L	New York
916	July	Cinemart	Alterations	730 Fifth Ave.
917	Aug.	Republic Steel Corp.	Penthouse	Cleveland, Ohio
918	Jan.	Mrs. Geo. Skouras	Apartment	233 W. 49th St.
919	Jan.	Boughton Cobb	Addition	Falls Village, Conn.
920	Feb. 1951	Andrew King	Alterations	Pierre Hotel
921	Feb.	Oscar Serlin	Alterations	53 E. 91st St.
922	Feb.	Hy Chesler	Dune Deck, kitchen alterations	Westhampton, L.I.
923	Mar.	J. Walter Thompson	Photos near stairs	New York
924	Mar.	International Monetary Fund	Board room	Washington, D.C.
925	Apr.	Paul W. Kesten	Apartment	860 Fifth Ave.
926	Apr.	Maytag Atlantic Co., Inc.	Addition	34-18 Northern Blvd., L.I.C.
927	May	George V.T. Burgess	Country house	Scarsdale, N.Y.
928	**May**	Sculptors Guild	1952 Exhibition	New York
929	June	Fred Nash	Additions and alterations	Minneapolis, Minn.
930	July	Porcelain Enamel Institute	Research	
931	July	Webb & Knapp Inc.	Addition	385 Madison Ave.
932	July	J. Walter Thompson Co.	11th fl. radio reception room	420 Lexington Ave.
933	Aug.	J. Walter Thompson Co.	11th fl. audition room	420 Lexington Ave.
934	Aug.	Richard Davis	House	Riverdale, N.Y.
935	Aug.	French Embassy	Office building	Washington, D.C.
936	Aug.	Henry Morgenthau III	Apartment	Sutton Terrace 63rd & York Ave.
937	Sept.	India Exchange Ltd.	Office building	Calcutta, India
938	Sept.	Dr. Joan Morgenthau	Apartment	1700 York Ave.
777	Oct.	Rikisutvarpid	New start - Studio building	Reykjavik, Iceland
939	Oct.	Lou Cowan	Alterations	46 E. 73rd St.
940	Oct.	New India House	Alterations	3 E. 64th St.
941	Nov.	Cinerama	Theater alterations	New York
942	Dec.	M. Shroder	Project - Apt. house [Sutton House]	New York
943	Dec.	J. Walter Thompson Co.	Conference - TV room, 10th fl.	420 Lexington Ave.
944	Jan. 1952	20th Century Garage	Alterations	48th St.
945	Jan.	Medical Arts	Small office building	Great Neck Plaza, L.I.
946	Feb.	J. Walter Thompson Co.	Cabinet work - 12th floor Hawes' office	420 Lexington Ave.
947	Feb.	Cinemart	Alterations	322 E. 44th St.
948	Feb.	Hy Chessler	"Hurricane" - new lounge	Westhampton, L.I.
949	Feb.	Henry Morgenthau, Jr.	Alterations	1133 Fifth Ave.
950	Apr.	J. Walter Thompson Co.	Alt. motion picture booth	420 Lexington Ave.
951	May	M. Kaufman	Office building	711 Third Ave.
952	Aug.	J. Walter Thompson	Vent. assembly room	420 Lexington Ave.
953	Aug.	J.L.	Project	New York
954	June	Mr. & Mrs. Kaufman	House	Mamaroneck, N.Y.
955	Sept.	Cinerama	Prefab	
956	Oct.	Buttenwieser	Alterations	New York
957	Oct.	Aaron Copland	Studio	Ossining, N.Y.
958	Oct.	Eddie Vanicky	Addition to house	Sharon, Conn.

Job No.	Date	Client	Description	Location
959	Nov.	Hy Chessler	New deck for 873	Westhampton, N.Y.
960	Nov.	Clinton Blume	Office building	New York
961	Nov.	Cinerama	Theatre alterations	Chicago, Ill.
962	Nov.	Government of India	Tourist office information	11 E. 58th St.
963	Dec.	Cinerama Inc.	Palace Theatre alterations	Chicago, Ill.
964	Dec.	Cinerama Inc.	Alteration to tennis court	Glen Cove, N.Y.
965	Jan. 1953	Cinerama, Prod.	Theatre alterations - Wilson Theatre	Detroit, Mich.
966	Jan.	Cinerama Inc.	Cinerama installation Warner Theatre	Hollywood, Calif.
967	Feb.	Cinerama Inc.	Research building	L.I., N.Y.
968	Feb.	Cinerama Inc.	Installation - Boyd Theatre	Philadelphia, Pa.
969	Feb.	Cinerama Inc.	Installation - Warner Theatre	Pittsburgh, Pa.
970	Feb.	Cinerama Inc.	Installation - Warner Theatre	Okla. City, Okla.
971	Feb.	Cinerama Inc.	Installation - Warner Theatre	New York
972	Feb.	Government of India	Secretary office	New York
973	Feb.	Barber & Menotti	Window	Mt. Kisco, N.Y.
974	Mar.	Cinerama Inc.	Theatre installation	Miami Beach, Fla.
975	Mar.	Cinerama Inc.	Printing building	New York
976	Mar.	E.W.	Study - office building 175 E. 45th St.	New York
977	Mar.		Stores and parking	Queens Village, L.I.
978	Mar.	Cinerama Inc.	Installation	St. Louis, Mo.
979	Apr.	Cinerama Prod.	Theatre	Sao Paolo, Brazil
980	Apr.	Board of Education	School of Industrial Art [High school of art and design]	New York
981	Apr.	J.W. Thompson	Miscellaneous offices	New York
982	Apr.	J.W. Thompson	Offices	Washington, D.C.
983	Apr.	Spel Prentice	Motel	Florida
984	Mar.	Cinerama Prod.	Ticket booth - colors Warner Theatre	New York
985	May	Salamanca Housing Authority	Housing project	Salamanca, N.Y.
986	May	Clinton Blume	Office building project	New York
987	June	Robt. Bernhard	Apartment	New York
988	Aug.	Produce Exchange	Study and analysis for Produce Exchange	2 Broadway
989	Sept.	Grobet File Co.	Mfg. building	
990	Sept.	Mr. Urban	Alteration - 143-5 Waverly Pl.	New York
991	Oct.	Isbrandtsen Co., Inc.	Study and analysis - 26 Bdwy.	New York
992	Oct.	Hy Chessler	Dune Deck - 1954 alteration	Westhampton, L.I.
993	Oct.	Douglas Elliman	The Home Club	New York
994	Nov.	Irving Trust	Study - 2 Broadway	New York
995	Nov.	Cotton Exchange	Study - 2 Broadway	New York
996	Nov.	Loomis-Suffern-Fernold	Study - 2 Broadway	New York
997	Nov.	Moller Steamship Co.	Study - 2 Broadway	New York
998	Dec.	P.W. Kesten	Apt.-office (Lombardy Hotel)	New York
999	Dec.	Arthur H. Bienenstock	Office building	New York
1000	Dec.	City of New York	Court House	New York
1001	Dec.	Burlingham, Hupper & Kennedy	Study - 2 Broadway	New York
1002	Jan. 1954	Hudson Guild Farm	Infirmary	Netcong, N.J.
1003	Mar.		Project - office building 38th & 5th Ave.	New York
1004	Mar.	Commodity Exchange	Study - 2 Broadway	New York
1005	Apr.	Westinghouse Elec.	Study - 2 Broadway	New York
1006	May	Wm. Fitelson	Addition - summer house	Morristown, N.J.
1007	May	J.W. Thompson	Relocation of mimeo & addressograph dept.	New York
1008	June	Ethicon, Inc.	Plant & campus	Bridgewater, N.J.
1009	June	New York City Housing Authority	Manhattanville houses NYS-74	New York
1010	June	Temple University	WL exhibition	Philadelphia, Pa.
1011	July	Wm. Kaufman	Co-op apartment house	New York
1012	Aug.	David Hoyman	3 E. 76th St.	New York
1013	Sept.	Maurice Stone	18 E. 49th St. - alteration	New York
1014	Sept.	U.S. Mission to U.N.	Layout - 711 Third Ave.	New York
1015	Apr.		Plainview synagogue & community center	Plainview, L.I.
1016	Nov.	N.H.H.A.	Roslyn project	Roslyn, N.Y.
1017	Dec.	CBS	18th fl. lobby	New York
1018	Dec.	CBS	Prod. center lobby	New York
1019	Jan. 1955	Wm. Fitelson	46 Morton St. - entrance	New York
1020	Jan.	Mr. Lubin	Project U.N. site	New York

Job No.	Date	Client	Description	Location
1021	Jan.	J.W. Thompson	Alteration to audition room	New York
1022	Feb.	Harlem Mortgage & Improvement Council	Project #1	New York
1023	Feb.	Harlem Mortgage & Improvement Council	Project #2	New York
1024	May	Longfellow Building	Repairs to balcony	Washington, D.C.
1025	Aug.	Confidential	Office building [Borg Warner]	Chicago, Ill.
1026	July	J.W. Thompson	Mr. Strouse's office	New York
1027	Aug.	J.W. Thompson	Review board	New York
1028	Sept.	P.T.	Washington Square	New York
1029	Sept.	Reynolds Metal	Project	New York
1030	Sept.	J.D. Weiler	Addition - office building	New York
1031	Sept.	Phillip Nash	Addition	Tuxedo Park, N.Y.
1032	Sept.	Leonard Gans	Office building	New York
1033	Oct.	J.W. Thompson	342 Madison Ave.	New York
1034	Nov.	Clinton Blume	588 Fifth Ave.	New York
1035	Nov.	Irwin Kyle	2 Projects	New York
1036	Dec.	Myron Behrman	Project	New York
1037	Jan. 1956	J.W. Thompson	12th floor north wing	New York
1038	Feb.	Collins-Tuttle	42nd St. & Third Ave.	New York
1039	Feb.	Downtown Manhattan Association	Pearl St. widening	New York
1040	May	Produce Exchange	Trading floor and offices	New York
1041	May	J.W. Thompson	14th floor	New York
1042	June	Hudson Guild	Alterations	New York
1043	June	Sam Kootz	Alterations	New York
1044	July	Mrs. R.C. Kramer	Alteration, 32 E. 74th St.	New York
1045	Sept. 1955	Mr. Hy Chesler	Dune Deck - new lounge and new rooms	Westhampton Beach, N.Y.
1046	Nov.	Group Health Insurance		New York
1047	Nov.	Sidney Rivkin	Office building	Milwaukee, Wis.
1048	Nov.	J.W. Thompson	Plans - all floors	420 Lexington Ave.
1049	Nov.	J.W. Thompson	11th floor alteration	420 Lexington Ave.
1050 (old #986)	June	Chas. Noyes & Co.	Office building	2 Broadway
1051	Jan. 1957	N.Y. Produce Exchange		2 Broadway
1052	Jan.	von Schreiber	Office building	211 E. 51st St.
1053	Jan.	von Schreiber	Office building	140 E. 44th St.
1054	Feb.	Loew's Theaters	Office building	571 Lexington Ave.
1055	Mar.	J.W. Thompson	10th floor alteration	420 Lexington Ave.
1056	Mar.	Pierre Bader	Alterations	7 E. 80th St.
1057	Apr.	Embassy of Switzerland	Chancellory building	Washington, D.C.
1058	May	Mills College of Education	Alteration front	66 Fifth Ave.
1059	June	J.P. Carey & Co.	Garage	425 E. 61st St.
1060	June	Mac Belkin	Office building	Washington, D.C.
1061	June	Sidney Rivkin	Motor hotel	40 Seventh Ave.
1062	June	Lubin and partners	Apartment house	U.N. site
1063	July	Marshall Management Corp.	Consultant	Huntington, L.I.
1064	Aug.	Swig, Weiler, Haas, Haynie	Office building	111 Pine St., San Francisco, Calif.
1065	Aug.	J.D. Weiler, C. Benenson	Apartment house	First Ave.
1066	Sept.	J.D. Weiler	Alterations, office building	30 E. 42nd St.
1067	Sept.	Swig & Weiler	Office building	333 Bush St., San Francisco, Calif.
1068	Sept.	Philip Jamra	Alterations	862 Lexington Ave.
1069	Sept.	Sam Kootz	House	East Hampton, N.Y.
1070	Oct.	J. Walter Thompson	14th fl. west wing	420 Lexington Ave.
1071	Oct.	John Calamaras	Apartment house	200 E. 15th St.
1072	Dec.	Erwin Wolfson	Office building	30 W. Broadway
1073	Jan. 1958	Clifford Roberts	Apartment	535 Park Ave.
1074	Jan.	Wm. Fitelson	Kitchen	46 Morton St.
1075	Jan.	J.W. Thompson	9th fl. south wing	420 Lexington Ave.
1076	Mar.	Wm. Kaufman	Apartment house	86th St. & E. End Ave.
1077	Mar.	Joseph Bernstein	Alterations	Confidential
1078	Mar. 1957	Seymour Durst	Office building	625 Third Ave.
1079	Mar.	Wm. Kaufman	Apartment house	51st St. & Third Ave.
1080	Mar.	J.W. Thompson	7th floor	420 Lexington Ave.
1081	Mar.	Jewish Memorial Hospital	Additions	196th St. & Broadway
1082	Apr.	Jack Resnick	FHA 207	Riverdale, N.Y.
1083	May	Jerome Crowley	Alteration	South Bend, Ind.
1084	June	H. Clayton Smith	Alteration, lobby	305 E. 45th St.

Job No.	Date	Client	Description	Location
1085	June	Louis Greenblatt	Office building	235 E. 42nd St.
1086	June	Ben Buttenwieser	Apartment	1 Beekman Place
1087	July	Robert Highfield	Apartment house	18th & R Sts., Washington, D.C.
1088	July	Erwin Wolfson	JWT layouts	Grand Central City
1089	Aug.	Wm. Kaufman	Apartment house	69th St. & Second Ave.
1090	Aug.	Teck Constr. Co.	Office building	Silver Spring, Md.
1091	Sept.	J.D. Weiler	Office building	60 Broad St.
1092	Oct.	Swiss Embassy	Interiors	Washington, D.C.
1093	Oct.	Jack Resnick	Apartment house	305 E. 86th St.
1094	Oct.	Consulate of India	Structure investig.	3 E. 64th St.
1095	Nov.	Marvin Kratter	Large scale housing	Harding Blvd., Queens
1096	Nov.	Webb & Knapp	Alterations	65 E. 56th
1097	Nov.	Collins & Tuttle	Research & admin. building	Stamford, Conn.
1098	Nov.	Uniformed Sanitation Men's Housing Assoc., Local 831, IB of T	Housing project	Flushing Meadows, N.Y.
1099	Jan. 1959	Alfred Mannon, 20th Century Garage	Alterations	320 E. 48th St.
1100	Feb.	North Hempstead Housing Authority	Housing project	Manhasset, N.Y.
1101	Mar.	Dworman Assoc.	Apartment house	58th St. at Third Ave.
1102	Apr.	Citizens Fidelity Bank & Trust Co.	Alteration and addition	Louisville, Ky.
1103	Apr.	Allen Rabinowitz	Maxine Elliot's Theatre	New York
1104	June	Sam Minskoff & Sons	City Hall Plaza	New York
1105	June	J. Walter Thompson	General	New York
1106	June	J.D. Weiler	Office building	390 Fifth Ave.
1107	June	Jack Resnick	Mayfair Theatre	47th St. & Seventh Ave.
1108	July	William Kaufman	Synagogue [Brotherhood House]	40th St. & Seventh Ave.
1109	July	J.D. Weiler	Project	40th St. & Broadway
1110	June	Dworman Associates	Research	
1111	July	J. Walter Thompson	7th floor west	New York
1112	Aug.	Architectural League	Exhibition lobby	New York
1113	Aug.	Long Island Rail Road	Projects	Long Island
1114	Aug.	Columbia Artists Management, Inc.	Alteration	165 W. 57th St.
1115	Sept.	Zeckendorf & Hirsh	Office building	Sixth Ave. & 52nd St.
1116	Sept.	Erwin Wolfson	Office building	New York
1117	Oct.	Dworman Assoc.	Title 1 project	Amsterdam Ave. & Riverside Dr.
1118	Nov.	J.D. Weiler	House	New Rochelle, N.Y.
1119	Nov.	J.W. Thompson	Viewing and projection rooms, 10th floor	420 Lexington Ave.
1120	Nov.	Dworman Assoc.	Housing & marina [Shore Club Towers]	Detroit suburbs
1121	Nov.	Dworman Assoc.	Apartment house	Los Angeles
1122	Nov.	Francis Kleban	Apartment house (2 E. 60th St.)	New York
1123	Jan. 1960	Loew's Theatres	Apartment house and theatre	72nd St. & Third Ave.
1124	Jan.	William Lese	Business building apt. house	Columbus Circle
1125	Feb.	Francis Kleban	Office building	
1125A	Aug. 1962	Norman Bowie	Grand Central Palace	New York
1126	Feb.	Bernard Spitzer & Mr. Lipman	Apartment house	200 Central Park South
1127	Feb.	Erwin Wolfson	Office building, 375 Hudson St.	New York
1128	Mar.	Dworman Assoc.	Office building & apt. house	Brooklyn, N.Y.
1129	Apr.	Charles Beigel	Office building around "21"	New York
1130	Apr.	J. Walter Thompson	Cafeteria lounge	New York
1131	Apr.	Jack Parker	Office building 750 Second Ave.	New York
1132	May	David Heyman	Terrace room, 3 E. 76th St.	New York
1133	May	Assoc. of Contracting Plumbers	Office interior	Graybar Bldg., N.Y.
1134	June	Alteration for Nestle	Business machine installation	711 Third Ave.
1135	June	Lawrence Buttenwieser	Apartment	Fifth Ave. & 89th St.
1136	June	Sheppard Pollak	Limited dividend housing	E. 180th St. & Monterey Ave., Bronx
1137	June	The Oaklands, Sidney Rivkin	Limited dividend housing	Horace Harding Expressway & Springfield Blvd.
1138	July	Alteration for outdoor advertising	Tabulating department Eighth floor, 711 Third Ave.	711 Third Ave.
1139	July	I.D. Robbins	Apartment house	Hudson, W. Houston & Clarkson
1140	July	Dworman Assoc.	Motel, apt. house & offices	Near Lincoln Square

Job No.	Date	Client	Description	Location
1141	July	Harold Aibel	Office building	Sixth Ave. & W. 48th St.
1142	Aug.	Robert Murdock	New shower	14 Sutton Place S.
1143	Aug.	Sheppard-Pollak	West side redevelopment	
1144	Aug.	Wiley Tuttle	Motel	Over Queens tunnel
1145	Aug.	Wm. Fitelson	3 room addition	Morristown, N.J.
1146	Sept.	N. Hempstead Housing Authority	Playground, harbor houses	Port Washington, L.I.
1147	Sept.	Lewis Leader	Co-op apartment house	10 E. 70th St.
1148	Oct.	Francis Kleban	Office building	Back of Saks Fifth Ave.
1149	Oct.	Millard-Schroder	Apartment house	Wilshire Blvd., L.A.
1150	Oct.	Erwin Wolfson	Office building	Sixth Ave. between 53rd & 54th Sts.
1151	Sept.	Carl Morse	Zoning study, office building	Fifth Ave. & W. 56th St.
1152	**Nov.**	**Stanley Bruff**	**Zoning study, office building**	**Broadway & Fulton**
1152A		Gleckman	Larger site	
1153	Nov.	E. Wolfson	Zoning study	Park Ave. & 32nd St.
1154	Nov.	Louis Smadbeck	Consultation	63rd St. & Second Ave.
1155	Nov.	E. Wolfson	Apartment house	W. 72nd St. & Central Park West
1156	Dec.	Stanley Broff	Office building	Fifth Ave. & 52nd St.
1157	Jan. 1961	Francis Kleban	Apartment house	Beekman Place, N.Y.
1158	Jan.	Francis Kleban	Public garage and apt. houses	Welfare Island, N.Y.
1159	Jan.	Jack Perlman	Mitchell Lama housing	Riverside Dr. & 165th St.
1160	**Dec. 1960**	**Erwin Wolfson**	[See job 1285]	Washington Market, N.Y.
1161	Feb. 1961	NYCHA	Apartment house	W. 91st-92nd & Columbus Ave.
1162	Feb.	Dworman Assoc.		33rd-34th & Second Ave.
1163	Mar.	Mrs. Dorcas Draper	Exhibition	Philadelphia, Pa.
1164	Mar.	Dworman Assoc.	Apartment house	Third Ave. between 81st & 82nd Sts.
1165	Mar.	Barent Ten Eyck	Country house	Woodstock, Vt.
1166	Mar.	Bob Arnow	RCA office building	66th St. & Broadway
1167	Mar.	Sheppard-Pollak	Mitchell Lama housing	W. 166th & Ogden Ave., Bronx, N.Y.
1168	Apr.	Alfred Goldstein	Two apartment houses	Second Ave. & 47th-48th Sts.
1169	Apr.	Abi Kalimian	Apartment house	York & 83rd St.
1170	Apr.	Abi Kalimian	Office	770 Lexington Ave.
1171	May	Lester Dworman	Townhouse	11 East 81st St.
1172	June	Abe Ellis	Office building	133-39 E. 47th St.
1173	June	F. Kleban	Inspection apartment house	200 E. 57th St.
1174	June	Haber-Halpern-Rattner	Mitchell Lama housing	Rosedale Ave., Bronx, N.Y.
1175	Apr.	City of New York (with Harry Prince)	Youth House for Girls	Bronx, N.Y.
1176	May	J.W. Thompson	Relocation of addresso-mimeo dept.	420 Lexington Ave.
1177	June	Erwin Wolfson	Preliminaries, office building	Atlanta, Ga.
1178	July	Haber-Halpern-Rattner	Mitchell Lama housing	172nd-174th St., Bronx, N.Y.
1179	July	Kalimian Bros.	Apartment house	Third Ave. & E. 79th St.
1180	July	Clinton Elliott	Alteration apartment house	1281 Madison Ave.
1181	July	Haber-Halpern-Ratner	Mitchell Lama housing	Brighton Beach
1182	July	I.D. Robbins	Mitchell Lama housing	Essex St.
1183	Aug.	Erwin Wolfson	Church Center	E. 44th St.
1184	Aug.	J.W. Thompson	Moving of records dept. to 16th floor	420 Lexington Ave.
1185	Aug.	Aaron Rabinowitz	Office building	42nd St. & Second Ave.
1186	Aug.	Bob Arnow	Office building	45 E. 42nd St.
1187	Sept.	Dworman-Haber	Mitchell Lama housing	Broadway & W. 240th St., Bronx, N.Y.
1188	Sept.	Dworman-Haber	Apt. house FHA ?	94th St. & Madison Ave.
1189	Oct.	Dworman-Haber	LaGuardia house	116th St. at Second Ave.
1190	Nov.	W.R. Grace (H.T. Ford)	Office building	Water & Pearl Sts.
1191	Nov.	Francis Kleban	Office building	E. 51st & 52nd Sts.

155

Job No.	Date	Client	Description	Location
1191A	Aug. 1962	Donald Augenblick	Office building	E. 51st & 52nd Sts.
1192	Aug. 1962	Samuel Kootz	Bathroom	Yorktown Heights
1193	Nov.	J.W. Thompson	Cafeteria, eighth floor	420 Lexington Ave.
1194	Dec.	William Kaufman, J.D. Weiler	Office building	777 Third. Ave.
1195	Dec.	First National City Bank	Exhibition building	World's Fair 1964
1196	Jan. 1962	J.W. Thompson	Ninth floor renovation	420 Lexington Ave.
1197	Feb.	Bank for Savings	Bank and apartment house	Third Ave. & 72nd St.
1198	Feb.	CAMI	New C of O	161 W. 57th St.
1199	Aug.	J.W. Thompson	Seventh floor renovation and shifting partitions	420 Lexington Ave.
1200	Dec.		Apartments	S.W., Washington, D.C.
1201	Mar. 1961	Howeth T. Ford	Office building	Madison Ave. & 49th St.
1202	Mar.	Dworman Assoc.	Apt. house and office building	Sunset Boulevard, L. A.
1203	Apr.	Clearview Community Center	Alterations	Union Turnpike, Queens
1204	Apr.	Glickman Corp.	Office building	49th St. & Madison Ave.
1205	Mar.	J.D. Weiler Bob Arnow	Prelim. consultation, office buiding	1411 Broadway, N.Y.
1206	Apr.	J. Milner	Zoning study	68th St. & Third Ave.
1207	May	J.W. Thompson	Acoustic treatment 10th fl. conference room	420 Lexington Ave.
1208	May	Kaufman, Weiler, Swig	Phone booth lobby	711 Third Ave.
1209	June	CAMI	Lobby renovation	165 W. 57th St.
1210	June	F. Kleban	Apartment house	Lexington Ave., 67th & 68th St.
1211	July	J. Walter Thompson	Moving record center 16th to seventh floor	420 Lexington Ave.
1212	July	J. Walter Thompson	Enlarge info. center and study mailroom, 12th floor	420 Lexington Ave.
1213	July	J. Walter Thompson	Cabinet work for Mr. McAvity 12th fl. N.W.	420 Lexington Ave.
1214	July	F. Kleban	Office building	57th & 58th Sts. & Second Avenue
1215	July	Howeth Ford	21 floors community-type office building	64th to 65 Sts. Third Ave.
1216	July	Belkin & WL	Apt. houses - Seward Park Ext.	Grand Street
1217	July	J.W. Thompson	Move publicity dept. from seventh floor west wing and square to S.E. wing 14th fl.	420 Lexington Ave.
1218	Aug.	Howeth Ford	Alterations and additions	1920 Broadway
1219	Aug.	Donald Augenblick	FHA apartment house	Baltimore, Md.
1220	Oct.	William Fitelson	Zoning study	202-6 W. 58th St.
1221	Nov.	Howeth Ford	Office building	68th St. & Broadway
1222	Nov.	Speed-Park	Speed-Park study	Imaginary location
1223	Nov.	J.W. Thompson	12th floor N.E. wing cubicles	420 Lexington Ave.
1224	Dec.	Howeth Ford	Alteration	Stern's Dept. Store
1225	Nov.	Dept. of Public Works	Auditorium and chapels	Goldwater Mem. Hosp.
1226	Dec.	CAMI Realty	Cutting through driveway ground floor	161 W. 57th St.
1227	Dec.	J.W. Thompson	11th floor west wing, alteration to offices	420 Lexington Ave.
1228	Dec.	Vassello, Fine, Burack	P.O. and apartment house	Yonkers
1229	Dec.	John Stuart	Showroom and offices	979 Third Ave.
1230	Jan. 1963	J.D. Weiler	Consultation	111 Pine St., San Francisco, Calif.
1231	Jan.	Mr. Weiss	Rezoning	Milton Point, N.Y.
1232	Jan.	J.D. Weiler	Addition to First Nat'l. Bank	Atlanta, Ga.
1233	Jan.	J.W. Thompson	Computer room, seventh floor	420 Lexington Ave.
1234	Feb.	J.W. Thompson	Elevator lobbies and reception rooms all floors	420 Lexington Ave.
1235	Mar.	Ruberoid "Competition"	Housing	E. River Dr. & 110th St.
1236	Mar.	Mr. & Mrs. Barnes	C. of O.	430 W. 22nd St.
1237	Mar.	Fred F. French	Tenants layout	300 E. 42nd St.
1238	Mar.	J.W. Thompson	South end west wing alteration, 11th floor	420 Lexington Ave.
1239	Mar.		Project air rights	Queens
1240	Mar.	Morgan Guaranty Trust	Processing facilities	30 W. Broadway
1241	Apr.	Bob Arnow	Office building	Chicago, Ill.
1242	Apr.	Jack Resnick	Office building	110 E. 59th St.
1243	Apr.	Longfellow building	Repairs	Washington, D.C.

Job No.	Date	Client	Description	Location
1244	Apr.	Harry Richmond	House	Brooklyn, N.Y.
1245	Apr.	Farmer's Bank of State of Delaware	Bank and small office building	Wilmington, Del.
1246	May	J.W. Thompson	Alteration of Mr. Strouse's office - 11th floor S.W.	420 Lexington Ave.
1247	May	J.W. Thompson	Alteration of Devine's office, room 1135	420 Lexington Ave.
1248	May	Kinney (Wm. A. White)	Office building	1195 Ave. of the Americas
1249	June	Frank Kleban	Office building Post Office	905 Third Ave.
1250				
1251	June	J.W. Thompson	Alteration 11th floor, north end west wing	420 Lexington Ave.
1252	July	Larry Tish	Garage and office building	53rd St. & Seventh Ave.
1253	July	J.W. Thompson	TV casting dept. 14th floor, N.E. wing	420 Lexington Ave.
1254	Aug.	J.D. Weiler, Bob Arnow	Alteration	42nd St. & Broadway
1255	Aug.	Roy S. Thurman	Office building	Washington, D.C.
1256	Sept.	J.D. Weiler	Bronze door	Cartier, Fifth Ave. & 57th St.
1257	Sept.	J.D. Weiler & Bob Arnow	Theatre, garage and offices	150 E. 58th St.
1258	Oct.	J.W. Thompson	12th floor N.W., desk plan	420 Lexington Ave.
1259	Oct.	CAMI	Storage room	165 W. 57th St.
1260	Oct.	First Federal Savings & Loan	Bank and office building	Miami, Fla.
1261	Nov.	American Radiator	Office building	40 W. 40th & 39 W. 39th St.
1262	Dec.		School and apartment house	Ogden Ave.
1263	Dec.	Taylor Woodrow Blitman	**Mitchell Lama (old 1178)**	Stratford Ave., Bronx, N.Y.
1264	Mar. 1964	Larry Tish	Building for RCA	53rd St. & Seventh Ave.
1265	Nov. 1963	See 1280	Office building	345 Park Ave., 580 Lexington Ave.
1266	Jan. 1964	Francis Kleban	City planning	Columbus Circle to Lincoln Center
1267	Jan.		Mitchell Lama	Near Forest Hills, N.Y.
1268	Jan.	Jackie Gleason	Remodeling for TV studio	Miami Beach, Fla.
1269	Feb.	AIA competition		Washington, D.C.
1270	Feb.	William Kaufman	Double 711	New York
1271	Mar.	J.D. Weiler & Benenson	Hotel to apartment house	Detroit, Mich.
1272	Apr.	J.D. Weiler	Office building	
1273	Apr.	Carl Morse & Fred F. French	Alteration	100 Avenue of the Americas
1274	Apr.	Carl Morse, Con Edison & Fred F. French	FHA apartment houses	330 E. 40th & 335 E. 39th St.
1275	Feb.	Michigan Osteopathic University	New campus	Mason, Mich.
1276	Apr.	J.D. Weiler	Office building	545 Fifth Ave.
1277	Apr.	J. Walter Thompson	Miscellaneous (small jobs)	420 Lexington Ave.
1278	Apr.	Frank J. Rooney & Alan J. Lockman	Consultation, office building	North Capitol St., Washington, D.C.
1279				
1280 (formerly 1191 & 1265)	May	Richard Garfunkle & Nizar Raslan	**Office building**	**580 Lexington Ave.**
1281	May	J. Walter Thompson	Seventh floor N.E. wing transcr. secy. area	420 Lexington Ave.
1282	May	State Univ. Construction Fund	Garage - Downstate Medical Ctr.	Brooklyn, N.Y.
1283	June	J. Walter Thompson	Eighth floor Square Media Research	420 Lexington Ave.
1284	June	Carl Morse	Consultation Chatham Plaza Ctr.	Pittsburgh, Pa.
1285 (formerly 1160)	May	J.D. Weiler & Bob Arnow	**Commercial, industrial, warehouse buildings**	**Washington Market, N.Y.**
1286	July	Jack Resnick & Son	Office building	Park Ave. & 58th St., 485 Park Ave.
1287	July	Frank Kleban	Apartment house	Fifth Ave. & 61st St.
1288	Aug.	Julien Studley	Office building	245 E. 47th St.
1289	Oct.	Oliver Tyrone	Office building and parking	Manor Oak near Pittsburgh, Pa.
1290	Oct.	Frank Kleban	GM showroom	Fifth Ave. & 58th St.
1291	**Nov.**	**Larry Tisch**	**Modernization, Loew's building**	**46th St. & Broadway**
1292	Nov.	Jack Resnick	Conversion	48th St. & Lexington Ave.
1293	Nov.	Sharp & Dworman	Office building	William & Beaver Sts.
1294	Nov.	J. Walter Thompson	Tenth fl., conference room	420 Lexington Ave.

Job No.	Date	Client	Description	Location
1295	Nov.	Chatham Center	Rental mock-up	Pittsburgh, Pa.
1296	Nov.	Dworman Assoc.	Urban project	Buffalo, N.Y.
1297	Nov.	AIA	Honor awards	Washington, D.C.
1298	Dec.	Chatham Center	Hotel layouts	Pittsburgh, Pa.
1299	Dec.	Leon Falk	Apartment	Pittsburgh, Pa.
1300	Dec.	Board of Education	J.H.S. #24	Richmond, Staten Island
1301	Dec.	Chatham Center	Clubrooms	Pittsburgh, Pa.
1302	Dec.	Frank Kleban	Office building	410 Park Ave.
1303	Dec.		400 car automated garage	145 W. 54th St.
1304	Jan. 1965	Joe Milner	Office building	315 E. 48th St.
1305	Dec. 1964	Lescaze, Pichel & Lepkaluk	Post office	Hicksville, L.I.
1306	Jan. 1965	Atlas - McGrath	Office building	One New York Plaza
1307	Jan.	Chatham Center	Store layouts	Pittsburgh, Pa.
1308	Jan.	Herbert Fisch	Office building	New York
1309	Jan.		Office bldg., 53rd & Third Ave.	New York
1310	Jan.	Telegraph Square	Motor inn and offices	Pittsburgh, Pa.
1311	Feb.	Chatham Center	Design of lighting plans of Chatham Center	Pittsburgh, Pa.
1312	Feb.	Chatham Center	Bridges	Pittsburgh, Pa.
1313	Feb.	Chatham Center	Design of pantry at second fl.	Pittsburgh, Pa.
1314	Feb.	Chatham Center	Roof signs	Pittsburgh, Pa.
1315	Feb.	Chatham Center	Extra time	Pittsburgh, Pa.
1316	Mar.	Carlyle Const. Corp. (Ray Colcord)	Office building	New York
1317	Mar.	Dworman Assoc.	Office building	Charleston, W. Va.
1318	Mar.	NYCHA	Low cost housing	E. 101st St. & First Ave.
1319	Apr.	Francis J. Kleban	Office building	New York
1320	Apr.	William Lescaze	Branch office	880 Third Ave.
1321	Apr.	Helmsley-Spear	Addition	200 Fifth Ave.
1322	Apr.	Milton Quinn	Office building	Wall Street
1323	Apr.	Herbert Charles	Office building	Madison & 26th St.
1324	May		Van Wyck Brooks Library	Bridgewater, Conn.
1325	May	Mental Hygiene Dept.	Rehabilitation Center Creedmoor Hospital	Queens, N.Y.
1326	June	Frank Kloban	Office building	450 Park Ave.
1327	June	Chatham Center	Tenants layouts	Pittsburgh, Pa.
1328	July	Speed-Park	Towers around Madison Sq. Park	New York
1329	July	Bob Arnow	Office building	52 Wall St.
1330	June	O.T.	Project X	Pittsburgh, Pa.
1331	July	Alteration at 211		
1332	Aug.		Weiler-Benenson	Washington St. Apts.
1333	Sept.	Francis Kleban	Office building	Attached to 630 Third Ave., 144 E. 41st St.
1334	Sept.	Speed-Park	Automated garage	122 E. 48th St.
1335	Oct.	Atlas-McGrath	"Dummy Set"	One New York Plaza
1336	Oct.	Francis Kleban	Apartment house	Beekman Place
1337	Oct.	Atlas-McGrath	Tenant changes	One New York Plaza
1338	Nov.	Weiler-Arnow	Addition	Stern's Dept. Store
1339	Nov.	Fischback	Office building	Lexington Ave. & 55th St.
1340	Nov.	Alvin Weil	Master plan	Roosevelt Raceway
1341	Nov.	Dorothy Norman	Stair chair	124 E. 70th St.
1342	Dec.	Speed-Park	Automated garage	340 W. 31st St.
1343	Dec.	Francis Kleban	Large project	11th to 12th Aves.
1344	Dec.	Louis Smadbeck	Office building	45 W. 53rd St.
1345	Dec.	American Land Co. Charles L. Gleaves	Sketch layout	Nr. Norfolk, Va.
1346	Jan. 1966	Atlas-McGrath	Revision curtain wall	One New York Plaza
1347	Jan.	Peter Sharp	Apartment house	Beekman Place
1348	Jan.	Jack Resnick	Office building	545 Fifth Ave.
1349	Jan.	Oliver Tyrone	Revision garage and truck bays - Incorporate Press Club	Oliver Plaza, Pittsburgh, Pa.
1350	Jan.	Morton Wolf	FHA apartment house	Amsterdam Ave., W. 67th St.
1351	Jan.	Morton Wolf	Office building and apt. house	Central Park, West W. 61st & 62nd Sts.
1352	Jan.	Judge Beldock	Town house	Brooklyn Heights
1353	Feb.	Atlas-McGrath	Second additional floor	One New York Plaza
1354	Feb.	Beaux Arts Assoc.	Consultation re elevator cars	Peter Cooper, Mayflower, Beaux Arts, One Fifth Ave.

Job No.	Date	Client	Description	Location
1355	Feb.	Jack Resnick & Son	RCA requirements in Resnick building	58th & 59th Sts.
1356	Feb.	Sol Atlas	Alteration of Centennial bldg.	Broad & Water Sts.
1357	8 Mar.	Carl Morse	Consultant bank & office bldg.	Charleston, W. Va.
1358	12 Mar.	James Roe	Zoning study apartment house	E. 51st St. & First Ave.
1359	4 Apr.	F. Kleban	Bank and office building	Durham, N.C.
1360	21 Feb.	Jack Resnick	Office building	110 E. 59th St. & 111 E. 58th St.
1361	14 Mar.	Sol Atlas	4,000 lbs. elevator changes	One New York Plaza
1362	23 Mar.	Sol Atlas	Relocation of building	One New York Plaza
1363	23 Mar.	Sol Atlas	Site study of two buildings	N.Y.S.E. location
1364	4 May	DiLarenzo	Office building	Plaza site
1365	12 Apr.	Jack Resnick	Office building	499 Park Ave.
1366	29 June	Rachlin & Co.	Office building	East Orange, N.J.
1367	11 July	Weiler & Lubin	Office building	245 E. 47th St.
1368	12 July	Oliver Tyrone	Updated presentation	Pittsburgh, Pa.
1369	30 June	SUCF	Additional two floors garage	Brooklyn, N.Y.
1370	2 May	Sol Atlas	Larger building	Site #1
1371	14 July	Rube Ford	Stores and office building	Fifth Ave. & 57th St.
1372	19 July	Jack Resnick	Office building	Fifth Ave. & 46th St.
1373 (old 1238)	25 July	Weiler-Arnow	Office building	N.E. Sixth Ave. & 42nd St.
1374	2 Aug.	Fishbach-Kessler	Office building	26th St. & Madison Ave.
1375	10 Aug.		Office building	
1376	11 Aug.	Oliver Tyrone	Revisions due to incorrect survey	Pittsburgh, Pa.
1377	17 Aug.	Jack Resnick	Revisions due to floor height change	111 E. 58th St.
1378	12 Sept.	Sol Atlas	Drawings for potential tenants	
1379	28 Sept.	Gray Advertising Inc.	Tenant changes	777 Third Ave.
1380	28 Sept.	U.S. Plywood	Tenant changes	777 Third Ave.
1381	30 Sept.	Sol Atlas	Second try for #2 site at Jack Schuster's request	
1382	10 Nov.	Board of Education	Changes by Bd. on J.H.S. #24	Staten Island, N.Y.
1383	10 Nov.	Jack Resnick	Northeast corner Park Ave. and 58th St. added	
1384 (old 1326)	10 Nov.	Wylie Tuttle	Office building	Park Ave. & 56th & 57th St.
1385		Sol Atlas	Checking MHT drawings	New York
1386	28 Nov.	Morton Wolf	New York Academy of Science	New York
1337	9 Dec.	Jack Resnick	Extra revisions	Broadway & 63rd St.
1388	9 Dec.	Sol Atlas	Coordination SOM	One New York Plaza
1389	12 Dec.	Speed Park	225 car garage	115 E. 40th St.
1390	23 Dec.	Harry Helmsley	Apartment and/or office bldg.	36 Central Park S., 35 W. 58th St.
1391	9 Jan. 1967	Carl Morse	Nurses house	59 Beekman St.
1392	12 Jan.	Bill Zimmerman	Office building	205 E. 60th St.
1393	12 Jan.	Herb Papock	Office building	Columbus Circle
1394	16 Jan.	Lescaze, Pinchel & Lepkaluk	Post Office addendum	Hicksville, L.I.
1395	20 Jan.	Robert Cronheim	Office building	Sixth Ave. & 46th St.
1396	20 Jan.	Jack Resnick	Cutting down tower	110 E. 59th St.
1397				
1398 (old 1152)	27 Jan.	Dewey Carver	Office building	Fulton & Broadway
1399	31 Jan.	PNB	Tenant change	Pittsburgh, Pa.
1400	2 Feb.	William Zimmerman	Office building	1530 Broadway
1401	2 Feb.	Mb	Tenant change	Pittsburgh, Pa.
1402	7 Mar.	Audel Colloid Corp.	Tenant change	777 Third Ave.
1403	28 Mar.	Speed Park	Mihai Alimanestianu	315 W. 42nd St.
1404	5 Apr.	Mr. Solow	Project X	
1405	17 Apr.	Louis Pokrass	Office building	45 E. 59th St.
1406	1 May	Ferdinand Roth	Office building	80 Wall St.
1407	1 May	Ferdinand Roth	Office building	75 Water St.
1403	12 May	Board of Education	Incinerator revision	Jr. H.S. 24 Richmond, Staten Island
1409	17 May	Morton Wolf	Putnam Country Club	Mahopack, N.Y.
1410	29 May	Lescaze, Pichel, Lepkaluk	Change orders to Post Office	Hicksville, L.I.
1411	2 June	Sol G. Atlas	Office building	Broad & South Sts.
1412	6 July	Greek Orthodox Chancery	Sixth floor alterations	10 E. 79th St.
1413	13 July	Fishbach & Kessler	Town house	Riverdale

Job No.	Date	Client	Description	Location
1414	7 June	Francis Kleban	Office bldg., Saks Fifth Ave.	Second Time
1415	13 July	Cohen Bros.	Office building	475 Park Ave., South
1416	17 July	Oliver Tyrone	Tenants changes	Pittsburgh, Pa.
1417	31 July	Francis Kleban	Office building	Larger site - Saks - dropped
1418	14 Aug.	Paul Milstein	Offices and apartment house	W. 63rd & Broadway
1419	17 Aug.	Oliver Tyrone	Changes	Pittsburgh, Pa.
1420	30 Aug.	Jack Resnick & Son	Office building	Third Ave. & E. 57th St.
1421	12 Sept.	Jack Resnick & Son	Revisions to 110 E. 59th St. After completion dwgs.	
1422	3 Oct.	SUCF	Roofing for garage	Albany, N.Y.
1423	2 Oct.	WZ	Project X - Grand Central Terminal	New York
1424	14 Nov.	Board of Education	Water on site	Richmond, Staten Island
1425	23 Jan. 1968	Atlas	Cellar stores 9 and 10, rearrangement entrance from loading area	
1426	15 Nov.	Peter Sharp	Apartment house addition	325 W. End Ave.
1427	22 Nov.	Fishbach Mansion Associates	Small office building	30 E. 26th St.
1428	27 Dec.	Regina Laudis	Master plan	Bethlehem, Conn.
1429	4 Jan. 1968	Oestreicher Realty	Office building	160 Water St.
1430	7 Feb.	City of Hartford, Conn.	Conn. Capitol Center	Hartford, Conn.
1431	8 Feb.	Sol G. Atlas	Console	One New York Plaza
1432	8 Feb.	Sol G. Atlas	41, 42, 43, 44 floors - changes for Solomon Bros & Hutzler	One New York Plaza
1433	26 Feb.	Sol G. Atlas	Change granite to precast	One New York Plaza
1434	1 Apr.	Jack Resnick & Son	Zoning study	200 E. 48th St.
1435	4 Apr.	Zuckerman Bros.	Zoning study	855 Sixth Ave.
1436	4 Apr.	Sol G. Atlas	Changes for Bear Stearns 47th 48th 49th + 1/3 50th floor	
1437	11 Apr.	Mort Wolf (Riley)	Zoning study	325 Lexington Ave.
1438	10 Apr.	Sol G. Atlas	Stores 3 + 3A	One New York Plaza
1439	9 May	William A. White (Brownlie, J. Cohen)	Zoning study	60 Wall St., 66 Wall St.
1440	10 May	Ford Motor Company	Speed park studies	Several - New York
1441A	27 May	**Horn & Hardart**	Feasibility studies	105 W. 45th St.
1441B	27 May	**Horn & Hardart**	Feasibility studies	122 Pearl St.
1442	29 May	Allan Riley	Apartment house	N.E. corner 69th St. & Columbus Ave.
1443	13 June	Zimmerman & Scanlan	Office building	Tarrytown, N.Y.
1444	19 June	Jack Resnick & Sons	Miscellaneous tenants	110 E. 59th St.
1445	20 June	N.Y.C.H.A.	Housing project	Monterey - E. 180th St.
1446	9 July	Pace College	1155 Raymond Boulevard	New York
1447	11 July	J.I. Kislak, Inc.	Office building	Newark, N.J.
1448	17 July	Lou Smadbeck	Zoning study	885 Third Ave.
1449	18 July	Grand Central, Inc.	Consultation	Grand Central
1450	21 June	Jos. F. Bernstein	Office building	
1451	22 July	Oestreicher Realty	Modernization	1140 Sixth Ave.
1452	24 July	Atlas-McGrath	Moving mech. 50 floor - PH	One New York Plaza
1453	26 July	Barton's Candy Corporation	Complex building	80 DeKalb Ave., Brooklyn, N.Y.
1454	15 Aug.	Auerbach, Pollack & Richardson, Inc.	Tenants changes, 25th floor	One New York Plaza
1455	16 Sept.	Gourmet Magazine	Tenant change	777 Third Ave.
1456	19 Sept.	DPW	Lowering pt. cellar	Welfare Island
1457	1 Oct.	Coster Gerard Aeon Realty Co.	Zoning study	37th-55th W. 53rd St.
1458	1 Oct.	Donald R. Riehl	Zoning study	Liberty & Washington Sts.
1459	11 Oct.	Wm. F. Wallace	Zoning study	Lexington Ave. & 57th St.
1460	2 Dec.	Health & Mental Hygiene	Furniture (Creedmore)	Queens, N.Y.
1461	11 Nov.	Allan Riley	Offices and hotel	W. 57th-58th Sts. & Sixth Ave.
1462	13 Nov.	Michael Gillespie	Custodial care, Seagirth Blvd. - Beach Ninth St.	Far Rockaway
1463	10 Dec.	Lou Smadbeck	Office building	Next to St. Bartholomew
1464	18 Dec.	Landauer & Assoc.	Zoning study	39th-40th St., First Ave.
1465	16 Dec.	Mort Wolf	Office building	5 E. 61st St.

Job No.	Date	Client	Description	Location
1466	20 Dec.	Rube Ford & Sonnabend	Office building	N.J. Zinc, 160 Front St.
1467	26 Dec.	Arthur Leidesdorf	Movies and office building	41st-45th E. 59th Sts.
1468	13 Jan. 1969	David Baldwin	Office building	Cortlandt St. & Bdwy.
1469	13 Jan.	David Baldwin	Office building	Pearl & Maiden Lane
1470	23 Jan.	Mort Wolf	Office building and apt. hotel	Albany, N.Y.
1471	Feb.	Board of Education	Water Condition	Jr. H.S. #24, Richmond, Staten Island
1472	12 Feb.	U.S. Post Office	Extension	Hicksville, L.I.

Appendix E
Selected William Lescaze Furniture, Lighting, and Miscellaneous Product Design

Comments on the designs

Committed to a total design expression, Lescaze, like the Adams brothers, Charles Rennie Mackintosh, Frank Lloyd Wright, and others, recognized that new architectural forms required new interior furnishing designs. Thus, during the twenties and thirties, Lescaze designed furniture, lighting, interiors, and accessories for most of his apartment, house, and commercial commissions. In order to promote his philosophy of a unified architectural and furnishings statement, he also designed interiors for department store and museum exhibitions.

His earliest documented furniture consists primarily of designs styled in Art Déco profiles. Some of the designs in wood recall the Bauhaus works of Marcel Breuer from 1921 to 1924; others relate to French designs of the late twenties. During the twenties built-in furniture—divans, bookshelves, and cabinets—became popular. Lescaze designed them for almost every job between the wars, because good modern forms were hard to acquire commercially and it was otherwise difficult and expensive to purchase custom-designed furniture for a client's particular installation. Lescaze's designs for tubular metal furniture recall those by the Europeans Mart Stam, Marcel Breuer, Mies van der Rohe, Le Corbusier, Pierre Jeanneret, Charlotte Perriand, and J. J. Adnet; some have no counterparts.

Lescaze's lighting designs in the twenties consisted of triangular fixtures installed in corners, concealed fixtures installed in architectural reveals, and constructivist-styled fixtures. In the thirties, he frequently employed skylights, glass-blocks, and baffled bars of light.

Lescaze's most notable product-designs were made for the important 1930s PSFS and CBS commissions. Other designs of this period were as diverse as a cocktail shaker for Sam Kootz, an elevator cab for the Otis Company, a piano case for Steinway, and a billiard table for the Brunswick-Balke-Collender Company.

Soon after the War, as good modern furniture design became commercially available and as his residential commissions diminished, Lescaze discontinued his product-design work.

Comments on documentation and dating

Lescaze's furniture designs are variously documented. Job numbers and dates are indicated on some of his drawings. On others there is no reference to the job and date, and only various combinations of upper- and lower-case letters and arabic and roman numerals (with little apparent systematic organization) identify the work. Thus, while some designs are firmly documented, others are dated on the basis of drawing style, the inclusion of a drawing's identifying letter-number combination in a series of dated drawings bearing the same "code," or its appearance in an executed architectural work where it is documented by an entry in the Job List and a photograph. Where dates or job are not documented, they are approximated in parentheses in the Check-List, following. (Photographs of drawings, courtesy Mrs. Lescaze, New York.)

Check-List of Selected Product Designs by William Lescaze

Free-Standing Furniture

Photo No.	Description	Date	Jobs	Documentation
164	Wood and upholstered lounge chair	Nov. 1927 – by Rufenacht Jan. 1929 – redrawn by Lescaze	Phillips apartment, Maison Bertie, Loeser's exhibition	"Club" armchair Dwg. 1010 Comm. 262
165	Wood and upholstered couch with end tables	Nov. 1927		Drawing, "Couch"
166	Wood and upholstered stool	Nov. 1927		Drawing, "Stool"
167	Metal and glass tiered-table; Metal and glass wall-table; Glass corner shelves and lighting fixture; Metal floor lamp; wood stool; Sofa and lounge chair	(1927-1928)	Philllips apartment	Photograph of job
168	Metal and glass table, as fabricated	(1928)	Phillips apartment	Photograph of job
169	"Chinese" bookcase, sofa, and metal floor lamp	(1928)	Phillips apartment	Photograph of job
170	Wood and upholstered armchair	(1928)		Drawing, Chair #1 Attributed on the basis of drawing style and paper
171	Wood and upholstered side chair	(1928)		Drawing, Chair #6 Attribution as above
172	Wood, low, round table	1928	de Sièyes house, Geller Showroom	Drawing, Job #220
173	Wood and upholstered armchair "C"	1928	de Sièyes house, Unity Lap Robe Co.	Drawing, Job #220
174	Wood desk	(1928)	de Sièyes house	Drawing, attributed to Job #220 on basis of drawing style & paper
175	Wood desk	(1928)	de Sièyes house	Drawing, attributed to Job #220 on basis of drawing style & paper
176	Wood desk, chaise, and cabinet	(1928)	de Sièyes house	Drawing, attributed to Job #220 on basis of drawing style & paper
177	Upholstered barrel-shaped armchair with wood base	(1928)	de Sièyes house and Macy exhibition of 1928	Drawing, attributed to Job #220 on basis of drawing style & paper

164

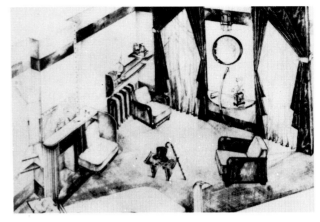

167

165

168

166

169

170

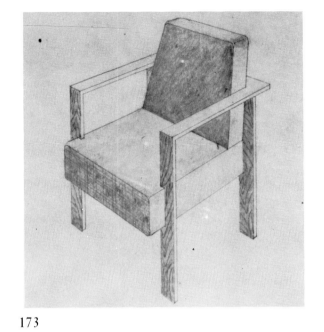

173

171

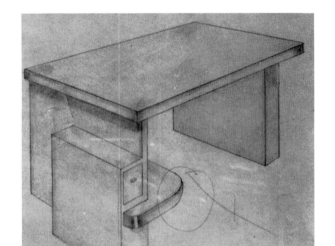

174

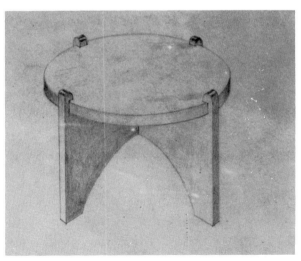

172

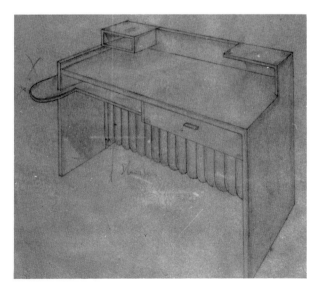

175

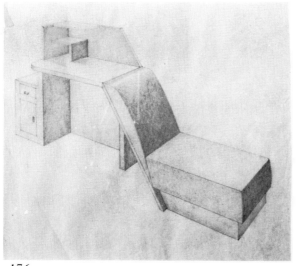

176

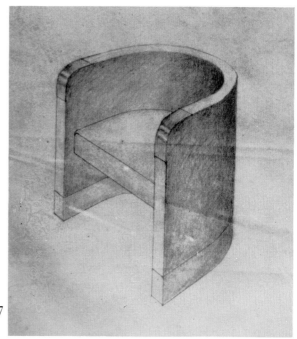

177

Photo No.	Description	Date	Jobs	Documentation
178	Upholstered barrel-shaped armchair with wood legs	(1928)	de Sièyes house	Drawing, attributed to Job #220 on basis of drawing style & paper
179	Upholstered easy chair with wood base	(1928)	de Sièyes house	Drawing, attributed to Job #220 on basis of drawing style & paper
180	Upholstered easy chair with wood base	(1928)	de Sièyes house	Drawing, attributed to Job #220 on basis of drawing style & paper
181 & 182	Upholstered armchair with wood arms and frame	(1928) (1928)	de Sièyes house, living room de Sièyes house, bedroom	Drawing attributed to Job #220 on basis of drawing style & paper
183 & 184	Wood corner tables and cabinet			Drawing, attributed to Job #220 on basis of drawing style & paper
185	Cabinet designs	(1928)	de Sièyes house	Photograph
186	Wood and upholstered armchair	(1928)	Macy Exhibition, Parrish Offices, Geller Showroom, Unity Lap Robe Co.	Photograph
187	Wood children's furniture	(1929)	Oak Lane Country Day School's nursery school	Photograph
188	High metal and upholstered armchair	11/14/29	Field house	Metal armchair "B" Drawing 1002
189	Metal and upholstered armchair	(1929)		Metal armchair "C" Drawing 1004, attributed on basis of number sequence
190	Metal and upholstered sidechair	(1929, probably redrawn after 1934)	Variation of design at PSFS	Chair Type No. 2, Drawing 1005
191	Low metal armchair with two-piece upholstered back	(1929)	Harding apartment, Field house, High Cross house, Hattie Carnegie showroom and offices, MMA, Loomis house, Lescaze house, Stokowski house, Unity Lap Robe Co., PSFS	Chair Type No. 1, Drawing 1006

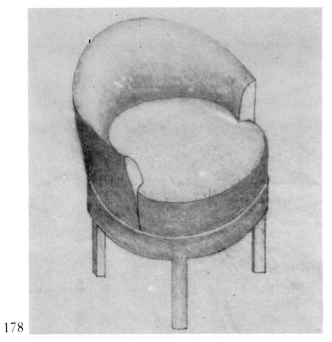

178

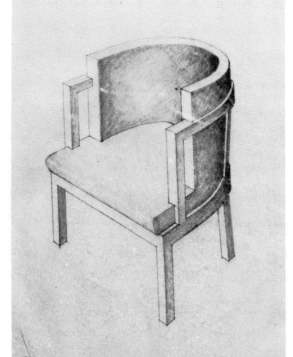

181

179

182

180

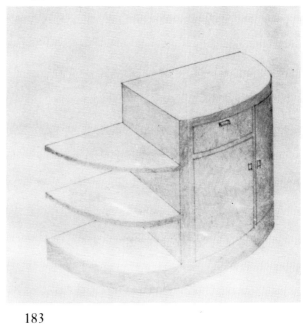

183

184

185

187

186

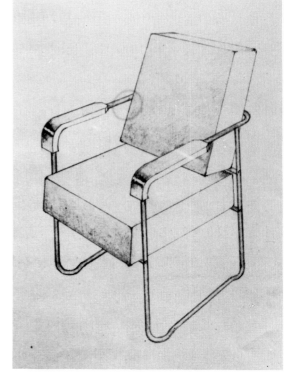

188

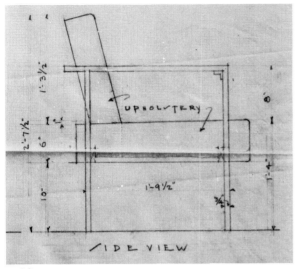

189

190

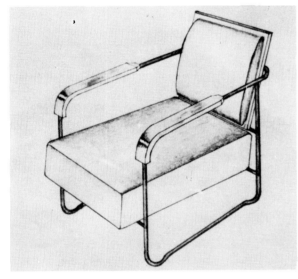

191

Photo No.	Description	Date	Jobs	Documentation
192	Low metal armchair with one-piece cushion back	(1929)	Lescaze house	Photograph of job, attributed on basis of style
193	Glass and metal nesting tables	4/2/29; rev. 12/5/29		Drawing 1013
194 & 195	Wood and metal armchair	4/5/29	Dreyfus apartment	Drawing 1014B
196	Metal and upholstered "writing-table" armchair	June-July 1930		Drawing 1049
197 & 198	Upholstered lounge chair; with rectangular wood legs	(1930)	Field house, PSFS's 33rd floor, Kramer house, CBS, Chicopee Sales Corp. Hobart house Kramer house	Drawing, Field Lounge Chair
199	Upholstered lounge chair with wood base	(1931); rev. 1937		Drawing, Chair Type No. 11
200	One-piece metal-framed chair and couch	8/4/30	Field house	Field couch and chair; drawing 1056

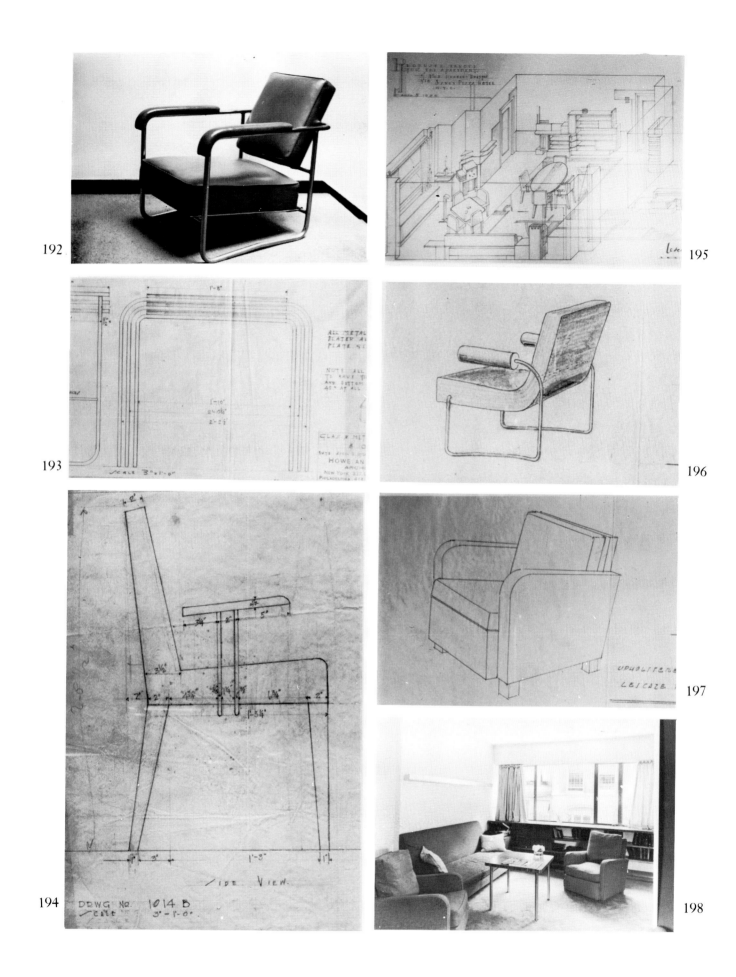

Photo No.	Description	Date	Jobs	Documentation
201	Metal, swivel, desk, sidechair	(1931)	PSFS, Field house, Time Inc., J. Walter Thompson Co.	Drawing, Chair Type 3
202	Metal, swivel, desk, armchair	(1931)	PSFS, Time Inc., J. Walter Thompson Co.	Drawing, Chair Type 4
203 & 204	Metal, upholstered armchair	1/29/31 rev. 4/2/31	PSFS, Hattie Carnegie showroom and offices, Lescaze house PSFS	Chair Type 5, Drawing 1062
205	Upholstered lounge chair with wood legs	(1931)	Lescaze house	Drawing, Chair Type 6
206 & 207	Metal and leather-upholstered arm chair	(1931)	Lescaze house, Loomis house	Drawing, Chair Type 10
208 & 209	Wood and upholstered armchair	(1931)	PSFS, 33rd floor PSFS, boardroom	Drawing 1066
210 & 211	Metal and upholstered stool	4/12/31	PSFS, Lescaze house Lescaze house	Drawing 1067 Photograph of job
212	Metal, swivel armchair with canvas seat and back	Mar. 1932 & Sept. 1933	PSFS	Drawing, C. 1
213	Metal, swivel sidechair with canvas seat and back	Mar. 1932	PSFS	Drawing, C. 2
214	Metal, cantilevered armchair with canvas seat and back	Mar. 1932	PSFS	Drawing, C. 3
215	Metal, cantilevered sidechair with canvas seat and back	Mar. 1932	PSFS	Drawing, C. 4
216	High cantilevered stool with wood seat	Mar. 1932	PSFS	Drawing, C. 5
217	High cantilevered stool with canvas seat and back	Mar. 1932	PSFS	Drawing, C. 6
218	Metal and leather upholstered lounge chair	Mar. 1932	PSFS	Drawing, C. 7
219	Metal and wood cantilevered sidechair	Mar. 1932	PSFS	Drawing, C. 8
220	Metal and upholstered armchair	(1932)	PSFS, Lescaze house	Photograph of job
221	Metal and upholstered roll-back sidechair	(1932)	PSFS, Lescaze house, Kramer house	Photograph of job
222	Metal and wood sidechairs	(1932)	PSFS	Photograph of job
223	Metal and upholstered armless couch	(1932)	PSFS	Photograph of job
224	Metal and leather swivel armchair	(1930-1934)	PSFS	Drawing
225	Metal and leather swivel sidechair	(1930-1934)	PSFS	Drawing
226	Metal and upholstered cantilevered armless lounge chair	(1932)	PSFS	Drawing, Chair 1A
227	Metal and upholstered cantilevered armless couch	(1932)	PSFS	Drawing, Couch 1B
228	Metal and upholstered lounge chair with arms	(1932)	Unknown	Drawing, Chair 11A
229	Variation on above	(1932)	Unknown	Drawing, Chair IVA
230	Metal and upholstered cantilevered armchair	(1932)	Unknown	Drawing, Chair IXE
231	Metal and fabric cantilevered sidechair	(1932)	Hessian Hills School, Field house	Photograph of job
232 & 233	Wood and upholstered armchair	(1934-1935)	Kramer house Kramer house	Drawing, Chair VC
234 & 235	Wood and upholstered armchair	7/19/35	Kramer house Kramer house	Drawing 78 Comm. 379
236	Wood and upholstered armchair	(1935)	Kramer house	Drawing
237 & 238	Wood and upholstered sidechair	(1935)	Kramer house Kramer house	Drawing Photograph of job
239 & 240	Metal and upholstered chaise	7/29/35	Buttenweiser apartment Buttenweiser apartment	Drawing

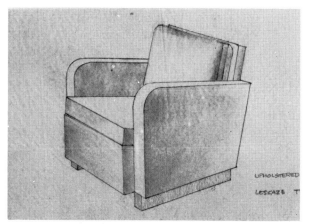

199

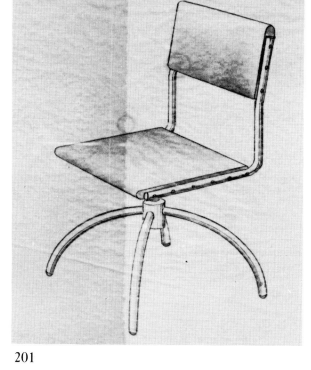

201

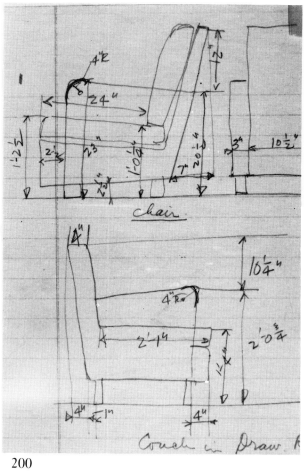

200

202

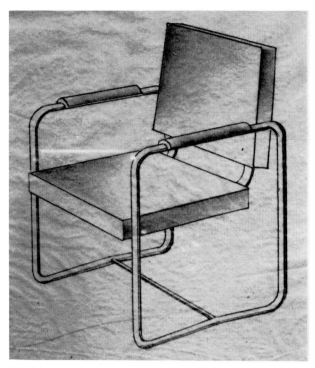

203

204

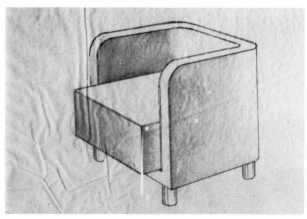

205

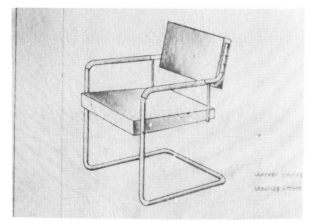

206

207

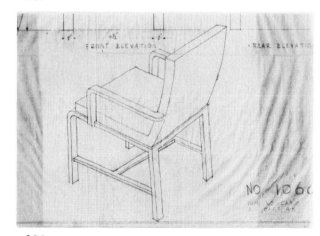

208

209

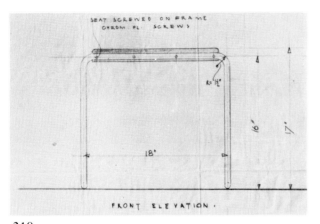

210

211

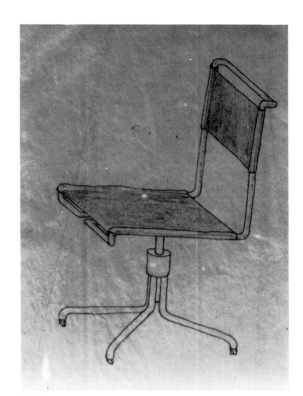

213

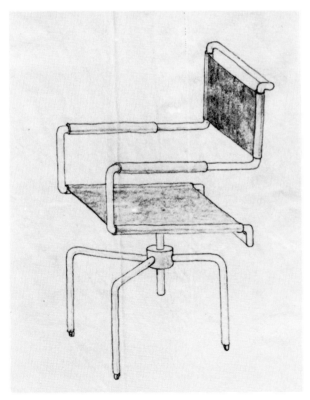

212

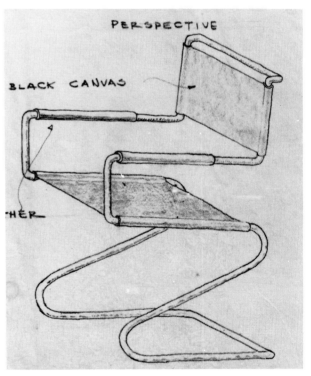

214

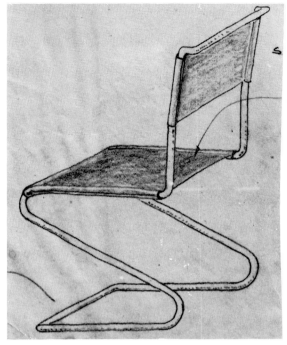

215

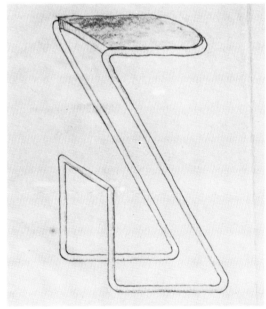

216

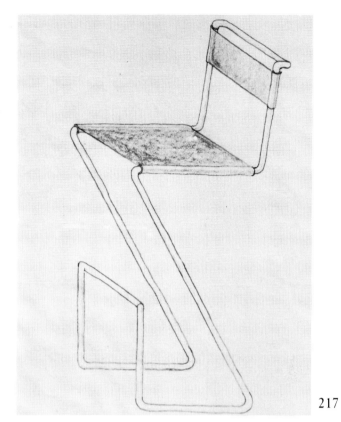

217

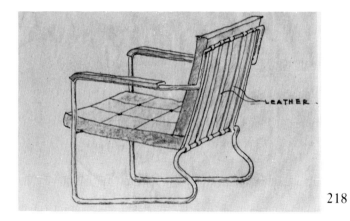

LEATHER

218

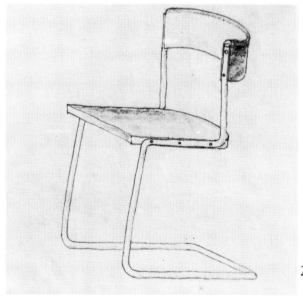

219

220

223

221

224

222

225

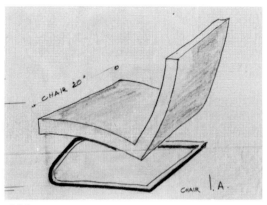

226

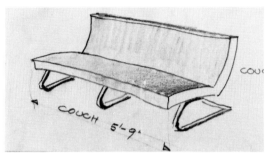

227

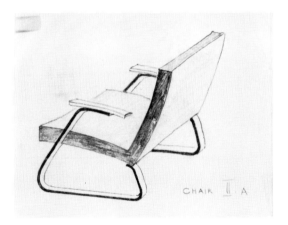

228

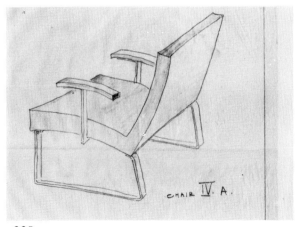

229

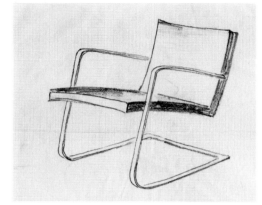

230

231

232

233

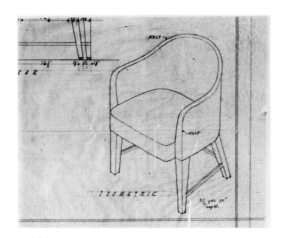

234

237

235

238

236

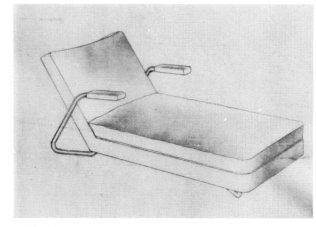

239

240

241

Photo No.	Description	Date	Jobs	Documentation
241	Wood and upholstered lounge chair	7/9/35	Buttenweiser (revised Field house chair)	Drawing 48, Comm. 396
		Rev. 12/30/41	Norman house	Drawing 117, Comm. 628
242	Wood and upholstered armchair	8/5/36	CBS	Drawing 28, Comm. 501
243	Wood and upholstered armchair with padded arm	8/5/36	CBS	Drawing 28, Comm. 501
244	Wood caned-back armchair	1/30/40	Norman house or Hobart house	Drawing
245	Bent-wood and upholstered chaise	5/18/42	Lescaze house addition at 209 E. 48th Street	Drawing, Comm. 671

"Built-In" Furniture

246	Custom cabinetry around couch and at wall	(1928-1929)	Leopold Stokowski	Photograph of job
247	"Built-in" seating and case pieces	1929	Harding apartment	Drawing
248	"Built-in" seating and case pieces	(1938)	Loomis house	Photograph of job
249	Typical case-piece design where drawer pulls form a continuous vertical bar	(Throughout the thirties)	Lescaze house, Dartington Hall boarding houses, High Cross house, Kramer house, Butler house	Photograph of job
250	Cabinets designed as space dividers	(1940-1941)	Norman house	Photograph of job
251	Wall storage, commercial application	(1931)	Carnegie salon	Photograph of job
252	Wall storage, residential application	(1930-1931)	High Cross house	Photograph of job

Lighting Design

253	Portable wall bracket	1928	de Sièyes house	Drawing, Comm. 220
254	Triangular corner fixtures	(1928)	Maison Bertie	Photograph of job
255	Lighting panels installed in bookcase	(1928)	Amos Parrish offices	Photograph of job
256	Ceiling lighting fixture	(1928)	Andrew Geller Shoe Stores	Photograph of job
257	Ceiling lighting system	(1928)	Andrew Geller Shoe Stores	Photograph of job
258	Ceiling lighting system	(1932)	PSFS	Photograph of job
259	Skylight	1934-1935	Raymond C. Kramer house	Photograph of job
260	Glass block	1933-1934	William E. Lescaze house	Photograph of job
261	Baffled-bar lighting fixture	1933-1934	William E. Lescaze house	Photograph of job
262	Ceiling lighting fixture	(1932)	PSFS	Photograph of job
263	Desk lamp	(1932)	PSFS	Photograph of job
264	Desk lamp	(1932)	PSFS	Photograph of job

Miscellaneous Designs

265	Clock	(1932)	PSFS	Photograph of job
266	Desk set	(1932)	PSFS	Photograph of job
267	Coat hooks	(1932)	PSFS	Photograph of job
268	Microphone	(1936)	CBS	Photograph of job
269	Mobile unit	(1945)	CBS	Photograph of job

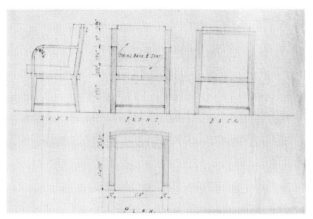

242

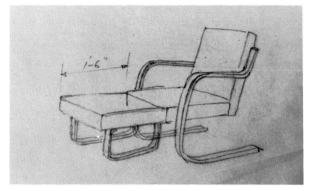

245

243

246

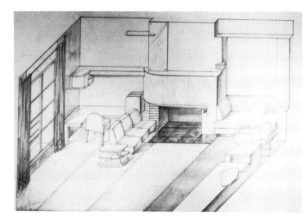

247

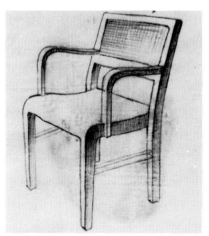

244

248

249

252

250

251

253

254

255

259

260

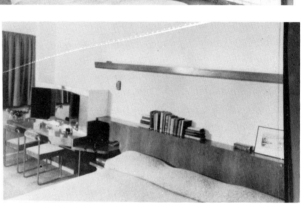

261

257

258

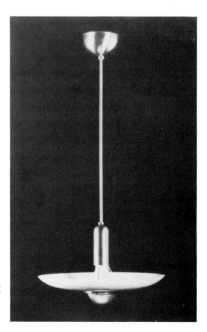

262

256

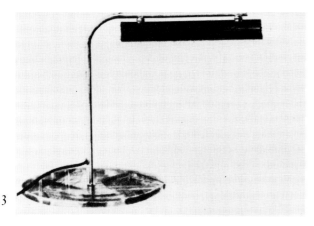

263

264

266

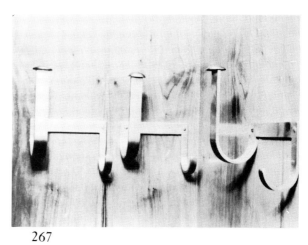

265

267

268

269

Bibliography

ABBREVIATIONS

Aronson   Aronson, Joseph. *The Book of Furniture and Decoration: Period and Modern.* New York: Crown Publishers, 1936.

Barbey   Barbey, Gilles. "William Lescaze (1896–1969): Sa carrière et son oeuvre de 1915 à 1939." *Werk* 58 (August 1971):559–63.

Cheney   Cheney, Sheldon. *The New World Architecture.* New York: Longmans, Green and Co., 1930.

Cheney and Cheney   Cheney, Sheldon, and Cheney, Martha. *Art and the Machine.* New York: Whittlesey House: McGraw-Hill Book Co., 1936.

Decorative Art Yearbook   *Decorative Art: Yearbook of the Studio.* London: Studio Publications, 1932–1937.

Ford and Ford   Ford, James, and Ford, Katherine Morrow. *Design of Modern Interiors.* New York: Architectural Book Publishing Co., 1942.

Ford and Ford   Ford, James, and Ford, Katherine Morrow. *The Modern House in America.* New York: Architectural Book Publishing Co., 1940.

Giolli   Giolli, Raffaello. "William Lescaze." *Casabella* 10 (January 1937):10–21.

Greif   Greif, Martin. *Depression Modern—The Thirties Style in America.* New York: Universe Books, 1975.

Hamlin I   Hamlin, Talbot. "Architecture." In *The New International Yearbook.* Edited by Herbert Treadwell Wade. New York: Dodd, Mead, 1930–1931.

Hamlin II   Hamlin, Talbot. "Architecture." In *The New International Yearbook.* Edited by Frank Vizetelly. New York: Dodd, Mead, 1932–1940.

Hitchcock   Hitchcock, Henry-Russell. "Howe and Lescaze." In *Modern Architecture: International Exhibition.* By Alfred Barr et al. New York: Museum of Modern Art, 1932; reprint ed., Arno Press, 1969.

McAndrew   McAndrew, John, ed. *Guide to Modern Architecture: Northeast States.* New York: Museum of Modern Art, 1940.

McGrath   McGrath, Raymond. *Twentieth Century Houses.* London: Faber, 1934.

Morancé   Morancé, Albert, ed. *Encyclopédie de l'architecture. Constructions modernes.* 3 vols. Paris, n.d. [ca. 1935].

Neutra   Neutra, Richard J. *Amerika.* Vienna: Verlag von Anton Schroll & Co., 1930.

Sartoris I	Sartoris, Alberto. *Gli elementi dell' architettura funzionale.* Milan: Ulrico Hoepli, 1932.
Sartoris II	Sartoris, Alberto. *Gli elementi dell' architettura funzionale.* 2nd ed. Milan: Ulrico Hoepli, 1935.
Sartoris III	Sartoris, Alberto. *Encyclopédie de l'architecture nouvelle.* Vol. 3. Milan: Hoepli, 1954.
Stern	Stern, Robert A. M. *George Howe: Toward a Modern American Architecture.* New Haven: Yale University Press, 1975.
Todd and Mortimer	Todd, Dorothy, and Mortimer, Raymond. *The New Interior Decoration.* New York: Scribners, 1929.
Year Book, Philadelphia Chapter A.I.A. and T-Square Club	*The Year Book of the Annual Architectural Exhibition Philadelphia.* Philadelphia Chapter of the American Institute of Architects and the T-Square Club.

SELECTIVE BIBLIOGRAPHY OF MAJOR WORKS, PROJECTS, AND COMPETITIONS ARRANGED BY DATE AND BY PROJECT

Dates indicate when the commission entered the job list and the time of its completion, when known.

1919   *DIPLOMA PROJECT,* Eidgenössischen Technischen Hochschule, Zurich, Switzerland.

Barbey, p. 559.

1923   *FORD HOUSE STUDIO AND REMODELING,* 2 Sutton Square, N.Y.C.

Barbey, p. 560.

"A Chapter Ends on Sutton Place." *New York Times,* 7 March 1965, Real Estate, pp. 1, 10.

Stern, p. 91.

1925   *EDGEWOOD SCHOOL ADDITION,* Greenwich, Connecticut.

"Boys' Dormitory." *Architecture* 55 (April 1927):207–208.

Stern, p. 92.

1927   *HALLE BROTHERS DEPARTMENT STORE EXHIBITION, "ART IN INDUSTRY" EXPOSITION,* Cleveland, Ohio.

"Halle Brothers Exposition Stresses Modernism." *New Review,* 19 August 1927.

Halle. Exhibitors Program.

1927   *LESCAZE APARTMENT AND STUDIO,* 337 East Forty-second Street, N.Y.C.

"A Bit of Old Spain in New York." *Arts and Decoration* 28 (November 1927):50–51.

Prussing, Lillian E. *Mid-Week Pictorial,* 12 January 1928.

Stern, p. 92.

1927   *CAPITAL BUS TERMINAL,* 239 West Fiftieth Street and 240–242 West Fifty-first Street, N.Y. [Destroyed prior to 1932].

"The Bus Grows Up." *The New Yorker,* 27 October 1928, pp. 20–21.

Hitchcock, pp. 144, 148, 150.

Stern, pp. 78, 94.

Stern, "PSFS: Beaux-Arts Theory and Rational Expressionism." *Journal of the Society of Architectural Historians* 21 (May 1962):91.

1927   *LEAGUE OF NATIONS BUILDING, COMPETITION PROJECT,* Geneva, Switzerland.

Architectural Competition for the Erection of a League of Nations Building at Geneva. Signed by the Jury and dated: Geneva, 1927, n.p.

"Competition for the League of Nations Headquarters at Geneva." *The Architect and Building News* 116 (13 August 1926):183, 184.

Ritter, John. "World Parliament, The League of Nations Competition, 1926." *Architectural Review* 136 (July 1964):17–28.

1927   *SOLDIERS AND SAILORS MONUMENT PROJECT,* Providence, Rhode Island.

Cady, John Hutchins. *The Civic and Architectural Development of Providence 1630–1950.* Providence, 1957.

———. *Program and Rules of the Second Competition for the Selection of an Architect for the Monumental Lighthouse.* Washington, D.C. Pan American Union, 1930.

1927–28 *JEAN DE SIÈYES HOUSE*, Mt. Kisco, New York

Barbey, p. 560.

Hitchcock, pp. 144, 148.

"Modernism Invades Even the Bucolic World of Camps and Hunting Lodges." *House and Garden*, June 1930, pp. 94–95.

Moore, Jennie. "Will Modernism Change our Houses?" *Building Developer*, June 1929, pp. 72–73.

Stern, p. 94.

1927–28 *R. COLFAX PHILLIPS APARTMENT*, 19 West Twelfth Street, N.Y.C.

"C. Phillips Apartment." *U.S.A.* 1 (Spring 1930), p. 42.

"The Modernistic Trend." *National Decorative Trade Service*, n.d., n.p.

1928 *CHRISTOPHER COLUMBUS MEMORIAL LIGHTHOUSE COMPETITION PROJECT*. Santo Domingo, Dominican Republic.

"Columbus Memorial Competition Awards." *Architectural Record* 70 (December 1931):56.

Howard, Edwin Laclede. "The City of Columbus." *Architectural Record* 64 (August 1928):145–149.

Kelsey, Albert, ed. *Program and Rules of the Competition for the Selection of an Architect for the Monumental Lighthouse*. Washington, D.C.: Pan American Union, 1928.

1928 *"PERMANENT" EXHIBITION, LOESER'S DEPARTMENT STORE*, Brooklyn, New York.

Glassgold, C. Adolph. "Decorative Art Notes." *The Arts* 13 (May 1928):296–301.

————. "The Decorative Arts." *The Arts* 14 (October 1928):215–217.

"Glimpse of New York Modernistic Apartment." *Arts and Decoration* 29 (September 1928):64.

Hitchcock, Henry-Russell. "Some American Interiors in the Modern Style." *Architectural Record* 64 (September 1928):38.

"The March of Decoration." *The American Sketch*, June 1928, p. 38.

"Modernistic Apartment." *Architecture* 58 (August 1928):89–92.

"Modernistic Apartment." *Mid-Week Pictorial*, 31 March 1928.

"Modernistic Interior." *Herald Tribune*, 5 April 1928.

Stern, p. 93.

Todd and Mortimer, pls. 66, 67.

"Victorian and Modern Side by Side Offer Striking Contrast at Loeser's." *Women's Wear Daily*, April 1928.

1928 *AMOS PARRISH AND COMPANY, OFFICES*, N.Y.C.

Glassgold, C. Adolph. "The Decorative Arts." *The Arts* 14 (October 1928):215–217.

Manufacturing Industries, December 1928, p. 603.

"Nineteen Twenty-Eight Contributes to a Modern American Style." *American Architect* 135 (5 January 1929):31–48.

Sanford, N. C. "Offices Decorated in the Modern Mode." *Good Furniture Magazine*, April 1929, pp. 193–194.

Storey, Walter R. "New Art Fashions Office Furniture." *New York Times*, 7 October 1928, Magazine Section, p. 10.

Todd and Mortimer, pl. 65.

"Twentieth Century Settings for the Modern Executive." *House and Garden*, February 1930, p. 82.

1928 *EXHIBITION OF ART IN INDUSTRY*, Macy's, N.Y.C.

"American Designs Prominent in Exposition at R. H. Macy's." *The World* (New York), 20 May 1928.

Glassgold, C. Adolph. "Art in Industry." *The Arts* 13 (June 1928):375–379.

"An International Exposition of Art in Industry, May 14 to May 26, 1928 at Macy's." Exhibition Catalogue.

"The Macy Exposition of Art in Industry." *Architectural Record* 64 (August 1928):137–143.

"Second Macy Art in Industry Exposition Reveals International Progress of Modern Art." *Women's Wear Daily*, 26 May 1928.

Stern, p. 93.

Storey, Walter R. "The Latest Art-in-Industry Exhibit." *New York Times*, 27 May 1928, Magazine Section, pp. 18–19.

1928 *NUDELMAN AND CONTI SHOWROOM*, N.Y.C., 224 West 45th Street, fourth floor.

Glassgold, C. Adolph. "The Decorative Arts." *The Arts* 14 (October 1928):215–217.

Manufacturing Industries. December 1928, p. 603.

Neutra, p. 102, pl. 141.

Stern, p. 93.

"Stress Modernism in New Dress Showroom."

Women's Wear Daily, 4 August 1928.

Todd and Mortimer, pl. 67.

1928   *COUNTRY HOUSE OF 1938, PROJECT.*

"Country Home of 1938 Has Airplane Facilities Built In." *New York Herald Tribune*, 23 December 1928, Magazine Section.

Hitchcock, p. 148.

Lescaze, William. "The Future American Country House." *Architectural Record* 64 (November 1928):417–420.

Moore, Jennie. "Will Modernism Change Our Houses?" *Building Developer*, June 1929, pp. 72–73.

Neutra, p. 131, pls. 205–206.

1928–29 *LEOPOLD STOKOWSKI APARTMENT*, East Seventy-first Street, N.Y.C.

Glassgold, Adolph. "The Stokowski Apartment." *Architectural Forum* 53 (August 1930):227–229.

Hoffman, Herbert, *Modern Interiors.* London: Studio Vista, 1934, p. 54.

"An Interior that Believes in Modernism," *Harper's Bazaar*, February 1930, pp. 106–107.

Kitchen, Karl K. "Up and Down Broadway." *New York World*, 23 April 1929.

1928   *ANDREW GELLER RETAIL SHOWROOMS*, Fifth Avenue, N.Y.C. and *FACTORY SHOW-ROOM*, Brooklyn, New York.

"Andrew Geller to Move to New Factory." *The Shoe Retailer.* 15 December 1928, p. 56.

Glassgold, C. Adolph. "The Decorative Arts." *The Arts* 15 (April 1929):269–273, 286, 288.

Hahn, Lew. "Art as a Selling Point." *American Magazine of Art* 23 (July 1931):44.

"Ideas in Search of Stores." *Retailing.* 6 April 1929, p. 13.

Kiesler, Frederick. *Contemporary Art Applied to the Store and Its Display.* New York: Brentano's, 1930, p. 144.

"A Modern Shoe Shop." *New York Telegram*, Magazine Section.

Morancé, 2:pls. 51–52.

1928   *GARAGE AND APARTMENT HOUSE PROJECT*, N.Y.C.

Gordon, Harry. "Wohin Mit Den Autos?" *Das Illustrierte Blatt.* Frankfurt a/Main, 23 January 1930.

Hitchcock, p. 148.

1928   *MAISON BERTIE BEAUTY SALON*, Fifth Avenue, N.Y.C.

Glassgold, C. Adolph. "The Decorative Arts." *The Arts* 15 (April 1929):269–273, 286, 288.

1929   *OAK LANE COUNTRY DAY SCHOOL, NUR-SERY SCHOOL BUILDING*, Oak Lane Road, near Philadelphia, Pennsylvania [destroyed ca. 1960].

"Architecture's Portfolio of Corner Windows." *Architecture* 73 (May 1936):304.

Barbey, pp. 560–561.

Cheney, p. 362.

"A Children's Day School and Two Country Houses in America by Howe and Lescaze." *Architectural Review* 71 (March 1932):92.

Curry, William B. "Modern Buildings for New Schools." *Graphic Survey*, 1 September 1931, pp. 486–498.

———. "Planning for Education." *Design for Today*, September 1934, pp. 319–322.

Dickson, Harold B. *One Hundred Pennsylvania Buildings.* State College, Pa.: Bald Eagle Press, 1954, p. 91.

Giolli.

Hamlin 1, 1931, pp. 52–58.

Hitchcock, pp. 141, 148, 151.

Hitchcock, Henry-Russell. *Modern Architecture, Romanticism and Reintegration.* New York: Payson and Clark, 1929, pl. 54.

Hoffman, Herbert. "Kleinkinderschule in Philadelphie." *Moderne Bauformen* 30 (1931):578–580.

Howe, George. "Modernism in School Architecture." *The American School and University Yearbook.* 4 vols. New York: American School Pub. Corp., 1931, 4:93–96.

"Ein Kindergarten." *Die Form* 5 (1 January 1930):15–17.

Lescaze, William. *On Being an Architect.* New York: G. P. Putnam's Sons, 1942, p. 243.

"The Little Red Schoolhouse of Tomorrow's Memories." *U.S.A.* 1 (Spring 1930):30.

McAndrew, p. 15.

McGrath, p. 118.

"Modern Buildings for Modern Schools." *School Management*, May 1937, pp. 240–241.

Morancé, 3:pls. 40–43.

"Nursery Building, the Oak Lane Country Day School, Philadelphia." *The Architectural Record* 67 (April 1930):360–363.

"Oak Lane Country Day School." *Der Baumeister*, November 1932, p. 382.

"Oak Lane Country Day School." *Mid-Week Pictorial*, 2 November 1929.

"Oak Lane School to Open Nursery." *The Philadelphia Inquirer*, 22 September 1929.

Sartoris I, p. 446.

Sartoris II, p. 549.

Sartoris III, 3:763.

Stern, pp. 96–98, 104n41, 107, 118n67.

"Stokowski School Opens Tomorrow." *Public Ledger* (Philadelphia), 22 September 1929.

"Trend: A New Schoolhouse that Looks Like a Penthouse on Mars." *News-Week* 6 (2 November 1935):20.

1929 *HERBERT DREYFUS APARTMENT*, N.Y.C.

"Should Architects Design Furniture?" *House and Garden*, February 1930, p. 86.

1929 *CHARLES HARDING APARTMENT LIVING ROOM*, N.Y.C.

Cheney, p. 210.

Decorative Art Yearbook 1935, p. 31.

Innen Dekoration, March 1932, p. 112.

"Living in Space." *Arts and Decoration* 40 (February 1934):23–26.

"Living Rooms." *Arts and Decoration* 39 (September 1933):20.

"Members Activities." *News of the Art Alliance of America*, February 1930, p. 2.

Patterson, Curtis. "Georgian Calm with Modernistic Repose." *Harpers Bazaar*, April 1931, pp. 105–106.

Rice, Norman N. "This Modern Architecture." *T-Square Club Journal* 1 (April 1931):23.

1929 *BEN HERZBERG APARTMENT*, N.Y.C.

"Apartment for Mr. Herzberg, N.Y.C." *Architectural Record* 67 (March 1930):259–260.

Decorative Art Yearbook 1935, p. 46; 1931, p. 61.

Herzberg Apartment. *L'architecture d'aujour-d'hui*, November–December 1933, pp. 69–75.

Kahn, Ely Jacques. "Modern Lighting Departs Radically from the Methods of the Past." *House and Garden*, August 1930, pp. 44–45.

"Modern Room by Howe and Lescaze Architects." *Arts and Decoration* 43 (January 1936):19.

"The New Decoration in America." *The London Studio*. 105 (January 1933):25, 30.

1929 *MRS. GEORGE PORTER HOUSE PROJECT*, Ojai, California.

"A Children's Day School and Two Country Houses in America by Howe and Lescaze." *Architectural Review* 71 (March 1932):93.

"House for Mrs. G. F. Porter, Ojai, California." *Architectural Record* 68 (November 1930):440.

"Roofs for Outdoor Living. House for Mrs. George French Porter, Ojai, California." *American Architect* 137 (March 1930):56.

1929–32 *PSFS BANK AND OFFICE BUILDING*. Twelfth and Market Streets, Philadelphia, Pennsylvania [with George Howe].

Aloi, Roberto. *L'arviedamento moderno*. Milan: Hoepli, 1934, pl. 581.

Annual Report. Investment Corporation of Philadelphia, 1933.

"Architecture Room." *Museum of Modern Art Bulletin* 1 (January 1934):4.

Auberjonois, Fernand. "La bâtiment de la Philadelphia Saving Fund Society." *Oeuvres Architecture Art Applique Beaux Arts*, August 1934, pp. 13–16.

"Bank and Office Building, Philadelphia Saving Fund Society." *Architectural Record* 69 (April 1931):308.

Barbey, pp. 560–561.

Bauer, Catherine. "Architecture: In Philadelphia." *Arts Weekly* 1 (23 April 1932):151–154.

Brooks, H. Allen. "PSFS: A Source for its Design." *Journal of the Society of Architectural Historians* 27 (December 1968):299–302.

"Building Facade Emphasizes Steel Frame." *Engineering News-Record* 109 (10 November 1932):549–552.

"Built in U.S.A. 1932–1944." *Architectural Forum* 80 (May 1944):96.

Carlman, Manne. "En Modern Bank-och Konitorsbyggnadi U.S.A." *Byggmastaren* 14 (January 1935):3–8.

Cheney, p. 158.

Cheney and Cheney, pp. 9, 148, 231.

"Clock Designed by Howe and Lescaze—Manufactured by Cartier, for the PSFS." *Industrial Arts* 1 (Spring 1936):83.

Conners, Kenneth Wray. "The Skyscraper Reaches Maturity." *The London Studio*. 105 (June 1933):380–382.

Cornwall, John E. "A Tool Goes to Work in Philadelphia." *Building Investment*, August 1932, pp. 18–20.

"Design Analysis: The Vertical Style." *Architectural Forum* 83 (July 1945):105–113.

Deskey, Donald. "The Rise of American Architecture and Design." *The Studio* 5 (June 1933):266–273.

"Filadelfia Saving Fund Society Building." *Neustra Arquitectura* 4 (May 1933):339–342.

Giedion, Siegfried. "Vers un renouveau architectural de l'Amerique." *Cahiers D'Art*, August 1933, pp. 237–243.

Giolli.

Gutheim, Frederick. "The Philadelphia Saving Fund Society Building: A Re-Appraisal." *Architectural Record* 106 (October 1949):88–95, 180, 182.

Hackett, R. Berkley. "Mechanical Equipment." *Architectural Forum* 57 (December 1932):548–550.

Hale, C. W. "Office Architecture with a Purpose." *Office Management*, September 1933, pp. 12–14.

Harbers, Guido. "Das Neue Burgogebäude PSFS." *Der Baumeister*, June 1933, pp. 195–202.

Haskell, Douglas. "The Filing-Cabinet Building." *Creative Art* 10 (June 1932):446–449.

Hitchcock, Henry-Russell. "Architecture Chronicle: The Brown Decades and the Brown Years." *Hound and Horn* 5 (January–March 1932):272–277.

———. *Architecture: Nineteenth and Twentieth Centuries.* Harmondsworth, Middlesex: Penguin Books, 3rd ed., 1968, pp. 381, 415, pl. 169.

———. "Howe and Lescaze." In *Modern Architecture: International Exhibition*, pp. 144–145, 148, 153. By Alfred Barr et al. New York: Museum of Modern Art, 1932; reprint ed. Arno Press, 1969.

———. "Wright and the International Style." In *Art in America in Modern Times*, pp. 70–72. By Holger Cahill and Alfred Barr. New York: Museum of Modern Art, 1934.

Hitchcock, Henry-Russell and Johnson, Philip. *The International Style: Architecture Since 1922.* New York: Museum of Modern Art, 1932, p. 159.

Houghten, F. S. "Comfort Conditions in Air Conditioning." *Real Estate Record*, 19 December 1936, pp. 38–40.

Howe, George. "A Design for a Savings Bank and Office Building." *T-Square Club Journal* 1 (March 1931):10–13.

———. "Functional Aesthetics and the Social Ideal." *Pencil Points* 13 (April 1932):215–218.

———. "New Departures in Philadelphia." *Building Investment*, March 1932, pp. 26–28.

International Architecture 1924–1934. London: Royal Institute of British Architects, 1934, p. 99.

Jordy, William. *American Buildings and Their Architects: The Impact of European Modernism in the Mid-Twentieth Century.* Vol. 4. New York: Doubleday and Co., 1972, chap. 2.

———. "PSFS: Its Development and Its Significance in Modern Architecture." *Journal of the Society of Architectural Historians* 21 (May 1962):47–83.

Jordy, William H., and Wright, Henry. "PSFS." *Architectural Forum* 120 (May 1964):124–129, 143.

Levinson, Maxwell. "The Most Outstanding Office Building in America." *Living Art*, January 1934, pp. 24–26.

Longees, E. F. "William Lescaze Defines Design." *Modern Plastics* 12 (April 1935):20–22, 58–59.

Machine Art. New York: Museum of Modern Art, 1934, pls. 81, 257.

McAndrew, p. 93.

Mieras, J. P. "De Philadelphia-Saving-Fund-Society, Architecten Howe and Lescaze." *Bouwkundig Weekblad Architectura* 55 (23 June 1934):258–263.

Mock, Elizabeth, ed. *Built in USA 1932–1944.* New York: Museum of Modern Art, 1944, pp. 100–101.

Modern Architecture U.S.A. New York: Museum of Modern Art, 1965, pl. 8.

"A New Shelter for Savings: The Philadelphia Saving Fund Society." *Architectural Forum* 57 (December 1932):483–498.

Nothing More Modern: The PSFS Building. (Rental Brochure). Philadelphia: Richard J. Seltzer Co., 1931.

Peter, John. *Masters of Modern Architecture.* New York: Braziller, 1958, p. 145.

"Le Philadelphia Saving Fund Building." *L'architecture d'aujourd'hui* 9 (January 1938):16.

Philadelphia Savings [sic] Fund Society Bank and Office Building." *Architectural Review* 81 (March 1937):126.

"Planning, Engineering, Equipment, the Philadelphia Saving Fund Society Building." *Architectural Forum* 57 (December 1932):543–550.

"PSFS." *Greater Philadelphia Magazine*, June 1964, p. 71.

"PSFS." *L'architecture d'aujourd'hui* 10 (June 1939):24–25.

"PSFS: Hollow Metal Equipment." *Metalcraft* 9 (July 1932):10–11.

Purdy and Henderson. "Structural Engineering." *Architectural Forum* 57 (December 1932):547–548.

Reilly, C. H. "The First Great Modern Bank Building: The Philadelphia Saving Fund Society's New Offices." *The Banker* 37 (February 1936):186–202.

———. "Philadelphia's Fancy." *Fortune* 6 (December 1932):65–69, 130–131.

Robertson, Howard. "An Office Building in Philadelphia." *The Architect and Building News* 137 (12 January 1934):66–68.

Santacilia, Carlos O. *A maquinismo la Vida y la arquitectura.* Mexico, 1939, pp. 25, 28, 43.

Sartoris I, p. 447.

Sartoris III, 3:765–767.

———. *Architettura funzionale*, pp. 550–552.

"The Saving Fund Society Building." *Architectural Forum* 56 (January 1932):97–102.

Scully, Vincent. *American Architecture and Urbanism.* New York: Praeger Pub., 1969, p. 154.

Stern, pp. 61–62, 87–89, 108–132.

———. "PSFS: Beaux-Arts Theory and Rational Expressionism." *Journal of the Society of Architectural Historians* 21 (May 1962):84–95.

Sterner, Harold, "International Architectural Style." *Hound and Horn* 5 (April–June 1932):452–460.

Tarleton, Leslie S. "Air Conditioning the Philadelphia Saving Fund Society Building." *Heating and Ventilating*, July 1932, pp. 27–30.

———. "Electricity and the Architect." *T-Square Club Journal* 2 (January 1932):26, 33.

———. "Heating and Cooking for a Modern Bank and Office Building." *Heating and Ventilating*, September 1931, pp. 57–60.

Tatum, George B. *Penn's Great Town.* Philadelphia: University of Pennsylvania Press, 1961, pp. 131–132, 203, pl. 136.

"The Unusual Philadelphia Savings [*sic*] Fund Building." *Engineering News Record* 109 (10 November 1932):549–552.

The Year Book. Philadelphia Chapter A.I.A. and T-Square Club, 1931 and 1949.

Zevi, Bruno. *Architecture as Space.* New York: Horizon, 1957, pp. 192, 194.

1929–31 *PECK HOUSE PROJECT*, Paoli, Pennsylvania.

"House for Arthur Peck, Paoli, Pennsylvania." *Architectural Record* 70 (November 1931):369.

The Year Book. Philadelphia Chapter A.I.A. and T-Square Club, 1931.

Sartoris I, p. 450.

Stern, pp. 107, 156.

1929–31 *MUSEUM OF MODERN ART PROJECT*, N.Y.C.

The Bulletin of the Museum of Modern Art 2 (March–April 1935):8.

The Bulletin of the Museum of Modern Art 6 (May–June 1939):7, 10.

Howe, George, and Lescaze, William. *A Modern Museum.* Springdale, Connecticut, 1930.

Lescaze, William. "A Modern Housing for a Museum." *Parnassus* 9 (November 1937):12–14.

"Museum Schemes for Congested City Area." *Pencil Points* 13 (October 1932):713.

"A Proposed Museum of Contemporary Art for New York City by Howe and Lescaze, Architects." *Architectural Record* 80 (July 1936):43–50.

Stern, pp. 104–106.

"Studies for a Modern Museum." *Trend*, May 1932, n.p.

1929–33 *PSFS GARAGE*, Twelfth and Filbert Streets, Philadelphia, Pennsylvania.

Garage Facilities. Philadelphia: Richard J. Seltzer, n.d. (Rental Brochure).

McAndrew, p. 94.

"PSFS Parking Garage, Philadelphia, Pennsylvania, Howe and Lescaze, Architects." *Architectural Record* 90 (July 1941):94.

1929–30 *WILLIAM WASSERMAN HOUSE, PROJECT*, Whitemarsh, Pennsylvania.

Brock, H. I. "Modern Architecture in Rural Settings," *New York Times*, 2 February 1930, Special Features, p. 8.

Carey, Elizabeth Luther, "League's Annual Exhibition." *New York Times*, 9 February 1930, Section 8, p. 12.

Cheney, p. 118.

"A Children's Day School and Two Country Houses in America by Howe and Lescaze." *Architectural Review* 71 (March 1932):93.

Glassgold, Adolph C. "House of William Stix

Wasserman, Esq., Whitemarsh, Pennsylvania."
Architectural Forum 53 (August 1930):23–32.

Hamlin I, 1930, pp. 52–58.

McBride, Henry. "Tendencies in City Buildings. Illustrated by the Exhibition." *New York
Sun*, 8 February 1930, p. 8.

Stern, pp. 108, 158, 159, 162–171, 232.

Year Book, Philadelphia Chapter A.I.A. and T-
Square club, 1929.

1930–31 *FREDERICK V. FIELD HOUSE*, New Hartford, Connecticut [Derelict in 1976].

Aronson, p. 301.

L'architecture d'aujourd'hui 4 (November–
December 1933):69–75.

Barbey, p. 561.

Coffin, Lewis A., ed. *American Country Houses of
Today*. New York: Architectural Book Publishing Co., 1935, p. 112.

"The Connecticut House of Mr. and Mrs. Frederick V. Field." *Arts and Decoration* 39 (October
1933):26–27.

Decorative Art Yearbook 1932, p. 131; 1934,
pp. 32–33.

Ford and Ford. *The Modern House*, p. 130.

"George Howe e William Lescaze architetti
americani." *Domus* 13 (May 1935):14–18.

Hamlin II, 1932, p. 52.

Hitchcock, p. 148.

"House for F. V. Field, Hartford, Connecticut,
and another for Arthur Peck, Paoli, Pennsylvania." *Architectural Record* 70 (November
1931):368.

"House in New Hartford, Connecticut." *Architectural Forum* 59 (November 1933):400–404.

"House of Frederick V. Field, New Hartford,
Connecticut." *Architectural Record* 72 (November 1932):326–329.

Jackson, Alan. "A New American Phenome-
non—Luxurious Smaller Houses." *Arts and
Decoration* 43 (February 1936):11–15.

Johnson, Philip. "The Modern Room" and
"The Modern House." In *Art in America in Modern Times*, pp. 72–76. By Holger Cahill and Alfred H. Barr, Jr. New York: Museum of Modern Art, 1934.

Lescaze, William. "Living Modern." *Junior
League Magazine*, April 1934, pp. 20–21.

"Living in Space." *Arts and Decoration* 40 (February 1934):23–26.

"A Logical House for Mr. Frederick Vanderbilt

Field." *Town and Country* 88 (1 April 1933):23–
25.

McAndrew, p. 22.

McGrath, pp. 117–118.

Man at Work: Arts and Crafts. Social Science
Series, vol. 7 of the Elementary School Course.
Boston: Ginn and Co., 1937.

Murchison, Kenneth. "Which Building Material Would you Prefer?" *Arts and Decoration* 46
(July 1937):14–17.

Sartoris II, pp. 553–554.

Sartoris III, 3:764.

Stern, pp. 107–108.

Whitaker, Charles. *Rameses to Rockefeller*. New
York: Random House, 1934, pl. 33.

Yorke, F. R. S. *The Modern House*. London: The
Architectural Press, 1934, pp. 150–152.

1930–32 *HEADMASTER'S HOUSE* (Curry House), Dartington Hall, Devon, England [restored].

"Architecture's Portfolio of Corner Windows."
Architecture 73 (May 1936):305.

Aronson, p. 318.

Barbey, p. 561.

"Circulation." *Architectural Forum* 67 (October
1937):345, 356.

Decorative Art Yearbook 1933, p. 24; 1935, p. 24.

Mid-Week Pictorial, 27 July 1935.

"Ein Neuzeitliches Haus in Sud-Devon." *Innen-
Dekoration* 1 (June 1934):196–197.

"An English Residence Designed by Two New
York Modernists." *House and Garden* 65 (February 1934):56–57.

"George Howe e William Lescaze architetti
americani." *Domus* 13 (May 1935):16.

Hening, Robert. "Building in Terms of Human
Beings." *Dartington Hall News*, 21 February
1967, p. 7.

"House in Devon, England." *Architectural
Forum* 59 (November 1933):405–408.

"House of William B. Curry, *Architectural
Forum* 58 (March 1933):177–180.

"House, Totnes, South Devon." *Architectural
Review* 77 (March 1935):108.

Hitchcock, p. 148.

Hussey, Christopher. "High Cross Hill, Dartington, Devon, The Residence of Mr. W. B.
Curry." *Country Life*, 11 February 1933,
pp. 144–149.

"Living in Space." *Arts and Decoration* 40 (February 1934):23–26.

Morand, Dexter. "Modern House in Devon." *Construction*, July–August 1934, pp. 93–96.

"Residencia privada del Señor W. B. Curry." *Revista de Arquitectura*, February 1936, pp. 68–72.

Sartoris II, p. 545.

Stern, pp. 97n25, 156.

Yorke, F. R. S. *The Modern House*. London: The Architectural Press, 1934, pp. 160–161.

1930–31 *FOXHOLE JUNIOR SCHOOL PROJECT*, Dartington Hall, Devon, England.

Curry, William B. "Modern Buildings for New Schools." *The Survey Graphic*, 1 September 1931, pp. 496–498.

Lescaze, William. "Letters About a Modern School." *Architectural Forum* 62 (January 1935):46–55.

1931 *HATTIE CARNEGIE SHOWROOM AND OFFICE*, Fifth Avenue, N.Y.C.

Decorative Art Yearbook 1932, p. 47.

Hitchcock, p. 148.

"New Interiors." *Creative Art* 9 (September 1931):240–246.

1931 *TRANS LUX THEATER INTERIORS*, Fifty-eighth Street and Madison Avenue, Forty-eighth Street and Broadway in N.Y.C., and Eighteenth Street and Market in Philadelphia.

"The Current Cinema." *The New Yorker*, 28 March 1931, pp. 75–76.

Hitchcock, p. 148.

Pawley, Frederick Arden. "Design of Motion Picture Theatres." *Architectural Record* 71 (June 1932):429.

"Trans-Lux Theater, New York City." *Architectural Record* 70 (August 1931):118–120.

"Trans-Lux Theater, New York, New York. Howe and Lescaze, Interiors." *Architectural Forum* 57 (October 1932):386.

1931 *EMIGRANT INDUSTRIAL SAVINGS BANK PROJECT*, N.Y.C.

Sartoris 1, p. 445.

Sartoris II, p. 548.

Sartoris III, 3:761

1931–32 *HESSIAN HILLS SCHOOL*, Mt. Airy Road, Croton-on-Hudson, New York [partially rebuilt in 1960 to become Temple Israel].

The American School and University Yearbook. Vol. 5. New York: American School Pub. Corp., 1932, p. 35.

Curry, William B. "Modern Buildings for New Schools." *Survey Graphic*, 1 September 1931, pp. 496–498.

Giolli.

"Hessian. Hills School." *National Business Review*, March 1931, p. 7.

Hessian Hills School." *Progressive Education*. "March 1933, p. 132.

McAndrew, p. 46.

McGrath, p. 118.

"Modern Buildings for Modern Schools." *School Management*, May 1937, pp. 240–241.

"Eine moderne amerikanische Schule." *Die Form*, July 1933, pp. 212–215.

"A New Schoolhouse That Looks Like a Penthouse on Mars." *News-Week*, 2 November 1935, p. 20.

"New School Plans are Exhibited Here." *New York Times*, 28 February 1932, section 2, p. 6.

Sartoris I, pp. 448–449.

Sartoris II, pls. 546–547.

Stern, pp. 96n23, 99n30, 98–101, 135, 152.

Sterner, Harold. "International Architectural Style." *Hound and Horn* 5 (April–June 1932):452–460.

"Ultra-Modern Design Accepted for School." *New York Times*, 30 April 1931, p. 26.

"Will Erect Functionalist Building." *Art Digest* 5 (1 June 1931):10.

1931–32 *EXHIBITION, PENNSYLVANIA MUSEUM OF ART* (now Philadelphia Museum of Art), Philadelphia, Pennsylvania.

"Design for the Machine." *The Pennsylvania Museum Bulletin* 27 (March 1932):115–119.

1931 *MAURICE WERTHEIM RESIDENCE PROJECT*, Cos Cob, Connecticut.

Gebhard, David, and Nevins, Deborah. *200 Years of American Architectural Drawing*. New York: Whitney Library of Design, 1977, p. 210. [Misidentified as the Peck House.]

McAndrew, p. 19.

Sartoris I, p. 451.

Stern, p. 107.

1931–32 *CHRYSTIE-FORSYTH STREETS HOUSING DEVELOPMENT PROJECT*, N.Y.C.

"Chrystie-Forsyth Street Housing Project." *T-Square Club Journal* 2 (April 1932):21.

"Explain Houses on Stilts." *New York Times*, 10 February 1932, p. 43.

Giolli.

"Governor to Veto City Bill to Lease Land for Housing." *New York Times*, 25 March 1932, p. 1.

Hitchcock, pp. 145–146, 148, 154–155.

"Model Housing." Editorial, *New York Times*, 4 March 1932, p. 18.

"Modern Housing in the Modern Manner." *East Side Chamber News* 5 (February 1932):7–9

Mumford, Lewis. "The Sky Line, Organic Architecture." *The New Yorker*, 27 February 1932, p. 45.

"Portfolio of Apartment Houses." *Architectural Record* 71 (March 1932):167–208.

"Proposed Chrystie-Forsyth Housing Development for New York City." *Architectural Record* 71 (March 1932):194–195.

"Proposed Housing Development, Chrystie-Forsyth Streets, New York." *Architectural Forum* 56 (March 1932):265–267.

"A Slum-Substitute Proposal for New York City." *The American City* 46 (March 1932):112.

Stern, pp. 101–104, 192.

Sterner, Harold. "International Architectural Style." *Hound and Horn* 5 (April–June 1932):452–460.

"The Trend of Affairs." *Technology and Review* 34 (March 1932):248.

Wright, Henry. *Rehousing Urban America*. New York: Columbia University Press, 1935, p. 110.

1932–36 *CHURSTON ESTATE HOUSING DEVELOPMENT*, Churston, Devon, England.

Churston [Sales brochure], England, 1935.

"Churston Development, South Devon, England." *Architectural Record* 81 (May 1937):bt31–bt34.

Cottis, Nicolas. "Time to Preserve This for the Future?" *Dartington Hall News*, 28 March 1969, p. 6.

Torbay Herald Express, 3 July 1933.

1932–33 *BOARDING HOUSE 1 (or A)*, Dartington Hall, Devon, England.

"Dartington Country School, South Devon, England." *Architectural Record* 75 (May 1934):384–385.

Heard, Gerald. "The Dartington Experiment." *Architectural Review* 75 (April 1934):119–122.

1933–34 *WILLIAM LESCAZE HOUSE AND OFFICE*, 211 East Forty-eighth Street, N.Y.C.

Aronson, pp. 150, 311.

Barbey, p. 561.

"Brownstone to Glass Brick." *House and Garden* 66 (December 1934):31–33.

"Casa Lescaze à New York." *Metron*, No. 9 (1946), p. 44.

Cheney and Cheney, pp. 169, 201.

"City House of William Lescaze, New York." *Architectural Forum* 61 (December 1934):388–399.

Cutts, A. B. "Residence of William Lescaze, New York." *Architectural Record* 77 (April 1935):171–174.

Decorative Art Yearbook 1936, pp. 21, 47, 74.

Decorators Digest, April 1935, pp. 42, 94.

Ford, pp. 51, 62, 72, 76.

Ford and Ford, p. 131.

"George Howe e William Lescaze architetti americani." *Domus* 13 (May 1935):14–15.

Greif, p. 148.

Handbook of the American Glass Industries Exhibition. March 1936.

Hopkins, Alfred. "Terrace from Terra, Close to the Earth." *Arts and Decoration* 44 (August 1936):18–20.

"House in New York City." *The Architect and Building News* 143 (5 July 1935):18–20.

Kramer, Ellen. "Designation Report." Landmarks Preservation Commission, 27 January 1976. No. 1 LP-0898, Mimeograph.

Lescaze, William. "City Home of William Lescaze." *The Technical Engineering News* (Massachusetts Institute of Technology) 16 (June, 1935):65–67.

———. "The Classic of Tomorrow." *American Architect* 147 (December 1935):11–13.

McAndrew, p. 69.

Modern Architecture U.S.A. New York: Museum of Modern Art, 1965, pl. 9.

Mumford, Lewis. "The Sky Line." *The New Yorker*, 15 September 1934, pp. 99–101.

Nelson, George, and Wright, Henry. *Tomorrow's House*. New York: Simon and Schuster, 1945, pl. 145.

New York American, 25 November 1934, p. 19.

"Odd Lots." *Creative Designs* 1 (Winter 1934–1935):33.

"Planning with Furniture." *American Architect* 148 (May 1936):68.

"Residence of William Lescaze, New York." *Architectural Review* 77 (April 1935):171–174.

"A Selected Review of the Year's Best Modern." *Arts and Decoration* 42 (January 1935):18–19.

Simonson, Lee. "Furniture into Walls." *House Beautiful* 78 (November 1936):48–49, 91.

Stern, pp. 166n18, 171, 171n27–29.

Storey, Walter Rendell. "William Lescaze, Interior Architect." *The London Studio* 116 (December 1938):304–307.

Williams, Herbert. "The Home of an Uncompromising Modernist." *Arts and Decoration* 51 (April 1940):5–7, 41.

1933–34 *GYMNASIUM*, Dartington Hall, Devon, England, [with Robert Hening; altered].

"The Gymnasium Block." *The Architects' Journal*, 3 October 1935, pp. 481–482.

"Gymnasium, Dartington School, England." *Architectural Record* 81 (May 1937):46.

1933–35 *CENTRAL OFFICE BUILDING*, Dartington Hall, Devon, England, [with Robert Hening; altered with major additions].

"The Offices, Dartington Hall, Devon." *The Architect and Building News* 149 (15 January 1937):76–78.

1933–34 *SPRETER STUDIO AND GARAGE*. Conshohocken State Road at Mill Creek Road, Lower Merion Township, Pennsylvania [altered with major additions].

Decorative Art Yearbook 1937, p. 16.

"Lighthouse for a Painter." *Arts and Decoration* 42 (January 1935):48–49.

"Spreter Studio." *Town and Country*, 1 April 1933, pp. 23, 31.

1933–34 *CHARLES EDWIN WILBOUR LIBRARY, BROOKLYN MUSEUM*, Brooklyn, New York [altered].

"Brooklyn Museum Uses Modern Style in Wilbour Library." *Art News* 32 (8 December 1934):11.

Hutchinson, Susan A. "The Wilbour Library Room." *The Brooklyn Museum Quarterly* 22 (January 1935):23–25.

McAndrew, p. 59.

"The New Wilbour Library—Brooklyn Museum." *The Bulletin of the Brooklyn Institute of Arts and Sciences* 39 (1 December 1934):102, 111.

"The Wilbour Library, Brooklyn Museum, Brooklyn, N.Y." *American Architect* 147 (December 1935):14–15.

Youtz, Philip. "Museum Planning." *Architectural Record* 80 (December 1936):417–422.

1933–38 *COTTAGES*, Dartington Hall, Devon, England, [with Robert Hening; altered].

"Churston Development, South Devon, England," *Architectural Record* 81 (May 1937):BT 34.

"Cottages at the Warren, Dartington Hall, Totnes." *Architectural Review* 80 (December 1936):263–264.

"Two Blocks of Cottages." *The Architects' Journal*, 3 October 1935, pp. 482–484.

1934–35 *BOARDING HOUSES 2 and 3* (or B and C), Dartington Hall, Devon, England, [with Robert Hening].

"Two Boarding Houses." *The Architects' Journal*, 3 October 1935, pp. 479–480.

1934 *ASTORIA-QUEENS HOUSING STUDY*, N.Y.C.

Aronovici, Carol. "Queensbridge Dwellings; Supplementary Report by The Housing Study Guild." Mimeograph. New York, 1934.

———. "A Study of a Regional Area Comprising 488 Acres in Astoria-Queens, N.Y.C." Mimeograph. New York, 1934.

"An Astoria-Queens Housing Project." *Savings Bank Journal* 18 (September 1937):5–6, 48.

Hamlin II, 1938, p. 38.

McAndrew, p. 65.

"New Colony Urged as Slum Solution." *New York Times*, 25 July 1937, General News, p. 5.

"Queens Project Urged to House East Side Poor." *New York Herald Tribune*, 25 July 1937, p. 4.

"Realistic Replanning." *Architectural Forum* 61 (July 1934):49–55.

1934–35 *R. C. KRAMER HOUSE*, 32 East Seventy-fourth Street, N.Y.C. [altered]

Cheney and Cheney, pp. 143, 195.

Decorative Art Yearbook 1937, p. 18–19, 67; 1935, p. 29.

Ford, pp. 51, 59, 62, 72, 76.

"House for Mrs. R. C. Kramer, New York City; William Lescaze, Architect." *Architectural Record* 81 (February 1937):30–38.

McAndrew, p. 81.

1934–35 *EDITORIAL PUBLICATIONS, INC.*, 40 East Forty-ninth Street, N.Y.C.

"Editorial Offices, Editorial Publications, Inc. *Architectural Record* 78 (September 1935):189–191.

1934–37 *BROOKLYN MUSEUM'S CHILDREN'S MUSEUM*, Brooklyn, N.Y.

"Brooklyn Children's Museum; P. W. A. Grant for a New Building." *Brooklyn Museum Quarterly* 22 (October 1935):194.

"The Proposed Children's Museum, Brooklyn, N.Y." *American Architect* 147 (December 1935):16–18.

"Proposed New Brooklyn Children's Museum Building." *Brooklyn Children's Museum News* 24 (May 1937):1.

"Proposed New Brooklyn Children's Museum Building." *Museum News* 15 (15 June 1937):8.

"Proposed New Building; W. Lescaze Architect. *Pencil Points* 18 (May 1937):supplement 20.

Report for the Year 1935, Museums of the Brooklyn Institute of Arts and Sciences. Brooklyn, New York, 1936.

1934 *METROPOLITAN MUSEUM OF ART'S CONTEMPORARY AMERICAN INDUSTRIAL ART EXHIBITION,* N.Y.C.

Aronson, pp. 257–258.

Bach, Richard F. *Contemporary American Industrial Art Exhibition, 5 November 1934–6 January 1935.* New York: Metropolitan Museum of Art, 1934, p. 25.

"Contemporary Quinquennial." *Architectural Forum* 61 (December 1934):408–420.

"A Museum Champions Modern Design." *Creative Designs* 1 (Winter 1934–1935):8–12.

"A Parade of Contemporary Achievements at the Metropolitan Museum." *Arts and Decoration* 42 (December 1934):12–24.

1934 *BROOKLYN MUSEUM ENTRANCE HALL AND AUDITORIUM,* Brooklyn, New York.

"Brooklyn Museum Will Now Greet Visitors with a New Face." *Art Digest* 8 (September 1934):32.

"Plans for New Auditorium and Landscaping the Museum Grounds; New Special Exhibition Galleries. *Brooklyn Museum Quarterly,* 22 April 1935. Also in: "The New Facilities of Brooklyn Museum Approach Completion." *Art News* 33 (25 May 1935):4.

Youtz, Philip. "Museum Planning." *Architectural Record* 80 (December 1936):417–422.

1934–35 *WARREN HOUSE* (Jooss House), Dartington Hall, Devon, England [altered].

"Architectural Portfolio." *The Architect and Building News* 148 (11 November 1936):Supplement.

"A House at Dartington." *The Architect and Building News* 148 (27 November 1936):254–256.

"The House of the Ballets Jooss." *Country Life* 83 (4 June 1938):590, supplement, p. xxx.

1934–35 *B. J. BUTTENWIESER HOUSE,* 17 East Seventy-third Street, N.Y.C.

Jackson, Alan. "To Suit the Family—A Streamlined Remodeling Job." *Arts and Decoration* 47 (October 1937):8–12.

1934–36 *UNITY HOUSE,* Near Bushkill, Pennsylvania [main building destroyed by fire in 1967].

Decorative Art Yearbook 1937, p. 19.

Kunz, Fritz. *Der Hotelbau von Heute im In und Ausland.* Stuttgart; Julius Hoffmann, 1937, pp. 99–100.

McAndrew, p. 91.

Stern, p. 161.

"Unity House, Forest Park, Pennsylvania." *Architectural Record* 79 (March 1936):185–193.

"Unity House, Forest Park, Pennsylvania." *Life* 5 (1 August 1938):42–53.

"Unity House." *Architectural Review* 74 (December 1938):296–297.

"Unity House." *Architect's Journal* 90 (13 July 1939):71.

1935–38 *WILLIAMSBURG HOUSES,* Brooklyn, New York [with others].

Barbey, p. 562.

Brock, H. I. "A Modernist Scans our Skyline." *New York Times,* 11 April 1937, Magazine Section, pp. 12, 24.

Hamlin II, 1938, p. 40.

Hamlin, Talbot. "New York Housing: Harlem River Homes and Williamsburg Houses." *Pencil Points* 19 (May 1938):281–292.

"Housing Project Shown in a Model." *New York Times,* 19 December 1935, p. 9.

McAndrew, pp. 59–60.

"Williamsburg Houses, Brooklyn, N.Y." *Architectural Forum* 67 (December 1937):495.

"Williamsburg Houses, Brooklyn, N.Y." *Architectural Forum* 68 (May 1938):356–359.

1935 *VINCENT CATES HOUSE,* Burrell Street, Melrose, Mass.

American Building Association News, April 1937, p. 215.

Decorative Art Yearbook 1937, p. 23.

The Boston Evening Transcript, 25 June 1935.

"House for Vincent K. Cates." *Architectural Forum* 65 (November 1936):454–455.

"The House Plan." *Architectural Record* 78 (November 1935):302–303.

McAndrew, p. 37.

The Melrose Massachusetts Leader, 5 July 1935.

"New England House on Modern Lines." *Arts and Decoration* 45 (January 1937):18–20.

"New in New England." *House Beautiful* 78 (December 1936):64–65.

"Planning the Minimum Home." *House and Garden* 172 (October 1937):40–41.

1935   *CBS STUDIOS*, N.Y.C.

"Columbia Broadcasting Station, New York." *Architectural Forum* 63 (August 1935):121–122.

"Columbia Broadcasting System, New York City." *Architectural Forum* 65 (October 1936):372–373.

McAndrew, p. 74.

1935–37 *ANSONIA HIGH SCHOOL*, Howard Avenue and Crescent Street, Ansonia, Connecticut [altered with major additions].

"Ansonia Goes Modernistic." Bridgeport (Conn.) *Post*, 6 August 1936.

Ansonia High School Dedication Program, 1936.

"Ansonia High School." *New York Times*, 3 October 1937, Magazine Section.

"Ansonia High School." *Architectural Review* 85 (March 1939):143–145.

"Ansonia High School, Ansonia, Conn." *Architectural Record* 81 (April 1937):13–15.

"Ansonia High School, Ansonia, Conn." *Architectural Forum* 67 (December 1937):487–492.

"Ansonia High School, Ansonia, Conn." *Journal, Royal Architectural Institute of Canada* 15 (January 1938):284–285.

"Ansonia High School, Conn. U.S.A." *Architect and Building News* 153 (18 March 1938):335–338.

"Ansonia High School, U.S.A. William Lescaze, Architect." *Architect's Journal* 83 (28 May 1936):826–827.

"Citizens Not Pleased with Pictures of Proposed New Ansonia School Building." *The Star News* (Ansonia), 22 November 1935, p. 1.

"The Functional Approach to School Planning, Ansonia High School, Ansonia, Conn." *Architectural Record* 79 (June 1936):481–486.

Hermant, Andre. "Constructions scolaires." *L'architecture d'aujourd'hui* 9 (August 1938):1, 95.

"Lescaze, Modernist, Chosen School Architect with Sears—Farrel Site Called Too Small." *The Evening Sentinel*, 31 July 1935.

"Lets' Build for Today." *Nations' Schools* 20 (December 1937):44–47.

McAndrew, p. 19.

"A Modern School." *School and Society* 47 (22 January 1938):121–123.

"The New Ansonia High School." *School Management*, October 1936, pp. 88–89.

"A New Schoolhouse That Looks Like a Penthouse on Mars." *News-Week*, 2 November 1935, p. 20.

Piccardi, Helen. "Ansonia, Connecticut, Goes Modern." *The School Executive*, January 1938, p. 215.

"School of Modern Design Now Under Construction in Ansonia Connecticut." *New York Herald Tribune*, 2 August 1936.

"Variety of Designs for New Ansonia High School." *The Evening Sentinel*, 24 July 1935.

1935–36 *LLOYD GOOD HOUSE*, Harvey Cedars, New Jersey [with George Daub].

Decorative Art Yearbook 1938, p. 60, 86.

"Domestic Interiors." *Architectural Forum* 67 (October 1937):271.

"House at Harvey Cedars, New Jersey." *Architectural Forum* 67 (August 1937):93.

McAndrew, p. 45.

"New Features in Modern Home." *North Shore Journal*, 7 July 1937.

1935   *PURDUE UNIVERSITY SMALL HOUSE PROJECT*

Betts, Benjamin F. "Purdue Begins Housing Experiment." *Architectural Record* 79 (January 1936): 64–65.

———. "Purdue Completes Year of Structural Research." *Architectural Record* 81 (March 1937):bt34.

———. "With $5,000; Costs and Construction Studies Undertaken." *American Architecture* 148 (February 1936):57–64.

"Low-Cost Housing Research at Purdue University." *Architectural Record* 80 (February 1936):142–144.

1935–36 *PAVILION OF THE MAGNOLIA PETRO-LEUM COMPANY, TEXAS CENTENNIAL EXHIBITION*, Dallas, Texas.

"Magnolia Petroleum Building." *Architectural Record* 80 (July 1936): 3.

"Magnolia Petroleum Company Building at Texas Centennial Exposition, Dallas—June 1936." *The Bulletin of the Museum of Modern Art* 4 (January 1936): 2.

1936 *CBS STUDIOS*, Chicago, Illinois.

"CBS, Chicago." *Architectural Record* 81 (March 1937): 118, 127.

"Columbia Broadcasting Studio." *Architectural Forum* 66 (May 1937): 443–446.

"Studios for Columbia Broadcasting System, Chicago." *Architectural Review* 81 (March 1937): 127.

1936 *OREGON STATE CAPITOL COMPETITION PROJECT*, Salem, Oregon.

"All Not Quiet on the Western Front." *Architectural Record* 80 (August 1936): 76–77.

Morin, Roi L. "Oregon Competition in Retrospect; Minutes of Jury Show Unusual Deliberations." *Architect and Engineer* 127 (November 1936): 11–26.

———. "Oregon's Capitol Competition." *Architectural Record* 80 (August 1936): 78–79.

"Oregon State Capitol Competition." *Architectural Forum* 65 (July 1936): 2–10.

"Oregon State Capitol Competition; Some Remarks Concerning its Results; with Winning and Mention Designs and Plans." *Pencil Points* 17 (July 1936): 352–374. Also, August 1936, supplement 14, 19–20.

"Oregon State Capitol Competition; Winning Design by Trowbridge and Livingston and F. Keally, with Five of the Runner-up Designs." *American Architect* 149 (July 1936): 27–34.

"Program for Open Competition for Oregon State Capitol." *Architect and Engineer* 124 (March 1936): 45–52.

1936–37 *FREDERICK S. DUNN HOUSE*, 19 Penrhyn Road, Woodbridge, Connecticut [minor alterations].

"Connecticut Contemporary, House of Professor F. S. Dunn, at Woodbridge, Connecticut." *House and Garden* 73 (January 1938): 54–55.

Decorative Art Yearbook 1938, p. 26, 43.

1936 *WILLIAM BUTLER HOUSE*, Harvey Cedars, New Jersey [with George Daub].

McAndrew, p. 45.

"Week-end House on Seashore." William Butler House, Harvey Cedars, N.J." *Architectural Record* 82 (August 1937): 73–74.

1936–38 *CBS STUDIOS*, Sunset Boulevard between Gower and El Centro Streets, Hollywood, California [with W. E. Heitschmidt, altered].

Barbey, p. 562.

"Broadcasting Studios." *Architectural Review* 85 (May 1939): 221–223.

"Broadcasting Studios." *Electronics* II (April 1938): 20–25.

"CBS Broadcasting Studios, Hollywood." *Architectural Record* 84 (July 1938): 108–111.

"CBS Broadcasting Studios, Hollywood, California." *Architectural Forum* 68 (June 1938): 454–464.

"Columbia Broadcasting Studios." *Architectural Forum* 64 (June 1936): 479–487.

"Columbia Broadcasting Studio." *Architectural Forum* 66 (May 1937): 443–446.

"Design for Broadcasting." *Engineering News-Record* 122 (5 January 1939): 12–15.

"Drawings of the '30's—William Lescaze: CBS Broadcasting Studios." *Royal Institute of British Architects Journal* 75 (May 1968): 228.

"Functional Design in a Broadcasting Studio; KNX, Columbia Broadcasting System in Hollywood." *Design* 40 (January 1939): 5–8.

Greif, p. 57.

"The New Home of the Columbia Broadcasting System at Columbia Square in Hollywood, California." *California Arts and Architecture* 54 (July 1938): 28–29.

"Plant for CBS—Hollywood." *Architectural Concrete* 4 (ca. 1938): 2–7.

Santacilia, Carlos O. *La maquinismo, la vida y la arquitectura*. Mexico, 1939, pp. 16–63.

"Station de la Columbia Broadcasting System à Hollywood." *L'architecture d'aujourd'hui* 20 (Mai 1949): 74–77.

"Un Studio d'émissions radiophoniques; la station C.B.S. à Hollywood." *L'architecture française* 9 (1944): 69–71.

"Utility Motive in Modern Design of Columbia Broadcasting Studios." *The Southwest Builder and Contractor* 91 (27 May 1938): 12–14.

1936–37 *ALFRED LOOMIS HOUSE*, Crows Nest Road, Tuxedo Park, New York.

"The Contemporary Domestic Interior." *Interiors* 109 (July 1950): 86–87.

"Experimental House Near Garrison." *Architectural Forum* 91 (November 1949):88.

Ford and Ford, pp. 71–73.

"House at Tuxedo Park, N.Y." *Architectural Review* 86 (November 1939):197–200.

"House for Alfred L. Loomis, Tuxedo Park, N.Y." *Architectural Forum* 71 (July 1939):36–41.

"House Within a House." *House and Garden* 75 (February 1939):48–51.

McAndrew, p. 86.

Nelson, George, and Wright, Henry. *Tomorrow's House.* New York: Simon and Schuster, 1945, pl. 123.

Stern, p. 169.

1936–37 *TIME, INC., OFFICES*, N.Y.C.

Greif, pp. 68–69.

"Office for Time, Inc., New York City." *Architectural Forum* 67 (November 1937):411–412.

1936–37 *BERNARD ROGERS HOUSE*, 291 Waymouth Drive, Rochester, New York [minor alterations].

McAndrew, p. 85.

1936–37 *KIMBLE GLASS COMPANY, OFFICE BUILDING*, Crystal Avenue, Vineland, New Jersey [alterations; entrance gate destroyed].

Barbey, pp. 561–562.

"A Glass Company's Offices, New Jersey, U.S.A." *Architect and Building News* 155 (29 July 1938):119, 130–132.

McAndrew, p. 46.

"Office Building for Kimble Glass Company." *Architectural Record* 82 (August 1937):124–125.

"Office Building for Kimble Glass Company, Vineland, New Jersey." *Architectural Forum* 68 (March 1938):200–204.

1936 *CBS STUDIOS, Cincinnati, Ohio.*

"Offices and Broadcasting Studios, Station WLW, Crosley Corporation, Cincinatti." *Pencil Points* 25 (July 1944):41–51.

1937–38 *FRED NASH HOUSE*, Wayzata, Lake Minnetonka, near Minneapolis, Minnesota [addition].

Ford and Ford. *The Modern House,* p. 74.

Golf and Sportsman, March 1938.

1937 *HOWARD MARKEL HOUSE*, Redding, Connecticut.

McAndrew, p. 22.

"Why Modern." *The Parents' Magazine* 13 (May 1938):45, 74.

1937–38 *AVIATION BUILDING, WORLD'S FAIR*, N.Y. [with Gordon Carr, destroyed].

"Aviation Buiding." *Architectural Review*, Special Issue, New York World's Fair 86 (August 1939):82, 87, pl. V.

"Aviation Building for New York Fair." *Architectural Record* 84 (November 1938):82–83.

"The Aviation Building." *Architectural Forum* 70 (June 1939):414.

Gutheim, Frederick A., "Buildings at the Fair." *Magazine of Art* 32 (May 1939):288.

Norton, Paul F. "World's Fairs in the 1930's." *Journal of the Society of Architectural Historians* 24 (March 1965):27–30.

Sartoris III, 3:768.

1938 *GARRET A. HOBART III HOUSE*, Lake Road, Tuxedo Park, New York.

"The Contemporary Domestic Interior." *Interiors* 109 (July 1950):84–85.

McAndrew, p. 85.

Sartoris III, 3:pl. 769.

1938 *WHEATON COLLEGE COMPETITION PROJECT*, Norton, Mass.

"An Architectural Competition." *Museum of Modern Art Bulletin* 5 (February 1938):2–3.

"Awards." *Architectural Forum* 69 (July 1938):1.

"Competition to Select an Architect for a Proposed Art Center for Wheaton College." *Architectural Forum* 68 (February 1938): supplement 6a–6d.

Hamlin, Talbot F. "Competitions." *Pencil Points* 19 (September 1938):551–565.

"Invited Participants Trail in Wheaton College Awards." *Architectural Record* 84 (July 1938):57.

"Report of the Jury for the Competition for an Art Center for Wheaton College." *Architectural Forum* 69 (August 1938):143–158.

"Two Young Draftsmen Win Wheaton Award." *Pencil Points* 19 (July 1938):supplement 37.

"Wheaton Prize Winners Shown." *Magazine of Art* 31 (July 1938):429–430.

1938–39 *SWISS PAVILION, WORLD'S FAIR*, N.Y. [with John Weber; destroyed].

Barbey, p. 562.

Gutheim, Frederick A. "Buildings at the Fair." *Magazine of Art* 32 (May 1939):289.

McAndrew, p. 63.

"Pavilion Swiss à New-York." *Vie, art et cité* 7 (September 1939):n.p.

"The Swiss Pavilion." *Architectural Review, Special Issue, New York World's Fair* 86 (August 1939):64, 65.

"Swiss Pavilion at the New York Fair." *Parnassus* 11 (March 1939):5.

"Switzerland Building." *Architectural Forum* 70 (June 1939):462.

1938   *GOUCHER COLLEGE CAMPUS COMPETITION PROJECT*, Towson, Maryland.

"Goucher College Campus Competition; Preliminary Studies Give Key to Winning Design." *Pencil Points* 19 (December 1938):735–750.

"Goucher College Campus Competition Program." 28 September 1938, Mimeograph.

"Goucher College Competition." *Architectural Forum* 68 (June 1938):supplement 58.

"Goucher College Competition; Moore and Hutchins, Winners." *Architectural Forum* 69 (November 1938):supplement 26.

"List of Architects to Compete for a General Development of Plan." *Architectural Forum* 69 (August 1938):supplement 77b.

"New York Architects Receive Goucher Award." *Pencil Points* 19 (November 1938):supplement 12.

Spencer, E. P. "College Builds a College; Goucher Competition." *Magazine of Art* 31 (December 1938):705–707.

1938   *HOUSE OF 2039 PROJECT*.

Gebhard, David, and Nevins, Deborah. *200 Years of American Architectural Drawing*. New York: Whitney Library of Design, 1977, p. 11. [misidentified as House of 2089].

1939–41 *LONGFELLOW OFFICE BUILDING*, Connecticut and Rhode Island Avenues, Washington, D.C.

"Longfellow Building, Washington, D.C." *Architectural Record* 89 (February 1941):44–45.

"Longfellow Building, Washington, D.C." *Architectural Forum* 74 (June 1941):394–401.

Sartoris III, 3:pl. 771.

Stern, p. 16.

1940–41 *EDWARD A. NORMAN HOUSE*, 124 East Seventieth Street, N.Y.C.

"Built in U.S.A. 1932–1944." *Architectural Forum* 80 (May 1944):87.

"Casa Norman, New York." *Metron*, No. 9 (1946):39.

"Edward Norman Residence, New York."

House and Garden 86 (October 1944):79–81.

"Town House, New York, N.Y." *Architectural Forum* 82 (March 1945):140–142.

1940   *MRS. GEORGE CRAWFORD GUEST HOUSE*, Greenwich, Connecticut.

"Guest House in Greenwich, Connecticut." *Architectural Forum* 83 (August 1945):138–139.

1941–46 *ELLIOTT (CHELSEA) HOUSES*, Twenty-sixth and Twenty-seventh Streets between Ninth and Tenth Avenues, N.Y. [with A. M. Brown; enlarged]

"Worth Fighting For: Decent Housing for All." *PM's Daily Picture Magazine*, 13 April 1943, p. 1.

1942   *WOODS END HOUSING DEVELOPMENT*, Roselle, New Jersey.

Lescaze, William. "Work Done in Field of Large Scale Planning and Housing" (typescript), 5 August 1949, WELA.

1942   *STUDIOS WLW*, Cincinnati, Ohio.

"Maison de la Radio à Cincinnati." *L'Architecture Française* 9/77–78 (1943):56–59.

"Offices and Broadcasting Studios, Station WLW, Crosley Corporation, Cincinnati, Ohio. *Pencil Points* 25 (July 1944):41–51.

1943   *CHESTNUT GARDENS*, Bridgeport, Connecticut.

Lescaze, William. "Work Done in Field of Large Scale Planning and Housing." (typescript), 5 August 1949, WELA.

1944   *WEST HARLEM HOUSING PROJECT*, Fifth Avenue to Morningside and 110th Street to 126th Street, N.Y.C.

"A Plan for Harlem's Redevelopment." *Architectural Forum* 80 (April 1944):145–152.

Uplifting the Downtrodden. New York: Revere Copper and Brass, Inc. n.d.

"Urbanisation de la zone Quest du parc d'Harlem, New York 1943–1944." *Architecture, Formes et Fonctions* 4 (1957):35.

1945–49 *JEROME CROWLEY HOUSE*, 1516 E. Washington Avenue, South Bend, Indiana [major addition, 1959].

Practical Houses for Contemporary Living. New York: F. W. Dodge Corporation, 1953, pp. 57–59.

1945–49 *CALDERONE THEATER*, Hempstead, Long Island, N.Y.

"Colorful Movie Theater." *Architectural Forum* 91 (November 1949):95–97.

Lescaze, William. "Light Color and Form in

New Theatre," *Lighting and Lamps* (January 1950):25, 39.

"Theater." *Pencil Points* 2 (August 1944):49.

"The 2500-Seat Calderone . . . ." *Better Theatres* (July 2, 1947):24, 29.

"The Years Work Commercial: William Lescaze, New York." *Interiors* 109 (August 1949):108–109.

1945–50 *CROSSETT HEALTH CENTER*, Crossett, Arkansas.

"Clinic and Group Practice." *Progressive Architecture* 32 (July 1951):62–63.

"Modern Health Center." *Architectural Forum* 91 (July 1949):44.

The Modern Hospital. June 1950.

1946–47 *CLARENCE LEVEY HOUSE*, Candlewood Lake, Connecticut.

"Three Bedrooms Plus Large Living Area Organized for Privacy, Sun, View," *Architectural Forum* 88 (April 1948):142–143.

1946–49 *RELIANCE HOMES, INC.*, Duke Street, extended, and Fort Worth Drive, West of Alexandria, Fairfax County, Virginia; Prospect Park, Roslyn, Pennsylvania.

"F.H.A. Approves 1st Prefabrication Loan; House Designed by William Lescaze." *Herald Tribune* (New York), 14 November 1948, p. VI, 5.

"A House in an Hour-and-a-Half." *The Evening Bulletin* (Philadelphia), 7 February 1948, p. 6.

"Newcomers." *Architectural Forum* 89 (October 1948):12.

"Prefab Stalled." *Architectural Forum* 88 (March 1948):11.

"Reliance Steel Products Company Key Plans of Types of Houses" (typescript), May 1947, WELA.

"Those Weren't Ducks Going South, They Were Houses." *Washington Daily News*, 14 November 1949, p. 24.

"Three-Bedroom Aluminum and Steel House is 'Built' Here in Hour and 5 Minutes." *The Evening Star* (Washington, D.C.), 11 June 1949, Section B-1.

1946–47 *NEW YORK HOUSING TRUST METAL CURTAIN-WALL RESEARCH.*

Creighton, Thomas. "Architecture and the Metal Curtain Wall." *Architectural Metals* (August 1961):7–12.

"The Curtain Wall." *Architectural Forum* 86 (May 1947):97–100.

1948–49 *DURISOL RESEARCH PROJECT.*

"Four Experimental Houses. . . ." *Architectural Forum* 91 (November 1949):86–89.

1947–52 *HARBOR HOMES*, Port Washington, Long Island, N.Y.

"Harbor Homes, Port Washington, New York." *Journal of Housing* 11 (August–September 1954):274–275.

1950–52 *SPINNEY HILL HOMES*, Manhasset, Long Island, N.Y.

"Long Island: State Aided Suburban Housing." *Architectural Record* 115 (June 1954):179–181.

1950–54 *DUNE DECK HOTEL*, Westhampton Beach, Long Island, N.Y.

"Seaside Hotel is Remodeled." *Architectural Record* 113 (January 1953):128–131.

1951–53 *PORCELAIN ENAMEL INSTITUTE RESEARCH PROJECT*

"Porcelain Enameled Curtain Walls Design Recommendations." *Architect and Engineer* 198 (July 1954):10–11+.

1952–53 *CINERAMA INSTALLATIONS:* New York, Los Angeles, Detroit, Chicago, Philadelphia.

"Lescaze Remodels an Old Broadway Theater to Accommodate the Latest in Entertainment." *Architectural Forum* 97 (November 1952):128–129.

1952–56 *OFFICE BUILDING*, 711 Third Avenue, N.Y.

"Color and Art Help an Office Building." *Architectural Forum* 105 (October 1956):154–155.

"Office Buildings." *Architectural Record* 121 (March 1951):227–249.

"Rivera and Lescaze in Review." *Interiors* 115 (March 1956):14.

1945–60 *CIVIL COURTHOUSE AND MUNICIPAL COURTS BUILDING*, 110 Center Street, N.Y. [with Matthew W. del Gaudio].

"Art and Politics Skirmish in City." *New York Times*, 30 April 1961, p. 82.

"Inside Courtrooms, Divided Circulation." *Architectural Record* 130 (August 1961):107–110.

"Proposed City and Municipal Courts Building, Foley Square, NYC." *Architectural Record* 118 (November 1955):188–191.

1964–65 *CHATHAM CENTER* (apartments, offices, hotel, garage, cinema), Pittsburgh, Pennsylvania.

"Building Complex Has Office-Hotel," *Architectural Record* 137 (January 1965):102.

SELECTED ADDITIONAL BIBLIOGRAPHY THAT DIRECTLY CONCERNS LESCAZE AND HIS WORK

American Designers Gallery Exhibition Catalogue, 1928.

"America's Interesting People." *American Magazine* 122 (August 1936):85.

"Architectural Tiff." *Art Digest* 6 (15 March 1932):3.

Architecture and Design, January 1953, entire.

Behrendt, Walter Curt. *Modern Building; Its Nature, Problems, and Forms.* New York: Harcourt, Brace, and Co., 1937.

"Biographical Sketch." *Architectural Forum* 61 (December 1934):399.

Blutman, Sandra. "Drawings of the 30's: William Lescaze, CBS Broadcasting Studios." *Royal Institute of British Architects Journal* 75 (May 1969):228.

Bonham-Carter, Victor. *Dartington Hall.* London: Phoenix House, 1958, pp. 112–115, 180.

"Building in the Spirit of the Age." *New York Times,* 14 October 1928, Amusement Section, p. 10.

Coates, Robert M. "Profiles—William Lescaze." *The New Yorker,* 12 December 1936, pp. 44–50.

Cutts, A. Bailey. "William Lescaze Discusses Contemporary Design." *The Master Builder* 39 (July 1934):212.

"Decorative Artists Form Union." *Architectural Record* 64 (August 1928):164.

"Denies League Curbed Architects Who Quit." *New York Times,* 1 March 1932, p. 43.

Fitch, James Marston. "William Lescaze." *Architecture, Formes et Fonctions* 6 (1959):96–103.

Frankl, Paul T. *Form and Reform.* New York: Harper Bros., 1930, pp. 84, 138.

"Genetrix, Personal Contributions to American Architecture." *The Architectural Review* 121 (May 1957):342.

Hening, Robert. "Building in Terms of Human Beings." *Dartington Hall News,* 21 February 1969, p. 7.

Hitchcock, Henry-Russell. "Architecture." *Arts Weekly,* 11 March 1932, pp. 12–13.

Horton, Philip, *Hart Crane,* New York: W. W. Norton and Co., 1937, pp. 109, 114–116.

"The House That Works: 1." *Fortune* 12 (October 1935):59–65, 94.

"Howe and Lescaze Quit League to 'Fight Alone' Rather Than 'Compromise With Crowd.'" *New York Times,* 28 February 1932, p. 1, 22.

Hubert, Christian, and Shapiro, Lindsay Stamm. *William Lescaze.* New York: Institute for Architecture and Urban Studies and Rizzoli International Publications, Inc., 1982, Catalogue 16.

"An Institution with a Future." *New York Sun,* 24 November 1928, p. 5.

Keller, Allan. "They Build New York: Lescaze a Modernist of Modernists." *New York World-Telegram,* 19 February 1938, Second Section, p. 19.

Lanmon, Lorraine Welling. "The Role of William E. Lescaze in the Introduction of the International Style to the United States." Ph.D. dissertation, University of Delaware, 1979.

Lewis, Thomas S. W., ed. *Letters of Hart Crane and His Family.* New York: Columbia University Press, 1974.

Longee, E. F. "William Lescaze Defines Design." *Modern Plastics,* April 1935, pp. 20–22, 58–59.

Machine-Age Exposition Catalogue, New York, 16–28 May 1927.

Obituary. *Architectural Forum* 130 (March 1969):89.

Patterson, Curtis. Review of *The New Interior Decoration,* by Dorothy Todd and Raymond Mortimer. "A Source Book on Modern Interiors." *International Studio* 94 (September 1929):72–73.

Pevsner, Nikolas. *Buildings of England: South Devon.* Harmondsworth, Middlesex: Penguin Books, 1952, pp. 100–101.

Pica, Agnoldomenico. "Lescaze." *Domus,* No. 476 (July 1969):1.

Platz, Gustav Adolf. *Die Baukunst Der Neuesten Zeit.* Berlin: Propylaen-Verlag, 1930.

Pommer, Richard. "The Architecture of Urban Housing in the United States during the Early 1930s," *Journal of the Society of Architectural Historians* 37 (December 1979):235–264.

"Re-Renderings." *Pencil Points* 21 (July 1940):422.

Rhoades, Eleanor. "The International Style in the U.S. as Represented by Richard J. Neutra, William Lescaze, and George Howe." Master's Thesis, New York University, 1938.

Richards, James M. *An Introduction to Modern Architecture.* Harmondsworth: Penguin Books, 1940; revised, reprint ed., 1965.

Stern, Robert A. M. "Relevance of the Decades." *Journal of the Society of Architectural Historians* 24 (March 1965):6–10.

"Symposium: The International Architecture Exhibition." *Shelter* 2 (April 1932):3–9.

Tallmadge, Thomas E. *The Story of Architecture in America.* New York: W. A. Norton and Co., 1927; revised, 1936.

Taylor, Helen Louise. "Modern Architecture." *The Vassar Review,* May 1934, pp. 13–15.

Third Annual Decorative Exhibition, 10 March—31 March, ca. 1925, Wanamaker's Gallery of Decorative Art.

Von Eckardt, Wolf. "William Lescaze Dies; Swiss-Born Architect." *Washington Post*, 10 February 1969, p. D3.

Weber, Brom. *Hart Crane*. New York: The Bodley Press, 1948, pp. 56, 63, 70, 77, 82, 91, 104.

———. *The Letters of Hart Crane*. New York: Hermitage House, 1952, pp. 56, 62–63, 66–67, 70, 77, 85, 91, 104.

West, Helen Howe. *George Howe, Architect*. Philadelphia: by the author, 1973.

"William Lescaze Architect Dies." *New York Times*, 10 February 1969, p. 39.

Wingert, Paul S. "William Lescaze: Modern American Architect." Typescript, ca. 1940.

Wodehouse, Lawrence. "Lescaze and Dartington Hall." *Architectural Association Quarterly* 8 (1976): 3–14.

———. Review of *George Howe: Toward a Modern American Architecture*, by Robert A. M. Stern. In *Journal of the Society of Architectural Historians* 35 (March 1976): 64.

WRITINGS BY WILLIAM LESCAZE

1918   "Réflexions que l'oeuvre, la vie, et la mort de Hodler suggérent en moi." *Zofingue Feville Centrale*. 58th Annual (July 1918), pp. 851, 859–865.

1928   "The Future American Country House." *Architectural Record* 64 (November 1928): 417–420.

1932   "A New Shelter for Savings." *Architectural Forum* 57 (December 1932): 483–498.

1933   "The Modern House." *Architectural Forum* 59 (November 1933): 393–394.

        "New Deal in Architecture." *The New Republic* 75 (26 July 1933): 278–280.

        "What is Modern Architecture." *The News Letter* (London), 3 April 1933, pp. 11–13.

1934   "Letters from an Architect to a Client." *Theatre Arts Monthly* 18 (September 1934): 684–695.

        "Living Modern." *Junior League Magazine* 20 (April 1934): 20–21, 98–99.

        Typescript of lecture at Vassar College, 9 May 1934.

1935   "The Classic of Tomorrow." *American Architect* 147 (December 1935): 10–13, 37–38.

        "A Community Theater." In *Architecture for the New Theatre*, pp. 71–86. Edited by Juliet R. Isaacs. New York: Theatre Arts, Inc., 1935.

        "Letters About a Modern School." *Architectural Forum* 62 (January 1935): 46–55.

        "Modern Architecture for Public Schools." *The School Executive* 55 (December 1935): 136–137, 153.

        Typescript of notes for lecture at Memorial Art Gallery, Rochester, New York, 5 November 1935.

        Typescript of lecture at Mt. Holyoke College, South Hadley, Massachusetts, 6 February 1935.

        Typescript of lecture at National Public Housing Conference, 16 March 1935.

        Typescript of notes for lecture at Swiss Society of New York, 16 October 1935.

1936   "The Classic of Tomorrow" (typescript). Lecture at the Art Institute of Chicago, 6 October 1936.

        "The Functional Approach to School Planning." *Architectural Record* 79 (June 1936): 481–486.

        "Modern Architecture" (typescript) for *L'Architecture D'Aujourd'Hui*, 24 December 1936.

        "Modern Architecture in the U.S.A." (typescript) for the *Architectural Review*, 24 December 1936.

        "Technique for an Architect" (typescript). 20 January 1936.

        "Technique of the Architect," in *Handbook of Contemporary Materials and Techniques of the Fine Arts*. Brooklyn Museum, 1936, pp. 84–93.

        "This Thing Called Modern" (typescript), n.d.

        Typescript for lecture at Contemporary Club, Philadelphia, 20 April 1936.

        Typescript for lecture at Pierson College, Yale University, 5 February 1936.

1937   "America is Outgrowing Imitation Greek Architecture." *Magazine of Art*, 30 (June 1937): 366–369. Abbreviated version in *Architectural Record* 82 (August 1937): 52–57.

        "America's Outgrowing Imitation Greek Architecture" (typescript). Lecture at Convention of the American Federation of Arts, Washington, D.C., 11 May 1937.

        "The Architecture of Tomorrow." *The Fashion Group Bulletin*, May 1937.

        "The Engineered House" (typescript), 9 May 1937.

        "4 Lectures on Modern Architecture" (typescript). Part of "A Symposium on Contemporary Art" at Summer Session of Columbia University, 19–22 July 1937.

        "Future of the Engineered House." Home

Week Supplement, *New York Herald Tribune*, 9 May 1937.

"Let's Build for Today." *Nation's Schools* 20 (December 1937):44–47.

"Meaning of Modern Architecture." *The North American Review* 19 (Autumn 1937):110–120.

"Modern Buildings for Modern Schools." *School Management*, May 1937, pp. 248–251.

"A New Architecture for a Changed World." *New York Times*, 3 October 1937, Magazine Section, pp. 12–13, 20.

"On Architecture" (typescript) for *PM* magazine, 1937.

"What Trees Could Mean to a City" (typescript). 4 March 1937.

"Why Modern Architecture" (typescript). 11 June 1937.

"Why Modern Architecture?" *Royal Architectural Institute of Canada Journal* 14 (April 1937):75–76.

1938   "Architecture to Fit the People, Not People to Fit the Architecture" (typescript). Radio talk on station WNYC, 15 August 1938.

"Modern Buildings for Modern Education." *Progressive Education* 15 (April 1938):332–336.

"A New Architecture for a Changed World." *Royal Architectural Institute of Canada* 15 (January 1938):271–273.

Typescript for lecture at the Civitas Club, Brooklyn, New York, 13 April 1938.

Typescript for radio talk for French Programs on W3XAL, International Division, NBC, 11 February 1938.

"Why Modern Architecture" (typescript). Lecture at the Century Club, Scranton, Pa., 11 January 1938.

"Why Modern Architecture." *Parent's Magazine* 13 (May 1938):45, 74.

1939   "Architecture Today." *Twice a Year*, No. 2 (Spring–Summer 1939):122–134.

"Buildings, School and Education" (typescript). 3 January 1939.

"Marginal Notes on Architecture." *Virginia Quarterly Review* 15 (Spring 1939):267–280. Excerpts published in *Architectural Forum* 71 (August 1939):24.

Typescript of a lecture at Columbia University, Summer 1939.

1940   "How Can I Be Useful?" *Pencil Points* 21 (September 1940): n.p.

"Reminiscences" (typescript). Talk delivered at the New York Architectural League, 25 January 1940.

Typescript of lecture at Columbia University, July 1940.

Typescript of lecture at University of California, Summer 1940.

1941   Lescaze, William. "These Documents Called Buildings." In *The Intent of the Artist*. New York: Russell & Russell, 1941. Reissued by Princeton University Press, a Division of Athenum Publishers, Inc., 1970.

"Building for Defense." *Architectural Forum* 74 (June 1941):127–128, Sup. 42.

1942   Lescaze, William. *On Being an Architect*. New York: G. P. Putnam's Sons, 1942.

1943   "Types of Schools to Serve Tomorrow's Needs." *American School and University* 15 (1943):35–36.

"Planning for Whom, How and When." Lecture at Worcester Art Museum (typescript), 16 February 1943.

"Service Station." *Architectural Forum* 78 (May 1943):132–133.

"Rambling Thoughts on Post-War Planning and Other Matters." *Ohio Architect* 4 (Second Quarter 1943):8–9+.

Homes of the Future. Office of War Information, 1943.

1944   "Such Stuff as Schools are Made Of." *Progressive Education* 22 (October 1944):24–25.

1945   "Postwar Community Planning—Art in a Free World." Lecture at the Museum of Modern Art (typescript), 24 February 1945, WELA.

"New Design for Living." Citizens Housing Council of New York (typescript), 26 April 1945.

1949   Review of *Architecture and the Spirit of Man*, by Joseph Hudnut. *Saturday Review*, 5 November 1949, p. 34.

1950   Review of *Switzerland Builds*, by G. E. Kidder Smith. *Saturday Review*, 2 September 1950, p. 39.

1951   "New York State Building Code Commissions: Aims and Accomplishments." *Architectural Record* 109 (June 1951):184–188.

1952   "Radio Stations," in *Forms and Functions of Twentieth Century Architecture*, 4 vols., 4:169–189. Edited by Talbot Hamlin. New York: Columbia University Press, 1952.

"The Correlation of the Arts." *A.I.A. Journal* 18 (November 1952):228–232.

1953 "The Story of Our Time," in the *Encyclopedia Yearbook*, vol. 16. New York: Grolier Society, Inc., 1953.

1954 "The Arts for and in Buildings." *Liturgical Arts* 22 (February 1954):49–51.

1964 "Another Look at PSFS." *Architectural Forum* 120 (June 1964):57.

1968 "Thoughts on Art and Architecture." *Art International*, XII/2 (February 1968):50.

INTERVIEWS

Clauss, Mr. and Mrs. Alfred, and Rice, Norman. Philadelphia. 10 April 1974.

Decent, Michael. Churston, Devon, England. 17 June 1973.

Harris, Charles A. New York City. 14 March 1974.

Hening, Robert. Dartington Hall, Devon, England. 16 June 1973.

Lescaze, Mrs. William. New York City. 6 November 1973; 8–10 October 1974; 17 July 1975; 29 June 1977; 28 July 1977.

Whittlesey, Julian. Wilton, Connecticut. 20 February 1974.

LETTERS TO THE AUTHOR

Bogatay, Todd C. 15 January 1974.

Clauss, Alfred. 10 July 1975, 9 August 1977.

Dumper, Henry A., 8 October 1980.

Fatula, John A. 16 May 1975.

Field, Frederick Vanderbilt. 13 June 1977.

Frey, Albert. 24 April 1974.

Fuller, R. Buckminster. 28 February 1974.

Hening, Robert. 2 August 1973.

Katz, Sidney L. 18 December 1973.

Lescaze, Mrs. William. 5 April 1972, 10 December 1973, 11 January 1974, 18 March 1974, 22 May 1974, 16 February 1976, 23 February 1976, Notes of June 1977.

Lightbown, Mary Jane. 14 September 1976.

Porter, William L. 5 May 1977.

White, William D. 3 September 1976.

Whittlesey, Julian. 27 February 1974.

MANUSCRIPT COLLECTIONS

Dartington Hall, Devon, England. Records Office. Lescaze Papers.

Syracuse University, Syracuse, New York. William E. Lescaze Archives, George Arents Research Library for Special Collections.

Index

Page numbers in italic type indicate illustrations.